Cycles of Spin

Strategic Communication in the U.S. Congress

How do politicians try to shape their news coverage? Patrick Sellers examines strategic communication campaigns in the U.S. Congress. He argues that these campaigns create cycles of spin: Leaders create messages, rank-and-file legislators decide whether to promote those messages, journalists decide whether to cover the messages, and any coverage feeds back to influence the policy process. These four stages are closely related; decisions at one stage influence those at another. Sellers uses diverse evidence, from participant observation and press secretary interviews to computerized content analysis and vector auto regression. The result is a comprehensive and unprecedented examination of politicians' promotional campaigns and journalists' coverage of those campaigns. Countering numerous critics of spin, Sellers offers the provocative argument that the promotional messages have their origins in the actual policy preferences of members of Congress. The campaigns to promote these messages thus can help the public learn about policy debates in Congress.

Patrick Sellers is currently a Professor of Political Science at Davidson College. He has also taught at Rice University and Indiana University and worked in the U.S. House and Senate in Washington, DC. He is coauthor (with Brian Schaffner) of the forthcoming book *Winning with Words: The Origins and Impact of Framing*. His research has appeared in the *American Political Science Review, American Journal of Political Science, Journal of Politics, Legislative Studies Quarterly, Political Communication*, and other leading journals.

Advance Praise for *Cycles of Spin*

"In this superb book, Patrick Sellers fills a major gap in the literatures about political communications, Congress, and representation. Sellers combines innovative statistical analysis, close personal observation of party message activities in Congress, and thoughtful case studies to provide the first comprehensive study of the strategic communications that occur between lawmakers, the media, and citizens. It is a major study that should be read by any serious scholar of American politics.

"First and foremost, *Cycles of Spin* is a book about how representation plays out on the ground. Teasing out the complex interrelations that exist between agenda setting and position taking in Congress, media coverage of lawmaking, and the policy attitudes of ordinary citizens is very difficult because the causal relations almost always are reciprocal. Sellers meets this challenge through innovative statistical tests of the 'feedback' that occurs between these actors. The work is very nuanced and rooted in an insider's understanding of party strategizing and the news business. And the book is extremely well written. It belongs on graduate student reading lists, but also would work well in upper-level courses about Congress and political communications."

– C. Lawrence Evans, College of William and Mary

"In *Cycles of Spin*, Sellers expertly constructs an elegant model describing how members of Congress create and promote their policy messages and predicting how successful those messages will be in gaining news coverage. *Cycles of Spin* fills a considerable gap in the study of strategic communication, illuminating the incentives and institutional constraints that shape how congressional leaders craft messages, why rank-and-file members either join the messaging effort or defect, and how news coverage feeds back into the policy debate."

– Regina Lawrence, Louisiana State University

"This is the most extensive study of media and policy agenda setting and framing in the U.S. Congress to date. It draws on a wealth of evidence that includes notes from weekly meetings of the Senate Minority Leader with Democratic legislative directors, more than 22,000 public statements by members of Congress, more than one million news stories from 12 national outlets and local newspapers in 43 states, and interviews with press secretaries of 41 Democratic senators. Professor Sellers's thorough analysis of this evidence specifies more precisely the actual relationships among politicians and journalists – and the effect of these relationships on public debate and policy outcomes. Highly recommended for all interested in political agenda setting and framing."

– David H. Weaver, Indiana University

COMMUNICATION, SOCIETY AND POLITICS

Editors

W. Lance Bennett, University of Washington
Robert M. Entman, The George Washington University

Editorial Advisory Board

Scott Althaus, University of Illinois at Urbana-Champaign
Larry M. Bartels, Princeton University
Jay G. Blumler, Emeritus, University of Leeds
Doris A. Graber, University of Illinois at Chicago
Regina Lawrence, Louisiana State University
Paolo Mancini, Universita di Perugia
Pippa Norris, Kennedy School of Government, Harvard University
Barbara Pfetsch, Freie Universitaet, Berlin
Philip Schlesinger, University of Stirling
Gadi Wolfsfeld, Hebrew University of Jerusalem

Politics and relations among individuals in societies across the world are being transformed by new technologies for targeting individuals and sophisticated methods for shaping personalized messages. The new technologies challenge boundaries of many kinds – between news, information, entertainment, and advertising; between media, with the arrival of the World Wide Web; and even between nations. Communication, Society and Politics probes the political and social impacts of these new communication systems in national, comparative, and global perspective.

Titles in the Series:

C. Edwin Baker, *Media, Markets, and Democracy*
C. Edwin Baker, *Media Concentration and Democracy: Why Ownership Matters*
W. Lance Bennett and Robert M. Entman, eds., *Mediated Politics: Communication in the Future of Democracy*

Continued after the Index

Cycles of Spin

Strategic Communication in the U.S. Congress

PATRICK SELLERS
Davidson College

CAMBRIDGE UNIVERSITY PRESS
Cambridge, New York, Melbourne, Madrid, Cape Town, Singapore,
São Paulo, Delhi, Dubai, Tokyo

Cambridge University Press
32 Avenue of the Americas, New York, NY 10013-2473, USA

www.cambridge.org
Information on this title: www.cambridge.org/9780521135801

© Patrick Sellers 2010

This publication is in copyright. Subject to statutory exception
and to the provisions of relevant collective licensing agreements,
no reproduction of any part may take place without the written
permission of Cambridge University Press.

First published 2010

Printed in the United States of America

A catalog record for this publication is available from the British Library.

Library of Congress Cataloging in Publication Data

Sellers, Patrick J.
Cycles of spin: strategic communication in the U.S. Congress / Patrick Sellers.
p. cm. – (Communication, society, and politics)
Includes bibliographical references and index.
ISBN 978-0-521-75599-3 (hardback) – ISBN 978-0-521-13580-1 (pbk.)
1. United States. Congress – Reporters and reporting. 2. Press and Politics – United States.
3. Communication in politics – United States. I. Title. II. Series.

JK1128.S45 2009
328.73001′4–dc22 2009010898

ISBN 978-0-521-75599-3 Hardback
ISBN 978-0-521-13580-1 Paperback

Cambridge University Press has no responsibility for the persistence or accuracy of URLs for external or third-party Internet Web sites referred to in this publication and does not guarantee that any content on such Web sites is, or will remain, accurate or appropriate.

Contents

Acknowledgments

This project is built from the contributions of many individuals. My initial education about the interaction between congressional politics and news coverage came from the staff of then–Senate Minority Leader Tom Daschle, particularly Randy DeValk, Joan Huffer, Joel Johnson, Laura Petrou, and Larry Stein. Staff members in the Senate and House Radio Television galleries also provided extensive insights and evidence. Rick Wilson, then at the National Science Foundation, provided valuable advice for exploring the unanswered questions that emerged from my experiences in the Senate.

My exploration of these questions has received funding from many sources, including the American Political Science Association (through its Congressional Fellowship and Small Research Grant programs), the National Science Foundation (SBR #9870841), the Dirksen Congressional Center and the Caterpillar Foundation, Indiana University, and Davidson College. Much of the data collection and analysis was possible only with the help of numerous research assistants, including Tiffany Allen, Emmanuel Amos-Abanyie, Patrick Brandt, Alana Calvin, Shelley Conroy, Jonathan Crooms, Dan Duggans, Sarah Hernley, David Holian, John Marion, Scott McClurg, Lauren Pierce, Brian Schaffner, and most recently, Taylor Ansley, Jarred Taylor, and Lydie White.

I received valuable feedback on the project from presentations at Indiana University, Davidson College, American University, Duke University, Vanderbilt University, and numerous conferences. A long list of individuals have provided useful suggestions for improving the project, including John Aldrich, Scott Althaus, Jeffrey Biggs, Patrick Brandt, David Canon,

Tim Cook, Chris Deering, Terry Firmin, Rich Forgette, Dan Lipinski, Bruce Oppenheimer, Dan Palazzolo, Phil Paolino, Laura Petrou, David Rohde, Barbara Sinclair, Tracy Sulkin, Elaine Willey, and three anonymous reviewers.

I should also mention the particularly valuable contributions of two individuals. As a graduate student, Brian Schaffner helped organize much of the initial data collection underlying this book. Since then, he has become a coauthor and colleague, while continuing to make helpful contributions to this project (including a last-minute but thorough reading of the full manuscript). Kathryn Firmin-Sellers read more drafts of chapters than I care to admit. She has always been willing to discuss vexing theoretical or empirical problems, as well as to help refine this project to reach its potential.

Finally, I dedicate this book to Kathryn, Maggie, and Ben, who help me explore the intricacies of persuasion and spin each day.

Cycles of Spin

Strategic Communication in the U.S. Congress

1

The Cycle

Politicians talk a lot. But, they don't talk too much, and that talk is rarely cheap. Communication is central to politicians' work, particularly in the U.S. Congress. Our senators and representatives often talk with each other in the structured, policy-rich environment inside Congress (Aldrich and Rohde 1995, 1996, Cox and McCubbins 1993, 2004, Denzau et al. 1985). They debate the overall policy agenda as well as legislative details of that agenda. Senators and representatives also talk extensively with constituents, often in the public, unpredictable, and unstructured context of election campaigns (Franklin 1991, Herrnson 2004, Jacobson 2004, McCombs and Shaw 1972, 1993, Sellers 1998). This interaction involves fewer policy details, as the politicians aim to explain and advertise Washington activities, rather than continue the "legislative combat" of committee and floor debate (Fenno 1978, xiii).

With increasing frequency, the politicians' legislative and electoral worlds are blurring together in "the permanent campaign" (Blumenthal 2008, Lawrence 2000, Ornstein and Mann 2000).[1] Policy debates between elections are extending beyond the structured arena inside Congress to a broader, less-structured, and more-public arena. Examples of these public debates abound. In January of 1995, a new Republican congressional majority aggressively promoted a bold legislative

[1] Other labels include "PR wars" (Sinclair 2006), "media politics" (Evans and Oleszek 2001), "crafted talk" (Jacobs and Shapiro 2000), "information cycles" (Bennett and Mannheim 2001), "crafted coverage" (Cook 1996), "spiral of opportunity" (Miller and Riechert 2001), and "recursive governance" (Crozier 2007). Also, Sulkin (2005) links agenda setting in elections and legislatures on the level of individual legislators.

agenda and used that agenda to win news coverage. Eight years later, members of Congress publicly debated the merits of launching the Iraq War. Their intentionally public deliberations helped spark a national discussion about the conflict. A similarly contentious public debate took place in 2005, when Congress considered President George Bush's plan to reform Social Security. In their attempts to shape the debate's outcome, legislators from both parties pitched carefully chosen arguments to the news media. During the next Congress, a newly elected Democratic majority again sought news coverage aggressively in an attempt to pass a specific legislative agenda.

When considered together, these public debates raise important analytical questions. How do congressional leaders decide which issues to bring up for debate inside and outside Congress? How do internal party divisions impact the powers of congressional leaders to set the agenda? What strategies effectively help legislators win news coverage of issues and arguments outside Congress? Does such coverage ever feed back to shape the legislative process and policy outcomes inside Congress? Finally, why do legislators' promotional campaigns sometimes succeed and sometimes fail?

These questions suggest the central theme of this book: how members of Congress use strategic communication[2] to shape the news coverage and agendas of policy debates. Politicians' promotional campaigns play a growing role in contemporary policy debates, from abortion and foreign policy to Social Security reform and tax policy (Crigler 1996, Graber 1996, Manheim 1991, 1994, 2008). Compared to deliberations inside Congress, debates in the public arena include many more participants, from interest group advocates to news journalists and members of the public (Kingdon 2003). The larger number of participants makes these broader debates less predictable than the structured deliberations of 535 legislators inside Congress.

[2] Mannheim defines "strategic political communication" as "the use of sophisticated knowledge of such attributes of human behavior as attitude and preference structures, cultural tendencies, and media use patterns – and such relevant organizational behaviors as how news organizations make decisions regarding news content and how congressional committees schedule and structure hearings – to shape and target messages to maximize their desired impact while minimizing undesired collateral effects" (2008, 106).

While all the participants may affect the broader policy debates, this book focuses on the role of the news media.[3] In these debates politicians share the goal of "dominating the news agenda, entering the news cycle at the earliest possible time, and repeatedly re-entering it, with stories and initiatives so that subsequent news coverage is set on [their own] terms." (Blumler and Kavanagh 1999, 214) As a result, the content of coverage "is really the imprint of power – it registers the identity of actors or interests that are competing to dominate the text" (Entman 1993, 53; see also Gamson 2001, Gans 2004, Pan and Kosicki 2001, Wolfsfeld and Sheafer 2006).

As politicians compete to shape news coverage of policy debates, that coverage can affect the progression and outcome of those debates in many ways. If news stories devote more attention to one party's arguments in a debate, the news audience may be more inclined to use those arguments when evaluating the parties' proposals in the debate. The party dominating the news coverage thus receives more favorable evaluations of its proposals (Druckman 2001, Iyengar 1991, Iyengar and Kinder 1987, Wanta et al. 2004). In addition to shaping the dimensions of evaluation, the news coverage may highlight attractive attributes of a party on those dimensions. With their attention drawn to these attributes, the public may evaluate the party and its proposals even more favorably (Aday 2006, Chyi and McCombs 2004, Dalton et al. 1998, Kahn and Kenney 2002, McCombs and Ghanem 2001). In light of these potential advantages, politicians may deliberately attempt to shape news coverage (Cook 1998, Entman 2004, Jacobs and Shapiro 2000). I argue that contemporary politicians carefully choose their public statements in anticipation of how the news media will cover those statements (Andsager 2000, Cook 2006, Gamson and Modigliani 1989, Kernell 1997, Lakoff 2004). By proactively anticipating journalists' needs, members of Congress in particular hope to shape their news coverage and thereby the agenda of policy debates outside and inside their chambers (Baumgartner and

[3] Opinions of the public, as captured in polls, certainly play a central role in political elites' strategic communication, both in the creation of messages and the assessment of their impact (Heath 1998, Jacobs and Shapiro 2000). In Congress rank-and-file legislators rely relatively little on polling, but congressional leaders make frequent use of surveys to "lead" both Congress and the public (Jacobs et al. 2002). The evidence in this book covers relatively short time periods (seven-month periods in two separate years), and the analysis focuses largely on four specific debates outlined in Chapter 2. It is unlikely to find substantial movement in public opinion about these debates during the short time periods. But, the evolution and outcome of the debates had the potential to shape longer-term perceptions of the two parties, thus providing a boost in the next election and beyond.

Jones 1993, Cobb and Elder 1983, Hilgartner and Bosk 1988, Lawrence and Birkland 2004).

These dynamics of strategic communication in congressional policy making are important for three reasons. First, greater internal unity gives congressional parties more influence over policy agendas and outcomes (Aldrich and Rohde 1995). We therefore need to understand how politicians use agenda setting inside and outside Congress to minimize division and thereby help themselves individually and collectively (Kingdon 2003). If we can understand the day-to-day mechanics of legislators' agenda setting, we can better explain how their efforts can lead to longer-term electoral success and realignment of political parties (Aldrich 1995, Carmines and Stimson 1986, Miller and Riechert 2001). In public policy debates, "the party which is able to make its definition of the issues prevail is likely to take over the government" (Schattschneider 1960, 73).

Second, if news coverage outside Congress is part of the agenda of legislative debates, we also need to understand the origins of that coverage (Dalton et al. 1998, Sigal 1973). Politicians' promotional and agenda-setting activities can act as one influence on news coverage (Cook 1989, 1998). Journalists themselves may be another influence on coverage, independent of what politicians say (Bennett 2007, Entman 2004). The journalists decide which politicians' messages to cover and how frequently to cover them. Because these decisions by journalists help determine whether the politicians' promotional efforts succeed, it is important to understand the interaction between politicians and journalists, particularly the type of coverage the journalists choose to provide (Graber 2006, Jasperson et al. 1998, Sheafer 2001, Shin and Cameron 2005).

Finally, we need to consider how the interaction among politicians and journalists affects the quality of the policy debates, and by extension, the information that the public receives about those debates. A functioning democracy requires citizens to be informed about their elected representatives, in order to hold those representatives accountable (Druckman 2005, Graber 2006, Lippmann 1920/2008, Page 1995). News coverage provides one source of that information (Baker 2007, Bennett 2007, Fox et al. 2005). As politicians and journalists continually exchange issues and arguments about public policies, their statements and stories could simplify and distort those debates, or make the debates more relevant and accessible to the public (Niven 2003). These sharply divergent outcomes underscore the importance of understanding how politicians use strategic communication, and how journalists respond to those efforts (Bennett and Entman 2001, Blumler and Kavanagh 1999).

This chapter lays a foundation for exploring strategic communication in the U.S. Congress. The next section explains why members of Congress increasingly rely on promotional campaigns. I then outline my core arguments about how politicians and journalists interact in cycles of spin. The final section describes the evidence used to evaluate my arguments.

1.1. THE CHALLENGES AND OPPORTUNITIES OF AGENDA SETTING IN CONGRESS

In recent decades members of Congress have grown increasingly independent in their pursuit of reelection and policy (Davidson and Oleszek 1998).[4] The growth in congressional staff and resources has allowed legislators to become legislative entrepreneurs, introducing bills often to their constituents' benefit. The members also have built independent fundraising organizations, allowing them to run candidate-centered campaigns (Jacobson 2004). Despite this growth in individual resources and opportunities, contemporary members of Congress still face obstacles to winning reelection by themselves.

In order to claim that they are working for constituents' interests, legislators need to produce successful policy initiatives. Position taking and bill introductions alone may prove insufficient for winning constituent support (Arnold 2004); legislators must also pass legislation earning that support. But, pushing legislation through Congress is not easy, as members may not agree on the most desirable policy (Kingdon 2003). The sharp partisanship and polarization of recent congresses suggest that policy agreement is growing rarer than ever (Oppenheimer 2002, Sinclair 2006). And within a party, even widespread agreement on a policy position does not guarantee that party members will act together to pass legislation (Aldrich 1995, Kiewet and McCubbins 1991). Members' preferences may not be self-evident. Legislators may prefer not to publicize their positions on certain issues, particularly controversial ones. Furthermore, no legislator has an incentive to gather this information and coordinate passage of legislation. Every member may prefer instead to free ride on the efforts of her colleagues, letting them do the necessary work to pass legislation while still enjoying the benefits of their efforts (the approved legislation). This temptation to free ride could discourage all

[4] A third individual goal, power, is also common (Fenno 1978). This book devotes little attention to pursuit of this goal, because those efforts usually take years, much longer than the seven-month periods of my analysis.

legislators from devoting effort to passing legislation, leading to the outcome of no bills passing Congress.

A legislative party may address this collective action problem by creating leadership positions and assigning valuable powers and resources to those positions. These benefits provide an incentive for individual members to work to become leaders, who must in turn advance the interests of their party members (Aldrich 1995, Cox and McCubbins 1993, 2004). The party leaders can assist rank-and-file members with tasks ranging from committee assignments to fundraising,[5] but one of the most important leadership responsibilities concerns the legislative agenda. Specifically, a party leader can use his institutional powers and resources to encourage consideration of legislation addressing the members' concerns and to prevent debate of bills that threaten their interests (Bachrach and Baratz 1962, Cox and McCubbins 2004, Riker 1986). As one observer put it, "the definition of alternatives is the supreme instrument of power" (Schattschneider 1960, 66).

Party leaders possess varying degrees of influence over the legislative agenda inside Congress. In the House, the majority's control of the Rules Committee and majoritarian rules governing floor debate give the Speaker extensive control over the legislative agenda. Those same rules prevent the minority party from exercising much influence over that agenda. The powers of Senate leaders lie between these two extremes. The Senate Majority Leader enjoys the right of first recognition on the floor, which bestows considerable influence over the chamber's agenda. But, the supermajority requirement for ending debate often forces the Majority Leader to obtain unanimous consent from other senators before bringing a bill to the floor for debate. Conversely, that need for unanimous consent increases the Senate Minority Leader's influence over the legislative agenda; the two Senate leaders often negotiate which bills to bring to the floor. In the House, the Speaker has no need to negotiate with the Minority Leader, which substantially reduces the latter's influence over the floor agenda.[6]

In addition to using these internal rules to shape the legislative debate, congressional party leaders often propose an agenda of policy issues and messages favoring their party at the start of each congress (Bader 1996, Sinclair 1997). The leaders then work to move these issues and arguments

[5] See Pearson (2005) and Sinclair (2006) for details on the leaders' nonpolicy assistance.

[6] See Sinclair (2006) and Davidson and Oleszek (1998). Evans and Oleszek (2001) document how congressional parties use internal Senate rules to further their public relations campaigns aimed beyond Congress.

to the top of the legislative agenda for active consideration. A prominent example of this type of agenda setting came after the 1994 elections in which the GOP won a majority of House seats for the first time since 1952. The newly elected Speaker Newt Gingrich (R-GA6) subsequently led a chamber majority committed to action on a number of issues important to conservative Republicans. Gingrich aggressively focused the House legislative agenda on these issues, using the institutional powers of the House majority to vote on bills implementing the GOP's preferred positions on these issues (Gimpel 1996).

Observers of Congress have studied extensively these efforts to shape the legislative agenda inside Congress. We know much less, however, about congressional leaders' attempts to influence the policy agenda outside Congress, particularly as captured in the news media. Just as presidents "go public," congressional leaders can hold press conferences and impromptu interviews in order to shape the public policy agenda (Kernell 1997). Such agenda setting is arguably more difficult for congressional leaders outside Congress than inside; the leaders lack institutional powers outside Congress to promote or discourage messages. The final decision about news coverage rests with journalists, and congressional leaders face extensive competition when trying to insert their issues and arguments into a gradually shrinking news hole (Kernell 1997, Sellers and Schaffner 2007).

Despite these obstacles, party leaders in Congress still endeavor to shape the news agenda outside Congress via strategic communication (Mannheim 1991, 1994, 2008). News coverage of Congress often focuses narrowly on a small subset of all the issues and arguments that legislators consider. The coverage makes the subset of issues and arguments stand out to the general public, relative to other elements of the "policy primeval soup" inside Congress (Kingdon 2003, 200). If a party's leaders successfully shape this policy agenda reported in news coverage, that coverage can encourage the public to focus on the party's preferred issues and arguments (Dalton et al. 1998, Iyengar 1991, Iyengar and Kinder 1987, Kahn and Kenney 2002, Lacy 2001). The public agenda setting mobilizes individuals and groups concerned about those issues and arguments, which in turn pressure Congress to act. If one party more effectively broadens the conflict to include supporters, that party is more likely to win (Schattschneider 1960).

By making an issue more prominent on the external media agenda and more salient to the public, party leaders can also increase the pressure on Congress to address the issue (Arnold 1990). The leaders can use news coverage of the issue to increase the costs to individual members of not supporting the leaders' arguments and legislative proposal on the issue

(Cook 1998, 2001). Changing the public salience of an issue alters how members address it, even if the level of division inside Congress remains unchanged. Doing nothing on a newly salient issue is more costly and difficult to explain than taking action on that issue (Sigal 1973, Price 1978).[7]

In addition, congressional leaders use news coverage for communicating with each other and other political elites about the legislative agenda (Cook 2001, Sigal 1973). A congressional staffer explained the need for this communication:

> Congressmen and senators read the mass media. The big problem on the Hill is the oversupply of information. They have no way of dealing with it. So they don't, mostly. We can write reports and papers and they don't read it. But if the *Times* or *Post* picks up our report and does a story on it, they do read that, and it gets their attention. (Quoted in Kingdon 2003, 60.)

The topics of this communication range from the composition of the legislative agenda to disagreements about individual issues. When liberal House Speaker Nancy Pelosi (D-CA8) shares a press conference podium with moderate Representative Gene Taylor (D-MS4),[8] the two Democrats hope that news coverage of the event will signal both ideological wings of their party that both legislators consider their policy proposals and accompanying arguments acceptable and worthy of further action. In all these ways, news coverage of issues and arguments can raise their prominence on the legislative agenda inside Congress. Congressional leaders thus target the news media and its coverage in hopes of affecting the legislative agenda inside Congress.[9] News making becomes a central part of policy making (Cook 1998).

[7] President Bush began his second term as president by proposing fundamental reforms to Social Security. In his (ultimately unsuccessful) efforts to get these reforms through Congress, a central goal was to raise the American public's concern about the impending threats to Social Security. Republicans hoped that raising the public's concern would increase pressure on Congress to pass reforms to the program (Toner 2005). In March of 2005, 18% of the public viewed Social Security as the most important problem facing President Bush and Congress. Social Security was the most highly ranked individual issue (Lake et al. 2005). Chapter 4 discusses why Bush's reforms failed.

[8] In 2004, Pelosi earned a vote rating of ninety five from the Americans for Democratic Action; Taylor's rating was sixty (http://www.adaction.org/ADATodayVR2005.pdf, last accessed December 1, 2006).

[9] These efforts to add issues to the legislative agenda constitute positive agenda control (Cox and McCubbins 2004, Finocchiaro and Rohde 2002). Congressional leaders may also exert negative control over the policy agenda inside Congress, by preventing their chamber from considering a bill or issue. The leaders lack such negative control over the policy agenda outside Congress, because journalists, not politicians, hold the final say over the composition of this agenda.

To the extent that party leaders can shape the policy agenda in the news media, they thus exert greater influence over the legislative agenda and debates inside Congress. That influence further strengthens the leaders' ability to help their individual party members by pushing legislation addressing the members' policy interests and slowing bills threatening those interests. The leaders' efforts also help these legislators electorally. When communicating with constituents, the rank-and-file legislators can go beyond mere position taking to claim credit for any legislative accomplishments that favor their constituents.

The leaders' agenda-setting efforts provide additional benefits beyond those for individual party members. The leaders also help shape their party's collective reputation (Jacobs et al. 2002). Each time Republican leaders in Congress help muscle a tax cut through both chambers, their success encourages both elite and mass observers of Congress to view the GOP as more committed to reducing taxes (Evans and Oleszek 2001, Pope and Woon 2005). Constituent groups benefiting from tax cuts grow more likely to support the Republican Party, as well as to expect further tax cut proposals in the future. In this manner, multiple Republican tax cuts over the last three decades have helped the party develop ownership of the issue (Petrocik 1996). In a similar manner, Democrats have built a strong reputation on issues such as health care and the environment. A party's legislative accomplishments and reputation on issues combine into an overall "brand name" different from that of the opposing party (Cox and McCubbins 1993, 2004).

Each congressional party attempts to focus voters' attention on favorable issues making up its brand name. This "priming" encourages voters to evaluate the party on those issues, making it more likely that the voters will evaluate the party's members positively and vote for them (Iyengar and Kinder 1987, Krosnick and Kinder 1990). If a congressional minority party can focus enough attention on its favorable issues, that minority may win enough additional seats in the next election to control Congress. Chapter 3 describes how Gingrich and his fellow Republicans succeeded in this task in the late 1980s and early 1990s. Since winning control of both congressional chambers in the 1994 elections and winning the presidency in 2000, the Republicans have continued working to strengthen their party's collective reputation and to weaken that of the Democrats. The *New York Times* described the plans of a leading Republican strategist:

> [RNC] Chairman [Ken] Mehlman talked big and thought big about the Republican Party: about how he and his allies could fundamentally redraw the political architecture of America, change the way Americans conceptualize the two parties and establish Republicans as the dominant party in America long after George Bush returned to Texas.... This was nothing short of a campaign to marginalize the Democratic Party and everything that Mehlman, reflecting Bush and Rove, said it stood for: big government, high taxes, liberal judges, a timorous foreign policy. (Nagourney 2006)[10]

Republican leaders have encouraged voters to focus on the strong points of the GOP's collective reputation, and to use these issues as the basis for evaluating all politicians.

Collective party labels may also benefit individual members of Congress in a more immediate, short-term manner. Legislators and journalists may give more serious consideration to a tax cut proposal from a Republican than one from a Democrat. The GOP has successfully passed more tax cuts than the Democrats have, and Republican constituents call more frequently for more tax cuts than their Democratic counterparts do. These differences encourage a public perception that the Republicans are more capable of passing tax cuts. This reputation and ownership of the issue (Petrocik 1996) suggests that a Republican tax proposal stands a greater chance of passage. In an electoral context, voters who believe taxes are too high will be more likely to support Republican candidates. The tendency exists even if the voter knows nothing about the candidates except partisan affiliation.

1.2. CYCLES OF SPIN

These diverse benefits thus create an incentive for members of Congress to employ strategic communication in legislative debates. This section outlines the main components of legislators' strategic communication campaigns, and how these promotional campaigns create cycles of spin. A central element is the message, which I define as the issue and arguments about the issue that a politician promotes. In launching a strategic communications campaign and promoting the message, the politician hopes to win a favorable outcome related to the issue. That issue often

[10] See also Bumiller (2004). Edsall (2006), and Hamburger and Wallsten (2006).

involves a specific policy choice, such as how much the federal government should spend. The arguments include the politician's preferred position on the issue, as well as reasons to adopt that position. The arguments frame the politician's position in a manner intended to attract greater support from target audiences, ranging from other legislators to the general public.[11]

It is important to note that, in terms of strategic communication, every issue and its component policy choices are subject to definition by participants in the policy process, from politicians to journalists to the public (Kingdon 2003). Politicians in particular try to define issues to gain political advantage and win their preferred policy outcomes (Jerit 2005, Riker 1986, Rojecki 2008). These definitions of issues vary widely, from broad and encompassing to narrow and specific. For example, Republicans frequently discuss budgetary politics as an issue in terms of overall government spending, which they wish to limit. Democrats define the issue of budgetary politics in terms of specific government programs that they wish to maintain (Jacoby 2000). If one party succeeds in focusing the policy agenda on that party's definition of budgetary issues, the party is advantaged in the subsequent budget debate. The dominant definition and implicit policy choice favor the party promoting the definition. If the debate focuses on the Republican definition, for example, that debate is likely to become a choice between decreasing and increasing the size of government and its spending. The public often finds the former position (that of the Republicans) more attractive than the latter (that of the Democrats) (Jacoby 2000). Reflecting their constituents' preferences, legislators often share these opinions. Alternatively, the policy debate may focus on the Democratic definition of budgetary issues. Along this dimension of the issue, the public and legislators commonly find the Democratic position (maintaining or expanding spending on Social Security or Medicare) preferable to the

[11] Gamson and Modigliani (1989) define a "frame package" as similar to a "message." Their definition suggests additional characteristics of messages that become relevant in the analysis that follows: "A package has an internal structure. At its core is a central organizing idea, or *frame*, for making sense of relevant events, suggesting what is at issue.... a package offers a number of different condensing symbols that suggest the core frame and positions in shorthand, making it possible to display the package as a whole with a deft metaphor, catchphrase, or other symbolic device" (3).

Republican position (reducing or limiting those specific programs) (Jacoby 2000).[12]

Politicians certainly face important constraints in their definition of issues (Rottinghaus 2008). Past accomplishments or external events can limit politicians' efforts to define issues (Alexseev and Bennett 1995, Wolfsfeld 2001, 2004). Continuing instability and American casualties in the Iraq War made it harder for President George Bush to frame the conflict as a victory for the United States. The reputations of political parties may also constrain their members' efforts to frame issues. The Democratic Party's long-perceived weakness on national defense hindered its members' efforts to focus discussion of the Iraq War on the continuing instability and American casualties. The American public did not view the Democrats as capable on national defense, and therefore was hesitant to accept the Democrats' description of the war (Petrocik 1996).

Despite these various constraints, I argue that politicians can still use strategic communication to shape policy debates for political advantage. When politicians initiate strategic communication campaigns, the

[12] These dynamics of campaigns and message demonstrate how the distinct concepts of agenda setting and framing may overlap. Riker (1986) describes the former concept as the art of heresthetics, "setting up situations – composing the alternatives among which political actors much choose – in such a way that even those who do not wish to do so are compelled by the structure of the situation to support the heresthetician's purpose ... structuring the world in order to win" (ix). In contrast to the heresthetician's manipulation of distinct policy alternatives, one type of framing focuses on equivalent alternatives: "how the use of different, but logically equivalent, words or phrases (e.g., 5% unemployment or 95% employment, 97% fat-free or 3% fat) causes individuals to alter their preferences" (Druckman 2001, 228, Tversky and Kahneman 1974). Another type of framing, "emphasis framing," more closely captures the individual-level thought processes implicit in agenda setting: "by emphasizing a subset of potentially relevant considerations, a speaker can lead individuals to focus on these considerations when constructing their opinions" (Druckman 2001, 230). If a legislator must choose between a Democratic and Republican budget, accepting one party's definition of the budget issue can lead the legislator to focus on the considerations in that definition and therefore support that party's budget. The party that defines budgetary politics wins the debate. A third variety of framing concerns the positive or negative attributes provided with each frame (McCombs and Ghanem 2001). When focusing on this "second-level agenda setting," a party is likely to include positive attributes in its description and definition of an issue. Thus, Democrats would define the budget issue by describing both specific government programs and the benefits of continuing to fund those programs. If the public accepts this definition of the budget, the public is more likely evaluate the Democrats favorably for two distinct reasons. Defining the issue in terms of specific programs improves the evaluations; mentioning the positive attributes of those programs also boosts evaluations.

resulting cycle of spin contains four stages. The first is the creation of a message. When choosing the issues and arguments to emphasize in public relations campaigns, congressional leaders prefer a message that appeals to diverse audiences, ranging from other legislators to the news media and the public. One path to this goal is to focus the message on a favorable issue, that is, one in which their own party is unified and the opposing party divided. Partisanship also influences the creation of messages, via issue ownership and the two parties' varying reputations across issues. A leader's message may prove more appealing and persuasive if it incorporates issues on which the leader's party possesses a relatively favorable reputation. When a party's message and promotional campaign fail, party members often must address issues favoring their opponents. As illustrated in this book's policy debates, it often proves difficult for a party to fashion a persuasive and appealing message on such unfavorable issues.

After creating a message, legislators must promote that message for it to have any effect.[13] More promotion by more people maximizes that effect. In this second stage of promotional campaigns, politicians face a daunting obstacle to collective promotion: An individual legislator can benefit from others' promotion of a message without joining their efforts. But if all legislators free ride, no one promotes the message. To overcome this collective action problem, congressional party leaders often play a central role. They attempt to choose messages that provide both collective and particularly individual benefits to their followers, in hopes that these benefits lead the followers to promote those messages. In this respect, the creation and promotion of messages are closely intertwined. The leaders work to avoid discussing issues and arguments that divide their party and discourage promotion, although sometimes the leaders have no choice but to do so. The followers respond to leaders' efforts by promoting the party message, at least in certain debates. The reasons behind their

[13] Legislators' promotional efforts fall along a continuum from events to statements. If a legislator introduces a bill or launches a filibuster, that action constitutes a promotional event that may yield news coverage. In this case, the legislator's public statements about the action help shape its framing in the coverage. At the opposite end of the continuum, a public statement itself may be a promotional event that wins coverage. The venue of the statement, such as a news conference or the floor of a chamber, may be quite unremarkable and not newsworthy. The content of the statement itself attracts reporters' interest and coverage. Thus, it is difficult to categorize politicians' statements as distinct from, and always intended to, frame events. Sometimes, simply making a statement becomes an event (Cook 1998). Accordingly, promotional efforts include legislators' actions across the entire continuum from events to statements.

decisions to promote a message (or remain silent) consistently reveal a concern for their party's collective interests.

The third step in promotional campaigns links politicians and journalists, asking which messages win news coverage. If members of Congress frequently talk about a particular message in news releases and at press conferences, that message is more likely to attract attention and coverage from journalists. The reporters build stories around how frequently politicians promote messages, with the most frequently discussed issues and arguments getting the most coverage. As a result, party leaders win more coverage for a message if they persuade rank-and-file members to promote that message. Journalists' own decisions also affect that coverage, independently of the politicians' strategic communications (Bennett 2007, Entman 2004). At times, reporters craft their coverage as outlined previously, to mirror the ebb and flow of legislators' promotional campaigns (Graber 2006, Sigal 1973). In these situations, messages promoted more frequently by politicians receive more mentions in news stories by journalists. At other times, reporters frame their coverage in a more balanced manner, giving equal attention to both sides' messages regardless of how frequently the politicians promote those messages (Gans 2004). And at yet other times, journalists exert a different type of independence from politicians, structuring news coverage to fit the preferences of their audience (Niven 2002).

In the final stage of promotional campaigns, news coverage feeds back to influence politicians' promotional efforts and policy debates (Baumgartner and Jones 1993, Lawrence and Birkland 2004, Miller and Riechert 2001, Wolfsfeld 2004). This feedback is a central component of a strategic communication campaign. When such a campaign is successful, the extensive coverage of a message encourages its proponents to promote it more frequently. Coverage of the message discourages its opponents, who either remain silent or attempt to shift attention to different, more favorable issues. Greater coverage of the message also makes it more likely that legislators support the policy outcome advocated in that message.

Overall, these four stages constitute a cycle. Politicians create messages, promote them, win coverage of them, and then respond to that coverage. The promotional campaigns driving a cycle are often competitive. In a particular debate, each party in Congress offers and promotes its own message. I argue that this "spin" is more than shallow rhetoric. In its message, each party attempts to draw attention to the issues and arguments that the party considers most relevant. As a result, the competing messages can provide useful signals to voters about the parties' policy priorities and proposals. By more closely linking legislators and their messages to journalists and news coverage, cycles of spin offer a useful window into the actual content of debates that traditionally took place only within the halls of Congress (Pan and Kosicki 2001).

1.3. EVIDENCE

Many observers focus on only a portion of the cycles of spin (Aday 2006, Sheafer 2001). Analyses of Congress or the presidency often focus on how dynamics inside each institution lead to the creation of messages; actual news coverage of those messages receives relatively little consideration (Evans and Oleszek 2001, Kernell 1997, Kingdon 2003, Sinclair 1997, 2006). Conversely, other observers focus extensively on the creation and content of news coverage, devoting less attention to explaining politicians' creation and promotion of messages entering that coverage (Gentzkow and Shapiro 2007, Hoffman 2006, Jasperson et al. 1998, Jerit 2005, Lawrence 2000, Lim 2006, Luther and Miller 2005). This book analyzes the complete cycle of agenda setting and strategic communication, from the creation of messages to their coverage and feedback. Thus, the breadth of this argument makes the book unusual among studies of Congress and political communication.[14]

The breadth of supporting evidence and analysis make the book unique.[15] As the following chapters explain, my arguments about cycles of spin suggest specific patterns of behavior by politicians and journalists. To assess the validity of these expectations, I collected evidence from diverse but carefully chosen sources (Iyengar 1991, Reese 2001). This section describes those sources and evidence.

While working for Senate Minority Leader Tom Daschle (D-SD) for the first seven months of 1997, I assisted the leadership staff during debates on a variety of issues. Throughout this period, I also attended

[14] Other studies more completely addressing cycles of spin include Andsager (2000), Bennett (1990, 2007), Entman (2004), Jacobs and Shapiro (2000), Lawrence and Birkland (2004), Niven (2005), and Schiffer (2006).

[15] Jacobs and Shapiro (2000) incorporate a similar diversity of qualitative and quantitative evidence of politicians' statements and journalists' news stories. Their analysis focuses more heavily on how the president attempts to influence Congress, largely on a single issue (health care reform). My book examines strategic communication campaigns across a range of issues, from the standpoint of individual members of Congress and their leaders.

weekly meetings of the leadership staff and Democratic legislative directors in the Senate. These meetings provided a regular indication of the leadership's efforts to reach out to and persuade other Democrats in the Senate. Supplementing these meetings are editions of the *Daily Report*, a publication produced by the Democratic leadership also intended for outreach to Senate Democrats.

Other evidence of promotional campaigns came from interviews with press secretaries of forty-one senators that I conducted during the summer of 1998. I also collected a set of 22,170 public statements by members of Congress from the first seven months of 1997 and 2003, consisting of entries in the *Congressional Record*, and press releases and press conference transcripts collected by the Federal Document Clearing House. The evaluation of promotional campaigns includes analysis of roll call votes and public opinion data from the National Election Studies.

To capture news coverage of these promotional efforts, I selected twelve national outlets and a local newspaper in each of forty-three different states. For each outlet, I collected all news stories appearing in that outlet during the first seven months of 1997 and 2003. When combined, the stories numbered approximately 1.3 million. I used computerized content analysis to evaluate whether each story covered each party's message in each debate analyzed (Bichard 2006). To evaluate whether this coverage of promotional campaigns varied across local outlets, I measured each newspaper's editorial slant by collecting the endorsements that the paper made in recent statewide elections. In addition, I collected for each county in a paper's market the number of subscriptions and the number of Democratic and Republican votes in the 1996 and 2000 presidential elections. Combining the subscriptions and votes allowed me to capture the political leanings of each paper's market.

The chapters that follow utilize this diverse evidence in a variety of ways. The experiences from my work in Daschle's office sparked the basic insights of my arguments. The quantitative evidence, analyzed with several types of statistical analysis, suggests the broad applicability of the arguments (Bichard 2006). The evidence and analysis also helps specify more precisely the actual relationships among politicians and journalists. Finally, the qualitative evidence from the interviews helps explain the motivations and decision making behind legislators' promotional campaigns, as well as validate the generalizations from the quantitative evidence and analysis.

This chapter has presented a foundation for exploring strategic communication campaigns by members of Congress. I outlined why legislators initiate these campaigns, and how their interaction with journalists leads to cycles of spin. The final section outlined the diverse evidence in the chapters that follow, which provides a comprehensive picture of agenda setting in national political debates. Such a broad picture helps us learn critical information about the legislative process in Congress. The book illustrates how the interaction among congressional leaders and followers determines the terms of debate that underlie many aspects of the legislative process, from floor speeches to roll call votes. In addition, the chapters document how journalists mediate the relationship between elected official and constituent by sometimes adding an independent frame to coverage of politicians' statements. Most importantly, I explain how the cycles of spin among politicians and journalists shape dimensions of public debate and subsequent policy outcomes.

2

Building Blocks

During the 105th Congress, legislators held 1,187 recorded votes and passed 710 pieces of legislation (Ornstein et al. 2002). Even after accounting for routine and symbolic legislation, this legislative workload encompassed an overwhelming number of interrelated issues. Other recent congresses have borne similar workloads (Ornstein et al. 2002). In order to impose some order on this legislative mass of interrelated issues, legislators regularly endow their leaders with agenda-setting powers (Aldrich 1995). In turn, the leaders work to steer the legislative agenda toward issues favoring their parties' policy and electoral interests (Cox and McCubbins 2004, Jacobs et al. 2002). If rank-and-file members join their leaders in publicly promoting a particular issue and argument, that message is more likely to influence and persuade other members inside Congress and the news media and public outside Congress. The result is increased pressure for legislative action on the issue and policy position advocated in the message.

This chapter develops a framework for capturing these dynamics of agenda setting, particularly the roles of strategic communication and the news media. The first section discusses different ways to capture politicians' behavior and preferences about policy agendas. In the next section, I introduce four policy debates that provide and structure much of the subsequent evidence in this book. The final section of the chapter draws out unanswered questions that emerge from the debates. The remainder of the book uses evidence from the debates to address these questions.

2.1. MEMBERS OF CONGRESS

When striving to understand legislators' preferences, issue positions, and other aspects of their behavior, observers of Congress most frequently turn to roll call votes. Douglas Arnold cogently summarizes the benefits of using roll call votes to understand congressional behavior:

> The recorded vote is a superb way to apportion responsibility for specific congressional actions because each representative must stand up and be counted. Each roll call has only two sides – yea or nay – so a representative cannot be all things to all people. Each absence from a roll-call vote creates an electoral liability, so the prudent legislator seldom prefers abstention to choosing sides. Each representative has exactly one vote, so the powerful, the ambitious, and the eloquent play no greater role than the weak, the lazy, and the inarticulate. Each vote requires all representatives to make decisions on the same proposal, thus creating a standardized way for comparing representatives' decisions. Representatives are compelled to take sides on more than 500 issues each year. Their decisions are recorded for posterity (2004, 92).

Most importantly, the content of the roll call votes constitutes the actual legislative agenda, thus indicating which issues and arguments rise high enough on that agenda to receive floor consideration.

Yet, roll call votes are less useful for understanding legislators' preferences about the relative importance of issues, and their efforts to shape the legislative agenda. Representatives often must simply vote on the issues making up floor votes, with little opportunity to influence the selection of those issues. In the House, the Rules Committee, under the thumb of the Speaker, almost always determines which bills receive floor consideration and how to debate them. The lack of a germaneness requirement gives individual senators more leeway in bringing issues to the Senate floor for consideration. But, the Senate Majority Leader, in consultation with the Minority Leader, largely sets the floor schedule for considering most legislation (Davidson and Oleszek 1998, Sinclair 2006).

In addition to limited influence over the policy issues making up the floor agenda, many rank-and-file members have little input into the structure of alternatives that they face in an individual roll call vote. When considering future funding for a particular government program, a moderate legislator may prefer to maintain its funding at current levels. But, the roll call vote on the issue may offer a choice between a Republican proposal to eliminate all funding for the program, and a Democratic proposal to double its funding. Neither option accurately represents the legislator's true preference, but she must choose one in order to cast a roll call vote.

When attempting to understand agenda setting in Congress, some observers have examined earlier stages of the legislative process, such as committee votes or bill introductions (Hall 1996). Other observers have captured how campaign ads from an election influences legislators' policy efforts in the subsequent congress (Sulkin 2005). In this book I use a new and different measure of legislators' agenda-setting preferences and efforts: the members' public statements. The legislators make these statements in a variety of public forums, from the *Congressional Record* to press releases to press conferences. All these statements contain extensive information, including the issues and arguments that the legislators prefer to address. To the extent that the statements contain these preferences about the legislative agenda, the statements become part of the legislators' actual efforts to set that agenda.

The statements also capture legislators' agenda-setting preferences more accurately than roll call votes do. To avoid criticisms of not doing their job, legislators need to participate in most, if not all, roll call votes that occur on the floor of their chamber. This obligation exists regardless of whether the legislator would prefer to avoid taking a public position on the issue under floor consideration. Legislators rarely face an electoral obligation to make a public statement. If a legislator believes an issue unimportant, or wishes to avoid embarrassing his party, he may simply remain silent. Conversely, the decision to speak publicly about an issue constitutes a more accurate indication of the legislator's belief in the issue's importance. In addition, public statements provide legislators with more flexibility in framing an issue and argument compared to roll call votes. The members can state their own preferred position on the issue, without having to fit that position into the fixed alternatives of a roll call vote.

In light of these strengths, the remainder of the book draws heavily upon legislators' public statements. Specifically, I examine leaders' and followers' efforts to shape the legislative agenda inside Congress and in the news media's coverage outside Congress. Much of the evidence comes from four specific congressional debates in 1997 and 2003. The next section introduces the four debates and outlines the most important events and overall promotional tactics for each. The differences among the debates enable useful comparisons for addressing central questions about strategic communications in Congress.

2.2. THE FOUR DEBATES

The first debate involved a ban on partial birth abortion and favored Republicans. The second concerned a supplemental appropriations bill and eventually favored congressional Democrats. The last two debates involved passage of the federal budget in 1997 and 2003. In these latter two debates, the encompassing nature of the budget provides both parties with multiple opportunities to shape the legislative agenda in advantageous ways.

2.2.1. Partial Birth Abortion

At the start of 1997, the congressional Republican leadership included a partial birth abortion ban as a central part of its agenda for the upcoming session (Koszczuk 1997). The House approved a version of the ban on March 20 by a 295–136 margin. Democratic representatives remained largely silent during floor debate of the legislation. Under the bill, individuals performing the procedure could face fines and prison terms of up to two years. The only exception to the ban applied if the procedure was needed to save the mother's life. The legislation, if passed into law, would be the first time that Congress had made a specific abortion procedure illegal. Supporters of the ban gained momentum from a statement by Ron Fitzsimmons, executive director of the National Coalition of Abortion Providers. He publicly acknowledged that "he had lied the previous year when he said that the procedure was rarely performed" (Austin 1998, 6–13). The momentum from this development raised conservatives' hopes of winning a veto-proof majority in both chambers.

The Senate considered the ban in May, as well as two main amendments. One, offered by Minority Leader Daschle (D-SD), would have outlawed all "post-viability abortions," that is, late-term abortions for a viable fetus, with exceptions for the woman's life or "grievous injury" to her health. Senators Barbara Boxer (D-CA) and Dianne Feinstein (D-CA) offered a second alternative, with a broader health exception for the woman. Republicans charged that the health exceptions in both amendments would create loopholes in the ban, thereby undermining or negating it. Democrats responded that a failure to include the health exception would make the bill unconstitutional (Carey 1997). The Senate defeated both amendments and approved the original ban in a 64–36 vote, falling three votes shy of the sixty-seven votes necessary for an override. President Clinton then vetoed the bill on October 10 (Austin 1998).

2.2.2. The Supplemental

In 1997, Democrats and Republicans also considered a supplemental appropriations bill. This legislation funded a variety of emergency needs, most notably relief for states and communities suffering from natural disasters that swept much of the country during the winter and spring of 1996–1997. Severe winter weather and record-level flooding devastated entire communities, particularly in the Midwest. The relief funding for these disasters gave legislative momentum to the supplemental, but the Republican congressional leadership attached a number of controversial provisions to the bill during the spring.[1]

The Republican majority in Congress faced significant internal divisions about the desirability of including these provisions. In late May, immediately before the Memorial Day recess, Gingrich, Senate Majority Leader Trent Lott (R-MS), and House Appropriations Committee Chair Robert Livingston (R-LA1) attempted to win House approval of a scaled-back "mini supplemental." The smaller bill focused more narrowly on disaster relief funding and omitted many of the more controversial provisions slowing the larger supplemental legislation. Introduced late in the day, the mini supplemental required unanimous consent to pass. House conservatives, led by Majority Leader Dick Armey (R-TX26) refused to consent, and the bill failed. After the vote, Armey apologized to disaster victims and their representatives in Washington. But, he argued that $2 billion was already flowing through the Federal Emergency Management Agency's pipeline, and that the delay in passing the supplemental would not slow relief efforts. Not all Republicans agreed. Republican John Thune, South Dakota's lone representative, complained that "[w]e have made a crucial mistake in putting politics and process in front of people" (Taylor 1997c, 1188).

On June 5, Congress finally passed the broader supplemental appropriations bill containing the controversial provisions. The Republican leadership and conservatives outside Congress believed that

[1] These provisions included reforms to the Endangered Species Act to assist upkeep of earthen flood levees; the amount of land that farmers can enroll in the Conservation Enrollment Program; and a provision making it easier to build and repair roads through federal lands. In addition, conservative legislators voiced concern about an initial lack of budgetary offsets to pay for the supplemental appropriations. In response, GOP leaders found sufficient funds in several areas, but even these offsets were controversial. Nearly $4 billion was to come from funds allocated for fiscal year 1998, which was essentially borrowing from the future to pay for spending in 1997 (Taylor 1997a, 1997b).

Clinton would back down and not veto the supplemental (Taylor 1997c). As *The Wall Street Journal* editorialized, "One reason the GOP lost its 1995–1996 budget fight with Mr. Clinton was that its leaders lost their nerve. If Republicans give in once again under Democratic pressure ... they'll be giving in from here to November 1998" (as quoted in Hager 1997b). The leaders were confident that they could win a veto war with the President (Hager 1997a).

After winning passage of the bill on a Thursday, Republican congressional leaders waited until the following Monday to send the bill to the White House. The leaders did not want to send it until they had come back to Washington after the weekend (Taylor 1997d). The President surprised the Republicans, however, by immediately vetoing the bill and sending it back to the Capitol. Apparently, "none of the four top House leaders were on duty to counteract the White House spin. Clinton got more unchallenged airtime to patiently paint the Republicans as crazy extremists" (Hager 1997b). He argued that "[t]he time has come to stop playing politics with the lives of Americans in need to send me a clean, unencumbered disaster relief bill that I can and will sign the moment it reaches my desk" (*CQ Weekly* 1997, 1393).

In his criticism of the bill, the President focused on two controversial provisions. The first would have prohibited the Census Bureau from using sampling in the 2000 census. The Bureau had proposed sampling as a way to avoid the undercounting of minorities and the poor that plagued the 1990 census. Republicans argued that sampling was prohibited by the constitutional requirement of an actual headcount. But, their opposition to sampling (and the Democrats' support for it) was also related to the greater numbers of Democratic voters that the census would count if sampling were used.

The second controversial provision attempted to prevent the possibility of the government being shut down if Congress and the president could not agree on appropriation bills. If such disagreement occurred, the "auto CR" provision (standing for automatic continuing resolution) would allow government departments and agencies to continue operating at the previous year's spending levels. This arrangement would continue until Congress and the president passed the necessary appropriation bills. Republicans hoped to use this provision to avoid a repeat of the government shutdowns of 1995 and 1996, when they received much of the blame for the inability to pass appropriations bills. Democrats strongly opposed the auto CR provision, because it would transfer substantial bargaining power on budgetary matters to the Republican congressional majority.[2]

Congressional Democrats joined the criticism of their Republican colleagues. Senate Minority Leader Daschle repeated many of the President's themes: "You've got people who are hurting. And now we've got legislators who are playing games, political games – very high stakes – in an effort to leverage their position. . . . And that is a travesty" (Taylor 1997b, 1009). On Tuesday, June 10, the leader and his colleagues held an all-night vigil in Daschle's office to draw further attention to the GOP tactics and the need for quick disaster funding. Rank-and-file legislators in the GOP also voiced public concern about their leaders' tactics. Senator Rod Grams (R-MN) wrote to both Senate party leaders, asking for the removal of the controversial provisions from the supplemental (Taylor 1997d). Republican Representative Fred Upton (MI6) received a concise warning from his mother: "You're getting killed." He added that "When your mom tells you that, you know you're in trouble" (Hager 1997b). Republican concerns and dissent grew stronger as the debate progressed.

On June 12, Congress approved a final supplemental appropriations bill with none of the controversial provisions attached. Democrats gloated. According to Senator Christopher Dodd (D-CT), "It doesn't get any better than this. The only victory [Republicans] had was that it ended today rather than next week" (Taylor 1997d, 1362). Republicans despaired. Representative Marge Roukema (R-NJ5) complained about her party's leaders: "I would hope that this is the last time that they paint themselves into a corner. I would have thought they understood better by now" (Taylor 1997d, 1362). Overall, the debate gave the Democrats a substantial policy and public relations victory over the Republicans.

2.2.3. The Budget Debates of 1997 and 2003

Unlike the debates over partial birth abortion or the supplemental, congressional deliberations about the federal budget offer no clear advantage to either party. Instead, the diversity of the budget offers both parties the opportunity to draw attention to favorable issues and arguments about

[2] The Republican leadership could refuse to agree to the president's request for higher spending levels. If the disagreement prevented passage of appropriations bills, the auto CR provision would allow the government to continue operating but at lower levels than requested by the president. The Republicans would win the disagreement without having to compromise with the president.

different aspects of the budget. The chronology of each year's budget debate illustrates how the two parties worked to shift focus to their own favorable messages.

In 1997, both Democrats and Republicans hoped to avoid the contentious budget debates and government shutdowns of 1995–1996. Continued economic strength had improved the federal balance sheet to the point where elected officials began to consider the actual elimination of the budget deficit. Democrats and Republicans had widely divergent plans for how to reach that goal. Republicans preferred to shrink the size of the federal government, through spending cuts and tax cuts. Doing so would return the public's "hard-earned dollars" to their own pockets, thereby strengthening the U.S. economy. But, the spending cuts would force Republicans to cut many programs that were politically popular, in areas from education to the environment to health care. Congressional Democrats opposed these cuts. The Democratic legislators were particularly concerned that the program cuts, combined with additional tax cuts, would unfairly benefit wealthy taxpayers. Some Democrats, particularly President Clinton, supported limited tax cuts aimed at middle- and lower-income taxpayers. At the same time, the Democrats also recognized that eliminating the budget deficit could strengthen both the economy and their own party's record of fiscal discipline.

In early February, the budget process began on a positive note as President Clinton sent his proposed budget for fiscal year 1998 to Congress. Republican leaders declared the proposal "alive on arrival," a sharp contrast with the "dead on arrival" verdict assigned to previous presidential budgets (Hager 1997c). The GOP appeared strongly motivated to negotiate a budget agreement with Clinton and the Democrats. Those negotiations lasted for several months. Republicans privately and publicly emphasized the need for spending and tax cuts. President Clinton and congressional Democrats defended specific programs, as well as the need for the benefits from any budget agreement to go to more than just the wealthy. At the same time, each party also faced internal divisions over how much to cede to the opposing side. Conservative Republicans worried that their leaders would agree to tax and spending cuts that were too small. Liberal Democrats feared that President Clinton would undermine programs benefiting the middle class by agreeing to substantial spending reductions and tax cuts favoring the wealthy (Rubin 1997).

Congress and the President overcame these roadblocks and reached agreement on a balanced budget plan on May 2. The plan combined $135 billion in tax cuts (over five years) with limits on entitlement and discretionary spending, as well as new initiatives in education and health care for children of the working poor. Republicans were ecstatic about the deal, celebrating the "political trifecta: a balanced budget in five years; significant, permanent tax cuts; and a plan to keep Medicare solvent for another decade" (Hager 1997e, 93). While President Clinton could celebrate a landmark achievement, congressional Democrats reacted more somberly. While they took satisfaction in the balanced budget and the new initiatives, Democratic legislators expressed frustration with being largely excluded from the final negotiations between Clinton and Republicans. For the rest of the spring and summer, both parties haggled over the details of the agreement but ultimately produced one reconciliation bill containing tax cuts and one detailing spending reductions (Elving and Taylor 1997).

Compared to these developments in 1997 that produced a balanced budget, much of the 2003 budget debate focused on Republican proposals to cut taxes. Some GOP legislators wanted tax cuts of $750 billion or more, in line with a proposal by President Bush. Other Republicans expressed concern about the costs of those cuts, particularly in light of the ongoing war in Iraq and a worsening federal budget deficit. Republicans also disagreed about which type of taxes to cut, with the options ranging from corporate dividends to capital gains taxes. Democrats also faced divisions; some members supported additional but moderate tax cuts, while others opposed any further cuts at all. Another division in the debate was the extent of recovery from the economic recession beginning in 2001. Republicans argued that many economic indicators pointed to growing strength in the economy, and that further tax cuts were necessary in order to maintain that momentum. Democrats responded by pointing to continuing high levels of unemployment and a lack of job growth. These arguments coincided with a broader Democratic theme that GOP economic policies favored the wealthy.

In April, congressional Republicans won passage of a budget resolution, although its content was initially a source of dispute. The conference agreement contained $550 billion in tax cuts, which the House approved largely along party lines. The Senate Republican leadership, however, could only win passage of the conference agreement by promising GOP moderates that the final tax cuts would not exceed $350 billion. This figure was the tax cut target in the Senate's original version of the budget resolution. In May Congress approved a $350 billion package, including $30 billion in aid to state governments struggling to balance their budgets (Ota 2003a, 2003b, Taylor 2003a, 2003b).

2.3. UNANSWERED QUESTIONS

The four debates differ in significant ways. The partial birth abortion debate favored the Republicans, while the debate over the supplemental eventually favored the Democrats. The budget debates initially favored neither party. The debates also varied in breadth, with the partial birth abortion and supplemental debates suggesting a narrower set of possible issues and arguments than the budget debates offered. These differences among debates raise three sets of important questions about cycles of spin. Each set of questions is the focus of a subsequent chapter.

Chapter 3 examines the first set of questions, which address how congressional parties and their leaders choose messages to promote, from the range of all possible issues and arguments before Congress. Why did the Republicans choose to focus legislative debate on partial birth abortion, while the Democrats worked to make the supplemental debate into a major issue? And why did both parties energetically engage in the budget debates? It is important to understand how partisan advantage guided the creation of party messages in these debates. That advantage could emerge from the advantaged party's relative unity in a debate. Alternatively, graphic arguments and images could themselves make an issue more attractive for a promotional campaign. In addition, legislators regularly attempted to link issues for partisan advantage. Each party regularly created messages tying together different aspects of the budget process, in hopes of gaining political advantage. But in the supplemental debate, GOP leaders attempted to link disaster relief funding to a number of other policy proposals, and their attempt ended in resounding failure. What logic guides these attempts at linking issues, and why does the linkage succeed at certain times while failing at others?

The promotion of party messages is the focus of Chapter 4 and the second set of questions. Why did rank-and-file Republicans embrace and promote their party's message in the partial birth abortion debate, but not in the supplemental debate? Why did Democratic legislators behave in an opposite manner, with enthusiastic calls for a "clean" disaster relief bill and near silence about partial birth abortion? In these patterns of promotion, the moderates in each party are of particular interest. While the moderates are more likely to defect to the opposing party when casting roll call votes, it remains unclear whether they also defect in promotional campaigns and promote the opposing party's message. In the partial birth abortion debate, for example, Democratic moderates could choose to vote for the Republicans' ban. Beyond voting, they could have done more to support the ban, such as speaking out in favor of it. In the supplemental decision, Republican moderates faced a similar dilemma about whether to speak out in favor of a "clean" disaster relief bill. The moderates' decisions to defect or remain silent may determine the success of a party's promotional campaign.

A different decision faced many Democrats in the supplemental debate. The most vigorous proponents of the Democratic message came from states hard hit by natural disasters. Democrats from states with few or no disasters had to make a different decision: While they did not oppose the party message, they could benefit from its promotion by others – without saying a single word themselves. This challenge of free riding extended across all four debates, as supporters of the party message could benefit from others' promotion while doing nothing to promote that message themselves. How do congressional parties overcome this temptation to free ride?

Chapter 5 addresses a third set of questions, which concern the interaction between politicians and journalists. In their coverage of the debates, do reporters mirror actual events and the varying promotional campaigns, or present competing arguments in a more balanced manner, or consistently favor one party across the debates? From the standpoint of politicians, which messages succeeded in winning coverage, which failed, and how did these messages differ? In addition, it is important to consider whether the news coverage feeds back to affect legislators' promotional efforts and policy making. Did unfavorable news coverage push congressional Republicans toward collapse in the final stages of the supplemental debate? When congressional Democrats reacted somberly to the 1997 budget agreement, did news coverage of their unenthusiastic reaction reduce their bargaining power in subsequent negotiations to fill in the details of the agreement? The extent of feedback suggests how much journalists and their coverage influence agenda setting and the policy process.

This chapter summarized the four congressional debates and raised three sets of questions about cycles of spin that emerge from the debates. The next chapter addresses the initial set of questions, those involving the creation of party messages. I first develop in greater detail my argument about the origins of promotional campaigns. I then evaluate that argument and its implications, using the diverse evidence outlined previously.

3

Creation

Republican candidates for the U.S. House crowded the steps of the U.S. Capitol on September 27, 1994. Three-hundred-sixty-seven incumbent and potential House members had gathered together to promote the Contract with America. Republicans had carefully crafted a set of policy proposals into a public relations campaign centered on the contract. Republican legislators hoped that the day's event and the broader campaign would help set the agenda of the fall elections and win control of Congress for the GOP (Gimpel 1996). These hopes became reality as the Republican Party won majorities in both congressional chambers for the first time in forty years (Ornstein et al. 2002). During the opening weeks of the 104th Congress, House Republicans built on their fall campaign and passed legislation on nearly every plank in the contract, with overwhelming coalitions that were often bipartisan (*CQ Almanac Online Edition* 1996). These early successes painted a picture of a strong and dominant Republican majority. But as 1995 progressed, that picture gradually dissolved, as congressional Republicans struggled to turn the provisions of the contract into law, as well as to pass other legislation. The year ended with an embarrassing shutdown of the federal government, which helped set the stage for President Clinton's reelection in 1996 (*CQ Almanac Online Edition* 1996). Why did the Republicans' legislative momentum in January slow to painful gridlock by December?

A similar puzzle emerged twelve years later during the 110th Congress. In the November elections preceding this Congress, the congressional minority party, this time the Democrats, created their own public relations campaign, organized around a set of policy proposals collectively named "Six for '06" (Nather 2006b). The congressional minority hoped that this campaign would build on already favorable Democratic trends created by an unpopular president and war and a series of scandals involving the Republican congressional majority. The trends and the promotional campaign again coalesced into widespread electoral victories and new congressional majorities, this time for the Democrats. During the opening weeks of this Congress, the new House majority passed legislation from their campaign agenda, attracting unified Democratic support and at least twenty-four Republican votes on every bill (Epstein 2007). As happened twelve years before, however, the majority's early momentum soon slowed. Pushing agenda-related legislation through the Senate proved difficult. While legislation related to some agenda items became law, other related bills stalled due to Republican opposition or disagreements among congressional Democrats (Epstein 2007, Nather 2007a). Observers derided the Democrats' agenda and accomplishments as "very small potatoes": "the Democrats would be hard-pressed to argue that they've accomplished a lot of big things" (Nather 2007b).

In both the 104th and 110th congresses, partisan opposition in the White House and Senate certainly slowed the ability of the new congressional majorities to implement their election agendas (Nather 2007a). But even in the House, where rules strongly favored the majority, the newly dominant party in each congress struggled to maintain its momentum and unity as the congressional term progressed. Why did the unity of the new congressional majority decline in each congress? More generally, why can party unity vary dramatically across votes even within a single congressional term, and what can legislators do to encourage (or discourage) that unity?

Such variation in party unity depends on the content of the legislative agenda (Cox and McCubbins 1993, 2004, Riker 1982, 1986). In this chapter and the next, I explore ways in which the interaction of party leaders and followers can shape the legislative agenda, both inside and outside Congress.[1] The first section of this chapter explains how this complex interaction can create obstacles to agenda setting, and how each

[1] Other political actors also influence the legislative agenda. The remainder of this book includes analysis of the president's role in the promotion and coverage of party messages. Interest groups also help shape and promote these messages (Baumgartner and Leech 1998, Gerrity 2007). Several of my colleagues in Daschle's office worked extensively to maintain relationships with Democratic-leaning interest groups and to coordinate promotional campaigns with those groups. In 2008, Senate Democrats used the Democratic Steering and Outreach Committee to serve as "a liaison between Senate Democratic offices and advocacy groups and intergovernmental organizations" (http://democrats.senate.gov/steering/index.cfm?pg=1, last accessed June 12, 2008).

type of legislator might overcome those obstacles. The remainder of the chapter presents evidence of party leaders' actual agenda-setting strategies; Chapter Four does the same for rank-and-file members of Congress. The evidence comes from my experiences in Daschle's office, as well as more comprehensive records of legislators' promotional efforts in 1997 and 2003.

3.1. THE CHOICE OF ISSUES

Congressional leaders work to shape the policy agenda inside and, I argue, outside Congress, thereby helping the individual and collective interests of their fellow partisans in Congress. Yet, the leaders' agenda-setting powers are far from perfect, with a range of constraints limiting their efforts to shape debate. Events outside Congress often force other issues ahead of the leaders' preferred agenda (Alexseev and Bennett 1995). The attacks on September 11, 2001, for example, moved the issue of homeland security to the top of the congressional agenda. Regularly scheduled events inside Congress also require legislators to address certain issues. The budgetary calendar specifies several dates each year when the congressional parties must pass bills that raise and spend federal revenues. When Senate leaders attempt to bring their preferred issues and legislation to the floor, rank-and-file members may use filibusters and unanticipated amendments designed to alter the floor debate and agenda (Evans and Oleszek 2001). Members' uneven use of these procedural powers points to the most fundamental challenge – and opportunity – for congressional leaders wishing to shape the legislative agenda: the varying issue preferences and alignments of legislators in Congress.

Congress addresses a wide number of potentially interrelated issues. In order to fulfill the responsibilities of their position, congressional leaders work to focus congressional debate on issues that further their party's individual and collective interests. The difficulty is that their followers may not share a single set of collective interests (Riker 1986). It is certainly true that recent congresses have seen growing levels of partisan unity on many roll call votes.[2] But, congressional parties are far from

[2] Party unity votes are roll call votes in which a majority of Republicans vote in opposition to a majority of Democrats. The percentage of floor votes falling into this category has risen from an average of 39% in the 1970s to an average of 58% in the 1990s (calculated from Ornstein et al. 2002, 172). See Kady (2006) for further evidence. The rising partisan unity could certainly result from party leaders' agenda setting and strategic communication.

unified across all issues. Throughout their histories, each party has at times faced deep internal divisions (Aldrich 1995). And in the most recent congresses, each party has struggled to maintain voting unity, particularly on issues favoring the opposing party. Democrats often must work to remain unified in opposition to Republican tax cut proposals. In turn, the GOP has found it difficult to maintain unity while legislating reforms to Medicare or immigration policy (Nather 2006a, Sandler 2006).

Such varying challenges across issues arose often during my work in Daschle's office. Debates about certain issues, such as partial birth abortion, regularly produced division and tension among Democratic senators and their staff. On other less divisive issues, the Democratic caucus at times responded with enthusiastic promotion of a party message. At other times, however, the caucus largely ignored these issues. To make sense of these issues and the Democrats' varying reactions to them, I developed four categories of issues that Congress might face. Each category produces different alignments of legislators and offers different incentives for congressional parties.

The first category contains issues on which one congressional party is unified, while the opposing party is divided (Hall 1996, Sinclair 2006). Issues meeting both criteria (homogenous preferences within the party and heterogeneous preferences within the opposing party) offer the best opportunity for furthering the party's collective interests (Aldrich and Rohde 1995, 1996). On each such issue, members of one party unify in support for a position that is often popular among the general public. In the opposing party, extreme members may support one position, while more moderate members are often torn between that position and the one receiving unified support from the first party. The cross-pressured moderates in the opposition give the first party the opportunity to use the issue for political advantage. Schattschneider (1960) emphasizes the utility of finding and using such favorable issues: "The effort in all political struggle is to exploit cracks in the opposition while attempting to consolidate one's own side" (67).

Congressional debate over the Iraq War illustrates this type of issue, at least during the war's initial year. Republican legislators' support for the war (*CQ Weekly Online* 2003a, 2003b, 2003c) mirrored that of the public (*Time* et al. 2004, *ABC News* 2003), while congressional Democrats split among various degrees of support and opposition. Almost one year after the outbreak of the Iraq War, the House passed a resolution affirming "that the United States and the world are safer with the removal of Saddam Hussein and his regime from power in Iraq." Republican representatives supported the resolution almost unanimously (97%), while Democrats split relatively evenly between supporting (51%) and opposing (44%) the resolution (*Congressional Quarterly* 2006). The issue captured in this vote, and the related arguments, favored Republicans by providing an effective message for dividing the Democrats while broadening the GOP's public support and strengthening the "national security" aspect of their brand name.[3]

Issues with different alignments of party preferences offer less potential for a party seeking political advantage. A second category of issues includes topics on which the two legislative parties unanimously disagree on an issue (i.e., homogenous preferences within each party and heterogenous preferences between parties). Each party can use this type of issue to develop a distinctive reputation and brand name. But if the general electorate's opinions reflect the disagreement between parties (which is likely), then neither party position wins widespread public support or causes divisions in the opposition. In 2005, the debate over reauthorizing the Patriot Act provides an example of this type of issue. In the Senate, 91% of Republicans voted in favor of reauthorization, while 93% of Democrats voted against (*Congressional Quarterly* 2005). A national survey during the same year found the public also equally divided over the merits of the Patriot Act (Pew Research Center for the People and Press 2005). While legislators from both parties offered numerous public statements on the issue, the widespread division made it hard for either party to win broad political advantage on the issue.

A third possible type of issue occurs when each legislative party is divided, and the preferences of the two parties largely overlap. In this case, both parties find it difficult to claim a single position and record, which by extension undermines their efforts to win public support. The broad issue of abortion offers one such example. Congressional Republicans are divided between a dominant pro-life faction and a smaller group of pro-choice members, such as Senators Olympia Snowe (ME) and Susan Collins (ME). Democrats split into similar factions, with dominant pro-choice legislators opposed by Senators Robert Byrd (WV), Ben Nelson (NE), and other conservative members (NARAL 2006). The split within both parties means that neither party can clearly benefit from

[3] President Ronald Reagan followed a similar strategy when negotiating with Congress over the federal budget. His public emphasis on taxing and spending helped unify congressional Republicans while attracting the support of conservative Democratic legislators (Kernell 1997).

promoting the issue. Typically, neither side can offer a unified position to the news media or benefit from divisions in the opposing party.

A final category of issues involves topics on which both sides unify around a single most popular position. On these valence issues, both sides are unanimous in support of a popular position, but little opportunity exists for seizing political advantage over the opposition. Such unified support occurred immediately at the outbreak of the Iraq War in 2003, when the public and congressional members from both parties voiced strong support for American troops and President Bush. Rep. Robert Menendez (D-NJ13) captured the sentiment spread throughout Congress: "Today there are no Democrats and no Republicans. There are only patriots" (Fessenden and Cochran 2003).

Issues fitting these latter alignments of legislators may prove relevant for a party's overall message strategy (Evans and Oleszek 2001). On issues such as the Patriot Act where the two parties unanimously disagree, politicians may still need to promote issues and arguments in order to further their own policy concerns and respond to party activists (Sinclair 2006, 306). On issues where both parties are divided, bipartisan coalitions may emerge, with legislators from both parties hoping to pass legislation that will further both their reelection and policy goals. These types of coalitions, however, may do little to further the interests of each party.[4] Finally, on valence issues such as the Iraq War, politicians from both parties need to promote their position publicly; failing to do so risks creating the public impression that a party is weak or less competent on the issue. Arguably, however, these concerns are largely designed to maintain a party's existing base of support. Issues with these alternative alignments offer less potential for gaining partisan advantage by dividing the opposition. For a party wishing to gain this type of advantage, the first category of issues offers the greatest potential.

Thus, party leaders are most likely to focus their agenda-setting efforts on issues where their own legislative party is unified around a single position on the issue, while the opposing party is not (Hall 1996, Sinclair 2006). While issues meeting these criteria may be few in number, they

[4] The partisan and bipartisan strategies offer competing ways to achieve the reelection and policy goals. As suggested in the text, reliance on each type of strategy depends on the partisan and ideological composition of the legislative chamber. Internally heterogeneous, externally homogeneous parties encourage bipartisan coalitions, while internally homogeneous, externally heterogeneous parties encourage partisan coalitions (Aldrich and Rohde 1995, 1996).

offer the greatest potential for partisan advantage to the party that owns them.[5] Yet, the awareness and use of these favorable issues do not guarantee the success of a party's promotional campaign. The leader's choice of message and the follower's decision to promote that message are closely related, which creates challenges to the collective promotion of party messages. The next section explains these interactions and challenges.

3.1.1. Remaining Challenges of Persuasion and Promotion

When choosing issues and arguments to promote inside and outside Congress, party leaders and followers engage in a complex interaction. I witnessed many examples of this interaction while working in Daschle's office. Additional examples occur every day in Congress, as leaders and followers negotiate the pursuit of their individual and collective interests. In this subsection and the next (3.1.1 and 3.1.2), I describe the details of the interaction among leaders and followers, including the specific decisions that they face, their preferences across possible outcomes, and their strategies for realizing preferred outcomes. The argument is largely deductive, building on theories of cost-benefit analysis and collective action (Olson 1965, Riker and Ordeshook 1968). If the argument is accurate, we can expect leaders and rank-and-file members in Congress to follow specific patterns of behavior. I use diverse evidence to evaluate these expectations in the remainder of this chapter and the next.

When launching a promotional campaign, party leaders and followers make three important decisions that are interdependent.[6] First, a leader must select an issue(s) to emphasize in the party message. She prefers to choose an issue favoring her party, where the leader's message and position receive wide support in the legislative party. But, external events or the opposing party may force the original leader to choose for the party message an issue favoring the opposition. This decision creates a second choice for the leader. As described in the first category of issues developed previously, the leader's party is divided on this unfavorable issue, with

[5] Petrocik (1996) uses public perceptions of parties to determine ownership of issues. My analysis attempts to unpack the origins of this ownership and to understand how party elites attempt to shape public perceptions of parties' strengths and weaknesses. See Carmines and Stimson (1986) for a similar analysis of racial politics over a longer period of time.

[6] For more extensive and formal analysis of the interaction among leaders and followers in Congress, see the literature surrounding Aldrich and McGinniss (1989), Aldrich and Rohde (1995, 1996), Cox and McCubbins (1993, 2004), and Krehbiel (1991, 1998).

factions supporting different positions. The leader must therefore decide which faction's position to use in the party message. On such an unfavorable issue, the leader could also decide against choosing a party message, thus making it easier for party members to follow their own individual preferences in public statements and roll call votes. But while I worked in Daschle's office, rank-and-file Democrats appeared to look to the Minority Leader and his staff for guidance and assistance in avoiding these unfavorable issues (June 7, 2007, Washington, D.C.). The followers expected Daschle to bear the brunt of any negative publicity on the issue. If he chose not to issue a party message and take a public role in a debate, any negative publicity more directly affected all members of the caucus.

The third and final decision belongs to the follower: whether to promote the party issue and argument, an alternative message, or no message at all.[7] Each actor bases her decision(s) on how she fares across the various possible combinations of messages and promotion. Significantly, achieving any particular combination depends on both individuals' decisions. Thus, a leader's creation of a message is closely linked to persuading a follower to promote it. The diverse strands of this linkage become clearer by comparing the various outcomes, from the standpoint of both the leader and the follower.

When comparing the various possible outcomes, the leader most prefers those where the follower promotes the party message. Such promotion increases the likelihood of the message receiving press coverage.[8] In turn, the coverage generates collective benefits for the party in the form of greater influence over the internal legislative agenda in the Senate (policy benefits), and greater public support for the party (electoral benefits). Greater coverage of the party message may also generate individual benefits for the leader. This coverage encourages the perception that the

[7] This framework does not attempt to explain how a leader chooses from the set of issues favoring her party. In Congress and the White House, a common strategy is to emphasize a different issue regularly, rotating through a set of issues to create a new and fresh message each day or week. Feedback from news coverage (documented in Chapter 5) can affect a leader's choice of issues. Extensive coverage of a message may encourage a leader to continue promoting the issues and arguments in the message, and to delay rotating to another issue and message. If a message receives little coverage, the leader may change to another message more quickly.

[8] If more legislators promote a message, a greater proportion of the legislature supports the issue and argument(s) in that message. The size of this group of legislators gives it a corresponding influence over the legislative process, which makes their message promotion worthy of news coverage. Chapter 5 provides extensive theoretical and empirical support for this assumed linkage between promotion of the party message and coverage of that message.

leader effectively promotes party interests, which in turn solidifies the leader's position at the head of the party.

The least desirable outcome for a leader is when the follower promotes an alternative message, particularly that of the opposing party. Such efforts reveal intraparty conflict. Moreover, assisting the opposing party gives its message a bipartisan strength. The public dissent yields individual benefits of attention and influence for the disloyal follower, but that dissent detracts from the collective goals of the leader. As a result, the leader prefers the follower to promote no message, if the alternative is to promote a competing one detracting from the party's message.

Overall, the leader is more likely to achieve a desirable outcome if she emphasizes messages on issues favoring her party. Followers are more likely to promote these messages, which are in turn more persuasive to the press, members of the opposing party, and the general public (Aldrich 1995, Cox and McCubbins 1993, Petrocik 1996, Pope and Woon 2005, Sellers 1998). Significantly, a leader selecting issues may face the constraint of being a minority in the chamber. The majority's control of the floor may hinder the minority's efforts to emphasize issues that it owns. In response to this disadvantage, the minority may work harder at building in-party loyalty, by considering rank-and-file members' opinions and ideas early in the legislative process and thereby encouraging those members to hold more ownership of the party's eventual proposals and messages (Sinclair 2006).

At the same time that the leader is choosing a party message, the follower must decide whether to promote that message. Three factors are central to the follower's decision. First, the follower considers the costs of promotion, which consist of the personal time required to participate in message-related activities (such as press conferences), and the staff and resources required to organize and promote such an event. The second component of the follower's decision is the probability that the party message receives press coverage, because such coverage is necessary for receiving any benefits from the party message. This probability is often small, reflecting the limited coverage of most congressional events in Washington (Hess 1991, Sellers and Schaffner 2007).[9] If the follower decides to support the message, the probability of receiving any benefits from coverage of that message will be higher than if she does not support the message.

[9] Individual legislators may win more coverage in their local news coverage (Arnold 2004, Vinson 2003). See Chapter 5 for more detailed discussion of national versus local coverage.

These benefits form the third component of the follower's decision, and they can be collective or individual in nature. The collective benefits may extend to all members of the party, and are realized if the party's message receives coverage. If the message emphasizes an issue on which the party is unified, coverage of that message provides collective policy and electoral benefits for the entire party. But if the message focuses on an issue favoring the opposing party, that message provides benefits for only a portion of the party. The particular faction that benefits depends on the issue position in the message that the leader chooses.

The follower may also receive her own individual benefits from promoting the party message. Promoting the message allows the follower to draw attention to an issue and position that she personally supports. In addition, she can link herself more closely to that issue and position, helping establish a policy reputation for activity on the issue (Cook 1998). Finally, the press coverage may produce electoral benefits among constituents.

For each possible outcome, the follower combines the costs, the individual and collective benefits, and the probability of receiving those benefits. This thought process helps the follower determine and reach preferred outcomes. In the follower's decision making, the collective benefits are particularly noteworthy (Hardin 1982). Generating the collective benefits of news coverage requires collective action by party members, because the media may ignore a message if few or no followers support it. But, the collective nature of the benefits means that a follower may still receive those benefits without helping promote the message. The temptation to free ride applies to all followers and may result in no promotion of the party message, no coverage of that message, and no provision of the collective good (Olson 1965). This collective action framework helps explain the promotional challenges facing a party even on favorable issues where members are unified in support of a message.

Beyond these collective considerations about favorable issues, legislators follow a similar logic of decision making in two other aspects of their promotional decisions. The first concerns the individual benefits of message coverage. A follower receives individual benefits from message coverage only if she helps promote the party message. If she chooses not to support that message, she cannot personally link herself to the message's issues and arguments, thus preventing provision of these individual benefits.

Second, on issues where the party is divided, only part of the party supports the issue position in the party message. For this subsection of the party, coverage of that message remains a collective good. Other members of the party, however, do not benefit from coverage of the message, because they do not support the issue position in that message. These opponents may be torn between hoping to present a unified party to the press and voters, and wanting to promote their own position publicly. The latter strategy can attract news coverage and thus individual benefits for defectors from the party, but pursuit of this strategy can diversify and possibly undermine their party's collective reputation (Domke et al. 2006, 293, Groeling 2005). The potential defectors must balance the collective benefits from remaining silent and allowing a more unified public presentation from their party, and the individual benefits from publicly stating their own dissent and undermining the party's collective image. This type of defection has grown more difficult in recent years, as parties have grown more polarized and the partisan margins in each chamber have shrunk (Sinclair 2006, 131).

These concerns illustrate how collective action remains a problem for legislative parties, even after leaders receive incentives and resources to further their party's collective interests. A leader must still persuade followers to support the party message. Such support is far from guaranteed, given the followers' temptation to free ride on the efforts of others, and the potential intraparty disagreement over the most desirable position in the message. In addition, the leader is unlikely to possess complete information about the followers' preferences and interests in issues. As a result, the leader cannot simply calculate backwards from followers' preferences and interests to the best issue for the party message. Instead, the leader must work in other, less certain ways to overcome the obstacles to collective promotion of the party message.

3.1.2. Strategies of Leaders and Followers

In her efforts to encourage promotion of the party message, the leader focuses on the three components of the follower's decision to support the message: the benefits of promotion, the costs, and the probability of receiving coverage (and therefore benefits). When working to influence the follower's beliefs about the first component, the leader tries to select messages on issues favoring her own party, that is, where her own party members are unified and the opposing party is divided. The follower is more likely to perceive benefits from promoting this type of message. The coverage of the message can provide collective and individual benefits. Significantly, the collective benefits are unlikely to induce the follower to promote the message: a free-riding party member can receive those benefits without helping promote the message. But, the follower can still receive individual electoral and policy benefits from promoting this message (if it receives coverage). When attempting to overcome the collective action problem surrounding promotion of the party message, the leader may therefore attempt to increase these individual benefits by emphasizing issues favoring the party.

The leader can also structure a media event so that a participating follower is more likely to receive the individual benefits of media coverage. These individual benefits are less likely at "cattle call" press conferences, where the leader receives all the press attention, to the exclusion of other party members (Sellers and Schaffner 2007). Instead, the leader can organize message promotion events where party members are more likely to interact individually with reporters and therefore to receive coverage.[10]

In addition to influencing the follower's beliefs about the benefits of promoting the party message, the leader can also target the costs of promotion and the probability of receiving press coverage. Most simply, the leader works to minimize the costs involved in promoting the party message (Pan and Kosicki 2001). These efforts involve adjusting promotional events to fit the follower's schedule, and using leadership staff to meet all logistical and promotional needs of such events. The leader also encourages the belief that the party message has a high probability of receiving press coverage. If this persuasion is successful, the follower is more likely to believe that she will receive the collective and individual benefits of message promotion.[11]

[10] Congressional leaders and followers can structure press events in a variety of ways. Records of the Senate Radio Television Gallery list four types of events: press conferences, studio interviews, stakeouts, and photo ops (Sellers and Schaffner 2007).

[11] A leader can also use selective incentives to influence legislators' beliefs about the benefits and costs of participating in leadership-sponsored events. By offering to expedite a bill important to a legislator, the leader could increase the legislator's perceived benefits of participating in the event. Threats to stall legislation could exert a similar effect on the perceived costs of not participating. While these activities underlie many traditional conceptions of congressional leadership (Aldrich and Rohde 1995, Evans and Oleszek 1997), the activities are extremely difficult to document systematically, particularly in the Senate. See Pearson (2005) and Sinclair (2006) for evidence of leaders' reliance on selective incentives.

3.1.3. Summary of Expectations

The previous arguments suggest a number of specific expectations about legislators' promotional activities. Party leaders work in four ways to encourage promotion of the party message:[12]

- The leaders
  → are more likely to select messages on issues favoring their party than on those where the opposing party holds an advantage,
  → help their followers receive individual coverage of the promotion efforts,
  → provide logistical services to reduce the costs to their followers of promoting the party message, and
  → encourage followers to believe that the message is likely to receive coverage.

In response to the leaders' efforts, the rank-and-file party members must decide whether to promote the party message.

- When that message uses issues favoring the party,
  → the follower is more likely to promote the message, and to perceive benefits than costs from promoting the message.
- When that message uses issues favoring the opposing party, if the follower agrees with the position in the party message,
  → the follower is more likely to promote that message, and to perceive benefits than costs from promoting the message.
- But if the follower disagrees with the message's position,
  → the follower is less likely to promote the message, and more likely to perceive costs than benefits from promoting the message.

The remainder of this chapter and the next provide evidence evaluating these expectations about leaders' and followers' promotional efforts. The

[12] In their attempts to encourage promotion of the party message, party leaders may also turn to their own individual powers of personal persuasion. Lyndon Johnson was only one of many congressional leaders talented in this respect (Caro 2003; see also Frisch and Kelly 2008, Loomis 2001, and Rosenthal and Peters 2008). In the contemporary Congress, it is difficult to document such persuasion systematically, because the interaction between leader and follower often occurs in private, impromptu meetings with no documentation. In the debate over partial birth abortion described in Chapter 2, I watched Daschle and his staff use this tactic of personal persuasion to try to build support for his own legislative proposal in the Democratic caucus.

next section of this chapter turns to party leaders' decision making in creating messages, including an explanation of how the leaders use favorable issues in hopes of eliciting greater promotion of party messages by followers. In the two subsequent sections, I document how this strategy is only somewhat effective across broad issues owned by parties, but much more effective in narrower debates that clearly favor one party. I then turn to evidence of leaders' reliance on other strategies for encouraging the promotion of party messages, such as shaping the costs and individual benefits of promotion for legislators and raising expectations that a message will succeed in winning coverage. The chapter concludes by examining how partisan control of the legislative and executive branches influences congressional leaders' promotion of messages. Finally, Chapter Four explores how rank-and-file members respond to their leaders' attempts at persuasion.

3.2. THE CREATION OF MESSAGES

When politicians create messages, what guides their thinking? My work in Daschle's office revealed a range of considerations. One central concern is the target of the message. Three distinct audiences are important (Kedrowski 1996, Kernell 1997, Mannheim 1991). The first target is the electorate. Politicians hope to persuade voters to focus on certain issues and arguments. A staff member of the Democratic leadership explained to me that their goal is to "give voters a clear image of the Democratic Party, so that they can have a clear reason to vote Democratic (personal notes, May 22, 1997). As part of this effort, the promotional campaigns may target individual groups within the electorate. In the summer of 2006, for example, Senate Democrats launched a four-week public relations campaign highlighting five different issues:

> Stem-cell research is supported by a majority of Americans, ... while the rise in college costs and gas prices affects voters of any political affiliation. The [Voting Rights Act] plays well with base Democratic voters, while Democrats believe the war in Iraq can play well with Democrats and independents who are disaffected by the Bush administration's policies related to the conflict. (Billings 2006)

Despite overlaps among the groups of voters, each issue appealed to a specific and different group.

A second target of messages is other elected officials (Entman and Herbst 2001). Politicians target other politicians for several reasons.

One is to encourage fellow members of the party (and their staff) to promote a particular message (personal notes, May 22, 1997). According one Democratic advisor, "our final audience is the public. But, we must get the caucus on board. They're the ones who will sell everything to the public" (personal notes, February 12, 1997). In addition, the public statements themselves may have policy-making implications; legislators may communicate with each other through their public statements and subsequent news coverage of those statements.

During one partisan conflict in 1997, congressional Republicans planned to send an appropriations bill to the White House in hopes of forcing President Clinton into a difficult choice: Sign the bill and thereby accept several riders favoring Republicans, or veto the bill and deny needed funding to Democratic constituencies. In an effort to preempt the Republicans' strategy and signal Clinton's resolve, Daschle made a public statement that the Republicans should "keep the car running" when taking the bill to the White House; Clinton signed the veto statement nineteen minutes after the bill arrived from Congress.

Gaining extensive coverage, Daschle's statement helped reduce the pressure on the President. Daschle redefined the alternatives that the Republicans hoped to present to Clinton. The senator's statement signaled that Clinton and congressional Democrats were unified in rejecting the alternative of signing the bill with the GOP riders attached. Daschle's support for a quick veto also signaled that congressional Democrats would accept (and indeed prefer) the veto of the bill and the accompanying denial of disaster relief funding to their constituencies. The Democrats believed that this denial would only be temporary (personal notes, July 8, 1997).

Public relations campaigns can also signal the positions of legislators on upcoming policy issues and thereby influence subsequent positioning and bargaining on those issues. In the Pelosi-Taylor example from Chapter One, the Speaker's appearance with a conservative member of her party signaled that their message was acceptable to both wings of the caucus (Cook 1998). Legislators' public statements of positions can also shape future negotiations between parties and chambers. Early in the 1997 budget debate, a Democratic advisor explained the logic:

> We need to set our message early, in order to make it credible. Even if there is an eventual deal, we need to set our message now. This will help us have clean hands in negotiations. A strong message from us improves the final outcome because it sets the terms of debate. It also keeps congressional Democrats relevant and gives us leverage. We can't wait and just float. (personal notes, February 18, 2007)

By clearly and publicly stating their arguments early, the Democrats hoped to influence the boundaries and outcomes of the subsequent policy debate.

News coverage also shapes these boundaries and outcomes, so a third target of promotional campaigns is the press (Sheafer and Wolfsfeld 2004). News coverage of politicians' messages helps communicate those messages to the public and other politicians. To encourage that coverage, the elected officials structure their promotional efforts to take advantage of the guidelines that journalists follow when producing news stories. Most notably, politicians can attempt to shape perceptions of the legislative importance of messages. If party leaders can persuade numerous members to promote a message, the news media is more likely to view the message's issues and arguments as important to the legislative process. That perception can lead to greater coverage. In an appeal for participation in a message event on the floor of the Senate, a leadership staff member made the link explicit: "Will your senator help on the floor during this hour today? If we can get four or five, maybe the press will notice. Call me" (personal email, March 19, 1997).

In addition to thinking about target audiences when creating a message, politicians also pay close attention to the language of the message. The words chosen for a message can influence whether the public, politicians, and journalists accept or reject the issues and arguments in the message (Aday 2006, Druckman 2001, Iyengar 1991, Iyengar and Kinder 1987, Lakoff 2004, McCombs and Ghanem 2001). Party leaders and followers increasingly devote great care and attention to the language in their messages (Rutenberg 2006). At a retreat in 2005, congressional Republicans received guidelines for how to discuss President Bush's proposed Social Security reforms:

> The blueprint urges lawmakers to promote the 'personalization' of Social Security, suggesting ownership and control, rather than 'privatization,' which 'connotes the total corporate takeover of Social Security.' Democratic strategists said they intend to continue fighting the Republican plan by branding it as privatization, and assert that depiction is already set in people's minds.... The Republicans' book, with a golden nest egg on the cover, urges the GOP to 'talk in simple language,' 'keep the numbers small,' 'avoid percentages; your audience will try to calculate them in their head,' and 'acknowledge risks,' because listeners 'know they can lose their investments.' (Allen 2005)

GOP leaders believed the specific language and its use could effectively counter Democratic criticisms and boost passage of the proposed reforms.

Congressional Democrats display a similar concern. In 1997, Republicans charged that President Clinton's budget contained a "$60 billion new entitlement." In a meeting to plan a response, one staffer in the Democratic leadership encouraged Democrats to "get beneath the phrase and point out that the President is proposing new spending on children's health and education." The staffer also addressed the Republicans' proposed $78 billion in tax cuts: "We need to peel back the term.... We need to get into the specifics of the proposals, such as how they would help Estee Lauder shelter $40 million of gains in the stock market" (personal notes, February8, 1997). These differing descriptions of the same policy proposals could certainly shape public perceptions and evaluations of the proposals.

The competing language reflects each party's goals and ideological orientation (Gamson 1996). The GOP's phrase "$60 billion new entitlement" brings to mind substantial spending for "entitled," that is, guaranteed, benefits. Eligible individuals could theoretically receive this entitlement regardless of effort. Conservatives often argue that these automatic benefits reduced or eliminated the need to work. GOP legislators instead wished to tie the provision of benefits to work, education, or other types of effort by recipients. This line of argument ultimately proved successful, culminating the Republican-sponsored welfare reforms of the 1990s (*CQ Weekly Online* 1996a).

The Democrats' competing argument made no mention of guaranteed benefits. Instead, the Democrats emphasized the specific targets of the new spending, appealing to public support for improving children's health care and education. Liberals often support increased government spending in these areas. The Republican and Democratic descriptions point to very different arguments about the spending proposals, with each argument appealing for support in a different manner (Jacoby 2000, Wanta et al. 2004).

Thus, when creating messages for their promotional efforts, leaders use language and targeted appeals to craft messages that draw the widest support (Gamson and Modigliani 1989). When creating these messages, the leaders often employ favorable issues, those in which one party is unified while the opposing party is divided. Numerous anecdotal examples illustrate how recent party leaders focus on this type of issue, thus providing initial support for my expectation about message creation presented earlier in this chapter.

Chapter 2, for example, described deliberations in 2003 about the federal budget. Congressional Republicans enthusiastically supported

President Bush's proposed tax cuts, while Democratic legislators struggled to craft a unified response. Many past debates about taxes have unified Republicans and divided Democrats in a similar manner (*CQ Almanac Online Edition* 1981, 1993, 1999, *CQ Weekly Online* 2001). The Iraq War posed a similar challenge for congressional Democrats, with party members splintering among options ranging from continuing current policy to immediately withdrawing U.S. troops from Iraq. In 2005, Reid urged "Democrats to limit their comments on the future of the Iraq war to areas where there is broad agreement within the party in an effort to quell increasing concerns both within the Democratic Caucus and the minds of the public that the ongoing conflict has caused deep intra-party divisions" (Stanton 2005b). A news account described the results of the Democratic split over Iraq:

> Reid's recent struggles with a small group of moderate Democrats has been a boon to Republicans in the chamber, who have used the Democratic leader's inability to keep all his Senators on the same page as a rallying point for their own splintered Conference.... Keen to quash any appearance of a rift within the party, Reid spent much of last week attempting to refocus public attention on the Bush administration's failures in Iraq and trying to craft a consensus critique of Bush that all Caucus members could agree to. (Stanton 2006)

Reid hoped somehow to create a message that could unify his caucus and turn the topic of Iraq into a more favorable issue.

In my interactions with Daschle's staff, they shared this goal of focusing on politically favorable issues. During private meetings with legislative directors in the Democratic caucus, the leadership staff often acknowledged the diversity of opinion within the caucus. But, the staff then encouraged the legislative directors to "try to find some stuff for Democrats to be unified on. This will have real message value" (personal notes, June 24, 1997). Again, the goal was to find a message that could unite the caucus.

In their attempts to focus on favorable issues, party leaders often create multipronged messages about those issues (Rojecki 2008). In 1994 the Contract with America contained ten separate components, and multiple issues and arguments within those components. This complexity allowed individual Republicans to craft a range of messages from the overall platform. Such flexibility encouraged more Republicans to endorse that platform (Gimpel 1996). Similarly, the head of the Democratic Senatorial Campaign Committee promised in 2003 that

Democratic candidates could individually tailor the Democrats' agenda (called "Operation Home Front") to fit their individual interests: "It fits differently in different states, but Operation Home Front will be right at the centerpiece of the Democratic message" (Billings and Preston 2003). On the floor of the Senate, the Democratic leadership also crafted multi-part messages, so that individual senators could speak on any one or more of them (personal email, May 19, 1997). Such flexibility makes it easier for legislators to find an argument or issue that they personally support, which in turn increases the likelihood of promoting the party message.

Party leaders can also unify their party behind a message by allowing and encouraging rank-and-file members to participate in the creation of the message (Sinclair 2006). In 2005, then-House Minority Leader Nancy Pelosi started having daily conference calls with leadership staffers, ranking members of House committees, and other active Democrats. The goal was "planning Democratic response to the day's news stories and coordinating strategy to tout the Caucus' message in the media.... One of Pelosi's goals, Democrats say, is to decentralize the dissemination of her Caucus' message so more members will feel invested in it" (Kornacki 2005). When planning messages and strategy in 1997, Daschle's staff also worked to "cast a wide net" and include many supporters. A central goal of the planning process was to energize these supporters (personal notes, May 29, 1997). Finally, House Republican John Boehner (R-OH8) pledged a similar commitment to inclusiveness when running for majority leader in 2006. After winning, he created six issue-based working groups to help improve coordination between the leadership and committees, and to help organize communication strategies and outside coalition work (O'Connor 2006). By including more rank-and-file members in the leadership's decision making, these strategies encourage greater ownership of the results of that decision making. In the area of public relations, greater ownership means that more members support the positions in the party's messages, which encourages greater promotion of those messages.

Congressional leaders thus refer to a variety of considerations when explaining the creation of the party's messages. The leaders aim their messages at the public, the news media, and other politicians. The latter target is the central and obvious focus of leaders' efforts to encourage promotion of party messages. To persuade rank-and-file legislators to promote those messages, the leaders carefully select language and issues that unify their party and divide the opposition. Such a concern with favorable issues fits this chapter's earlier expectation about how leaders selectively choose issues to encourage message promotion.

Despite the numerous anecdotal examples in this section, it remains unclear how widely congressional leaders seek and use favorable issues, beyond the individual examples. To provide a more widespread assessment of leaders' reliance on this strategy, the next section examines congressional leaders' public statements across all issues before Congress. This portion of the analysis focuses on Senate party leadership in 1997, particularly Daschle and his staff.

3.3. CHOOSING AMONG BROAD ISSUES

The first step in this analysis was to categorize how the different issues before Congress favored the two parties. I turned to the framework of issues developed by Baumgartner and Jones (1993).[13] Their framework helped me identify broad categories of issues favoring each party, that is, issues where one caucus was unified and the opposing caucus was divided.[14]

Four broad issues clearly favored one party: health, education, and environment for the Democrats, and defense for the GOP. These four issues are not the *only* ones that the leaders promote. Instead, the four offer the greatest potential for furthering followers' collective and individual interests and for winning political advantage over the opposition. I argue that the leaders therefore are most likely to promote messages involving these issues, although external events or efforts of the opposition may force each leader to turn to other issues.

In other broad categories of issues, either the two parties shared the advantage or no partisan advantage existed. For example, if discussions of social welfare emphasize specific poverty programs and the provision of benefits, Democrats are more likely to be unified and own the issue. But, the advantage switches to the Republicans if the discussion revolves around more general welfare reform. Because no party enjoyed a clear advantage on social welfare issues, party leaders perceived less political

[13] This dictionary spans twenty-seven pages, containing nineteen major issue categories, 169 subcategories, and multiple specific issues within each subcategory. The most recent version is available at http://www.policyagendas.org/codebooks/topicindex.html.

[14] See Appendix 3.A for further details on this classification.

gain in emphasizing these issues. Instead, the leaders are more likely to focus on issues that their party has a clear advantage.[15]

With this categorization of issues, I turned to the actual messages selected by Senate party leaders. I used several different sources of messages. The first and narrowest is the *Daily Report*, the daily newsletter produced by the Democratic Policy Committee in the Senate. I collected editions from March to July of 1997. The publication reviews recent developments in the Senate and describes upcoming floor action. It also presents substantive and rhetorical arguments from the Democratic leadership's message for the particular day and week. For example, the June 24th edition reprinted portions of a *New York Times* editorial that criticized Republican tax proposals. The *Daily Report* feature was titled "GOP Tax Tables Paint Misleading Picture of Who Benefits from House and Senate Tax Bills." In addition to frequent excerpts from newspaper editorials, the Democratic publication also uses quotes from Democratic legislators.

For a second source of Daschle's messages, I turned to my notes from weekly private meetings between Daschle's leadership staff and the legislative directors (LDs) of the Senate Democrats. Normally occurring on Friday afternoons, these meetings gave the leadership staff an opportunity to brief the LDs on expected developments during the upcoming week. Such regular meetings also allowed the leadership staff to (attempt to) persuade the LDs to support the leadership's strategies and messages.[16]

I attended every LD meeting from the start of February to the end of July, a total of sixteen meetings. At each meeting I took detailed notes, particularly of the leadership staff's presentations. Again, these presentations focused on events of the upcoming week. The leadership initiated

15 The unclear partisan advantage on some issues is partially a function of the Baumgartner and Jones issue categories. This framework performs very well for their own analysis. But, several categories include issues favoring each party. To address this potential problem, I also examine the four specific congressional debates described in Chapter 2.

16 During my tenure in Daschle's office, the LD meetings were only part of the Democratic leadership's attempts to distribute their interpretation of recent and upcoming events, and to persuade others to accept their strategies and support their messages. On Fridays, leadership staffers also held separate meetings with the Senate Democrats' administrative assistants, with their press secretaries, and with the minority chiefs of staff of the Senate committees. In addition, Democratic senators regularly met on Tuesdays in caucus meetings and on Thursdays in policy luncheons (often featuring guest speakers such as a cabinet secretary, author, or economist). The leadership's efforts to coordinate and promote the party's message have grown even more extensive in recent years (Sinclair 2006).

some events, while responding to or taking advantage of others. When focusing on specific legislation, the presentations were often detailed in nature and focused on legislative maneuvering in committee or on the Senate floor. Also common to many presentations was a message component: the issues and arguments that the leadership planned to discuss on the Senate floor or when talking with reporters and constituents.

These first two sources of messages aim for a relatively narrow audience: the LDs and general staff of Democratic senators. Party leaders also target their strategic communication efforts toward a broader, more public audience. To capture these broader efforts, I turned to the leaders' public statements. One source of statements was the *Congressional Record*. For another such source, I used the leaders' press releases, collected by the Federal Document Clearing House (FDCH).[17] Finally, I turned to transcripts of news conferences on Capitol Hill, also as compiled by the FDCH. For each private and public statement, I coded the issue(s) mentioned, using the Baumgartner and Jones directory of issues.[18]

3.3.1. Party Leaders' Statements

Table 3.1 summarizes Daschle's and Lott's statements across the broad issues. The patterns of issue emphasis are remarkably similar across the three sources of messages, but reveal only mixed evidence of leaders focusing on issues favoring their party. The most frequently mentioned issue was macroeconomics, including the federal budget. Both leaders devoted at least one third of their public statements to the issue (101 of Daschle's statements and 57 of Lott's). Nearly two thirds of the *Daily Report* editions (43 of 68) addressed microeconomics. And the issue arose in a message context in all 16 LD meetings. This emphasis undoubtedly reflects both parties' efforts to steer discussions of the budget toward specific topics favoring their interests. Democrats wished to discuss the federal budget in terms of specific governmental programs. Republicans, on the other hand, preferred to emphasize general revenue, spending, and

[17] From April through July of 1997, I also collected hard copies of any releases that party leaders distributed to the Senate press galleries. In addition, research assistants collected the titles of all press releases on legislators' congressional web sites during the first seven months of 2003. The patterns in these releases largely track those reported in the text.

[18] The coding process involved a combination of a computerized content analysis program and human coding with research assistants. See Appendix 3.B for more details about the sources and coding.

TABLE 3.1. *Statements of Senate Party Leaders on Broad Issues, 1997*

	Private Statements		Public Statements	
	Democrat (Daschle)			
Issue	*Daily Report*	Legislative Director Meetings	Democrat (Daschle)	Republican (Lott)
Macroeconomics	43	16	101	57
Civil rights and civil liberties	4	1	4	1
Health	20	9	59	33
Agriculture	0	0	7	2
Labor and immigration	7	0	21	12
Education	22	8	19	14
Environment	8	7	5	9
Energy	0	0	5	6
Transportation	2	0	4	12
Law, crime, and family issues	1	1	15	19
Social welfare	6	0	39	22
Community development and housing	0	0	12	7
Banking, finance, and domestic commerce	0	1	35	24
Defense	0	0	18	20
Technology	0	0	10	4
Foreign trade	0	0	4	4
International affairs	4	1	41	43
Government operations	10	0	61	39
Public lands	0	0	6	0
Total	68	16	177	170

Note: Each cell entry is the number of Daily Report editions, LD meetings, or public statements mentioning a particular issue. The number of statements in each column may sum to more than the total in the bottom row, because each statement may have addressed more than one issue.

deficit targets, along with innovations such as the line-item veto and balanced budget amendment to the Constitution.[19] While these issues and

[19] These competing arguments significantly affect public opinion about government spending. Support for that spending rises or falls depending on whether one hears the Democratic or Republican arguments, respectively (Jacoby 2000).

arguments were important to the parties, an equally plausible explanation for the frequent discussion of macroeconomics is the importance of the budget process on Capitol Hill. The budget calendar forces both parties to discuss budgetary issues throughout the year. These discussions serve both as the context for many other issues and as the most prominent battleground for conflicts between the two parties.

In their private statements, the Minority Leader and his staff gave much more emphasis to Democratic issues than Republican ones. The *Daily Report* mentions the three Democratic issues relatively frequently (twenty, twenty-two, and eight editions of the sixty-eight total editions). The issue of government operations was a topic in ten editions, reflecting ongoing investigations of campaign finance irregularities and a dispute over the 1996 Senate election in Louisiana. Notably, the publication never mentioned the issue of defense, an issue favoring the Republicans. At the LD meetings, Daschle's staff followed similar patterns of issue emphasis. After macroeconomics, the three Democratic issues received the most frequent mentions (nine, eight, and seven meetings). The staff mentioned no other issue more than once, with defense never mentioned as a message issue.

Daschle's public statements deviated from this narrow focus on politically favorable issues, reflecting his responsibility as Minority Leader to address a wide range of issues. His sixty-one statements about government operations again reflect the investigations mentioned above. Among other issues, he also made thirty-five public statements about banking, finance, and domestic commerce. This broad issue includes federal relief for natural disasters, and Chapter Two has already discussed how the topic became a central public relations theme for the Democrats.

Within his public statements, Daschle only somewhat emphasized issues favoring his party, compared to the statements of Lott. On the Democratic issue of health, Daschle made fifty-nine public statements, while Lott made only thirty-three. The Republican leader made more statements on the environment (nine to Daschle's five), while Daschle was more active on education (nineteen to Lott's fourteen). Finally, Lott made only two more public statements on the Republican issue of defense (twenty to Daschle's eighteen).

Daschle's and Lott's public statements reflected their parties' relative advantages on only two of the four broad issues. Other pairs of party leaders also appeared to base their promotional activities only moderately on the varying partisan advantages across issues, as Table 3.2 indicates. In 1997 House Democratic Minority Leader Richard Gephardt (MO3) made more public statements on health and education than his

TABLE 3.2. *Public Statements of Congressional Party Leaders and the President on Broad Issues, 1997 and 2003*

	1997			2003				
	House		President	Senate		House		President
Issue	Democrat (Gephardt)	Republican (Gingrich)	Democrat (Clinton)	Democrat (Daschle)	Republican (Frist)	Democrat (Pelosi)	Republican (Hastert)	Republican (Bush)
Macroeconomics	74	60	209	38	14	43	4	150
Civil rights and civil liberties	1	10	24	2	0	6	1	7
Health	45	27	123	28	24	34	3	105
Agriculture	0	2	10	0	0	2	0	3
Labor and immigration	15	9	107	13	5	14	1	44
Education	24	12	103	10	1	12	2	39
Environment	5	5	26	5	0	9	1	18
Energy	0	4	25	13	7	10	2	61
Transportation	1	5	35	4	1	8	0	26
Law, crime, and family issues	16	19	147	2	1	2	0	34
Social welfare	26	24	129	17	7	20	0	100
Community development and housing	5	10	32	2	1	5	2	22
Banking, finance, and domestic commerce	15	24	68	7	2	6	1	88
Defense	2	6	121	11	5	12	2	108
Technology	2	8	81	6	1	3	0	26
Foreign trade	4	3	33	1	0	1	0	21
International affairs	32	40	362	33	25	37	4	465
Government operations	29	26	128	19	11	7	1	106
Public lands	2	1	16	6	1	3	0	3
Total	130	153	724	85	78	95	8	739

Note: Each cell entry is the number of public statements mentioning a particular issue. The number of statements in each column may sum to more than the total in the bottom row, because each statement may have addressed more than one issue.

counterpart, Republican Speaker Newt Gingrich (GA6). The GOP leader spoke out slightly more frequently on defense. In 2003, both Democratic leaders (Daschle and Pelosi) made more public statements than their Republican counterparts on Democratic issues. The Democrats were also more publicly vocal on defense. Overall, across the four broad issues and four pairs of Democratic and Republican congressional leaders, the relative frequency of those leaders' public statements reflected broader partisan issue advantages in twelve of sixteen comparisons.

Overall, the evidence in Tables 3.1 and 3.2 provides only modest support for the argument that party leaders devote greater attention to issues favoring their party. The limited support for the argument may result from two factors. First, the tables do not address the possibility that leaders may strategically link two or more issues in a single statement. The linkage of divergent issues is important to agenda setting but difficult to discern. To address this concern, I next consider how frequently Daschle and Lott combined issues in their statements. The second concern involves the broad nature of each issue, which often encompasses diverse proposals by members of both parties. In the 105th Congress (1997–1998), for example, Democratic and Republican representatives and senators introduced 1,603 bills and resolutions related to education.[20] Both parties are interested in the broad topic of education but often approach the topic differently. The diversity of legislation makes it harder to find evidence that one party dominates promotional activities on a broad issue like education. I address this second concern by examining the leaders' promotional efforts in the four specific debates described in Chapter Two.

3.3.2. Leaders' Linkage of Issues

The leaders' efforts to link issues were most evident when they discussed macroeconomics. Tax cuts were central to the 1997 budget debate, particularly during the summer months. Because Republicans are often more unified than Democrats on this issue, Daschle attempted to steer the debate to more Democratic issues. Specifically, one third of his 101 public statements on macroeconomics emphasized how paying for the tax cuts would force Republicans to cut health, education, and

[20] This figure comes from a search for the Standard Subject Term "education" at the Library of Congress's THOMAS website (http://thomas.loc.gov/bss/d105query.html, last accessed May 28, 2008).

environmental programs. The Minority Leader also emphasized tax cut proposals targeted to these areas, such as tax credits for college tuition. Finally, a majority of his statements dealing with macroeconomics contained a distributional argument that the Republican tax and budget plans would help the wealthy and hurt low- and middle-income working families.

Similar Democratic messages appeared in the *Daily Report*. Of the forty-three editions that addressed macroeconomics, twenty one of them linked the issue to education, health, or environmental protection. And in twenty-eight of the forty-three issues mentioning macroeconomics, the DPC added the same distributional argument about the Republican tax and budget plans. The *Daily Report* discussed only macroeconomics and no other issues in only seven editions.

These attempts to link tax cuts to more Democratic issues also occurred in the LD meetings. As already mentioned, macroeconomics was a topic of every meeting. In particular, the leadership staff discussed the issue of taxes at the last seven meetings, reflecting summer debate over a tax reconciliation package. But, these issues of macroeconomics and taxes were linked to Democratic issues in nine of the sixteen meetings. And in the last seven meetings, the discussion of taxes was always tied to the distributional argument described previously.

Daschle's linkage of taxes and Democratic issues differs significantly from the message efforts of the Majority Leader. Lott linked these issues less frequently, discussing macroeconomics, the budget, and taxes in isolation. Thirty-four percent of the Majority Leader's public statements mentioned macroeconomics. Most of these fifty-seven statements emphasized how the Republicans' economic proposals would benefit all Americans: "Our goal is the total dismantling of today's tax system, replacing it with a new system that is fair, simple, uniform, and most important, a system that lowers the tax burden on working men and women" (Lott 1997g). Eighteen of the fifty-seven statements addressed health, education, or the environment. When the Majority Leader did address one of these Democratic issues, it was either to highlight the Republican proposal for an education tax credit, or to defend against Democratic attacks on Republican budget and tax proposals. The tax credit proposal represented an attempt to link taxes and education in a manner more favorable to Republicans. The proposal would purportedly make education more accessible, instead of harming education as charged by the Democrats. Lott's responses to Democratic attacks marked a capitulation to discussing taxes and macroeconomics on their terms instead of his own.[21]

3.4. SPECIFIC DEBATES

In the evidence thus far, party leaders' promotion and linkage of issues reveals a moderate emphasis on issues offering partisan advantage. These patterns, however, emerge from broad categories of issues encompassing many different narrower proposals. To investigate partisan competition and advantage within these broad categories, I next discuss the four specific congressional debates introduced in Chapter Two: a partial birth abortion ban and a supplemental appropriations bill in 1997, and the budget resolutions and related reconciliation legislation in 1997 and 2003. The four debates provide stronger and clearer evidence of party leaders' inclination to promote messages on politically favorable issues. For each debate, I discuss the content of the leaders' messages, the frequency of their promotional efforts, and the motivations behind those efforts.

3.4.1. Partial Birth Abortion

During the debate over the partial birth abortion ban, Democratic and Republican party leaders emphasized sharply different issues and arguments, reflecting broader trends within their parties. The issue of abortion has long proved divisive for both parties. But in recent years, pro-life

[21] The evidence of linkage thus far emerges from press releases and party publications, whose lack of structure makes it relatively easy to link any two issues. One might expect similar flexibility on the Senate floor, where the lack of a germaneness requirement allows senators to amend nearly any bill with unrelated legislative language. But when trying to plan the promotion of messages on the floor, scheduling considerations may constrain this approach to linking issues. A Democratic leadership staffer described one example of this constraint. During the spring of 1997, Senate Democrats hoped to add a campaign finance reform bill as an amendment to a bill on the Senate floor. The problem was that none of the bills forthcoming on the floor were appropriate vehicles for such an amendment. A supplemental appropriations bill funding disaster relief was too popular to slow down with a controversial campaign finance bill. The Democrats wanted to end debate on a partial birth abortion ban as quickly as possible. The only possible legislative vehicle was a bill allowing employers to substitute time off for overtime pay. But, the Republicans scheduled debate on this "comp time" bill on Mondays and Fridays, when most senators are out of town. This timing meant that "Democrats never had enough members around to make an effective message on adding campaign finance reform as an amendment to comp time. So, they didn't do it." (personal interview, May 30, 1997).

advocates in the Republican Party have enjoyed more success on the issue by narrowing their focus to the specific procedure that they commonly called partial birth abortion (Kingdon 2003). Graphic descriptions and images of this procedure have helped pro-life Republicans unify their party in support of banning the procedure. GOP leaders' arguments in the debate[22] are certainly graphic: "Partial birth abortion is a procedure performed primarily in the second trimester in which a living baby is partially delivered before the abortionist stabs the baby's head with scissors and sucks out his brain contents" (Canady 1997a). The name "partial birth abortion" vividly depicts the nature of the procedure. Due in part to the powerful language, Democrats have found it harder to oppose this procedure than other limitations on abortion. Pro-choice advocates have unsuccessfully attempted to give the procedure a less provocative name in public debate: "dilation and extraction." The alternative name is an attempt to remove the gruesome implication that the procedure involved the partial birth of a child. This alternative label is also more scientific in tone, thereby placing the procedure closer to established medical science, and further from the connotation of a murder or crime.

Despite the Republican advantage on the issue, neither Democratic nor Republican leaders made many public statements in the debate. As Table 3.3 indicates, Daschle made a total of sixteen public mentions of either party's message in the debate; Gephardt made only two such mentions.[23] Among Republicans, Gingrich made one public statement in the debate, and Lott totaled only five such mentions. The Republican leaders may

[22] The arguments making up each party's message came from the leaders' press releases in this debate; I relied on similar releases by the leaders in the other three debates. (Appendix 3.B contains the complete text of a sample release from a party leader.) These releases accurately capture any arguments in a debate that the leaders wished to promote. In the partial birth abortion debate, for example, the arguments in the Democratic message were an important part of a presentation by Daschle's staff to an LD meeting (personal notes, May 9, 1997). In the other two debates in 1997, the arguments in the Democratic messages were central to the leadership staff presentations in LD meetings. The Republican leadership likely followed a similar consistency in distributing their individual arguments and overall messages privately and publicly.

[23] As noted in Chapter 1, I define a message as "the issue and arguments about the issue that a politician promotes" (7). Appendix 3.C lists the specific arguments (quoted from legislators' press releases) making up each party's message in each debate. In the partial birth abortion debate, for example, the Democratic message includes any of the specific Democratic arguments listed in Appendix 3.C for the debate. My analysis counts Daschle as promoting his party's message in the debate each time that he mentions any of those specific Democratic arguments. This same framework applies to all four specific debates and any politician's mention of any argument (and therefore party message) in those debates.

TABLE 3.3. *Public Statements of Congressional Party Leaders and the President in Specific Debates, 1997 and 2003*

	Senate		House		
	Democrat	Republican	Democrat	Republican	President
Debate	(Daschle)	(Lott/ Frist)	(Gephardt/ Pelosi)	(Gingrich/ Hastert)	(Clinton/ Bush)
Partial birth abortion (1997)					
Democratic message	13	2	2	1	1
Republican message	3	3	0	0	0
Supplemental (1997)					
Democratic message	36	3	15	5	19
Republican message	25	20	12	0	10
Budget (1997)					
Democratic message	108	23	133	20	144
Republican message	144	189	144	183	159
Budget (2003)					
Democratic message	44	9	129	3	65
Republican message	28	11	46	3	140

Note: Each cell entry is the number of public statements mentioning the party message in a particular debate.

have chosen to let other GOP legislators take the public lead on this issue. As explained in more detail as follows, this move by the leaders makes it more likely that these followers receive the individual benefits of media coverage. Evidence in Chapter 4 suggests that many Republican senators deferred to policy leadership of Senator Rick Santorum (R-PA) on the issue.[24]

The reasons for the Democratic leaders' near silence appear more complicated, particularly for Daschle. The issue split congressional Democrats between strong pro-choice supporters and more moderate and conservative Democrats. Daschle himself needed to address the issue in advance of his reelection in 1998. Pro-life forces had already begun to run campaign ads in South Dakota, attacking Daschle for an expected vote against the partial birth abortion ban.[25] His late-term abortion amendment aimed to address both these concerns. The amendment attempted to ban late-term abortions, instead of just a single procedure (partial birth abortion). If Daschle succeeded in restructuring the debate along these lines, he might have been able to build a larger coalition within the Democratic caucus, as well as split the GOP caucus.[26] The success of his amendment could also have forestalled home-state criticisms that he was out of touch with constituents on abortion. After the amendment failed, Daschle likely wanted to put the difficult issue behind as quickly as possible.

3.4.2. The Supplemental

The political advantage switched sharply during the 1997 debate over the supplemental appropriations bill. Disaster relief funding often passes Congress with little controversy (*CQ Almanac Online Edition* 1970, 1992; Healey 1994). But as Chapter 2 points out, the Republican leaders decided to take advantage of the 1997 bill's must-pass status, and they attached a number of controversial provisions to the bill. Lott and

[24] Given the Republican party leaders' limited public statements in the debate, I also selected the GOP messages from statements by the most prominent Republicans leading the debate, Santorum and Rep. Charles Canady (R-FL12).

[25] Personal notes, April 7, 1997.

[26] At a staff meeting, a Daschle staffer expressed concern about attacking Republicans for undermining the Supreme Court's Roe v. Wade decision legalizing abortion. The staff member noted that many Democratic senators may do the same when voting for the partial birth abortion ban. This concern indicates an effort to avoid alienating these Democratic senators (personal notes, April 7, 1997), which is consistent with the goal of building a broader Democratic coalition.

Gingrich made arguments defending many of the provisions, apparently hoping that at least one of them would survive in the final version of the bill. The GOP arguments ranged from the peace-keeping effort in Bosnia (Lott 1997e) to concerns about the economic and social costs of the Endangered Species Act (Lott 1997a). The Republican leaders even linked the supplemental to broader concerns about the federal budget and their "auto CR" proposal: "In simplest terms, the President came out against disaster relief and in favor of government shutdowns" (Gingrich 1997f). As Chapter 2 indicated, none of these arguments appeared successful, as none made it into the final bill.

The controversial provisions created an opportunity and a challenge for Democratic leaders. The GOP strategy exposed Republicans to the potential criticism that they were slowing the provision of needed disaster relief, by "playing politics" arguing for proposals better debated outside the supplemental. But in taking advantage of this vulnerability, the Democrats risked criticism of politicizing the debate themselves. The Democratic leaders had to link their party and message to natural disasters and related need for funding assistance, but not in an overtly political manner (Wolfsfeld and Sheafer 2006). To accomplish this goal, Daschle and Gephardt used fewer arguments and built them around the call for a "clean" bill (Daschle 1997h). As Gephardt put it, "we've said for many days now that the bill should be about disaster relief. It should be about helping the people out there who need the help right now and take off extraneous provisions like the census provision and like the continuing appropriation" (Gephardt 1997m). This message helped the Democrats attach their party and their arguments to the widespread and graphic coverage of natural disasters across the country. By "riding the wave" (Ansolabehere et al. 1993, Wolfsfeld 2001), Daschle and Gephardt won even more coverage for their party and message.

The relevant rows of Table 3.3 reflect this advantage. Daschle discussed both party messages more frequently than Lott did, particularly Democratic issues and arguments. A similar disparity occurred in the House between Gephardt and Gingrich. The Democratic leadership worked hard at pressing their advantage in the supplemental debate. During their all-night vigil, leadership staffers searched for Democratic representatives from states with Republican senators and with many disaster problems. The staffers hoped that the representatives would bring even more public pressure to bear on these GOP senators (personal notes, June 2, 1997) and thereby deepen the existing split among Republicans.

In explaining their focus on this debate, Daschle's staff emphasized that "it's so useful to drive the wedge down." (personal notes, June 2, 1997) The Democratic message could unify Democrats in Congress, while splitting Republican legislators. Consistent with my argument at the start of this chapter, Daschle and Gephardt publicly discussed the issue and debate much more frequently than Lott and Gingrich did.

3.4.3. The Budget Debates of 1997 and 2003

Unlike the debates over partial birth abortion or the supplemental, congressional deliberations about the federal budget offer no clear advantage to either party. Instead, the diversity of the budget offers each party the opportunity to draw attention to favorable issues and arguments about different aspects of the budget. As a result, both years of budget debates saw the parties' congressional leaders linking issues and arguments to build an advantage, in a manner consistent with my previous argument. Daschle, Gephardt, and Pelosi emphasized the unequal distribution of benefits and the substantial cuts in specific government programs that would occur under the GOP budget and tax cut proposals. The Senate leader concisely summarized their arguments: "Republicans insisted on a misguided scheme to cut Medicare, Medicaid, education, and the environment in order to pay for generous new tax breaks for the richest Americans" (Daschle 1997g). Gephardt provided even more detailed criticism: "After the Republicans voted to cut 32 million kids off from the school lunch program, we thought their assault on children was over. But last week, the Republican leadership was back in force, cutting 180,000 women, infants and children from the WIC nutrition program" (Gephardt 1997k).

In contrast, the four Republican party leaders (Lott, Gingrich, Frist, and Hastert) focused on the need for greater tax cuts, which would shrink the wasteful federal government and return taxpayers' dollars to their pockets. In a national radio address in June of 1997, Lott used a holiday to drive home these arguments: "Here in Washington ... Father's Day is like every other day on the calendar: just another opportunity for the federal government to reach into your family's pocketbook and spend YOUR hard-earned money" (Lott 1997c).

The leaders used the same arguments throughout 1997 and 2003. In July of 1997, Congress and the President were nearing approval of a series of tax and spending cuts that would help balance the federal budget. Gingrich expressed disapproval of the cuts' magnitude by returning to the original GOP message: "Will these cuts alone be enough to reverse years of high liberal taxes and big government? No" (Gingrich 1997e). Six years later, Hastert used the arguments yet again when describing Bush's budget proposal for 2004: "It includes measures that will boost consumer confidence by putting more money in the pockets of the average American family. It will speed up the tax cuts put into place in the last tax relief package" (Hastert 2003e).

The differences between the Democratic and Republican arguments illustrate how each party was attempting to steer the budget debate toward its own priorities and ideological concerns. Reflecting the differences in content, the party leaders varied significantly in their promotion of the competing messages. As indicated in Table 3.3, in 1997, each party's leaders promoted their own message more frequently than the opposition did. In 2003, the Democratic leaders discussed both party messages more often. Overall, the party leaders largely chose and promoted issues and arguments that were most favorable, that is, where their own party was unified and the opposing party was split.

Daschle's staff explicitly mentioned this reasoning at a number of points in the 1997 budget debate. In early February, one staff member explained to me the Democratic leadership's initial strategy on the budget:

> We will try to use the budget to get back to our message.... The Republicans still want a big tax cut, and hate education and the environment; they are just trying to figure out how to realize these goals.... They will have to do something, if we can keep them from negotiating an agreement [with Clinton]. We aren't divided on the main points, but they are and are covering up the disagreements by focusing on other issues where they're unified. (personal notes, February 15, 1997)

The staff member believed that if the Democrats could refocus the debate on their favorable issues (such as education and the environment), the Republicans would no longer be able to hide their internal divisions.

One month later, another staffer outlined the connection among the Democrats' message, favorable issues, and the upcoming elections:

> Before making a deal, we must remind people who's fighting for what. We have to do this if we want electoral benefits from this, and if we want message points from the message. Democrats want to prolong the budget negotiations, so that they can move the debate on to favorable issues, so that they can raise Democratic numbers nationwide, so that they can do better in the next election. (personal notes, March 12, 1997)

Both statements illustrate the Democrats' concern with focusing congressional debate on issues and arguments advantageous to Democrats.

Thus far, this chapter has presented extensive evidence supporting the expectation that party leaders tend to focus on favorable issues and arguments when creating party messages. Targeting fellow partisans in Congress, the leaders choose issues and arguments for party messages that unify those members and divide the opposition. The *Daily Report* editions, the LD meetings, and the leaders' public statements documented their pursuit of this strategic goal, particularly in the linkage of issues and in the four narrower debates. By structuring party messages in this manner, each leader created a message with greater potential to provide collective and individual benefits for followers, which in turn persuades them to promote that message.

3.5. ADDITIONAL STRATEGIES

For party leaders seeking to mobilize rank-and-file members in promotional campaigns, emphasizing favorable issues and arguments is only one of several possible strategies that I outlined at the start of this chapter. A leader can also help followers receive individual benefits of promotion and coverage, reduce their costs of promoting the party message, and encourage them to believe that the message will receive coverage. This section examines each of these strategies, drawing evidence from a range of party leaders' activities.

3.5.1. Individual Benefits of News Coverage

When Frist focused his party's budget message on tax cuts, he steered that message toward issues and arguments unifying his congressional party. Rank-and-file members' support and promotion of the message was likely to translate into greater coverage of the message, which in turn created collective benefits for the entire party. Promoting the message could also yield individual benefits for Republican members of Congress. If those legislators received coverage themselves, they could leverage that coverage into greater support among constituents, more influence over budget outcomes, and expanded influence in the budget process. So, if Frist worked to facilitate individual senators' coverage, those senators were more likely to promote the party's message.

One path to this goal is simply to step back. Party leaders often dominate congressional news coverage, even if other rank-and-file legislators appear with them at a news conference (Kuklinski and Sigelman 1992, Sellers and Schaffner 2007). A leader can help followers win coverage by stepping back and letting the followers lead promotional efforts (Epstein 2007). Observers noted Frist's adherence to this strategy early in his tenure as Senate Majority Leader: "Where Lott, Daschle and other previous leaders dominated news conferences and the television cameras, Frist routinely steps back and lets others do the talking.... stepping back and letting others take the limelight gets Frist 'tremendous credit from his colleagues'" (Cochran 2003)[27] In his plan to improve the House Republicans' message process, Majority Leader Tom DeLay (R-TX22) also worked to share the limelight; according to his spokesperson, "We want [committee chairs and members] to carry the message from the cradle to the grave, from the time the bills are marked up to the time the bill is signed by the president" (Crabtree 2003). All these strategies can help loyal followers receive the individual benefits of news coverage.

Congressional leaders must also deal with another type of individual benefit: news coverage of defecting from the party (Groeling 2005, Groeling and Kernell 2000). A defector can either criticize the party or complement the opposing party. If a member of a congressional party disagrees with the party message, that potential defector faces several options. The legislator could promote the party message despite disagreeing with it. As a result of the disagreement, the legislator would receive no individual benefits from promoting a preferred position. But, the legislator might win individual benefits of coverage, and his party might receive collective benefits through strengthening the party's reputation. Alternatively, the legislator might promote the opposing party's message. Such promotion might yield individual benefits through individual news coverage and through promoting a preferred issue position. In addition, reporters may find the dissent newsworthy, thus providing more individual benefits through news coverage for the legislator. The dissenting message and accompanying publicity can undermine the reputation of the legislator's own party, thereby creating collective costs. A third alternative is to remain silent, promoting neither message. The legislator would not receive individual benefits or coverage, but the legislator's party would not face collective costs or a weakening of its reputation.

[27] But, the same news article quotes Wendy Schiller, who offers a different interpretation: "'Frist hasn't shown that he has the capacity or the willingness to lean on [i.e., put pressure on] chairmen, so his style de facto has had to be conciliatory. Most of the people he would lean on have been in the Senate a lot longer than he has. They have a great deal of independence and are electorally secure.' One senior Democratic aide complains that Frist is letting committee chairmen and senior members pursue their own agendas to such a degree that the Senate increasingly will be tied in knots" (Cochran 2003).

When faced with potential party defectors in a debate that splits a party, a leader is unlikely to persuade the potential defectors to promote the party's message. The likely benefits are too small relative to the expected costs. The leader must instead try to convince these legislators to remain silent and not to promote a competing message. The leader must argue that individual benefits of defecting are smaller than the collective costs to the party's reputation.

When leaders undertake this task of persuasion, their failures are more prominent and noticeable than their successes. In 2002, the House Republican leadership strongly opposed floor consideration of legislation to reform campaign finance regulations, while Democrats supported the legislation and pushed for a floor vote. A group of Republican moderates, led by Rep. Christopher Shays (CT4), disagreed with their party leaders. GOP leaders encouraged the moderates to cease pushing for the legislation, but the moderates refused. By continuing to support campaign finance reform publicly, the moderates received extensive publicity and eventually succeeded in winning a floor vote (Foerstel 2002).

Successful discouragement of defection receives less attention because the potential defectors either remain silent or decide not to defect. An example of this successful persuasion occurred among Senate Democrats in February 1997. With President Clinton soon to send his proposed budget to Congress, Democratic congressional leaders were anxious to avoid the "dead on arrival" (DOA) assessment that greets many presidential budgets on Capitol Hill. If Clinton's budget was a viable alternative, congressional Republicans would have to negotiate more seriously with the President about budgetary priorities. But if the president's budget did not receive serious consideration, GOP legislators could write a budget closer to their own preferences. To help ensure the viability of Clinton's budget, Daschle and his staff contacted moderate Democrats who would be most likely to criticize that budget. The leader argued that if these moderates withheld negative assessments and outright criticism, even if only for several days, the president's budget would be less likely to be declared DOA. The argument apparently worked, as the moderates muted their criticism. As noted previously, Republicans declared Clinton's budget "alive on arrival" (personal notes, February 5, 1997).

Overall, congressional leaders do help rank-and-file members realize individual benefits from promoting the party message. The leaders also appear concerned about the individual benefits that their followers may receive from defecting and promoting the opposition's message. Chapter 4 illustrates how the followers often share these concerns about the costs of defection for a party's collective reputation.

3.5.2. Costs of Promotion

For a third strategy to encourage rank-and-file promotion of party messages, leaders may assume many costs of promoting those messages. Individual legislators and their staff face numerous obligations and follow extremely busy schedules. As a result, these demands may force each office to focus narrowly on its own unique needs and messages, leaving little time or resources to learn about important issues and arguments involving the entire caucus, or to promote the party's messages. Congressional leaders and their staff make contributions in both areas, by helping individual offices obtain the details of the caucus messages and by providing low-cost opportunities to promote those messages.[28]

In the first area, the leadership devotes extensive time and resources to collecting useful information about current congressional debates and sharing it with rank-and-file members in a timely fashion. Each party caucus has a policy committee that produces numerous publications summarizing bills before Congress and presenting the party's interpretation of the legislation.[29] These publications are often available over internal congressional intranets (Stanton 2006b). Emails from leadership staff announce newly available information on a daily basis (Pershing 2006). The staff members also produce recess packets, containing the party message on issues that constituents are likely to mention during legislators' trips back to their home states and districts. The packets suggest ways to publicize that message, from examples of issue-based events to potential topics for newspaper columns (Billings and Preston 2003, Preston and Billings 2004). These combined materials aim to reduce the costs of promoting the caucus message, because the legislators and their staff receive the descriptions of the caucus message, rather than having to search for that information on their own. The policy committee publications also provide substantive details to back up the caucus message, in the event that a senator receives a more detailed question about the message.

[28] See Harris (2005) for a review of party message organizations from the 1970s to the early 1990s.

[29] See Sinclair (2006) for more details about each committee.

In the second area, the leadership coordinates and facilitates its caucus members' promotion of party messages, both on and off the House and Senate floors. On the floor, the leadership directs the use of procedural tactics to further both legislative and public relations goals (Billings and Preston 2003, Evans and Oleszek 2001, Sinclair 2006). Earlier parts of this chapter explained how congressional leaders create messages for their caucuses to promote. The leaders in both chambers then organize floor events to draw attention to these messages. In each caucus one or more staff members may have as their sole responsibility the organization and coordination of these events (Pershing 2005).[30] In addition to recruiting members to participate, this staff also prepares material for members to use on the floor, from compelling arguments and statistics to oversized graphs and vivid photos. The resulting "floor show" can consume extensive time for participating members. In 2004, the House Republican leaders had organized so many floor events during special orders that younger GOP representatives "were getting worn out." In response, the leadership launched a new effort to encourage senior members to participate more often. According to a leadership spokesperson, "[i]t lets our freshmen and sophomores who've been running on overdrive take a breather. This is a way to sort of jump-start those [members] where apathy might have set in" (Pershing 2005). The leaders turn to these strategies to make the floor events effective.

[30] Some staffers focus solely on responding to breaking events, particularly public statements by the opposition. Most recently, Senate Democrats agreed to coordinate their public messages through a newly created Senate Democratic Communications Center, led by then-Senate Minority Leader Harry Reid (D-NV). The war room's staff sent daily talking points to Democratic senators' staff and arranged television and radio appearances (Klein 2005b). A spokesman for Reid explained the Democrats' focus on public relations: "Republicans control the House, Senate and White House. They have the megaphone of the White House, we do not. So, what we need to do is get our best people out there to talk about the message, day in and day out" (Billings 2006b). In response to the Democrats' effort, Senate Majority Leader Bill Frist (R-TN) assembled a Republican "peace room" to counter the Democrats' "war room." The "rapid-response and message-development team [was] designed to enhance the Republican Conference's existing policy and messaging efforts.... The effort might be considered a backhanded compliment to the success of Reid's caucus communications center, which is tasked with providing Senators with a more unified message and agenda than in years past. On many occasions, the Democratic Caucus, instead of coming off as disorganized and dispirited, presented Republicans with a largely united, energized party that came out swinging" (Stanton 2006b). The Democrats' promotional campaigns were apparently so effective that the Republicans could not let those campaigns go unanswered.

Off the floor, the leadership provides a variety of other services to help members' public relations efforts. Both senators and representatives have access to recording studios in the Capitol, an adjacent building, or nearby campaign and party committee headquarters. Crews from these studios can also film a news conference on the Capitol grounds or elsewhere. After taping an interview or speech, these studios can distribute the audio or video clips through blogs, podcasts, and websites. (Billings 2005b, personal notes, July 6, 1997, Stanton 2006b) The studios may also upload video footage to satellites, for downloading and use by television stations in legislators' home districts or states. While the studios can polish these clips into "video press releases," the local stations may prefer raw footage of an event. One bureau chief argued that "It's a journalist's job to edit," instead of relying on "an unchallenged viewpoint." (Katz 1997; Sellers and Schaffner 2007) To help make the members' promotional efforts more effective, the leadership staffs also work to coordinate those efforts with supportive individuals and groups outside Congress. Potential partners in the parties' public relations campaigns range from mayors and governors (Drucker 2006) to grassroots groups and talk show hosts (Firestone 2003).

The leadership staffs often use a combination of these tactics in specific debates. An excellent example occurred during the debate over the supplemental appropriations bill, when Senate Democrats organized the all-night vigil in Daschle's Capitol office to protest the Republicans' tactics. The leadership mounted a diverse public relations offensive. The staff recruited senators to participate in three-hour shifts throughout the late afternoon, night, and early morning. These senators promoted the Democrats' message through a variety of media. Nationally, the Democrats targeted the evening network news shows, late-night coverage on CSPAN and Nightline, and then early morning talk shows such as Good Morning America. The Democrats also set up interviews with the senators on late-night and early morning radio shows across the country, such as "The Trucking Bozo." Senators competed for attention in Internet chat rooms set up specifically for the vigil. A set of phone banks allowed senators to take and receive calls from disaster victims. To make this interaction even more vivid to reporters in Daschle's office that night, the Democrats used a big-screen television to display disaster victims as they talked with the Democratic senators. Images of these senators and victims went out to local stations across the country. The staff of the Democratic leadership organized every aspect of the event, substantially lowering the costs of participating for individual senators.

Practically the only costs facing the senators were lost time and sleep.[31]

All these examples support the expectation developed earlier in this chapter about the costs of promotion. Congressional leaders devote extensive time and resources to reducing these costs for their followers in hopes of increasing the followers' promotion of party messages.

3.5.3. Probability of Coverage

The previous sections have illustrated how party leaders in Congress attempt to influence caucus members' perceptions of both the costs and benefits of promoting the party's message. The provision of these benefits is not certain, however; a message must receive coverage for any member of Congress to receive the associated benefits. Thus, a legislator's beliefs about the probability of coverage are an important aspect of her decision whether to promote the caucus message. These beliefs about coverage provide the fourth strategy outlined earlier for increasing rank-and-file promotion of the party message: The leader may argue that there is a high probability of receiving coverage.

To examine the frequency with which the Democratic leadership resorted to this strategy, I turned to two sources described previously: the *Daily Report* and the LD meetings. As an earlier quote suggests, the DPC publication uses evidence and arguments already published in news outlets. Such a reliance on published material makes sense, because it can make the *Daily Report*'s arguments more authoritative and therefore more compelling. Another benefit of published material is that it demonstrates that the caucus message has already received coverage. By showing that the *New York Times* or a state newspaper has covered a message, the leadership can suggest that the message has already received some coverage and is likely to receive more. Despite these reasons, the *Daily Report* used already-published material with surprisingly low frequency. Only twenty of the sixty-eight editions quoted evidence and arguments that had already appeared in news outlets.

The Democratic leadership also addressed the probability of coverage relatively infrequently in the LD meetings. In only six of the sixteen meetings, the leadership staff offered an argument about the probability of the caucus message on an issue receiving coverage. These arguments took a

[31] For additional examples of coordinated promotional events, see Preston and Crabtree (2002) and Stanton (2006).

variety of forms. The most straightforward held that "the press is ready to write stories with our message." One such appeal occurred in the midst of the Senate debate over the supplemental appropriations bill. During the last week of the debate, a Democratic leadership staffer made an appeal for participation in the all-night vigil. His argument focused on the potential for receiving coverage:

> We now have an opportunity to make a major breakthrough with our message.... We can highlight the Republican extremists and how they're holding lives hostage.... We can define ourselves in contrast to the Republicans.... The Republicans have no strategy. They're counting on us not to pull the trigger.... The President cleared his schedule on Tuesday, and he's willing to help us. He realizes that it's a dead cat scenario, and it shouldn't be found on his door.... Unless you have a doctor's note, we're hoping to have everyone there. (personal notes, June 9, 1997)

The staffer hoped the chance for "a major breakthrough" in coverage would encourage Democratic legislators to come to the vigil and help promote the party message.

After the Democrats' success in the supplemental debate (Taylor 1997), another leadership aide framed the upcoming fight over taxes as

> the definitive debate for the two parties. We need to remember the context. We have them [the Republicans] on the run. Last week we landed a significant blow that divided them.... they're frightened of what we can do. We demonstrated who we are. It's crucial that we continue the definition of Democratic priorities on the Senate floor. (June 13, 1997, Washington, D.C.)

The staffer was attempting to persuade the legislative directors that the Democrats' success in the debate over the supplemental made future victories more likely.[32] During the same budget debate, the leadership staff also cited extensive poll results to bolster their argument about their budget message's potential for earning coverage (personal notes, June 21, 1997).[33]

[32] Kingdon (2003) explains the mechanism underlying this linkage: "Success in one area contributes to success in adjacent areas.... These spillovers, as we have called them, occur because politicians sense the payoff in repeating a successful formula in a similar area, because the winning coalition can be transferred, and because advocates can argue from successful precedent. These spillovers are extremely powerful agenda setters, seemingly bowling over even formidable opposition that stands in the way" (203).

[33] See Hearn (2005) and Jacobs et al. (2002) for other examples of using polling to shape expectations.

Yet another approach to this same goal targeted perceptions of the opponents' media efforts. The Democratic leadership argued that the Republicans' message strategy was not working, which meant that the Democrats' strategy stood a better chance of winning coverage. During an LD meeting about the supplemental, a leadership staffer declared that "The Republicans are under it on the supplemental message. They're getting horrible press.... They're being controlled by their kooks again. We have the opportunity to remind [the public] of the kooks" (June 4, 1997, Washington, D.C.). In another LD meeting, a leadership staffer argued that a stalemate in budget negotiations was starting to resemble the situation two years earlier (1995), when the press had written numerous negative stories about the Republicans' responsibility for the government shutdown. The Republicans were beginning to receive blame again for the current stalemate (March 7, 1997, Washington, D.C.).

These appeals suggest the diverse ways in which the Democratic leadership attempted to persuade the caucus that the leadership message would win coverage. The evidence provides only modest support, however, for the expectation above that the leadership would rely upon this strategy. Only one third of the *Daily Report* editions and the legislative director meetings contained attempts to influence beliefs about the probability of coverage. Why did the leadership use this strategy so infrequently? The claims about the probability of coverage may have amounted to "cheap talk," lacking credibility with the target audience. It is difficult for the leadership to monitor local coverage in the states and districts of all their party members. In addition, each rank-and-file legislator can obtain independent and arguably more accurate information about the amount of local coverage of a particular issue and message (by reading the newspaper and watching television herself). She is therefore likely to have her own beliefs about the probability of coverage. The independent source of information makes it more difficult for the leadership to influence these beliefs. Given this difficulty, the leadership resorts more frequently to the other strategies of persuasion described earlier.

3.6. PARTISAN CONTROL OF GOVERNMENT

Thus far, this chapter has focused on the promotional activities of the party caucuses in Congress. I have explored how the internal dynamics of those caucuses guide their promotional activities, particularly those of their leaders. The legislators' efforts do not take place in a vacuum, however. In particular, a party's institutional context may shape its promotional campaigns, and two aspects of that context appear particularly important.

The first is the president and his bully pulpit (Kernell 1997). While this book focuses on Congress, it is impossible to ignore the role of the president in policy debates (Bond and Fleischer 1990, Canes-Wrone 2006, Edwards 2007). In public relations the president has an incentive to coordinate his efforts with members of Congress, particularly legislators from his party. As with coordination inside Congress, joint efforts between the president and legislators face a collective action problem. Each can prefer having legislation passed, without having to pay the costs of lobbying and persuasion that are often necessary for winning approval of a bill.

Members of the president's party in Congress may be particularly susceptible to free riding on the promotional efforts of the president. The president's appearance at a public relations event substantially boosts the probability of that event receiving news coverage. The president's powerful role in the legislative process makes his statements more newsworthy in the eyes of the press.[34] In contrast, an individual member of Congress, even a party leader, has less influence and is therefore less newsworthy. The member's attendance at a news event provides a much smaller boost to the probability of the event receiving coverage. The greater impact of presidential appearances suggests that the president is likely to promote a party message more frequently than members of Congress do.[35] In fact, legislators from the president's party may rely on the president to promote a party message, instead of doing it themselves. Such reliance may lead the president's fellow partisans in Congress to engage in less public promotion than legislators from the opposition party do.

This argument finds only mixed support in the evidence of leaders' promotional activities previously presented. Using the records about broad issues (Tables 3.1 and 3.2), one can compare the total public statements of the two party leaders in each chamber and year. In three of the four possible chambers and years, the congressional leaders from the

[34] Chapter 5 explains this link between policy influence and newsworthiness in greater detail.

[35] An appropriate analogy would be the decision whether to vote in an election. An individual is more (less) likely to vote if that individual's own participation substantially (minimally) affects the probability of a particular election outcome occurring, and of the individual receiving benefits from that outcome (Riker and Ordeshook 1968).

president's party made fewer public statements than the opposition leaders did. Only Daschle in 1997 made more statements than his Republican counterpart. In contrast, the specific debates (Table 3.3) provide much less support for the argument about deferring to the president. In six of the eight possible debates and chambers, the leaders from the president's party actually promoted party messages *more* frequently than the opposition leaders did. The exceptions occurred in 2003, when Frist and Hastert were relatively inactive in the budget debate and may have been deferring to the more effective promotional efforts of Bush.

A second important aspect of the institutional context facing legislators is whether their party controls Congress. The majority party can use congressional rules and procedures to promote its message, only bringing to debate, for example, bills addressing issues that it owns (Evans and Oleszek 2001, Sinclair 2006). The debate of these bills may effectively win news coverage of the issues. The party's majority status and control of legislative rules allows it to exert a strong influence over the policy-making process and outcomes of debates. As a result, the majority may be content to limit policy debates to internal deliberations inside Congress, thus making fewer attempts to promote messages in those debates outside Congress.

In contrast, the minority party in Congress lacks such institutional advantages, particularly in the House. With limited influence over rules and procedures, the minority may rely more heavily upon public relations campaigns. Promoting party messages beyond Congress can help the party win support from outside the institution, thus reducing its disadvantage in the debates inside the institution (Schattschneider 1960). These dynamics suggest that the minority party in Congress will promote messages more frequently than the majority party, across all debates and regardless of the president's party (Graber 2006).[36]

The party leaders' promotional activities strongly support this argument. When discussing broad issues, the leader of the minority party made more public statements than his or her counterpart in the majority in three of the four possible chambers and years. Only Gingrich made more public statements than Gephardt did in 1997. An even stronger

[36] Consistent with this argument, the analysis in Chapter 5 suggests that the minority party's news coverage outside Congress exerts the strongest feedback on the activities and public statements of legislators inside the institution. Thus, if the minority party can win news coverage, that party wins greater influence in a policy debate inside Congress. Coverage of the majority party exerts little feedback into the internal policy process.

pattern emerges in the public statements about specific debates (Table 3.3). In every chamber and debate, the leader of the minority party made more public statements (about either party message) than the majority party leader did. Across all the topics, chambers, and years, the minority party appears to work harder than the majority party at expanding and "socializing the conflict" beyond the confines of Congress (Schattschneider 1960).

In sum, the institutional context facing congressional parties appears important for their promotional activities. Party leaders in Congress demonstrate only a modest inclination to defer to the more effective public statements of presidents from their party. More importantly, the leaders' promotional activities appear closely tied to whether their party controls Congress. Minority party leaders consistently are more active in promoting party messages, perhaps in order to overcome the institutional limitations of their minority status and to "socialize" legislative debates beyond the unfavorable context inside Congress.

3.7. CONCLUSION

Leaders of political parties in Congress work in diverse ways to shape the legislative agenda inside Congress and the public agenda outside the institution. Influence over those agendas increasingly requires effective public relations campaigns, in which congressional coalitions join together to promote a preferred set of issues and arguments. As agents of their rank-and-file members, party leaders often initiate and coordinate these campaigns, with the goal of furthering the collective and individual interests of their members.

This chapter began by developing a series of expectations about leaders' strategies in enlisting rank-and-file participation in promotional campaigns. The remainder of the chapter provided diverse evidence in support of most of the expectations. Most notably, to encourage followers to promote party messages, the leaders often create those messages on favorable issues, where the party is unified and the opposing party is split. Even if faced with a divisive issue, a leader may attempt to link that issue to a more favorable one, in hopes of nullifying the disadvantage and creating more incentives for party members to promote the message. The party leaders also try to encourage greater promotion by providing greater individual benefits of promotion, such as news coverage, and by reducing the costs of promotion. The fourth and final strategy found less use; the leaders only sometimes worked to shape followers' beliefs about the probability of a message succeeding.

The first of these strategies helps us understand the varying fortunes of the new congressional majorities in 1995 and 2007. For congressional Republicans in the 104th Congress, the Contract with America focused on favorable issues and arguments that unified their party while splitting the minority Democrats. As a result, the House GOP easily passed legislation on nearly all planks of the contract during the first one hundred days of the term (*CQ Almanac Online Edition* 1996). But during the summer and fall of 1995, the Republicans began to address the details of their budget proposals, which created greater division within their party. Efforts to reduce federal agricultural subsidies drew strong resistance from rural Republicans (*CQ Almanac Online Edition* 1996). Newly elected GOP representatives attached riders on abortion and the Environmental Protection Agency to appropriation bills, slowing their passage and dividing their colleagues (*CQ Weekly Online* 1996b, Koszczuk 1995). These efforts were part of a broader Republican division on budgetary issues between the confrontational House freshmen and senior colleagues who often preferred more accommodation (*CQ Almanac Online Edition* 1996). Congressional Republicans struggled to remain unified on these divisive, unfavorable issues.

Congressional Democrats encountered similar problems twelve years later. In 2007, the new congressional majority remained largely unified on issues in its campaign agenda ("Six for '06") and passed a number of related bills, particularly in the House (Epstein 2007). But, other more divisive issues arose later in the term, creating deep challenges for keeping Democrats unified (Epstein 2007). In the debate over the Iraq War, Democratic representatives and senators endorsed divergent positions, making it nearly impossible for their leaders to create a unified party message (Nather 2007a, Stanton 2006). On the issue of immigration, Democrats also faced deep divisions about whether to provide any sort of "amnesty" to illegal immigrants (Nather 2007d). These debates split Democratic legislators, in contrast to the earlier, more favorable issues.

The examples from 1995 and 2007 illustrate how the varying content of legislative debates dramatically shapes legislative parties' ability to remain unified. By carefully focusing the legislative agenda on favorable issues, a party can maintain unity and realize preferred policy outcomes. Failing to focus the agenda on such issues makes the goals harder to achieve. This chapter has illustrated how party leaders work to set the legislative agenda by initiating promotional campaigns on favorable issues and encouraging their followers to help promote party messages. It remains an open question whether the leaders' persuasive efforts actually work. Rank-and-file members could conceivably ignore their leaders and base their public relations on whether they individually like or dislike a bill. To examine the effectiveness of the leaders' strategies, the next chapter considers how the rank and file respond to those strategies.

APPENDIX 3.A. PARTISAN ADVANTAGE ON BROAD ISSUES

To determine the parties' relative advantage on broad issues before Congress, I turned to records of recent roll call votes, supplemented by two sources of public opinion data. The latter evidence provides a broader picture of partisan advantages across the issues, beyond the confines of Congress.

First, the Senate cast 306 roll call votes in 1996 (according to *Congressional Quarterly*'s Washington Alert electronic database). I coded these votes according to the Baumgartner and Jones issue framework,[37] and I then examined the caucuses' relative unity on votes dealing with each issue in the framework. I focused specifically on votes where one party was relatively unified (at least 80% of voting members supporting the same position) and the other party was relatively divided (less than 80% of voting members supporting a single position). As previously argued, the contrasting patterns on these votes indicate an advantage for the unified party over the divided one. The patterns below hold if votes are categorized with a threshold of 85%. Also, all issue categories contain roughly the same percentage of votes where one party is advantaged, relative to those where both parties are unified or divided.

[37] I checked the reliability of this coding, following Neuendorf (2002) and Riffe et al. (2005). An additional coder practiced assigning the Baumgartner and Jones issue categories to roll call votes from 1995, and we discussed any discrepancies. After the coder and I refined the coding framework and reached an appropriate level of agreement in the practice tests, the coder then went back through all the 1996 votes and assigned issue codes. For each of the nineteen issue categories, I calculated the percentage agreement, that is, the percentage of votes in 1996 on which the additional coder and I agreed on whether to assign a particular issue category. Across the nineteen categories, the percentage agreement ranged from .91 to 1.00. I also calculated Cohen's *kappa* for the coding for each of the issue categories, to account for the possibility of chance agreement. This statistic ranged from .33 to 1.00 across the nineteen issue categories. Thirteen of the nineteen issue categories produced a *kappa* value of .70 or greater, including all four issues where one party enjoyed strong ownership. These statistics suggest a high level of reliability in the coding.

Second, John Petrocik assessed the partisan advantage of a range of issues in his original investigation of issue ownership (1996). His analysis relied upon survey data and content analysis of newspaper articles from 1958 to 1992.

Third, the 1996 National Election Study asked respondents which party was more capable on ten issues. These general assessments of parties' issue reputations are more appropriate for my analysis than more detailed survey questions about specific policy proposals. Few publicly available surveys ask the latter type of question, particularly about all specific proposals in the roll call votes. The questions about capability summarize how the public rates the two parties on an issue, using whatever information from the roll calls (and other sources) that respondents may encounter and retain. Senators appear to incorporate similar information into their decisions about legislative strategy and message promotion. During a number of meetings with staff from other offices, the Democratic leadership presented survey data on public assessments of the two parties. The survey questions often addressed general proposals (such as Medicare funding or tuition tax credits), instead of detailed proposals from roll call votes.

Using the three bodies of evidence, I examined each of the nineteen general issues in the Baumgartner and Jones framework. I separated the nineteen issues into four categories. The first category contains issues clearly favoring the Democratic Party, which number only three: health, education, and the environment. The issue of health demonstrates how I classified the issues. Five votes found the Democrats unified and the Republicans divided. The GOP had a corresponding advantage on only one vote. A similar advantage appeared in the public opinion evidence. The health issue is part of Petrocik's "social welfare/spending" category, which he assigns to the Democratic Party. In the 1996 NES, the percentage of respondents rating the Democratic Party better on making health care more affordable was thirty-four points greater than the percentage preferring the GOP on this issue. Thus, the issue of health appeared to belong to the Democrats, although the Republicans attempted to minimize this advantage by linking health to other issues.

A second category of issues includes those favoring the Republican Party. The only issue in this category is defense. Of all the roll calls on defense, Republicans held the advantage on seventeen (i.e., they were relatively unified, while the Democrats were relatively divided). On this same issue, the Democrats enjoyed an advantage on only three votes.

Petrocik assigns the issue to the GOP, while the NES did not ask about defense. In light of this evidence, I assigned defense to the GOP.

A third category of issues are those where the advantage is shared between the two parties; these issues include social welfare, macroeconomics, labor and immigration, and civil rights and civil liberties. Democrats enjoy an advantage on some aspects of each issue, while Republicans are more unified on other aspects. The issue of social welfare illustrates this third category. In 1996, the Senate took ten votes on social welfare where the Democrats were unified and the Republicans were divided. All these votes favoring the Democrats focused on specific welfare programs, such as low income energy assistance (#41, March 19, 1996). There were sixteen votes related to social welfare where Republicans were unified and Democrats were not. Of these sixteen roll calls, four dealt with welfare reform. The remaining twelve votes were linked to other issues. Overall, Democrats appeared more unified on social welfare when the vote focused on a specific welfare program. But, Republicans held an advantage when the vote shifted to welfare reform or included other issues outside welfare. Petrocik assigns "social welfare/spending" to the Democratic Party. In the 1996 NES, the percentage of respondents rating the Democratic Party better on eliminating poverty was twenty-eight points greater than the percentage preferring the GOP on this issue. Along similar lines, the Republicans faced a thirty-eight-percentage-point disadvantage on cutting Social Security benefits. But when the questionnaire moved from providing specific benefits to making general reforms to welfare, the parties were more evenly matched. Here, the Democrats enjoyed only a four-point advantage.

It is important to note that for some issues in this third category, I was able to assign ownership to only a small subset of the possible topics. For example, the issue of civil rights and civil liberties includes many more topics than discrimination against racial minorities (Democrats) and partial birth abortion (Republicans). The specific topics listed were the only ones for which evidence of partisan advantage (survey and/or roll call data) existed.

The final category of issues involves those where I was unable to find empirical evidence, neither in roll call votes nor in the NES. This category includes agriculture; law, crime, and family issues; energy; transportation; community development and housing issues; banking, finance, and domestic commerce; space, science, technology, and communications; foreign trade; international affairs and foreign aid; government operations; and public lands and water management.

APPENDIX 3.B. CODING POLITICIANS' STATEMENTS AND NEWS STORIES

This book relies heavily on analysis of the content of numerous statements by politicians and news stories by journalists. Recovery of this content required four different approaches, which varied by the method of coding and the source of the statement or story.

3.B.1. The Senate Democratic Leadership and Private Statements About Broad Issues

To assess the Senate Democratic leadership's emphasis of broad issues in 1997, I turned to two sources: editions of *The Daily Report* and my notes of the LD meetings. The sources do not cover identical periods because I discovered each source at a different time during my work in Daschle's office. For each edition and LD meeting, I coded each issue that was mentioned as part of the leadership's message.[38] Each mention could take a direct form: "Our message on this bill is...." Or, the message component could be less direct: "When you are talking with your constituents about this issue, it's more effective to emphasize.... " I then calculated the percentage of meetings in which each issue was mentioned; Table 3.1 reports those percentages. I also coded the notes for mentions of issues regardless of whether there was a message component. The resulting percentages parallel those in the main text, except that issues not owned by the Democratic Party receive more frequent mention. These noisier findings make sense. The Democratic leadership focuses its message efforts on issues owned by its party. But when trying to give the caucus an accurate idea of upcoming events in the Senate, the leadership must broaden its presentation and include issues owned by Republicans or by no party.

3.B.2. Public Statements About Broad Issues

Records of politicians' public statements came from four sources: *The Congressional Record* (www.CQ.com), press releases (FDCH, www.nexis.com), and press conference transcripts (FDCH, www.nexis.com)

[38] I also evaluated the reliability of this coding. The same additional coder evaluated the editions of *The Daily Report* and my notes of the LD meetings, using the Baumgartner and Jones issue categories. For each of the nineteen issue categories, the percentage agreement ranged from .84 to 1.00. The value of Cohen's *kappa* was again greater than .70 for the large majority of issue categories.

for members of Congress, and *The Presidential Papers* (FDCH, www.nexis.com) for the president. I collected all the politicians' public statements in each source in each seven-month period in 1997 and 2003.

To code mentions of broad issues in each statement, I turned to a computerized content analysis program called Context, produced by Oracle Corporation. The program operates in a manner similar to many Internet search engines. If given a specific word or phrase as a search, the Context program calculates the importance or "relevance" of the word or phrase in each document in its database (or legislator's statement in my work). Ranging from 0 to 100, the relevance score for each document depends on a range of factors, such as the number of mentions of the phrase or its placement near the start of the document (more relevant) or the end (less relevant). Context employs a built-in dictionary of more than one million words, allowing searches to incorporate synonyms; a search for "disaster relief" will also include "disaster assistance."[39]

Content analysis of a sample statement can further illustrate these various abilities of the Context program. In the following statement, House Speaker Gingrich extols the virtues of further tax cuts:

SPEAKER GINGRICH APPLAUDS DEBT REPAYMENT ACT AS ROAD MAP FOR SMALLER, SMARTER GOVERNMENT

(Washington, D.C.) House Speaker Newt Gingrich (R-GA) joined Rep. Mark Neumann (R-Wl) in introducing the National Debt Repayment Act today with 95 cosponsors. The bill, which has bipartisan support, directs future surpluses in the federal budget towards paying off the federal debt, providing tax relief and restoring solvency to federal trust funds. Gingrich stated his strong belief in the bill's objectives, 'The Debt Repayment Act takes us in exactly the right direction to lead a national dialogue on how best to deal with a surplus once the budget is balanced. Rep Mark Neumann's leadership in initiating this dialogue reflects tremendous foresight on behalf of the American people. As we move towards finalizing the first balanced federal budget in 30 years, the first tax cut in 16 years and reforms to save Medicare from bankruptcy, it is entirely appropriate that we now begin to outline our plan for when we have a budget surplus. I believe that the broad-based support for balancing the budget translates into support for eliminating the national debt. Not only will this bill ensure that we fully repay our debt, it establishes a clear priority for lowering taxes. Republicans are committed to cutting Americans' taxes every year because lower taxes equal more take-home pay. And this is not just an economic issue. Tax cuts are a moral issue. The question is how do we give back to the American people more of their hard-earned money so they can have more time to be better parents, better citizens,

[39] For other examples of computerized content analysis of politicians' statements, journalists' stories, or blog postings, see Andsager (2000), Hopkins and King (2008), Jasperson et al. (1998), Miller (1997), Miller and Riechert (2001), and West (2001).

better entrepreneurs. That is what cutting taxes is all about. The National Debt Repayment Act will play a significant part in making the federal government smaller by eliminating wasteful Washington spending and smarter by providing permanent tax relief.' (Gingrich 1997d)

A Context search for "tax relief" produces a relevance score of 29. The phrase occurs twice, once near the start of the release and once in the final sentence. I also searched for "government" occurring within 10 words of "spending" or any form of the word "waste." This search yielded a relevance of score of 14. Only the last sentence of the release meets these search criteria, so the relevance is lower.

In searching for broad issues, I used the same nineteen categories of general issues in the Baumgartner and Jones framework (1993).[40] This categorization groups all specific policy issues into nineteen broad categories; health care, education, environment, and defense are four such categories. Applying the Context program to the public statements yielded a relevance score for each broad issue for each statement. I considered any relevance score greater than 0 to indicate that a statement mentioned the issue in the search.

In these relatively simple searches for specific phrases, the computer appeared to outperform humans. For example, the FDCH collected eighty-two congressional releases issued on January 21, 1997. I personally searched these releases for mentions of "education" and related issues. I missed two of the seven releases with these mentions that the Context program correctly found. The program produced no false positives, that is, incorrectly assigning a mention of education to a statement. Repeating this test for other issues and statements produced similar results: the computer coding performed as well as or better than human coding, while producing a small number of false positives.[41]

3.B.3. Public Statements and News Stories About Specific Debates

The coding for the four specific debates differed from that of broad issues. While politicians' statements came from the same four sources, the coding also included all news stories appearing during each seven-month period in twelve national outlets and one newspaper from each of forty-three

[40] See note 13 in this chapter.

[41] See Gentzkow and Shapiro (2007) and Quinn et al. (2006) for more inductive computerized approaches to categorizing and retrieving politicians' messages.

different states. The coding of statements and stories again used Context, but searched this time for specific arguments making up the parties' messages in the four debates. Appendix 3.C summarizes these arguments and messages.[42]

Searching statements and stories for so many issues and messages was only feasible using the computerized content analysis of the electronic evidence. This approach made it possible to refine the search terms and rerun the searches with relatively minimal expenditure of time and resources. Such flexibility is not possible with human content analysis. Of course, the latter approach provides greater detail in coding of content, allowing the analyst to go far beyond the search for specific phrases, to assessing the context and tone of those phrases. This more detailed coding is only feasible with smaller numbers of cases (as described in the next section).

42 The book's website (http://cyclesofspin.davidson.edu/) lists the specific news outlets, the sources of the party messages, and the specific search terms used in the content analysis. The news stories from the fifty-five outlets come from the individual source files in the Nexis database (www.nexis.com). Each outlet's source file contains only stories produced by that outlet, thus excluding any wire service stories that appeared in the outlet (Druckman 2005). National news outlets tend to publish only internally produced stories. So, the exclusion of wire service stories is unlikely to cause a problem for the measures of the twelve national outlets' coverage included in my analysis. The remaining forty-three outlets in this study are local newspapers. These outlets tend to rely much more heavily upon wire service stories. The exclusion of such stories from Nexis could create a problem for my measures of these outlets' coverage. My measures of local coverage could understate the level of congressional coverage that actually appears in local outlets, due to wire service stories on Congress that the outlets publish. This problem likely biases the measured level of local coverage downward from its actual level. But, the measurement error does not appear to affect the analysis of news coverage in Chapter 5. Given the exclusion of wire service stories from Lexis Nexis, one might expect the patterns reported in the text to differ between national and local outlets. But, separate analysis of the two sets of coverage reveals little difference. Members of Congress may receive more positive coverage in local outlets than in national outlets (Schaffner 2006). My analysis, however, focuses on the balance of coverage between Democratic and Republican messages in congressional debates. This balance appears similar in national and local coverage. In the 1997 budget debate, for example, the average national coverage of congressional Democrats and their message was 36% of that of congressional Republicans and their message. In local outlets, the coverage of congressional Democrats and their message was 31% of that of congressional Republicans and their message. In VAR analysis of national and local outlets, national coverage of the parties' messages strongly and consistently drove local coverage of those messages. While national coverage often appeared initially, local coverage followed with stories of their own. As explained in Appendix 5.A, I am concerned with identifying whether coverage exerted or was influenced by a significant impact, regardless of whether that impact is over the short or long term. Thus, the different timing of national and local coverage does not appear important in my results.

It is important to distinguish clearly between the measures of promotion and coverage. In the measures of promotion, each event mentioning a different argument in the Democratic message counts as one public statement of the message on a particular day. Thus, an event mentioning two different Democratic arguments would count as two statements on that day. Two events mentioning the same Democratic argument would also count as two. Each legislator attending an event also affects the frequency of mentions. If one legislator attended the first event described earlier, the total number of mentions would still be two. But if three legislators attended that event, the total number of mentions would be six. The measures of coverage are calculated slightly differently. If a story refers to at least one Democrat and to one argument in the Democratic message, that story counts as a single mention. References to two different arguments in the Democratic message mean that the story counts as two mentions. The number of references to Democratic legislators does not affect how the story is counted, as long as the story refers to at least one Democratic congressman. I assume that that reference to the Democratic legislator effectively links the mentions of the message to the Democratic Party.

3.B.4. The Tone of Public Statements About Specific Debates

Two research assistants undertook this coding for the supplemental and partial birth abortion debates, again following Neuendorf (2002) and Riffe et al. (2005). This human coding captured whether politicians (in their public statements) referred to the debates' messages positively or negatively (Kahn and Kenney 2002). After several rounds of practice coding of sample statements, we developed a coding framework with six possible categories for each statement:

- the author of the statement supports, agrees with, or believes in the party's message in the debate;
- the author criticizes, does not support, disagrees with, or does not believe in that message;
- the author expresses a mixture of support for and criticism about the message;
- the author expresses indifference or neutrality about the message;
- the statement is unrelated to the particular debate; or
- the author's reference to the message is unrelated to the particular debate.

We continued the practice coding on sample statements until we reached at least 80% agreement on coding each possible argument in the debates.

After refining the coding framework and completing the practice coding, the research assistants began coding the entire set of statements in each debate (including the randomly chosen statements from the practice coding). After the assistants coded more of the statements,[43] I calculated their level of agreement for each possible argument in the two debates (these additional calculations excluded any cases used in the earlier practice coding). Across these twenty-eight arguments, one argument produced a percentage agreement of .81; the corresponding statistic for the rest of the arguments was .95 or higher. Cohen's *kappa* reached a value of .70 or higher for twenty-three of the twenty-eight arguments; the lowest value was .57. Because of this level of agreement (and also funding constraints), only one assistant coded each of the remaining statements.

APPENDIX 3.C. CONGRESSIONAL LEADERS' MESSAGES AND COMPONENT ARGUMENTS IN SPECIFIC DEBATES

This appendix lists the arguments making up the Democratic and Republican messages in the four specific debates. Each entry contains the unique word or phrase capturing the specific message (highlighted in bold), as well as the context in which that word or phrase occurred. See the book's website (http://cyclesofspin.davidson.edu/) for the specific terms used to search for that message.

Partial Birth Abortion Debate, Democratic Arguments

- "Sincere efforts to find **common ground** have been labeled as 'shams,' as 'political cover,' and 'deceptive' by many who passed judgment without having even read the legislation." (Daschle 1997i)
- "I haven't looked at each one of the 41 states' prohibitions in this regard, but they're all as comprehensive and as restrictive as ours is. In fact, most states have already outlawed the **health exception** completely." (Daschle and Landrieu 1997)
- "It is likely that doctors wishing to perform **late term abortions** will simply choose another option." (Daschle 1997i)
- "Recurring efforts to pass and veto a bill which is likely to be found to be unconstitutional only delays meaningful progress in an effort to ban not just **one procedure** but all of them once a fetus is viable." (Daschle 1997i)

[43] They coded the remaining 143 statements in the partial birth abortion debate, and 512 more statements in the supplemental debate.

- "This was not an easy decision, because it is highly likely that H.R. 1122 will be declared **unconstitutional** should it be enacted into law." (Daschle 1997i)
- "It is not an easy decision because I favor a **woman's** right to consult the physician of her **choice** to decide the most appropriate course of action on matters directly affecting her health and her most personal circumstances." (Daschle 1997i)

Partial Birth Abortion Debate, Republican Arguments

- "Partial-birth abortion is a procedure performed primarily in the second trimester in which a living baby is partially delivered before the **abortionist** stabs the baby's head with scissors and sucks out his brain contents." (Canady 1997a)
- "This report by the **AMA** confirms what we have been saying all along," said Santorum. "This procedure is not a medically recognized procedure." (Santorum 1997a)
- "We are talking about a barbaric procedure, where, very often, healthy babies are partially delivered and then killed. This is not a choice. This is **infanticide**." (Santorum 1997b)
- "Partial-birth abortion is never **medically necessary** to protect a mother's health or her future fertility." (Canady 1997b)
- "This legislation, proposed by Minority Leader Daschle, is nothing more than **political cover** for those who are feeling the heat from their constituents at home." (Santorum 1997b)
- "Earlier this year, **Ron Fitzsimmons**, the Executive Director of the National Coalition of Abortion Providers, confirmed that partial-birth abortions are performed as often as 5000 times a year, mostly during the second trimester of pregnancy on healthy mothers and healthy babies." (Santorum 1997b)

Supplemental Debate, Democratic Arguments

- "My preference, as I said to our caucus, and then I reported our caucus position to Senator Lott just a few minutes ago, that our position is a **clean bill**. But regardless of what happens – whether it's clean or not – our uncompromising position is not a dollar comes out of emergency money." (Daschle 1997h)
- "Well, we've said for many days now that the bill should be about **disaster relief**. It should be about helping the people out there who need the help right now and take off extraneous provisions like the

census provision and like the continuing appropriation, which are important matters but really not connected with the supplemental appropriation. We ought to be having an appropriation that supplements past appropriation bills in this year." (Gephardt 1997m)

- "Dear Mr. Speaker, It has been two months since President Clinton first requested that Congress act on legislation to support clean-up and rebuilding efforts in the wake of several floods and other **natural disasters** especially in North and South Dakota, and Minnesota. We call on you today to drop the legislative riders that are currently under consideration by you and the majority members of the House-Senate Conference Committee and have precluded final action on this emergency funding bill." (Gephardt 1997b)
- "Senate Democratic Leader Tom Daschle and other Senate Democrats have vowed to keep the Senate in session around the clock Tuesday, June 10, unless Congress passes the disaster-relief conference report in a form the President can sign.... Additional Senators will also take part in the **vigil.**" (Daschle 1997c)

Supplemental Debate, Republican Arguments

- "We think the census issue – in some respects – is, may be more difficult to resolve than how we deal with **continuing resolutions**. And there are a couple of other points of disagreement. But there really are only about four of them that really are still pretty hard to resolve." (Lott 1997d)
- "Well, I do think this is an important issue, how do we do the next **census**? I'm concerned about this sampling idea. I do think that an accurate, full count is preferable. I'm willing to – I think we ought to take the time to ask questions about how would this work, and how effective has it been in the past, and you ask legitimate questions about the best way to have a complete and thorough census." (Lott 1997d)
- "I know you're concerned and interested in the **Endangered Species Act**. The Endangered Species Act has been on the books since the 1970s. I know you support reauthorization. But I also know that you would like to make sure that it considers economic and social costs for these actions. And we're going to make sure that happens." (Lott 1997a)
- "Help is on the ground, the waters are receding and emergency financial aid **is flowing** to thousands in the Dakotas and Minnesota." (Lott 1997b)
- "In simplest terms, the President came out against disaster relief and in favor of **government shutdowns**." (Gingrich 1997f)

- "Good afternoon. At 6 o'clock, or thereabouts, the Senate will be voting on the supplemental appropriations bill, which does include funds for the Department of Defense to reimburse costs to **Bosnia.**" (Lott 1997e)
- "Senate Republicans have also put themselves on a collision course over two provisions that have whipped up environmental activists and gained a veto threat from Interior Secretary Bruce Babbitt. The first would block Interior from its ongoing rulemaking procedure for approving **rights-of-way** claims on federal lands." (Taylor 1997g)
- "Another controversy involves the popular Women, Infants and Children (**WIC**) program, which provides food vouchers to poor pregnant women and children. The administration says an additional $76 million must be added to the program, which received $3.7 billion for the ongoing fiscal year. Republicans included one-half of the request, saying there should be money carried over from prior years." (Taylor 1997f)

1997 Budget Debate, Democratic Arguments

- "The goal of this legislation is to help working families purchase private health insurance for their children through age 18. It is targeted to **children who 'fall through the cracks.'**" (Daschle 1997a)
- "The Democratic **children's health** initiative is targeted to children who fall through the cracks–those who don't have employer-based insurance and whose parents earn too much to qualify for Medicaid." (Daschle 1997e)
- "Medicare works - and must keep on working for generations to come. That is why I am so disturbed to see Medicare put on the **chopping block** in the reconciliation conference that convened yesterday." (Gephardt 1997i)
- "There is a national need to build and rebuild our nation's schools to create the positive learning environment for our children. Our **school buildings are crumbling.**" (Gephardt 1997g)
- "The **Democratic Tax Bill** provides 20% tax credit for tuition and fees for part-time students seeking to acquire or improve job skills...." (Daschle 1997d)
- "At a time when we're trying to balance the budget, the last thing we need to do is **dig a deeper hole.**" (Gephardt 1997e)
- "Democratic Leader Richard Gephardt . . . will join the Democratic freshman class tomorrow at a press conference to release a report

detailing the lack of accomplishment in the **'Do-Nothing' 105th Congress.**" (Gephardt 1997c)

- "We were able to stop them from indexing capital gains - which would have enriched the wealthiest 5% of all taxpayers and **exploded the deficit** in years to come." (Gephardt 1997h)
- "When we introduced the **Families First** Agenda, we invited Republicans to join with us in implementing it." (Gephardt 1997j)
- "Republicans have worked hard to **hide their budget.**" (Daschle 1997g)
- "The President's proposal treats **Medicare** as what it's supposed to be: a health care program, not **an ATM machine for other government spending.**" (Daschle 1997f)
- "Republicans insisted on a misguided scheme to **cut Medicare**, Medicaid, education, and the environment in order to **pay for generous new tax breaks** for the richest Americans." (Daschle 1997g)
- "Well, the flat tax, again, in my view, if you have one rate, say a 15 percent rate, that's a huge tax cut for people at the top. It is not a **progressive** tax system." (Gephardt 1997m)
- "After the Republicans voted to cut 32 million kids off from the school lunch program, we thought their assault on children was over. But last week, the Republican leadership was back in force, cutting 180,000 women, infants and children from the **WIC** nutrition program." (Gephardt 1997k)
- "America can't afford Newt Gingrich's **tax giveaway.**" (Gephardt 1997f)
- "We need to reform Medicare, not raid it to pay for taxes for **those who need them least.**" (Daschle 1997b)
- "We have to ask ourselves what this effort is all about – is it about economic experimentation – giving the wealthy, who already have a huge advantage over middle class taxpayers – the lion's share of the benefit with the hopes that it **trickles down** to the rest of the economy?" (Gephardt 1997d)
- "There has been a refusal to consider expansion of health coverage for the 10 million **uninsured** children in this country." (Gephardt 1997a)
- "To once again provide tax breaks for the **wealthy** few at the expense of the many." (Gephardt 1997l)

1997 Budget Debate, Republican Arguments

- "Out of a desire to achieve a true **bipartisan** approach to balancing the **budget** . . . " (Gingrich 1997b)

- "We believe these levels provide enough room for important reforms, including broad-based permanent **capital gains tax** reductions, significant death tax relief, $500 per child tax credit, and expansion of IRAs." (Gingrich 1997c)
- "We believe these levels provide enough room for important reforms, including broad-based permanent capital gains tax reductions, significant death tax relief, $500 per **child tax credit**, and expansion of IRAs." (Gingrich 1997c)
- "We believe these levels provide enough room for important reforms, including broad-based permanent capital gains tax reductions, significant **death tax** relief, $500 per child tax credit, and expansion of IRAs." (Gingrich 1997c)
- "Now I would think any party, Republican or Democrat, that could have the **first tax cut in 16 years** and the first balanced budget in 28 years is in pretty good position – 29 years, actually – is in pretty good position to go home – and has also saved Medicare for a decade – is in a pretty good position to go home and say, this is a remarkably successful session of Congress so far." (Gingrich and Archer 1997)
- "Here in Washington, however, Father's Day is like every other day on the calendar: just another opportunity for the federal government to reach into your family's pocketbook and spend YOUR **hard-earned money.**" (Lott 1997c)
- "Will these cuts alone be enough to reverse years of **high** liberal **taxes** and big government? No." (Gingrich 1997e)
- "But the essence of what we wanted to do was to increase your right to choose, to increase your control over the health care you got, to increase the competition so there were more ways of you getting health care, so your hospital, your doctor and others could work together, in addition to health maintenance organizations, and in addition to fee-for-service medicine, and to give you a number of options, including **medical savings accounts**, so you could literally have a greater ability to shop." (Gingrich 1997g)
- "They specialize in the **politics of envy and resentment.**" (Lott 1997c)
- "We've kept our focus on three basic goals: a guaranteed balanced budget by the year 2002, tax relief especially for hard-pressed, middle-income families. And the reform of government entitlement programs that have had America on the fast track to insolvency. The keystone of that effort is our commitment to **preserve and strengthen Medicare.** (Lott 1997c)

- "Here in Washington, however, Father's Day is like every other day on the calendar: just another opportunity for the federal government to **reach into your family's pocketbook** and spend YOUR hard-earned money." (Lott 1997c)
- "The **reform** of government **entitlement** programs that have had America on the fast track to insolvency." (Lott 1997c)
- "Our **tax cut** will provide for taxpayers at every stage of life." (Gingrich 1997e)
- "**Tax cuts are a moral issue.**" (Gingrich 1997d)
- "We are committed to providing **tax relief** to families and helping more people find jobs." (Gingrich 1997a)
- "The President, on the other hand, wants a hefty portion of tax reduction to go to people who pay no income taxes. **That's not tax relief; that's welfare.**" (Lott 1997c)
- "The National Debt Repayment Act will play a significant part in making the federal government smaller by eliminating **wasteful Washington spending** and smarter by providing permanent tax relief." (Gingrich 1997d)

2003 Budget Debate, Democratic Arguments

- "For every dollar spent on unemployed benefits, **$1.73** is infused **into** the **economy**. For every dollar spent on the dividend taxation reduction, the centerpiece of the Republican proposal, nine cents will be injected into the economy. Nine cents for the Republican tax plan, $1.73 for extending unemployment benefits." (Pelosi 2003j)
- "This number, 563, drives home the point in a personal way. Since President Bush became President, every working hour of every working day **563 Americans lose their jobs**. A little more than the number of people who serve in the Congress, House and Senate combined, lose their jobs in every working hour of every working day since the President has taken office." (Pelosi 2003k)
- "This morning, the Republican leadership will officially introduce the President's dividend tax proposal, promising that it will revitalize the struggling American economy. But with each passing day, it becomes clearer that the President's so-called stimulus package is nothing more than **a sham, wrapped in spin, shrouded in deception.**" (Daschle 2003e)
- "Finally, the report by the Committee for Economic Development, a blue-ribbon organization of corporate CEOs stated, 'The budget deficits, the President's plan, would be akin to '**arsenic poisoning**' for the

economy.' A vote for this budget is a vote for arsenic poisoning for the economy." (Pelosi 2003m)

- "We will urge the House to move quickly to enact this **fair**, fast-acting, and fiscally responsible **plan**." (Pelosi 2003h)
- "The President's budget is worse than a bad movie that no one wants to see twice. It's a **budget-busting epic disaster**." (Daschle 2003f)
- "**States** face the worst **fiscal crisis** in a half century." (Daschle 2003d)
- "Unfortunately, the Republican leadership in the House of Representatives is blocking consideration of this vital legislation. Your immediate intervention with House Republicans is required to ensure that the working and military families of 12 million children are made eligible for the **child tax credit**. These families need the money today, but this tax relief will not be made available to them unless you personally urge the Republican Leadership to pass this extension immediately." (Pelosi 2003d)
- "You guessed it – it is that **credibility gap** again – the gap between the President's lofty political rhetoric and the harsh realities of his policies. And this time it is affecting America's seniors very directly." (Pelosi 2003i)
- "House Republicans passed a budget in the **dead of night** on March 21 that dishonors our veterans by making deep cuts in veterans' benefits." (Pelosi 2003a)
- "The support of one Senate Democrat does not negate the criticism of Chairman Greenspan, the condemnation of 10 Nobel laureates, the unenthusiastic response of dozens of elected Republicans, and the unfairness to the majority of Americans. This plan is still the wrong plan for the country and it is **dead on arrival**." (Daschle 2003h)
- "Last year when he proposed his budget, the President promised that the deficit would be 'small and short-term.' Instead, we are now looking at a $304 billion deficit this year – exceeding the previous record deficit rung up by the first President Bush – another $307 billion deficit next year and continued **deficits as far as the eye can see**." (Daschle 2003i)
- "It is simply wrong to pass a budget that fails veterans, fails students, fails seniors, fails children, and fails the **disabled**. The American people deserve better." (Pelosi 2003c)
- "The President's response has been to offer a controversial proposal that will do almost nothing to create jobs in the near term, is drastically tilted toward the wealthiest, and will significantly worsen our

long-term economic outlook by increasing deficits and raising interest rates. Under the Bush proposal about 200,000 millionaires and multi-millionaires will get more in total tax relief than the 92 million Americans who make $500,000 a year or less. In addition, more than 90 percent of the President's $670 billion package will hit in the years beyond 2003-**driving us** steadily **deeper into the deficit ditch** his policies started digging in 2001." (Daschle 2003g)

- "Finally, the president's plan, when it does go into effect, will **explode the deficit** over the next decade. The 10-year impact of our plan, $100 billion, allows the budget to recover as the economy recovers." (Pelosi 2003h)
- "Daschle noted that the U.S. economy is in its longest job slump since the **Great Depression** - unemployment has risen to 6.0% and more than 2.7 million jobs have been lost since the beginning of the Bush Administration." (Daschle 2003c)
- "The tax cut is a tragedy. It does not create jobs and it does not grow the economy– the only thing it **grows** is **the deficit**." (Pelosi 2003o)
- "Yesterday, without a ceremony, President Bush signed a bill allowing the federal government to increase its debt to a record $7.4 trillion. Our children will be stuck with this bill. Is that why there was no signing ceremony – because the President did not want the country to see that he is **indebting our children** for years to come?" (Pelosi 2003n)
- "The Democratic plan will pump $136 billion into our economy this year. The plan includes the proposals to not only put this money into the economy, but it directs the money to crucial needs and to those Americans most hurt by the Bush recession and **jobless recovery**." (Pelosi 2003h)
- "Cutting emergency home heating assistance while calling for hundreds of billions of dollars in new tax breaks for the very wealthy is absolutely indefensible. Taken together, these two proposals are a brazen demonstration of how misplaced this Administration's priorities are – and how out of touch President Bush is with the needs of ordinary Americans. Democrats will offer an amendment on the Senate floor to restore **LIHEAP** funding at the earliest opportunity." (Daschle 2003a)
- "Unfortunately, President Bush's proposals will only exacerbate the crisis and will undermine the fundamental guarantees in our health care system. He has proposed a radical overhaul of **Medicaid** (MediCal in California) that, if enacted would end the guaranteed benefit for low-income individuals and families. His plan would shift the ultimate

fiscal responsibility for Medicaid onto the states at a time when they can ill afford it, and encourage states to limit their liability by capping enrollment and cutting benefits for some of their most vulnerable populations." (Pelosi 2003g)

- "The hallmark of American history has been the willingness of our leaders and our citizens to sacrifice today for the liberty, security, and prosperity of our children, and our children's children, tomorrow. Therefore, I am asking Democrats and Republicans to come together to support the **Patriotic Pause Amendment**, which puts aside costly tax cuts and, with the exception of national defense and homeland security, freezes spending levels. Given the uncertainty of the times we're living in, this approach is both fair and responsible." (Daschle 2003b)
- "Their **reckless** budget makes room for $90,000 a year in **tax** breaks for millionaires, while irresponsibly piling up long-term debt for our children and grandchildren." (Pelosi 2003e)
- "Tomorrow, the President will give a speech in Chicago to announce a Republican plan that is none of the above. Instead of helping all working Americans, the vast majority of the benefits will go to the wealthy. Instead of a fast-acting plan that boosts the economy now, the bulk of its provisions will take effect years from now. And instead of being fiscally responsible, it will explode the deficit over the next decade just as the Baby Boom generation becomes eligible for **Social Security** and Medicare." (Pelosi 2003h)
- "The 9.4 million people in this country who are out of work and can't find a job are not being helped by an economic plan that gives enormous **tax breaks to those who need them least**. And neither are the working and military families of 12 million children who did not get the expanded child tax credit other families are receiving, nor the record number of homeowners faced with losing their homes." (Pelosi 2003l)
- "It's not just Democrats who recognize the deficiencies in the Bush plan. A group of 434 prominent economists, including **ten Nobel Laureates**, has taken out a full-page ad in the New York Times to express opposition to the plan." (Pelosi 2003f)
- "There's some concern as to whether it will come to the floor because there's some unrest in the Republican caucus because of the initiatives we have taken for **veterans**. In light of our salute to men and women in uniform has I think made the Republicans nervous. So they may have to try to improve the bill, which is definitely, in its present form, unfair to veterans." (Pelosi 2003p)

- "President Clinton, 22 million jobs in 8 years. President Bush, losing 2.7 million jobs in the first two years of his term. That was the result of his failed economic policy. And what is his answer to this record unemployment? The same **warmed-over stew**, the same recipe for economic disaster." (Pelosi 2003k)
- "But he asks no contribution from the **wealthiest**. Instead, he proposes an 'economic growth package' that doles out $88,000 a year to millionaires." (Daschle 2003f)
- "The new job loss numbers from the Bureau of Labor Statistics show that the economy lost another 189,000 jobs over the last two months. That means that since President Bush took office two years ago, a total of 1.7 million jobs have been lost – the **worst record on job creation** for any president in the past 58 years." (Pelosi 2003b)

2003 Budget Debate, Republican Arguments

- "Some of my Democratic colleagues will oppose this jobs bill and support even more unemployment compensation. They will oppose this bill because it increases the deficit, as they demand that we spend trillions of dollars for a **bigger government**. This misguided philosophy will lead us only to bigger government, bigger deficits and no jobs." (Hastert 2003a)
- "Tonight the Senate approved a fiscal year 2004 budget resolution that provides essential **funding** for important national priorities such as our national **defense**...." (Frist 2003b)
- "It includes measures that will boost consumer confidence by putting more money in the pockets of the average American family. It will speed up the tax cuts put into place in the last tax relief package, including getting rid of the marriage penalty even faster. The President also proposes to boost investor confidence by getting rid of the **double taxation of dividends**." (Hastert 2003e)
- "This budget reflects two realities. First, we have a responsibility to defend our nation from enemies who want to attack it. Second, in order to get back to a balanced budget, we must **grow the economy**." (Hastert 2003b)
- "We have to take dramatic action to get this economy growing again. The **President's plan is dramatic and bold**, and it will work if we give it a chance." (Hastert 2003d)
- "It includes measures that will boost consumer confidence by putting more money in the pockets of the average American family. It will **speed up the tax cuts** put into place in the last tax relief package,

including getting rid of the marriage penalty even faster. The President also proposes to boost investor confidence by getting rid of the double taxation of dividends." (Hastert 2003e)

- "What we will vote on today combines the best elements of many proposals into a **tax relief** package that will truly provide stimulus quickly." (Frist 2003a)
- "Explosive **medical liability** insurance rates have led to dire consequences." (Hastert 2003c)

4

Promotion

After the 2004 elections, newly reelected President Bush launched a major initiative to reform Social Security. The centerpiece of his plan was a proposal to allow voters to place a portion of their Social Security contributions in individual accounts to allow more diverse and potentially more profitable investment opportunities. Republicans were initially quite hopeful about the President's plan. As one advisor put it, "If this is successful, this will define the Bush administration for the next 100 years. People who are more independent and don't feel dependent on the government are more likely to be available to the Republican Party" (Rosenbaum 2005, 20).

Democrats, in contrast, were wary and fearful about the President's plan, particularly after their wrenching electoral defeat the previous November. Democratic leaders in Congress created a carefully worded response, using simple narratives to attack the Bush proposal: "The first, titled 'Privatization: A Gamble You Can't Afford to Take,' stressed the insecurity of middle-class families and compared Bush's plan to a roll of the dice. The second, 'The Magical World of Privatization,' spun out a metaphor that centered on Bush as 'an old-fashioned traveling salesman, with a cart full of magic elixirs and cure-all tonics'" (Bai 2005, 8). The Democratic leaders hoped that the rank-and-file members of their party would adopt and discuss these themes as their own.

But, the Democratic followers certainly enjoyed other options. The legislators could have kept silent, free riding on others' promotion of the themes while receiving the partisan benefits of that promotion. Or, the followers might have disagreed with their leaders' negative themes and viewed Bush's reform proposals more favorably. If so, the followers could have remained silent, this time to avoid a public display of internal party discord. A final option would have been to promote a Democratic plan for individual accounts or Bush's own proposal, because either plan might be closer to the followers' own policy preferences. In the end, most congressional Democrats chose to remain "on message" and to read "from the designated talking points even after it got excruciatingly boring to do so" (Bai 2005, 8). The Democrats' united front appeared to make a difference: Bush's reform proposal gradually lost momentum.

The Democrats' public relations success contrasted sharply with their defeats in earlier legislative battles. As detailed in Chapter 2, Bush issued another broad proposal in 2003, this time involving tax cuts. Congressional Republicans largely endorsed the President's proposal, but the Democrats' response was more divided. While many in the Democratic Party criticized Bush's plan, Senator Max Baucus (D-MT), the ranking minority member of the Senate Finance Committee, helped write the legislative language implementing Bush's proposal (Barshay 2003). The divided Democratic Party failed to stop the tax cut proposal, which passed Congress and became law in May. Why did the Democrats' promotional efforts succeed in 2005, when they had frequently failed before? More generally, why do members of Congress sometimes work together to promote their party's message, and other times remain silent or promote competing issues and arguments? How frequently are these promotional efforts coordinated with the White House?

This chapter addresses these questions, using congressional policy debates from 1997 and 2003. The first section of the chapter examines how frequently rank-and-file members promoted the messages constructed by party leaders. The second section asks why legislators promoted those messages. Their decision making provides compelling evidence of legislators' concern for their party's collective reputation, beyond the narrow motivations of their own individual policy preferences.

4.1. THE PROMOTION OF PARTY MESSAGES

Recall the expectations developed in Chapter 3 about rank-and-file legislators' decisions whether to promote a party message:

- When that message uses issues favoring the party,
  → the follower is more likely to promote the message, and to perceive benefits than costs from promoting the message.

- When that message uses issues favoring the opposing party, if the follower agrees with the position in the party message,
  → the follower is more likely to promote that message, and to perceive benefits than costs from promoting the message.
- But if the follower disagrees with the message's position,
  → the follower is less likely to promote the message, and more likely to perceive costs than benefits from promoting the message.

To evaluate these expectations, I again turn to the broad categories of issues and the four specific debates of the previous chapter. In my examination of legislators' promotional efforts surrounding these issues and debates, I used two sets of evidence. The first is a set of 22,170 public statements by all members of Congress, taken from the same electronic sources as the previous chapter (the *Congressional Record* and the FDCH).[1] For this chapter's analysis, I only used statements by rank-and-file members. Using computerized and human coding, I assessed whether each public statement (i.e., each floor statement, press release, or transcript) referred to one of the four broad issues, or either of the party messages in each of the four specific debates.[2]

The second set of evidence consists of comments by the press secretaries of forty-one different senators, made during interviews that I conducted on Capitol Hill during June and July of 1998. The interviews

[1] The number of statements from each source for 1997 and then 2003 are as follows: *Congressional Record* (7,848; 4,256), releases from the FDCH (7,872; 910), and transcripts of news events from the FDCH (774; 510). The FDCH contains relatively fewer statements from Democratic legislators. This source collects the most important or newsworthy releases. As the congressional minority with fewer members, the Democrats (despite their more strenuous efforts) were likely to produce fewer such releases than the majority Republicans, who controlled the levers of congressional power. The partisan distribution of statements falls closer to parity in the *Congressional Record*, reflecting its inclusion of all statements by Democrats and Republicans on the House and Senate floors.

[2] Again, see Appendix 3.B for details on the human and computerized content analysis. For April through July of 1997, I also collected copies of any releases that members of Congress distributed to the House and Senate press galleries, as well as records of televised news conferences on Capitol Hill, compiled by the House and Senate Radio-Television galleries. While this additional evidence covered only part of the seven-month period in 1997, the evidence indicated that members promoted the same issues as the comprehensive evidence suggested.

ranged in length from ten minutes to one hour.[3] Rather than using the interviews to ask general questions about senators' press activities, I focused my questions on the two specific debates over partial birth abortion and the supplemental appropriations bill.[4]

Using two such different sources of evidence allows each source to serve as a check on the validity of the other. The contextual information from the interviews can suggest whether senators actually made promotional decisions for the reasons suggested by the public statements. In addition, these public statements exist for all 535 members of the House and Senate. I can therefore ascertain whether the insights from the forty-one interviews with Democratic senators' press secretaries apply to the rest of the Senate and to the House. Finally, the press releases and events capture the actual promotion of messages, which provides a useful check on the press secretaries' recollections of their activities a year earlier.

4.1.1. Broad Issues and Specific Debates

While one might expect each party to dominate public discussion of its favored issues, legislators' public statements from the two periods again revealed limited evidence of emphasizing favorable broad issues. Democrats averaged slightly fewer public statements on health care than Republicans (2.45 versus 2.63, $p = .70$). An opposite tendency occurred on education, with Democrats making more statements (1.54 versus 1.34, $p = .10$). Republicans were significantly more outspoken about the

[3] I conducted interviews with the press secretaries of fifty-one senators. But, ten of the press secretaries had started working in their office since the previous summer, when the events of interest to my analysis occurred. I therefore was unable to use the results of these ten interviews in the current analysis. The forty-one remaining offices that provided access were representative of the overall Senate. I interviewed eighteen Democrats and twenty-three Republicans. This sample included at least one senator from thirty seven of the fifty states. Among the Democrats that I interviewed, the average seniority was 13.26 years; the equivalent for all Senate Democrats was 13.00 years. I also calculated the average of DW-NOMINATE ideology ratings produced by Poole (2005), where values close to −1 indicate more liberal legislators, and values close to 1 suggest more conservative ones. Democrats in the sample averaged −.38, while the mean for the Democratic caucus was −.40. The Republicans that I interviewed were equally representative. Their average seniority was 7.79 years, while that of the GOP caucus was 9.85. The sample of Republicans had an average ideology score of .41; the equivalent for all Republicans was .39.

[4] A potential concern with interviewing only press secretaries is that they may exaggerate the role of their work (public relations) in their office. But, Kedrowski (1996) interviewed administrative assistants on Capitol Hill and replicated many of the findings that emerged from Cook' s (1989) interviews of press secretaries.

environment (1.00 versus .58, p = .006) and defense (1.43 versus 1.15, p = .04). Similar to their party leaders, the rank-and-file members tended not to speak out more frequently on broad issues favoring their party. Following diverse interests and constituencies, the followers appear to have made more public statements on issues where their party traditionally lacked an advantage. Such diversity underscores the difficulty for leaders trying to coordinate their party's promotional efforts.

Stronger evidence of partisanship emerges from the promotion of party messages in specific debates. Unlike the broad issues encompassing a wide range of possible arguments and proposals, each specific debate generated clearly defined partisan messages about individual legislation that Congress was considering. In the debate over partial birth abortion, for example, Republican party leaders spoke of "infanticide" and "abortionists." Democratic leaders countered that message with their own argument that the Republicans' proposed "ban is unconstitutional." (See Appendix 3.C for a list of arguments that each party used.) In each debate, the components of the party messages varied in their attractiveness to rank-and-file members of Congress. Legislators frequently adopted some arguments, while completely ignoring others. Their selective acceptance of the party messages sheds light on what rank-and-file legislators believed to be an effective message.

First consider the 1997 debate over partial birth abortion. Figure 4.1 summarizes each party's promotional efforts in the debate, both overall and on individual arguments in the parties' messages. The figure lists the number of mentions by congressmen from each party of each *individual* argument in each party's message in the debate, as well as mentions of the party's overall message (i.e., of *any* argument in that message). The arguments are ordered, first by party and then by promotional advantage, that is, the number of Democrats promoting an argument compared to the number of Republicans doing so. The phrases with the greatest Republican advantage are at the top of each party's section, and those with the largest Democratic advantage are at the bottom.

In the partial birth abortion debate, Republicans discussed the Republican message much more frequently than their Democratic colleagues did (115 versus 7 statements). These mentions were more favorable than unfavorable.[5]

[5] Research assistants coded the tone of all legislators' statements in the debates over partial birth abortion and the supplemental appropriations bill. See Appendix 3.B for details. The text's discussions of tone only include statements with a clear positive or negative reference to a particular issue or argument. The lengthy time required to code the tone of statements by hand prevented capturing the tone of legislators' numerous statements in the two budget debates or in the news stories in Chapter 5.

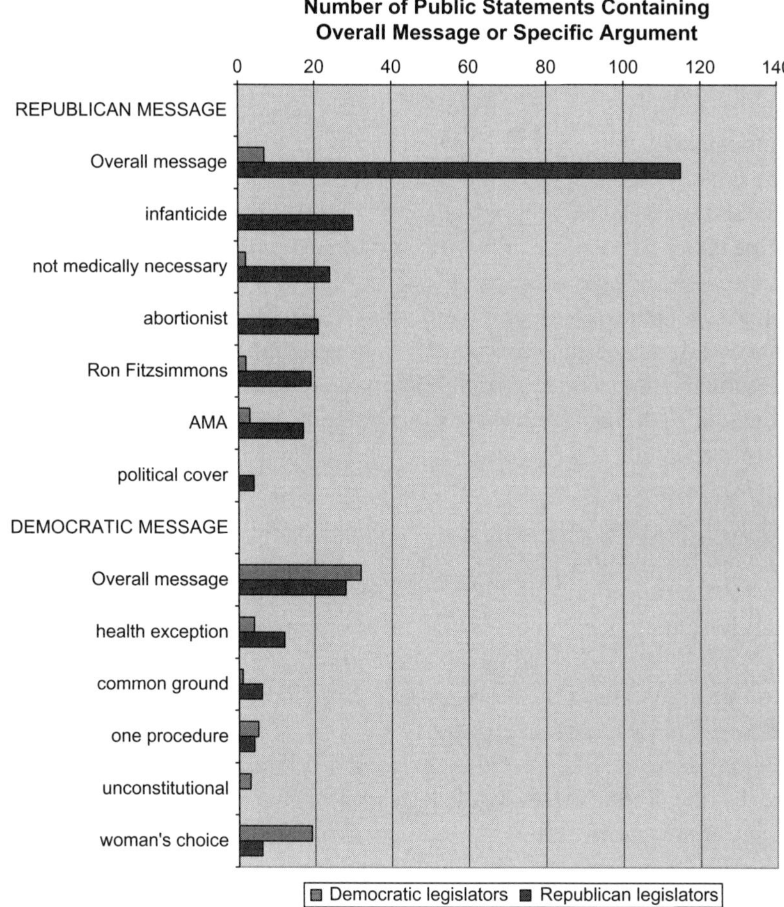

FIGURE 4.1. Messages and Public Statements About Partial Birth Abortion.

Of the GOP legislators' mentions of the Republican message, 108 clearly supported that message. Democrats were less uniformly positive, with two positive mentions of the GOP message and two negative mentions. Discussion of the Democratic message produced a similar advantage for Republicans. GOP legislators mentioned the Democratic message nearly as frequently as Democrats did (28 versus 32 mentions), albeit more negatively. The Republicans discussed the Democratic message positively three times and negatively eleven times. In contrast, Democratic legislators made sixteen positive mentions of their party message and no negative mentions.

Among the specific Republican arguments about partial birth abortion, vivid phrases such as "infanticide" and "abortionist," found frequent use in Republican legislators' statements. Democrats never used these terms. Democratic legislators also embraced their own party's message much less enthusiastically. The overall levels of promotion are lower, and Republicans used two phrases in the Democratic message ("health exception" and "common ground") more frequently than Democrats did. The aggregate measures of tone previously discussed suggest that the GOP legislators were mentioning these phrases in order to attack them. On three other phrases in the Democratic message, the Democrats enjoyed a slight promotional advantage, particularly "woman's choice."

The most telling evidence of the Democrats' promotional disadvantage in this debate emerged from the distinct names that the two parties used to describe the medical procedures underlying the debate.[6] To avoid false positives (such as references to "common ground" in other political debates), the content analysis only selected statements that mentioned a particular argument (such as "common ground") AND either party's name for the procedures. Republicans used their preferred name, "partial birth abortion," 927 times, while mentioning the Democratic names ("late-term abortion" or "dilation and extraction") only 68 times. Democratic legislators used the more graphic Republican phrase 79 times and their own party's names 112 times.[7]

These patterns, when combined, paint a picture of a debate dominated by the Republicans. GOP legislators promoted their own party message much more frequently and in more positive terms, while attacking the opposition's message. Democrats defended their party's

[6] It is important to note that the Republican and Democratic legislation targeted different procedures. The GOP ban would have ended a particular abortion procedure, while Daschle's legislation targeted a broad set of abortion procedures late in pregnancy.

[7] Many references to either name likely contained a positive or negative tone, defending or criticizing the particular procedure. As presented immediately above, human coding was able to capture the tone of references to party messages in the debate over partial birth abortion; similar evidence is available as follows for the supplemental debate. But, it proved difficult (and expensive) to extend this human coding to every reference to partial birth abortion or the supplemental or terms from the budget debates. Such positive and negative references can include a variety of wordings and forms. As Appendix 3.B explains, I instead relied on computerized content analysis to search for unique words and phrases making up references to issues and arguments. This focus on mentions ignores the tone of the mentions, but instead captures the extent of legislators' reliance on the different issues and arguments making up the parties' messages in each debate. This selective focus on issues and arguments constitutes the parties' efforts to set the agenda of each debate.

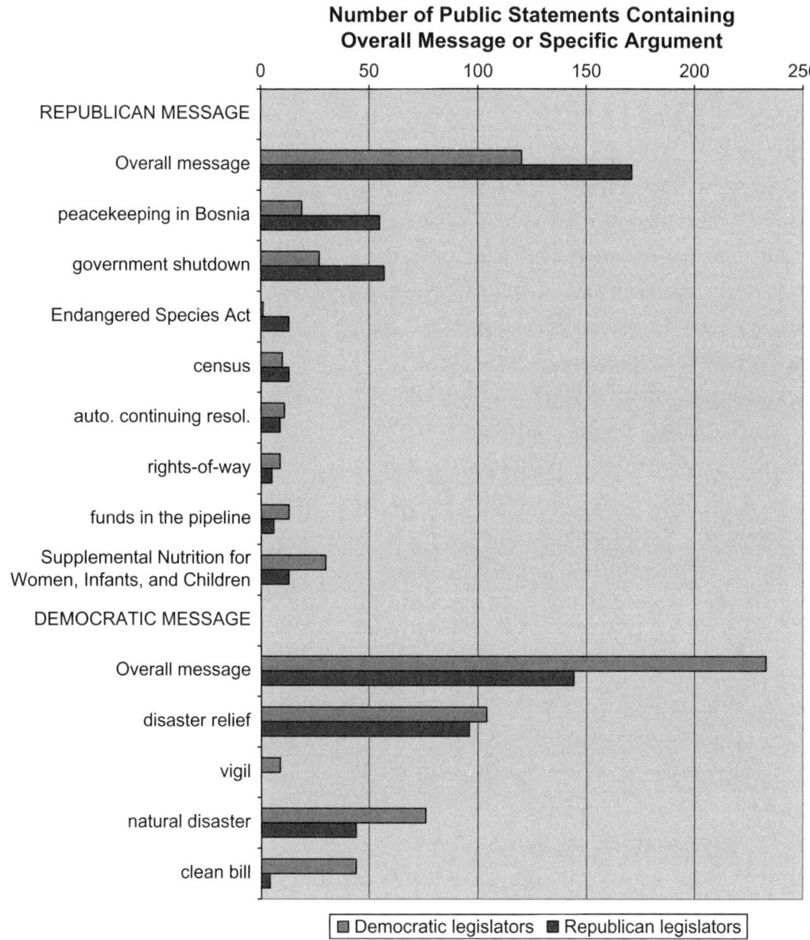

FIGURE 4.2. Messages and Public Statements About the Supplemental.

message with much less vigor, while saying little positive or negative about the Republican message. Much of the debate employed the Republicans' issues and arguments, illustrating in detail the GOP advantage.

A significantly different scenario emerged during the debate over the supplemental appropriations bill (see Figure 4.2). This debate drew much more participation from both parties. Democrats mentioned the Democratic message more frequently than Republicans did (233 versus 144 statements). Significantly, the tone of these mentions was overwhelmingly positive in both parties. Democratic legislators made 185 positive references to the Democratic message and no negative references. Their GOP counterparts made 96 positive mentions of that message and only seven critical mentions. The Democrats' message thus proved popular among legislators from both parties. The Republicans' message did not find such widespread support. Republicans made 171 mentions of their message, while Democrats mentioned it 120 times. GOP legislators mentioned their message in more positive than negative terms (85 clearly positive mentions versus 23 clearly negative ones). Democrats, in contrast, were much more critical (three clearly positive mentions versus 90 clearly negative ones). The tone of the legislators' statements suggests that the Democratic message found bipartisan support, while the Republican message was more divisive.

Among specific issues and arguments in the debate, Democratic themes about "disaster relief" and "natural disaster" attracted the most mentions from legislators in both parties. But as the measures of tone previously suggested, both parties discussed the Democratic arguments in a supportive tone; thus, neither party enjoyed a large promotional advantage on any of the specific Democratic arguments. The Republican leaders won the most promotional help from followers with their arguments about the need to address the ongoing Bosnian conflict and to prevent future government shutdowns. But despite this GOP support, congressional Democrats were highly critical of GOP attempts to add the various provisions to the supplemental appropriations bill. This criticism of the Republicans meshed well with the Democrats' own message. By drawing attention to the ongoing natural disasters and the growing need for disaster relief funding, the Democrats increased pressure on GOP legislators to assist disaster victims by passing a "clean" relief bill as soon as possible. As the press secretaries reveal as follows, GOP legislators faced growing constituent pressure to address the disasters (instead of the unrelated policy provisions). The Republicans did so, thereby helping the Democrats win the promotional battle inside and outside Congress.

The last two specific debates involved the federal budget in 1997 and 2003. These debates were extremely complex, involving issues from health care to tax cuts. This complexity made it harder for either party to enjoy a clear advantage, as the Republicans did with the partial birth abortion ban and the Democrats did with the supplemental. Instead, the complexity created the opportunity for each side to shift the budget debates toward politically favorable terms.

The debates over the budget attracted high levels of promotional activity, reflecting the topics' importance. Each year saw both parties using

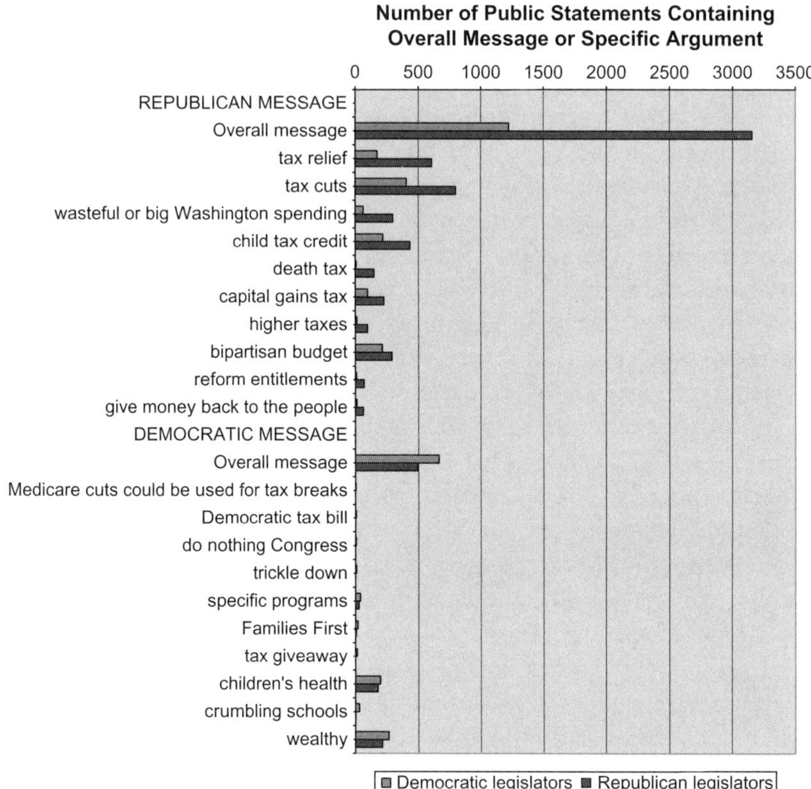

FIGURE 4.3. Messages and Public Statements About the 1997 Budget Resolution.

many different arguments in their public relations efforts. The large number of arguments makes it cumbersome to discuss them individually. Accordingly, the figures summarizing legislators' statements include for each party the five arguments where the party held the largest promotional advantage, and the five arguments producing the greatest disadvantage.[8] These sets of arguments were nearly always the most common topics of the rank-and-file legislators' messages in the debates.

In 1997, the Republican Party message focused on general budgetary arguments about spending and taxes. Across the ten main Republican arguments listed in Figure 4.3, only one type of government program

[8] Unlike the figures for the budget debates, my subsequent analysis of these debates includes all the budget-related arguments listed in Appendix 3.C, not just those with the greatest promotional advantages and disadvantages.

receives mention, and only in a carefully chosen way. The phrase "reform entitlements" highlights the idea that recipients of certain government benefits believe that they are automatically entitled to those benefits, as well as the need to reform such automatic government spending. Significantly, the phrase makes no mention of specific programs (such as Social Security) whose reform might spark controversy.

Most of the arguments in the Republican Party message emphasize taxes and general government spending. The GOP enjoyed sizeable promotional advantages on all these arguments, although the Democrats made a number of public statements on them too. Members of both parties discussed the need for a "bipartisan" budget package. The Republicans more frequently expressed a desire for such an agreement. GOP politicians allegedly wanted any budget agreement to emerge by "immaculate conception," resulting from private negotiations between President Clinton and congressional leaders. Increasingly common, this unorthodox legislative maneuver (Sinclair 1997) would spare the congressional Republicans from having to issue their own deficit reduction package. Such a package would undoubtedly entail painful, unpopular cuts in specific government programs. A bipartisan budget package emerging from private negotiations would allow Republicans to share blame for the unpopular cuts, as well as focus attention on broader government spending and taxes and away from specific programs (Hager 1997c).

Such specific programs made up four of the ten main arguments in the Democratic message. The Democrats worked to protect programs involving "crumbling schools," "children's health," "school lunches," "Headstart," "WIC," and "Medicare." Many of the party's promotional advantages emerged on these specific arguments. The greatest advantage occurred on distributional themes involving the "wealthy."

In general, members of both parties spent more time discussing arguments in the Republican message than those in the Democratic message. The Democratic legislators made nearly twice as many public statements mentioning Republican arguments as Democratic ones (1,223 versus 663 statements, respectively). Republicans were even more focused on their party's themes (3,152 versus 495 statements). An important part of my argument is that congressional parties obtain political advantage when they focus on issues where their members are unified and the opposition is divided. The issue of taxes provides such an advantage for Republicans. GOP legislators are largely unified on the issue, while Democrats are often divided about whether and how hard to push for tax cuts. Republicans help their electoral and policy goals when they make tax cuts a

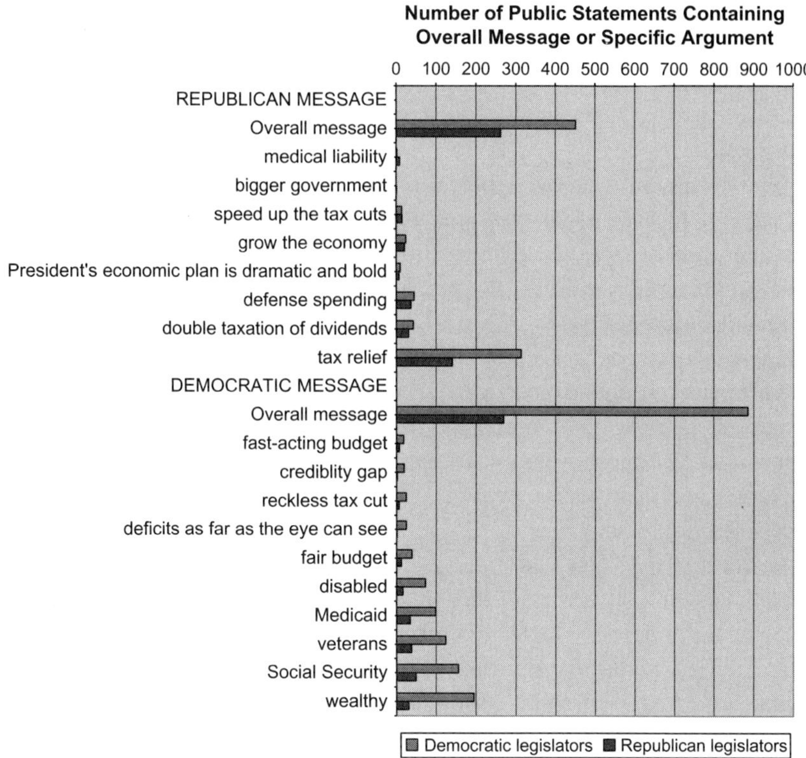

FIGURE 4.4. Messages and Public Statements About the 2003 Budget Resolution.

central part of budgetary debates. Democrats resist by shifting focus away from general budgetary matters like taxing and spending to specific government programs. In 1997, the budgetary debate focused more frequently on Republican issues and arguments involving taxes. Democratic leaders may have more effectively persuaded rank-and-file Democrats to promote their party message to the extent that that message attacked the Republican "budget" for favoring the wealthy in areas of government spending, instead of attacking Republican tax cuts for doing so.

Six years later, the debate over the budget resolution generated similar partisan arguments but lower levels of promotion, particularly among Republicans (see Figure 4.4). The economic recession starting in 2001 shaped congressional Republicans' message, leading to proposals to "speed up the tax cuts" and "grow the economy." Democrats discussed these arguments as frequently as the Republicans did, perhaps in an attempt to pin blame for the economic difficulties on the Republican

White House. The overall Republican message still focused on general statements about government spending and the economy. The arguments include only two specific areas of spending: national defense, and health care (specifically, the costs of "frivolous" medical liability lawsuits).

The Democrats enjoyed promotional advantages on nearly all the arguments in their own message. Republicans discussed many Democratic arguments much less frequently than six years earlier. Statements mentioning the "wealthy" theme, for example, fell from 265 to 195 among Democrats, and from 213 to 31 among Republicans. On the theme of "tax relief," Democrats made more statements in 2003 than in 1997 (increasing from 174 to 313 mentions), while the Republicans discussed their own plan much less frequently (declining from 607 to 141 mentions). The most common Democratic arguments (and those providing the largest Democratic advantage) fell into three groups: specific types of spending ("Social Security," "veterans" programs, "Medicaid," and programs for the "disabled"), Republican fiscal irresponsibility involving "deficits as far as the eye can see," and the distributional argument about wealthy millionaires. The Democrats continued focusing on specific areas of spending and discussing overall government spending in distributional terms. Overall, Democrats' total statements in the debate fell 29%, declining from 1,886 statements in 1997 to 1,336 in 2003. GOP legislators dropped 86%, from 3,647 to 527.

4.1.2. Deference, Coordination, and the President

The two parties' decline in promotional efforts may be tied to a consideration discussed in Chapter 3: the changes in institutional context from 1997 to 2003, specifically the party controlling the White House. That chapter found only mixed evidence of congressional leaders of the president's party deferring to his bully pulpit. A similar pattern emerged in this chapter. After their party won the presidency in 2003, rank-and-file Republicans followed their leaders in Congress, reduced their promotional efforts, and appeared to defer to Bush's bully pulpit. Democratic legislators, on the other hand, made more public statements under Clinton than Bush. Instead deferring to Clinton, congressional Democrats spoke out frequently.

Reflecting these varying patterns of deference, the presidents and their congressional parties displayed different levels of coordination in their promotion of messages. The president and his party colleagues in

Congress could conceivably agree to publicize a party message on the same day. In the 1997 budget debate, Clinton and congressional Democrats both promoted the Democratic budget message on 49 of the 213 days (23%) covered in the analysis. In 2003, Bush and GOP legislators both promoted their budget message on only 18 days (8% of all days covered). While both years saw the president and his fellow partisans in Congress rarely promoting their party's message on the same day, the level of coordination appears higher in 1997.

The limited day-to-day coordination is not surprising, given the widely divergent schedules of Congress and the White House, and the intrusion of unexpected events such as foreign policy crises. A picture of greater coordination emerges when one considers promotional efforts from week to week. The period of analysis in 1997 covers thirty-one different weeks. In the 1997 budget debate, Clinton and congressional Democrats both mentioned the Democratic message in twenty-six weeks (84% of the thirty-one weeks analyzed). In 2003, in contrast, Bush and his fellow partisans in Congress both promoted the GOP budget message during sixteen weeks (52%). From two different standpoints, therefore, coordination between the White House and its fellow partisans in Congress appears greater in 1997.

How can we explain the differences in deference and coordination between the two years? In 1997, Clinton was the most prominent Democrat in government and overshadowed his fellow partisans in Congress. In turn, the Democratic congressional minority enjoyed relatively few powers. As Clinton directly negotiated with the Republican majority, congressional Democrats were often forced to argue publicly for their relevance to the policy-making process while pushing the president to remain true to traditional Democratic principles and issue positions (Palazzolo 1999). Thus, Democratic legislators spoke out frequently on the same issues that Clinton discussed. The need to demonstrate relevance changed in 2003 when the congressional Democrats, while still a minority, became the highest ranking Democrats in government. They still worked to promote the Democratic message in policy debates, but their status as the highest ranking opposition strengthened their relevance, and they did not need to work to keep a Democratic president supporting Democratic issue positions. These changes may explain the moderate decline in congressional Democrats' promotional efforts from 2003 to 1997.

Congressional Republicans never faced a need to demonstrate their relevance, because their majority in both years gave them extensive influence in the policy process. At the same time, however, their incentive to promote Republican messages changed substantially between 1997 and 2003. During the first year, GOP legislators were the highest ranking opposition to Clinton, and the Republicans in Congress were best able to counter Clinton's bully pulpit and the Democrats' promotional efforts. This incentive weakened in 2003 when Bush became president. While no longer the highest ranking Republicans in government, the GOP legislators still controlled Congress and could use the majority's powers to influence the policy process. At the same time, they could rely on Bush and the presidential bully pulpit to promote the GOP message in policy debates. These factors reduced congressional Republicans' incentive to engage in promotional campaigns and encouraged them to free ride on the public statements of Bush.[9]

4.1.3. Discussion

From health care to the federal budget, the issues and debates in this section highlight the central role of partisanship in legislators' public relations. Members of each party only sometimes devoted more attention to broad issues favoring their party, thus providing mixed support for the expectations about rank-and-file legislators' promotional efforts developed in Chapter 3. But, these expectations found stronger support in the promotional campaigns surrounding the four specific debates. In each of these debates, the leaders of each party used very different arguments. Their rank-and-file followers often discussed those arguments in expected ways, reflecting the particular partisan advantage in each debate. The debate over the partial birth abortion ban favored the Republican Party, and GOP legislators often repeated their leaders' graphic and effective arguments. Democrats, in contrast, mounted a relatively limited public defense, rarely mentioning any of their leaders' arguments. In the debate over the supplemental appropriations bill, the advantage switched to the Democrats. Republicans joined the Democrats' efforts to draw attention to the natural disasters, thus assisting the Democrats' efforts to pass a

[9] Coordination between the president and his partisans in Congress may also occur unintentionally, as they all respond to an unexpected outside factor. For example, the United States launched the Iraq War in March of 2003. As this conflict progressed, congressional Republicans likely helped promote and defend Bush's arguments about the war, and the legislators needed little encouragement or direction from the White House.

clean bill. In each debate, one party enjoyed greater promotion of its message, creating a clear promotional advantage.

The two remaining debates offered a different pattern of public statements. The complexity of the federal budget made it harder for either party to enjoy a promotional advantage in these debates. With no clearly dominant message, members of each party tried to steer the budget debates toward arguments favoring their interests. Republicans tended to emphasize taxes and general government spending, while the Democrats focused on distributional themes and specific government programs.

Across the four debates, the legislators aimed their promotional activities at each other, hoping to influence the policy outcome of each debate. Another important target was the public. Here, the varying promotional advantage across the debates could shape what voters learned about the debates.[10] When Congress took up the partial birth abortion ban and the supplemental, the message of the advantaged party in each debate won more mentions from legislators than did the message of the disadvantaged party. As a result, voters were more likely to encounter the former message than the latter one. In the more competitive debates over the budget, voters more likely encountered both sides' messages because neither party had a clear promotional advantage. These examples illustrate how variation in legislators' promotional efforts may influence whether voters hear one or both sides of a debate. The final flow of messages, however, depends on journalists' decision to cover the competing messages.

4.2. WHO PROMOTES PARTY MESSAGES?

The four specific debates paint a picture of sharply divided political parties. This picture is often accurate, particularly on issues favoring one party. It is important, however, to remember the nature of this advantage. In Chapter 3 I argued that on the most favorable issues, one party is unified around a popular political position, while the opposing party is divided. The favored party will enthusiastically promote the party message capturing that popular position. In the disadvantaged and divided party, the party message contains the preferred position of only a portion of the party members, who are most likely to promote that message.

To evaluate these expectations in greater detail, I consider how promotion of the party message varies across politicians' partisanship, policy

[10] Chapter 5 links the promotional efforts to news coverage of the messages, which in turn can impact voters (Iyengar 1991, Iyengar and Kinder 1989).

preferences, and institutional position. In the debate over the partial birth abortion ban, for example, which Republicans publicly supported their party's message on this GOP-leaning issue? Which of the disadvantaged Democrats provided the meager support for their party's message reported above? Did President Clinton help promote that message or remain silent? To address these questions, I briefly examine legislators' overall promotional activities across all issues, showing how a statistical technique called multiple regression can assess competing influences on legislators' promotional activities. I then use that technique to consider how legislators' policy preferences and partisanship interact to shape the promotion of party messages in the four specific debates. The final section of this chapter considers how legislators coordinate these promotional efforts with presidents sharing their party.

4.2.1. Identifying Show Horses

Among all members of Congress in 1997 and 2003, the average annual number of public statements (on any issue) was 46.05. Twelve House members (four Democrats and eight Republicans) made no public statements in a particular year, while Senate Minority Leader Daschle made the most public statements of any legislator in a single year (417 in 1997). Daschle's public relations efforts suggest that the legislative work horses of Congress may now also act as show horses in order to further policy and electoral goals (Cook 1998).[11] With public relations efforts playing a central role in the legislative process, it becomes important to understand who is engaging in these efforts, and why (Sheafer 2001).

One possible influence on promotional activities is the office held by each legislator. Senators could easily mount more extensive public relations efforts than representatives, given the greater resources, powers, and newsworthiness of the former (Arnold 2004, Hess 1986). To investigate this idea, one could compare the average number of statements of senators and representatives. Yet, other factors may also explain the variation in public statements, and the comparison of only the two averages prevents consideration of these other factors.

[11] The terms "work horse" and "show horse" originated in Matthews' (1959) quote of the *Washington Post* and *Times Herald* from February 19, 1956: "There are two kinds of Congressmen – show horses and work horses. If you want to get your name in the paper, be a show horse. If you want to gain the respect of your colleagues, keep quiet and be a work horse" (1067).

I examine the variation in legislators' public statements by using a different statistical technique: multiple regression. This approach can suggest how one factor may influence a quantity of interest, while controlling for the influence of other possible factors on that same quantity of interest. Regression can suggest whether and how each factor (i.e., each independent variable) influences the quantity of interest (i.e., the dependent variable). A useful way to present these estimates of influence is with expected values (King et al. 2000). Regression can suggest what value we expect the dependent variable to take if an independent variable has a particular value. If we wish to understand how the branch in which a legislator serves (an independent variable) influences her number of public statements (the dependent variable), it is possible to estimate the expected number of public statements of a member of Congress if that legislator is a member of the House. A similar numerical estimate is available for a legislator in the Senate. These two numbers are more useful than a comparison of means, because we calculate the expected values after controlling for other possible influences on legislators' public relations efforts that we wish to consider in our analysis. Readers with a statistical background may recognize that the dependent variable and various independent variables make up a regression model. See Appendix 4.A for more details on the regression models producing the expected values in this chapter (including a description of variables, the method of estimation, estimated coefficients, and their significance).

In the first regression model that I estimated, the expected number of public statements for a typical House member was 30.44. The corresponding estimate for a typical senator was 119.17. These expected values control for a variety of other possible influences on legislators' promotional activity; both expected values assume that these other influences are at their average level for each hypothetical legislator in question. The expected values themselves appear far apart, suggesting that senators make many more public statements than representatives do. Despite this large difference, an important question remains: How far apart must the two expected values lie in order to conclude that the pattern is statistically significant? In other words, how can we decide that the pattern results from true differences between senators and representatives and not from random variation in the evidence?

To answer this question, it is important to remember that each expected value (of the dependent variable) is only an estimate of the true value of that dependent variable (when the independent variables have particular values). If our estimate is good, the expected value will be close to the true value; a poor estimate will be far from the true value. We can understand the proximity of the expected and true values by calculating a confidence interval around the expected value. With a 95% confidence interval, we can be 95% confident that the interval around the expected value includes the true value of the dependent variable. Any of the wide range of values inside the confidence interval could be the true value of the dependent variable.

This logic helps us interpret the expected numbers of events for an average senator and representative. The confidence interval for the representative's expected value is 28.34 to 32.50, and that for the senator's estimate is 96.20 to 146.92. If the two intervals overlapped, then a real possibility would exist that the true number of statements for an average senator is not significantly different from that of a typical representative. But in this case, the two confidence intervals are far from overlapping. The difference between intervals suggests that the promotional activity of a senator is higher (most likely, much higher) than that of a representative. While not surprising (Arnold 2004, Cook 1998, Hess 1986) the pattern helps illustrate the statistical techniques and interpretation used in the remainder of this chapter.[12]

4.2.2. Partisan Messages and Party Loyalty

When examining which legislators promote particular messages and why, it is important to evaluate carefully the role of the parties' collective reputations. This book has thus far assigned a central role to those reputations. Chapter 3 argued that rank-and-file legislators base their promotional decisions on both individual policy preferences and collective concerns about the party's overall reputation. In this argument, a rank-and-file member will promote a party message if she agrees with it and receives individual benefits from promoting it. If the legislator disagrees with a message from her party (such as the one recommended by her leader), the legislator will not promote it; she receives no individual benefits from doing so. But when considering whether to promote the opposition's message, the legislator must balance the costs to her party's

[12] In the regression model in Appendix 4.A, other significant influences on legislators' overall promotional activities include the proximity of a legislator's next election, whether the legislator is a congressional leader, and the legislator's partisanship and ideology. See also Cook 1998, Hess 1986, Kuklinski and Sigelman 1992, and Sellers and Schaffner 2007.

collective reputation of such defection, with the individual benefits of promoting a message that she more strongly supports.

This balancing is likely less necessary for legislators at a party's outer ideological extremes (such as liberal Democrats or conservative Republicans). These members are very likely to support their own party's message, and to oppose that of the opposition.[13] More moderate party members, in contrast, are more likely to disagree with their own party's message and to agree with that of the opposition. So, these moderates must more frequently balance the individual and collective considerations. Chapter 3 suggested that the collective concerns will sometimes lead these moderate legislators to remain silent and forgo promoting the opposition's message.

Many observers have questioned such a party-based explanation, asking whether collective considerations about parties' reputations are truly important for legislators' decision making. In their critique, these observers suggest a high, if counterfactual, standard for assessing the effects and strength of congressional parties and their leaders: whether party leaders actually lead legislators to behave differently than they would in the absence of such efforts (Aldrich and Rohde 1995, Krehbiel 1998). Even the high levels of partisanship in contemporary congresses could result from the sharp division among members' preferences, with party leaders playing no role in the growing partisanship. Those leaders may have been following the rank-and-file members of their parties, instead of leading. Promoting the issue positions and preferred message of the median party member may be the easiest and safest way to remain a party leader. As party members' preferences diverge further and further from those of their leader, those members are less likely to support or help promote the leader's message. In this preference-based explanation of congressional behavior, legislators base their public relations efforts solely on their own individual policy positions and electoral concerns. Collective concerns about the party message and brand name play no role.[14]

[13] This argument assumes that party leaders choose messages close to the preferences of the median member of their caucus. Such a median message draws support from more caucus members than a nonmedian message does (Downs 1957).

[14] This explanation suggests that members of Congress campaign for reelection by emphasizing individual position taking and credit claiming, while shying away from the party brand name. As a noted observer put it, "the party label seems more like a bad-luck charm than a treasured brand name" (Krehbiel 1998, 223). Reflecting this candidate-centered campaigning, legislators rarely win local news coverage associated with their party label. They "seldom claim to be either party supporters or party opponents; they seldom invoke party as a reason for their roll-call votes" (Arnold 2004, 259).

In such a scenario, legislators at the outer ideological extremes of a party will still find their own party's message more appealing than that of the opposition party. The key difference from the party-based argument occurs among moderates. The preference-based explanation suggests that the moderates' individual policy preferences always make them more likely to support the opposition's message than their more extreme caucus colleagues do. Across all debates and issues, the moderates will display little concern about collective partisan considerations.

The difference between these party- and preference-based arguments boils down to the moderates in each party. Do their individual policy preferences alone make them always more likely to promote the opposition's message, or do collective partisan considerations sometimes encourage these legislators to forgo that message and sometimes remain silent? To assess the accuracy of these two competing expectations, I turned to the press secretary interviews and the legislators' actual public statements, focusing on the four specific debates in 1997 and 2003.[15] The two bodies of evidence indicate that legislators base their promotional decisions on both the individual and collective considerations outlined earlier, and not on their individual preferences alone.

4.2.3. Partial Birth Abortion

In the debate over the partial birth abortion ban, Republican legislators spoke publicly about both parties' messages more often than Democrats did. To understand whether the members of Congress balanced individual policy preferences and collective partisan concerns, it is necessary to capture the legislators' individual policy preferences on the issue. I turned to the congressional votes in 1996 to override President Bill Clinton's veto of a partial birth abortion ban (Senate vote #301 and House vote #422, http://thomas.loc.gov/). These votes allowed me to classify 90 (of 100) senators and 358 (of 435) representatives serving in 1997 as supporters or opponents of their leadership's position and message. If a Democrat voted to support the president's veto, I classified her as a supporter of the Democratic leadership's message and position.

[15] I also used regression analysis to examine partisan dynamics in message promotion on the four broad issues described previously. Democratic and more liberal legislators tended to make public statements more frequently on health care and education. Discussion of the environment and defense did not vary significantly by party or ideological perspective.

A vote to override designated a Democrat as an opponent. The reverse applied to Republicans.

The Republican caucus was largely unified on this vote and issue. Of the 48 Republican senators whom I was able to classify as a supporter or opponent of their leadership, 45 of them voted to override the Clinton veto in 1996. In the House, 184 of 196 GOP representatives cast votes to override. Despite the leadership supporters' dominance of the GOP, they and the leadership opponents mentioned the leadership's message with a similar low frequency. After controlling for other factors that might influence message promotion, regression analysis suggested that each supporter of the GOP leadership message made .47 public references to that message, while each opponent made .16 references. The confidence intervals around these two expected values overlap (.24 to .89, and .01 to .90), suggesting an insignificant difference between the two groups. A similar pattern occurred in Republican legislators' statements about the Democratic message on partial birth abortion: supporters of the GOP leadership made an expected .08 public mentions (.04 to .13), while the corresponding expectation for opponents was .20 (.02 to .84). The interviews with Republican press secretaries provided a third indication of similar promotional efforts by the two party factions. I asked the press secretaries to describe how frequently their offices nationally promoted the leadership's message in the partial birth abortion debate in 1997. I labeled the responses as ranging from 0 (no promotion) to 3 (very active promotion). Among the 18 leadership supporters in the interviews, the average level of promotion was .61; the single leadership opponent in the interviews never promoted the message.

These patterns suggest little difference in the public relations efforts of supporters and opponents of the GOP leadership. But, the per-legislator estimates conceal a larger overall difference. If the 227 leadership supporters average .47 public statements per legislator, their combined effort in support of the ban numbers approximately 107 statements. By the same logic, the 15 leadership opponents produced a total of approximately two statements in support of the ban. GOP leadership supporters also made approximately 18 statements referring to the Democratic message in the debate; opponents of the leadership made three such statements.

In sum, many Republicans did not make public statements about either message during the debate over the partial birth abortion ban, which meant that GOP supporters and opponents of the leadership produced similar low per-legislator averages. But, the total statements by the two Republican factions differed substantially, with the more numerous supporters of the GOP leadership generating the bulk of the statements.

The motivations behind these patterns emerged from the interviews with the Republican press secretaries. Their responses focused almost exclusively on individual electoral considerations. Among supporters of the ban, the partial birth issue solidified and energized the electoral base of many senators, particularly conservatives and pro-life activists. Remarkably, no Republicans supportive of the ban mentioned any policy benefits from promoting the leadership's message. The only mention of policy benefits came from the press secretary of the sole Republican opponent. The staffer justified the vote with the argument that it was promoting the "right" policy.

The Republican press secretaries also mentioned a number of factors which might limit the individual electoral benefits. The press secretary of the sole opponent also feared a loss of Republican fund raising support for voting against the partial birth abortion bill. In addition, many staffers expressed concern that the leadership's message would mobilize pro-choice forces and alienate the general electorate. Abortion has been one of the most contentious topics in American politics, splitting the general public and each party (Carmines and Woods 2002, Koch 2001). As one staffer put it,

> Abortion is the most divisive, most difficult issue here. This is because you automatically piss off half the electorate. This is particularly the case in a diverse state like [ours]. But partial birth is slightly different; we felt confident we could promote the issue. It's a more populist issue, with more general appeal. (July 15, 1998, Washington, D.C.)

The Republican press secretaries hoped that framing the issue in terms of the partial birth procedure would provide greater benefits for their party.

Other individual concerns appear unrelated to partisanship and policy preferences. The press secretaries were sensitive to Senator Rick Santorum's (R-PA) leadership on the issue; they expressed a desire not to encroach on "his issue" (Miller 1977). Several of the offices were busy promoting their own issues, and focusing on partial birth abortion would take time and resources away from these issues. According to one press secretary, for press activities to win coverage, they must focus on issues related to a senator's committees and on which the senator has been a leader. Otherwise, the staffer argued, "you're just whistling in the wind" (July 17, 1998, Washington, D.C.). Another press secretary voiced a similar opinion: "In the eyes of the press, you look silly if you try to get publicity on issues that you aren't closely linked to" (July 17, 1998, Washington, D.C.). By focusing press activities on an issue where a senator has developed expertise and a record, press staffers believed that they could help their senator own that issue.[16] Building such a reputation can help legislators win more coverage with the same effort, which effectively lowers the individual costs of promotion. By extension, the reputation helps legislators win the individual benefits of news coverage in Washington (Cook 1989, 1998, Hess 1986; Schiller 2000) and constituent support at home (Fenno 1978, Sellers 1998).

These explanations suggest a number of unanticipated extensions to my argument. The Republican press secretaries often explained their work on partial birth abortion by focusing on individual benefits of promoting the issue. A senator can receive greater policy and electoral benefits by promoting issues on which she has developed a personal record and reputation. Both the issues and accompanying reputation are often tied to a senator's home-state reelection constituency. For example, Senator Pete Domenici (R-NM) took a leading role on Energy Department appropriations, reflecting the importance of that department's research laboratories for his state's economy. Emphasizing issues without this personal reputation is less likely to produce coverage and benefits for the senator. The benefits of personal reputation may help explain why legislators often concentrate time and resources on a small set of issues (Schiller 2000).

The Republicans' discussion of partial birth abortion begins to illustrate how the issue fits the criteria outlined earlier for a politically favorable issue. The Republican caucus and their constituencies were largely unified around a ban. In addition to these homogenous preferences, many GOP senators believed that their position on the issue could win the support of the general public.

For partial birth abortion to provide maximum advantage to the GOP, the issue also needed to divide the Democrats. Democratic legislators displayed such division. Of the 42 Senate Democrats whose policy position I was able to classify, 34 senators joined their leader and voted

[16] A substantial number of press secretaries illustrated this point by referring to China. Each argued that no senator had yet become the acknowledged expert on this largely ignored issue. Each hoped her boss would become that expert.

against overriding the President in 1996.[17] In the House, 104 of 162 Democrats voted against override. While Democratic legislators appeared more divided on the issue, neither supporters or opponents of the Democratic leaders were frequent contributors to the debate. Regression analysis indicates that the factions averaged .08 public statements or less about the Democratic or Republican issues; the confidence intervals around these expected values all overlapped. Even as a group, supporters of the Democratic leadership's position made a total of approximately three statements in support of that message. In the interviews, the Democratic press secretaries reported similarly low levels of activity on the issue. On the same 0-to-3 scale used above, the thirteen supporters of the Democratic leadership message averaged .15. The four opponents reported no promotional activity at all.

The limited public statements reflected the concern of all the Democratic press secretaries about how the issue risked splitting their senators' electoral coalitions. The opponents of their party leaders' message expressed concern about creating a public conflict within the party. These Democrats viewed the threat of divisive conflict as particularly serious on partial birth abortion. The press secretary for a southern Democrat said that her boss did not do any public relations work on the issue; he just voted for the pro-life position. "He didn't beat his chest on this issue.... [The senator] didn't support the Democrats, but he didn't trample on their message either" (July 2, 1998, Washington, D.C.). Another press secretary explained the silence of her boss in greater detail:

> Reporters try to get him to talk when he goes against the leadership. But unless he really cares about the issue, he doesn't talk to reporters. He just votes against the leadership and is quiet about it. It's selective opposition.... He feels that these are

[17] In the Senate, the Democratic leadership sought to make partial birth abortion "a Daschle issue, instead of a leadership issue." Several Democratic press secretaries mentioned that their bosses were given free rein to vote with their consciences. Among the opponents, some preferred the more conservative Santorum bill, while others desired a more liberal alternative (written by Senators Boxer and Feinstein) than either the Santorum or Daschle proposal. But, Daschle's position as Minority Leader made it difficult to consider his proposal without thinking of his position. In addition, Daschle and his staff promoted his alternative ban in caucus and staff meetings. Such opportunities for persuasion might have been less available for a rank-and-file Democratic senator. In the House, the minority's weaker influence over the floor agenda prevented the Democrats from offering a more moderate alternative to the GOP ban. The lack of influence and moderate alternative appeared to contribute to a greater GOP advantage in news coverage during the House debate. Chapter 5 documents this advantage.

his only options because they are in the minority and can't afford lots of public conflicts and debates within the party. (July 10, 1998, Washington, D.C.)

Such a balancing of individual and collective concerns is central to my arguments about why legislators engage in message promotion. These senators voted for their own preferred policy positions, but they saw few individual electoral or policy benefits in promoting that position to the media. Instead, they feared creating a divided image of their party. In the decision whether to go public with the opposition's message, collective partisan concerns trumped individual policy preferences.

Supporters of the Daschle alternative were also unenthusiastic about discussing the issue. They appeared to prefer to vote for that legislation but not publicize it. When explaining the few statements that their bosses did make, the press secretaries mentioned only individual benefits. Some senators were motivated by a desire to promote the "right" policy, one that they believed in. The Daschle alternative provided electoral benefits to one southern Democrat. The vote and related promotional efforts allowed the senator to remain true to a campaign commitment to support a partial birth ban. They also reinforced the senator's conservative reputation against charges of being a liberal.

Among the supporters, these benefits were outweighed, however, by concerns about promoting the Daschle alternative. Most frequently mentioned were electoral concerns, both collective and individual. Many Democrats viewed the issue as part of the Republicans' strategy for the next election. As one press secretary put it,

The Republicans presented the Democrats with a difficult situation. The Democrats didn't want to vote the way that they have traditionally voted, and that some traditional Democratic constituencies would want them to vote, because doing so would create perfect material for a 30-second spot. (June 25, 1998, Washington, D.C.)

The partial birth issue risked alienating activists in both wings of the Democratic Party: pro-choice women's groups and more conservative Catholic constituents. The press secretaries also lamented that the graphic pictures of partial birth abortions proved very effective: "It's really hard to combat those horrific images that the Republicans use" (July 2, 1998, Washington, D.C.).

Individual policy concerns also discouraged the Democrats from promoting the issue. Several senators were personally torn on the issue, facing costs regardless of their decision. This tension created a strong hesitancy to discuss the issue; one press secretary said that her senator would "rather go to the dentist than have a conversation about the issue" (July 9, 1998, Washington, D.C.). Two Democratic senators faced recall efforts over the partial birth issue, initiated by conservative voters in their state. The press secretary for one senator said that the recall effort made him decide to vote against the partial birth ban. Finally, the Catholic Church in another Democratic senator's state apparently excommunicated a woman over the partial birth abortion issue. The press secretary for this senator mentioned that this potential for excommunication was in their minds as they approached the issue.

The two groups of Democrats followed similar promotional strategies on partial birth abortion, but for different reasons. Opponents of the leadership saw no individual benefits to promoting its message, and they did not promote that message. At the same time, though, these opponents did not promote their own more liberal or conservative message on the issue. They feared that such a divisive debate would undermine the party's collective reputation. The supporters of the leadership promoted its message only slightly more frequently. These Democrats saw some individual benefits to promotion, but these were outweighed by collective and individual concerns.

Overall, the evidence about the partial birth abortion debate largely, but not completely, supports my expectations about legislators' promotional activities. First, Republicans were more active than Democrats, which reflected and further strengthened the GOP's advantage on the issue. The GOP was largely unified behind Santorum's ban, reflecting their constituencies' and the general public's support for that position. In contrast, the Democratic caucus was torn between the public's preferred position and more liberal ones supported by Democratic constituencies. It is therefore not surprising that the Republicans worked to move this issue onto the congressional agenda, while the Democrats remained largely silent.

Second, the Democrats' response on this unfavorable issue (for them) fits my argument about how individual and collective considerations guide legislators' public statements. When the Democrats faced the debate over partial birth abortion, legislators in the party were divided in their preferred positions and messages. As a result, the party was unlikely to realize collective benefits (for the entire party) by promoting a single message. Among opponents of the party's message, concerns about the party's collective reputation discouraged the promotion of alternative or competing messages. The only Democratic legislators who promoted the party's message on this unfavorable issue were those who could derive individual benefits from such promotion. Daschle was one of the few Democrats in this category. During the months leading up to the 1997 floor debate, the Minority Leader had faced advertisements in his home state that criticized his earlier opposition to a ban on partial birth abortions. With reelection approaching in 1998, Daschle and his staff worked to craft a moderate alternative that would attract both pro-life and pro-choice support. While his proposal failed, it helped defuse the issue for his 1998 reelection.

4.2.4. The Supplemental

While the partial birth abortion debate supports my arguments, a thorough test requires applying them to an issue where the parties' incentives are reversed, that is, to an issue favoring the Democrats. The debate over the supplemental is such an issue. As was the case with partial birth abortion, the first step of the analysis is to categorize the supporters and opponents of each party's message. This categorization is more complicated for the supplemental than for partial birth abortion. For the latter issue, the alternatives largely fell along a single dimension capturing the restrictiveness of each ban. The debate over the supplemental revolved around the Republican leadership's efforts to link disaster relief funding with other unrelated issues (such as sampling and the auto CR). It is difficult to determine directly whether each legislator supported this linkage of issues. As a proxy, I used the amount of relief funding that a legislator's state received from the supplemental.[18] Within the Democratic caucus, senators from high-funded states were likely to have more constituents facing disasters, which would make these legislators stronger supporters of their leadership's message to pass a clean bill. Democrats representing low-funded states would be weaker supporters of that message. Among Republicans, senators from low-funded states had the fewest constituent concerns about disasters. These legislators would therefore be the strongest proponents of their leadership's strategy of linking the supplemental to the other issues. But, their colleagues from high-funded

[18] I divided each state's funding from the supplemental by the state's number of House members. This per capita measure more accurately captures the importance of funding in each state; $500,000 is much more important in a relatively unpopulated state like North Dakota than in a populous state like California. I was unable to obtain the level of funding per congressional district.

states would be less likely to support this strategy, reflecting the more extensive disasters facing their constituents.

While controlling for other influences on promotional efforts, a regression model produced the expected number public statements mentioning the Democratic and Republican messages on the supplemental, for all Democratic and Republican legislators. Among the Democrats, legislators from high-funded states promoted their leadership's message more frequently than did their colleagues from states receiving little funding. For example, Congressman Earl Pomeroy (D) was the sole House member from North Dakota, which received the highest level of per capita funding from the supplemental ($321 million). According to the regression model, Pomeroy's expected number of statements of the Democratic message was 172 mentions. In contrast, Congresswoman Rosa DeLauro (D) represented the Third District of Connecticut, which received no disaster relief funding from the supplemental. DeLauro's expected number was .18 mentions, and the confidence intervals around the two expected values were nonoverlapping. We can therefore be more confident that the difference in the two legislators' promotional efforts was linked to their states' funding and not to random variation.

The interviews with Democratic press secretaries revealed similar patterns of promotional support. I asked the staffers how frequently their office promoted the leadership's message nationally. I categorized as strong supporters of the leadership message those senators whose states received above-average per-capita levels of disaster relief funding. Weak supporters were senators from states receiving below average levels of funding. On the same 0-to-3 scale, the promotional efforts of the twelve strong supporters averaged 1.75; the mean for the six weak supporters was 1.33.

A similar relationship appears to exist between state disaster funding and Democrats' statements about the Republican message. Again, legislators from high-funded states generated higher expected values with confidence intervals that did not overlap with the intervals of the lower expected values of legislators from low-funded states. Analysis earlier in this chapter suggests that the majority of these Democratic statements were criticisms of the Republican message. So, Democratic legislators with more natural disasters and funding in a state discussed the Democratic message and criticized the Republican message more frequently than Democrats from low-funded states did.

The strong and weak supporters' promotional efforts reflect the collective and individual benefits that each group might receive from coverage of the two competing messages. A national public relations victory could provide collective electoral benefits to all Democrats, regardless of the number of disasters in their states. But, the individual policy and electoral benefits of such a victory are much more likely to go to Democratic senators from states with many disasters. For their counterparts from states with few disasters, swift passage of the supplemental would make a difference for relatively few constituents. Thus, both groups of Democrats helped promote their leadership's message while criticizing the Republican leadership's arguments, because both strategies could bring to all Democrats the collective benefits of a victory over the Republicans. But, Democrats from high-funded states were more active in their promotional efforts, because they were more likely to realize individual benefits from doing so.

This interpretation of the Democrats' promotional activities finds support in their press secretaries' explanations of those activities. Frequently, the staffers initially mentioned the good media coverage that they received, both nationally and in their individual states. As one press secretary from a western state put it, "nothing beats a disaster for generating press.... We had a story to tell and pictures to show" (July 10, 1998, Washington, D.C.). The likelihood of press coverage made it easier to realize policy and electoral benefits. Several press secretaries mentioned individual policy benefits of promoting the leadership's message: helping speed disaster relief to constituents.

Even when representing states unaffected by natural disasters, Democratic staffers spoke of the need to assist the devastated communities and families: "While the disasters have mainly struck the Dakotas, the bill does affect [our state] too. [Our state] sometimes gets hit by hurricanes, by tornadoes, by drought. If we don't help the Dakotas, it could be [our state] that gets hit next" (June 30, 1998, Washington, D.C.). This explanation provides an additional rationale for why senators from low-funded states might work to provide collective policy benefits for the party. Instead of free riding on the efforts of others, these legislators helped push for prompt passage of relief funds for the disaster-stricken states. The legislators anticipated that other members might reciprocate if the low-funded states suffer in future rounds of disasters. (Shepsle and Weingast 1994).

When discussing electoral benefits of the leadership's message, the press secretaries referred to both the overall Democratic Party and their own individual senator. The leadership's message spelled out a clear Democratic position and helped unify the party. At the same time, the issue gave

Democrats an opportunity to attack. One press secretary summarized the situation:

> This was a freebie. The Republicans made a political miscalculation of the nth degree. Their actions reinforced the image that the Republicans were not in touch with the average citizen. I talked to as many reporters as possible, pushing the Democratic message: 'My God, here they go again. Didn't they learn their lesson from the government shutdown?' (June 30, 1998, Washington, D.C.).

These collective electoral benefits accrued to all Democratic senators, regardless of the disasters in their states.

The caucus message also provided individual electoral benefits to senators, helping them maintain or shore up political support among home state constituencies. Such efforts were particularly important for senators from states such as the Dakotas, hit hard by natural disasters. As a staffer from one of these states acknowledged, "we knew we'd sink or swim on this issue alone" (July 10, 1998, Washington, D.C.). Thus, senators from hard-hit states worked harder at promoting the caucus message. Their colleagues with few disasters did less promotion, because they would receive fewer individual benefits from doing so.

The leadership message also provided the opportunity for individual benefits within the Senate. The previous election of one Democratic senator had faced a legal challenge from Republicans. The senator participated in many leadership-sponsored activities on the supplemental, at least partially out of appreciation for Daschle's assistance in establishing the legality of her election. Another freshman senator had little or no disasters hit her state. But, she actively promoted the leadership's message, in hopes of accumulating favor with other more senior Democrats. These examples offer additional reasons why senators from low-funded states might promote the party message.

The Democratic press secretaries mentioned few drawbacks to promoting the leadership's message on the supplemental. One staffer mentioned that promoting the leadership's message nationally might tie her senator too closely to the national Democratic Party, which would not appear attractive in their conservative state. "They do get national news in [our state]. . . . [The senator] has sometimes looked more like a national Democrat and more liberal than many [state] voters liked" (July 10, 1998, Washington, D.C.). But, most of the Democratic staffers shared the following viewpoint: "There were no costs for us. The issue made the Republicans look like kooks again with their own extreme agenda" (July 1, 1998, Washington, D.C.).

The Democrats' responses about the supplemental reflected their party's overall advantage on the issue. Despite the wide variation in the number of natural disasters affecting their constituents, Democrats joined together to help promote their party's message, which also appeared popular among the general public. Senators from states with many disasters more actively promoted the message, reflecting their greater potential for realizing individual benefits. But, senators with few disaster-struck constituents did not completely free ride on their colleagues' efforts. These Democrats from low-funded states also helped promote the party message, out of a fear that their states "would be next," a desire to attack Republicans on a favorable issue, or a hope to repay or accumulate favor with more senior colleagues.

The Democrats' enthusiastic embrace of their leadership's message contrasts significantly with the Republicans' behavior in the supplemental debate. Recall that Republicans promoted the Democratic message less frequently than Democratic legislators did, but nearly as positively. The GOP legislators also discussed their own party's message more frequently and positively than Democrats did. The GOP's promotional efforts appear largely unrelated to the disaster relief funding allocated to each legislator's state. In the regression models of promotional efforts, increasing state funding for disaster relief appears unrelated to GOP legislators' discussion of either party's message in the debate. For each message, Republicans from high- and low-funded states produced expected values with overlapping confidence intervals. The Republican press secretaries reported similarly low levels of promotional activity. Among the eight GOP senators opposing the leadership message (i.e., from high-funded states), the staffers' reported promotional activity averaged .25 (on the same scale from no promotion (0) to very active promotion (3)). The staffers from the fifteen senators supporting the leadership (i.e., from low-funded states) said that they had not promoted the GOP message at all nationally.

Republican promotional efforts on the supplemental thus appear largely unrelated to the natural disasters occurring in some legislators' states. The lack of a link appears related to perceptions among Republicans that their party's message, and therefore the debate itself, were not politically advantageous for the GOP. These particular sentiments emerged from interviews with Republican press secretaries. Staffers working for both supporters (from low-funded states) and opponents (from high-funded states) of the GOP message reported similar perceptions of the benefits and costs of promoting that message.

First, consider two provisions that the GOP tried to attach to the supplemental, those involving sampling and the auto CR. Across the two groups of Republicans, the interviews revealed no substantial difference in support for leadership's positions on these two issues. None of the press secretaries mentioned any concerns about promoting the leadership position on these particular issues. Only one staffer mentioned a benefit of the leadership's message and position. Her senator represented a state with multiple national parks. The auto CR provision would protect park employees and the local economy against government shutdowns. In general, the lack of mentioned benefits suggests that the senators did not expect to realize individual benefits from discussing the sampling and auto CR issues by themselves.

The press secretaries referred more frequently to the lack of any benefit in *linking* such provisions to the disaster relief funding in the supplemental. Constituents did not accept the Republican argument about the need to link the issues. Many voters believed that the Republican leadership's message and strategy were preventing relief funds from reaching disaster victims. Such concerns were most common in states with extensive natural disasters. A Republican press secretary from one of these states described their dilemma:

> This was a difficult situation for us, because [our state] got lots of disaster relief funds. While the burned and flooded North Dakota town got most of the coverage, the flooding was also horrible for [our state]. We were in a spot. We wanted to support the leadership, because the White House and Democrats never pass anything 'clean.' But, the Republican strategy was ill-timed.... You can't tell someone whose house had fallen into [a local river] that the funds that they're going to get are not affected by this debate (July 15, 1998, Washington, D.C.).

The staffer saw electoral and policy costs in the GOP strategy linking disaster relief to the controversial policy provisions.

Significantly, these concerns about the leadership's strategy extended to states where few disasters had occurred. A Republican staffer from one of these states expressed frustration with their efforts to promote the leadership's message:

> We promoted the leadership message in [our state], but the coverage didn't reflect it. Reporters would ask [my senator] why we were adding the amendments. We would go into a long explanation of the need for the amendments. But then a reporter would ask, 'Why aren't the people in the Dakotas getting help?' It was like banging your head against a wall.... Every night in people's living rooms, they had these images of incredible destruction in the Midwest.... You'd be sitting in church, and when the minister asked members to contact Congress to

release the funds, everyone would turn around and look at you (July 9, 1998, Washington, D.C.).

While mentioning a variety of concerns, the Republican press secretaries offered few benefits of promoting the leadership's message.

In addition, several senators believed that they could generate greater benefits by pursuing other issues. These senators had no record of involvement on the issues in the supplemental, and they did not serve on committees with jurisdiction over these issues. They believed that their time and resources were better spent on issues where they had already been active and leading the debate. Such responses further illustrate the importance of individual policy reputations described earlier. Republicans appeared much more likely to mention this type of argument as a reason for not promoting their leadership's message. Democratic senators rarely mentioned these concerns. Perhaps the GOP's majority status in Congress provided more opportunities for such individual credit claiming.

Promoting the Republican leadership's message on the supplemental appeared to offer few benefits. This perception extended across both supporters and opponents of the position in the Republican leadership's message. The arguments in Chapter 3 suggested that the supporters and opponents would respond differently, so the two groups' similar responses require explanation. Press secretaries for both groups often discussed the issue in terms of their own state electorate, rather than national Republican constituencies or the general public. For Republicans from states receiving high levels of disaster relief funding, the Republican leadership strategy appeared to hold up funding of immediate importance to many constituents. As a result, these senators' individual concerns about meeting constituent needs outweighed any collective considerations about their party's overall message and reputation. The dominance of the individual concerns meant that these legislators were unlikely to help promote the leadership's message.

The same arguments in Chapter 3 suggested that Republicans from states with few disasters would have been more likely to promote the GOP leadership's message, given these senators' lack of local need for immediate funding. But in these low-funded states, national media coverage of disasters elsewhere encouraged public awareness of the need for immediate funding. This coverage made it difficult for legislators from the low-funded states to promote the party message. Localized, individual concerns emerging from these legislators' constituencies again appeared to outweigh any collective concerns about publicly dissenting from the GOP leadership's message and undermining the party's reputation.

In sum, the press secretaries' statements about the supplemental illustrated the Democrats' partisan advantage on the issue. Many members of Congress from that party supported their leadership's message, albeit with varying frequency. GOP legislators, in contrast, appeared much less supportive of their own leaders' attempts to add the controversial provisions, instead of passing a "clean" supplemental. Staffers from both parties suggested that the latter argument was more popular among the public. The combination of evidence vividly demonstrates the components of the Democrats' advantage in the debate.

4.2.5. The 1997 and 2003 Budget Resolutions

My final assessments of legislators' strategic communication campaigns focus on the debates over the federal budget in 1997 and 2003. Unlike partial birth abortion and the supplemental, the budget debates did not provide clear advantage to either party, due to the breadth of potential issues involved. This complexity created opportunities for legislators from each party to steer the debate toward favorable issues by promoting their party leadership's message. It is more difficult to assess the specific reasons behind legislators' promotional efforts in the two budget debates, because the press secretary interviews did not address these debates. Fortunately, the legislators from each party varied in their promotion of their party message and that of the opposing party. The relative frequency of these statements by different factions of a party suggests the extent to which each faction based its public relations efforts on individual policy preferences or collective concerns about the party's reputation.

Regression analysis of the 1997 debate produced the expected number of statements about each party's message by each party's legislators. Among the Democrats, promotion of the Democratic message declined significantly (with nonoverlapping confidence intervals) as one moved from liberal to moderate Democrats. During negotiations over the balanced budget agreement, liberals such as Senator Paul Wellstone (D-MN) proclaimed their support for Democratic goals:

> children must have good nutrition and health care, and there certainly must be affordable, good child care, however delivered, at the local community level, and we know it is going to require some funding and investment ... in any of our States in some of our inner-city neighborhoods, the school buildings are dilapidated, the toilets don't work, the heating doesn't work. We are saying to

these children: We don't care about you. We don't give a damn about you. Mr. President, that is a Federal responsibility. (Wellstone 1997)

Democratic moderates such as Senator Max Baucus (D-MT) were more restrained in discussing the Democratic message. The regression model suggests that Baucus made 1.09 mentions of the message; in contrast, the expected value for Wellstone was 5.72. The difference in expected values is not substantial, but it is significant (with nonoverlapping confidence intervals) while controlling for other possible influence on legislators' promotional activities. We can thus be confident that Wellstone and Baucus differed significantly in their promotion of the Democrats' budget message in 1997. The difference in promotional activities most likely reflects different perceptions between the two groups of Democrats about the benefits of promoting the party message. Liberal Democrats such as Wellstone could receive individual and collective benefits from promoting that message. Moderate Democrats like Baucus might receive fewer such benefits; these legislators still promoted the message with some frequency, however, suggesting that they receive at least some benefit from doing so.

No such difference between party factions occurred in the Democrats' public statements about the Republican Party's message. Here, liberal and moderate Democrats appeared equally likely to mention the GOP message; the two types of Democrats produced expected numbers of mentions with overlapping confidence intervals. Instead of following their policy preferences and promoting a message (that of the Republicans) that might better reflect those preferences, Democratic moderates refrained. Baucus never complained about "big government" or "wasteful Washington spending." While these phrases capture ideas that might have fit Baucus's own policy preferences, the phrases were also central to the Republican Party's message in the budget negotiations. Democratic moderates such as Baucus appear to have avoided these phrases, in hopes of minimizing public disagreements with other Democrats and maintaining their party's collective reputation. Instead of basing their promotional activities purely on their individual policy preferences, the moderates acted as if they also incorporated collective partisan considerations.

Similar patterns occur among Republicans in 1997 and among both parties in 2003. Regression analysis suggests that in all three cases the more extreme legislators in each party promoted their leaders' message more frequently than the moderates did. At the same time, both groups in each party promoted the opposing party's message with similar expected frequency. In a 1997 press release, Representative Phil Crane's (R-IL09) description of the Republicans' tax proposal provides a representative example of the party's message about "tax relief" and "wasteful spending":

> Following the release of the tax plan, which if enacted would be the first major tax relief plan in 16 years, Crane stated, "We have halted the course of the 'old Washington' – one that raised taxes to match wasteful spending – which bankrupted the futures of our children and grandchildren. We are on a new course: cutting taxes and letting people keep more of the money they earn, which will secure the future for generations to come." (Crane 1997)

Moderate Republicans mentioned these themes less frequently. Centrist Representative Connie Morella (R-MD08) made only 5.61 statements containing the Republican arguments; the corresponding expected value for Crane was 15.61 statements (with no overlap between the confidence intervals of the two expected values). In contrast, the two factions in each party varied little in their statements about the opposing party's message, suggesting concern among moderates about their party's collective reputation. When examining Republicans' public statements about the Democratic message, the regression model suggested that Morella and Crane each mentioned that message less than two times (with overlap between the expected values' confidence intervals).

In sum, the evidence from the four debates provides strong support for the party-based explanation described earlier in this chapter. Across the parties and debates, moderates promoted their own party's message less frequently than the more extreme party members did. Thus, individual policy preferences appear important for legislators deciding whether to promote their own party's message. The moderates refrained, however, from discussing the opposing party's message more frequently than their more extreme colleagues did. Significantly, a decision not to promote that message helps avoid drawing attention to dissension within a party; the overall message emerging from a party may still be unified. Promoting the opposing party's message does create such a public spat, and the public nature of the conflict is significant. As Chapter 5 explains, journalists often use conflict to produce newsworthy stories. Understanding that public disagreement can harm a party's collective reputation, moderates in each party appeared to refrain from promoting the opposing party's message.

4.3. CONCLUSION

This chapter has provided support for several expectations from Chapter 3 about the promotional activities of rank-and-file members of Congress. Most notably, these legislators promote their party's message more frequently when it focuses on issues favoring the party, such as the supplemental for the Democrats and partial birth abortion for the Republicans. When messages on such issues help the party's collective reputation, rank-and-file members can enjoy any such collective benefits without helping promote the message. To overcome this temptation to free ride, leaders construct a message that reflects the followers' policy preferences and therefore promises electoral benefits. Promoting such a message can provide individual policy and electoral benefits to rank-and-file legislators. These individual benefits encourage the legislators to promote the message, whereas collective benefits are less effective in providing such encouragement.

Congressional leaders must sometimes create party messages on unfavorable issues which divide a party (Ryan et al. 2001). Collective considerations may more strongly influence behavior with this type of message and issue. Rank-and-file members appear more likely to promote such a message if they agree with the position in the message. But if they disagree, the legislators must balance the individual benefits of promoting a competing message, against the collective costs to their own party's reputation that would result from their defection. If the individual benefits are greater, the members may decide to promote the competing message. Many Republicans followed this path in the debate over the supplemental. If collective costs are greater, the legislators will decide against promoting that message. Moderate Democrats reached this conclusion in the partial birth abortion debate.

In the 2005 debate over reforming Social Security, a similar group of moderate Democrats again chose to protect their party's overall reputation. They could have defected by publicly proposing an alternative to Bush's reforms. Such a course of action might have been more in line with their own individual policy preferences. The announcement of the alternative might have generated favorable news coverage and other individual electoral benefits in the moderates' home districts or states. But, these legislators decided not to defect from their party's promotional efforts. Concern for their party's collective reputation made them more loyal to their party and more disciplined in their statements to the public.

4.3.1. Strategic Communication and the Expansion of Advantage

The varying promotional efforts of these debates often suggested that one party held an advantage. Republicans dominated the partial birth abortion debate, Democrats held a strong advantage in deliberations about the supplemental, and neither party controlled the budget debates. It is important to clarify the origins and evolution of the parties' advantages, where they existed. In each debate, any initial advantage emerged from the original alignment of the politicians' policy preferences. The party that was unified around an issue and popular position enjoyed an advantage. If neither party unified around a single issue and position, no clear advantage existed. As the debates progressed, any advantage based on legislators' policy preferences led to a similar advantage in public statements. In the debates over partial birth abortion and the supplemental, the advantaged party enjoyed more frequent discussion of its message. No such pattern of promotion occurred in the budget debates, where neither party enjoyed a consistent advantage.

The varying public statements by legislators are important, because an advantage in strategic communication can reinforce and expand an advantage based on legislators' issue positions. The advantaged party uses public relations to pressure members of the disadvantaged party to concede and support the advantaged party's position. The most successful strategic communication campaign increases the party's advantage to the point where the disadvantaged party finds it difficult to remain in opposition. The advantaged party's message defines the issue underlying debate so that any opposition to that party's position on the issue appears unreasonable. It even becomes difficult to find language defending that opposition. In the partial birth abortion debate, Democrats found it extremely hard to oppose a ban on "infanticide." The party was also unable to convince its members to use a preferred term for the procedure ("dilation and extraction") instead of the more widely accepted Republican label ("partial birth abortion").

Why were the Democrats unable to interrupt the Republicans' graphic images and reframe the debate in more favorable terms? Part of the Democrats' inability stemmed from the Republicans' more frequent repetition of issues and arguments emphasizing the GOP's frames during the debate. In addition, the Republicans were the majority in both chambers of Congress, which gave them greater powers to shape the debate, particularly in the House. Finally, the GOP benefited from a longer-term public prominence of their definition of the debate. According to a search of the

LexisNexis Academic database, the *New York Times* first mentioned the phrase "partial birth abortion" in June, 1995. Between that month and the start of 1997 (before that year's congressional debate began), the paper published 100 articles mentioning that phrase, but only thirteen articles referring to the Democratic label for the procedure.[19] As the *New York Times* coverage suggests, public deliberation outside Congress emphasized the GOP definition of the debate well before the House and Senate took up the partial birth abortion ban.

The debates over the ban, the supplemental, and the budget underlined the importance of legislators' public relations campaigns more generally. In these promotional campaigns, party leaders' efforts at persuasion are far from irrelevant. In a logical and predictable fashion, the leaders successfully encourage their followers to promote the party message, particularly on favorable issues. As the next chapter shows, a party's promotional advantage often translates into a similar advantage in news coverage. As a result, voters are more likely to encounter that party's message. The issues and arguments of the opposing party may receive less attention. In this manner, the alignment of preferences and promotional activities inside Congress can affect public knowledge and opinion outside the institution.

APPENDIX 4. REGRESSION MODELS

The expected numbers of statements in this chapter come from a series of regression models. I estimated nine models: one for legislators' total statements, and then for each of the four specific debates, one model for statements mentioning the Democratic message, and one for statements mentioning the Republican message. In each model, the dependent variable was a count of statements, which did not have a normal distribution. These counts also exhibited evidence of overdispersion, which makes sense. The rate of making statements for a particular legislator may be heterogeneous, varying across the number of statements. There may be a substantial difference in the probability of a legislator making no statements versus making one statement. Once the legislator makes a single statement, the legislator may be more likely to make additional ones. So, the rate of making statements varies from zero to one to multiple

[19] The specific search terms were ("partial birth abortion") for the first search, and (("D&C") OR ("D&X") OR ("dilation & extraction")) and abortion) for the second one.

statements. To estimate models with dependent variables of this nature, I used a negative binomial regression model, specifically the *nbreg* command in *Stata 9.0*.

Table 4.A1 reports the estimated coefficients and associated results for each model. Each model of statements mostly uses the same set of independent variables.[20] One dummy variable captures whether a legislator is a member of the Democratic Party; I assigned Rep. Bernard Sanders (VT-I) to this party. A second dummy variable measures whether a legislator is a member of the Senate. Another independent variable is the legislator's vote percentage in her most recent election. A related variable is the number of years until the legislator's next election. The fifth independent variable is the population (in millions) of the district or state that the legislator represents. The final two independent variables are a measure of policy preferences in the particular debate,[21] and an interaction term between party and policy preferences. The latter term is necessary because my argument (as developed in the text) suggests that policy preferences will have a different relationship with promoting party messages, depending on whether a legislator is a Democrat or Republican.[22]

To calculate the various estimates of the expected number of statements, I used *Clarify 2.1* (King et al. 2000, Tomz et al. 2003). When calculating the expected values for a particular independent variable,

[20] The exceptions were the two models of mentions of the Democratic and Republican messages on partial birth abortion. The low number of statements in this debate appeared to prevent the model from converging. I therefore estimated a simpler model for these dependent variables, including only the Senate dummy and the three measures capturing the interaction of party and policy preferences.

[21] In the debate over the supplemental, the measure of policy preferences is the amount of disaster relief funding assigned to a senator's or representative's state, divided by the number of House members representing the state. In the model for partial birth abortion, I measured legislators' policy preferences using their vote (where available) in the 1996 attempt to override President Clinton's veto of a partial birth abortion ban. For the debates over the budget resolutions, I used a broader measure of legislators' policy preferences: their DW-NOMINATE scores for the particular chamber and year (Poole 2005). I also estimated the models using an alternative measure of legislators' ideology, the ratings compiled by the American Conservative Union from roll call votes. This alternative measure produced similar but less significant results.

[22] The data on election timing and vote percentage come from the Federal Election Commission (http://www.fec.gov/pubrec/fe1996/tcontent.htm and http://www.fec.gov/pubrec/fe2002/tcontents.htm). The populations of the legislators' districts and states come from the United States Census (http://www.census.gov/population/censusdata/apportionment/tabA.xls) and the CQ Electronic Library (http://library.cqpress.com). The measures of ideology are available courtesy of Keith Poole (http://voteview.com/dwnl.htm) and the American Conservative Union (http://www.acuratings.org/).

TABLE 4.A1. *Regression Models of Legislators' Public Statements (Standard Errors)*

		Partial Birth Abortion		Supplemental		1997 Budget Resolution		2003 Budget Resolution	
	All Statements	Democratic Message	Republican Message	Democratic Message	Republican Message	Democratic Message	Republican Message	Democratic Message	Republican Message
Democrat	−.82***	−.51	−1.94	−.21	−1.15**	−1.06*	−.57	.74	1.50**
	(.18)	(1.06)	(1.63)	(.31)	(.40)	(.42)	(.43)	(.46)	(.44)
Senate	1.62***	2.16***	1.64*	1.46**	1.49*	1.66***	1.62***	1.68***	1.58***
	(.15)	(.44)	(.74)	(.56)	(.67)	(.32)	(.34)	(.34)	(.28)
Previous vote percentage	−.004			.008	.02	−.002	.006	−.004	−.004
	(.003)			(.01)	(.01)	(.007)	(.007)	(.007)	(.006)
Next election	−.15**			.03	.15	−.05	−.07	−.08	−.12
	(.05)			(.18)	(.20)	(.10)	(.11)	(.11)	(.10)
Population	−.01			.05	.04	−.01	−.005	−.02	.01
	(.01)			(.04)	(.06)	(.03)	(.03)	(.03)	(.02)
Policy	−.27	−.52	1.39	.007	−.02	−.50	1.43*	.59	2.47***
	(.29)	(1.04)	(1.48)	(.007)	(.01)	(.68)	(.72)	(.70)	(.69)

(*continued*)

TABLE 4.A1. (*continued*)

		Partial Birth Abortion		Supplemental		1997 Budget Resolution		2003 Budget Resolution	
	All Statements	Democratic Message	Republican Message	Democratic Message	Republican Message	Democratic Message	Republican Message	Democratic Message	Republican Message
Democrat X policy	−.90*	−.50	−1.27	.008	.04*	−2.38*	−2.04*	−2.78**	−3.20**
	(.41)	(1.33)	(2.05)	(.009)	(.02)	(.99)	(.99)	(1.04)	(.95)
Constant	3.26***	−2.51*	−2.55	−1.99*	−2.68**	.47	1.08	−.38	−1.27*
	(.24)	(1.01)	(1.46)	(.88)	(.97)	(.55)	(.56)	(.64)	(.59)
N	1,059	444	444	531	531	531	531	529	529
LR χ^2	305.36***	25.59***	24.59***	71.41***	51.06***	99.86***	89.90***	112.86***	96.95***
Pseudo R^2	.04	.09	.08	.08	.07	.05	.03	.06	.06
α	1.11	6.55	20.95	5.84**	8.25	2.21	2.33	2.50	1.66
	(.05)	(2.41)	(5.35)	(.97)	(1.44)	(.22)	(.23)	(.26)	(.20)
χ^2 test for joint effect of Democrat, Policy, and Democrat X Policy	30.81***	2.06	20.80***	8.47*	9.45*	20.92***	42.82***	79.61***	34.80***

Note: See Appendix 4.A for details of estimating the models. * $p < .05$, ** $p < .01$, *** $p < .001$.

I set all other independent variables at their means. I then calculated the expected number of statements with the independent variable of interest set at different possible values. For the expected values associated with partisanship and ideology, I used the actual party and ideology score for all non-leaders, calculating an expected number of events for each legislator.

Examinations of legislators' promotional activities often focus on the House (Arnold 2004, Cook 1989, 1998, Harris 1998, Lipinski 2004) or the Senate (Hess 1986, Kuklinski and Sigelman 1992), but rarely on both simultaneously. To investigate whether partisanship and policy preferences vary in their influence on senators' and representatives' promotional decisions, I reestimated the models in Table 4.A1, once for the House and once for the Senate. In the current results presented in Table 4.A1, all nine models produced a significant chi-squared test for the joint influence of partisanship, policy preferences, and their interaction. When I reestimated the nine models only for representatives, the same chi-squared test was significant in eight models. The exception was the model for the Democrats' message on partial birth abortion. In the House-only models, coefficients were the same sign as those in the combined models for twenty-four of the twenty-seven relevant independent variables (three independent variables in each of nine models). In the reestimates for only senators, only four of the nine models generated significant chi-squared tests. Only eighteen of the twenty-seven relevant independent variables produced coefficients of the same sign as those in the combined model. The lowered significance for the senators' estimates is most likely due to estimating models with only 100 cases for the Senate, compared to 535 cases for the results in Table 4.A1.[23]

In several models, the number of cases is slightly less than 1,070 (for both years combined) or 535 (for a single year). The models for all types of messages omit the four party leaders, as well as three additional legislators. First, Senator Lisa Murkowski received appointment to the Senate in 2002. She did not have a previous vote percentage, and this missing evidence forced her omission from the model. Second, Representative Ron Paul received a DW-NOMINATE (i.e., ideology) score of 1.05 in 1997

[23] As an additional check, I reestimated the models after adding an interaction term between the Senate dummy variable and the legislator's vote percentage in the most recent election. Senators often have narrower margins of victory than representatives have, but the addition of the interaction term made little difference. The term was almost never significant, and the estimated coefficients for the three variables of interest (party, policy, and their interaction) remained nearly unchanged.

and 1.36 in 2003. In order to maintain comparability with alternative measures of ideology, I only included cases with a DW-NOMINATE score ranging from −1 to 1. Thus, I omitted both cases involving Paul from the model estimation. Including him does not alter the estimated patterns or significance.

The models involving partial birth abortion included considerably fewer members of Congress than the 535 serving in 1997. The omitted legislators are those who did not serve in 1996. They could not cast a vote in the effort to override President Clinton's veto, and those veto override votes are my measures of legislators' policy preferences on the issue in 1997. Finally, the models for the 2003 budget resolution omit two cases: Murkowski and Paul.

5

Coverage and Feedback

When the Iraq War began in March 2003, members of Congress from both parties strongly supported the war effort. The House and Senate passed multiple resolutions recognizing and commended the participating soldiers and their sacrifices.[1] Journalists had to decide how to cover the politicians' widespread statements of support. Some reporters crafted headlines such "American Power Inspires Dreams of Liberation" (Schmitt 2003). Other journalists attempted to balance their coverage by giving attention to arguments criticizing the war effort (Walsh 2003).[2]

As the conflict in Iraq continued and the 2004 elections approached, the voices of opposition inside and outside Congress grew as loud and frequent as the supporters of the military effort. Led by their presidential nominee John Kerry, many Democrats vigorously promoted issues

[1] On March 21, 2003, the House approved (by a 392–11 vote) House Concurrent Resolution 104, "[e]xpressing the support and appreciation of the Nation for the President and the members of the Armed forces who are participating in Operation Iraqi Freedom." On June 4, 2003, the House approved (by a 406–2 vote) House Concurrent Resolution 177, "[r]ecognizing and commending the members of the United States Armed Forces and their leaders, and the allies of the United States and their armed forces, who participated in Operation Enduring Freedom in Afghanistan and Operation Iraqi Freedom in Iraq and recognizing the continuing dedication of military families and employers and defense civilians and contractors and the countless communities and patriotic organizations that lent their support to the Armed Forces during those operations." On September 5, 2003, the Senate approved (by unanimous consent) Senate Concurrent Resolution 64, which "commend[ed] members of the United States Armed Forces for their services to the United States in the liberation of Iraq" (http://thomas.loc.gov/, accessed July 2, 2008).

[2] Such arguments and coverage were much more extensive outside the United States (Bennett et al. 2007, Dimitrova et al. 2005).

and arguments attacking the Republican execution of the war (Mason 2004). In Congress, the Democratic minority initiated floor debates to restrict funding and change war policy, albeit unsuccessfully (Broder 2005, Skorneck 2003). Journalists now had to decide how to cover the growing criticism. Their news accounts gave more attention to the Democrats' critical messages, but President Bush nonetheless won reelection and continued the Republicans' military strategy (Milbank and Deane 2005).

Over the next two years, however, that military strategy encountered growing obstacles in Iraq, and critics of the war effort began to outnumber supporters substantially (Kirkpatrick and Nagourney 2006). Journalists again faced the challenge of deciding how to cover events in Iraq and politicians' statements about those events. Some reporters increasingly focused on the continuing problems in Iraq, with headlines like "Bomber Attacks Baghdad Paper on Day When 52 Are Killed" (Von Zielbauer 2006). Other journalists actively searched for positive developments in Iraq to balance the numerous negative messages in their stories (Graham 2004). Over all these stages of the Iraq conflict, many reporters also faced criticism from conservative Republicans. The conservatives charged the "liberal media" with distorting actual events and framing coverage to provide a biased interpretation of the war (Bennett 2007, Media Research Center 2005, Watts et al. 1999).

As this account suggests, journalists faced difficult decisions about their coverage of the long-running Iraq debate. On the one hand, journalists might write stories that accurately and objectively reflected newsworthy developments in the debate, with coverage closely following and depending upon politicians' public statements. On the other hand, the reporters may have adopted a more independent approach, producing news that differed from the actual events and statements by politicians. The journalists' decisions about the content of their news stories are important, because that coverage could have fed back to influence the war debate. Legislators could have used coverage of their past promotional efforts to guide future decisions about whether to maintain their current message or switch to a new one. The news stories could also have impacted the actual policy process.

These dynamics of coverage and feedback are the focus of this chapter. The first section of the chapter develops expectations about how journalists decide to cover politicians' promotional efforts, and how that coverage can feed back to influence the policy process. The second section evaluates these expectations by comparing politicians' promotional efforts in the four specific debates to overall news coverage of those debates from throughout the United States. In its third section, the chapter assesses how coverage varies across outlets' medium (print versus broadcast), editorial stance (Democratic versus Republican), and audience (Democratic versus Republican).

5.1. CHOOSING WHAT TO COVER

Politicians' promotional efforts share a common goal: winning press coverage of desirable messages. But to understand the link between press events and news stories, we must consider more than the efforts of politicians. We must also incorporate the news media, particularly the decisions and incentives of reporters and their relationship with politicians. The press possesses its own internal dynamics, institutions, and constraints, all of which affect news coverage (Sparrow 1999, 2006). At the same time, the "Fourth Estate" is more than a distinct institution; it is also part of a larger political and policy process. Other parts of that process influence and respond to the press (Cook 2006). This section thus examines how journalists decide what to cover when interacting with elected officials, and how that coverage can feed back to influence the officials.

Observers of journalism agree little on exactly what constitutes "news" (Graber 2006, Sigal 1973), particularly "good news" (Niven 2003). Reporters can view many different aspects of events and statements as newsworthy (Breed 1955, Graber 2006, Tankard 2001). Reporters may focus their coverage on conflict (Bennett 2007, Jasperson et al. 1998, Paletz and Entman 1981, Zachary 2001) or strategic maneuvering (Druckman 2005, Lawrence 2000, Patterson 1994). They may also simplify complex issues that arise in the campaign (Blumler and Kavanagh 1999, Downie and Kaiser 2002, *The Economist* 2006, Graber 2006, Patternson and Donsbach 1996, Sigal 1973, Wolfsfeld 2001), as well as highlight any sensationalistic elements (Bennett 2007, Bennett and Mannheim 2001, Fox et al. 2005, Luther and Miller 2005, Patterson 1994, Wolfsfeld 2001, 2004, Zilber and Niven 2000). The reporters' stories can over-emphasize critical or negative elements (Niven 2001, 2002, Wolfsfeld 2004), a tendency which led former Vice President Spiro Agnew to label reporters "nattering nabobs of negativism" (Hofstetter 1976, 5). Compared to print or radio outlets, television news may provide more coverage of messages containing graphic visual images (Graber 2006).

In addition to these varying conceptions of the news, observers also disagree about the extent of journalistic independence, that is, whether reporters are mere conduits for others' messages or independent contributors to the evaluation of those messages (Entman 2004, Wolfsfeld 2004). An accurate understanding of coverage thus requires clear statements of exactly how reporters decide what to cover, and the mechanisms that encourage that coverage (Sheafer 2001). This section discusses four specific ways in which journalists may decide to cover politicians and their messages.[3]

5.1.1. Ignoring Politicians

The first way is to provide no coverage at all. In recent decades the consolidation of news outlets has brought more collaboration across those outlets. Media conglomerates such as the News Corporation or Time Warner acquire numerous individual outlets, in hopes of using fewer reporters to produce the outlets' coverage and thereby wringing greater profits from economies of scale (Downie and Kaiser 2002, *The Economist* 2006). Many news organizations have replaced their Washington bureaus with wire service subscriptions, again with the goal of maximizing efficiency and economic return (Druckman 2005, 477, Lim 2006, State of the American Newspaper 2006). The increased collaboration has also occurred less intentionally, as news organizations and individual reporters increasingly "ride the wave" and focus on only one or two prominent stories at a time (Ansolabehere et al. 1993, Reinemann 2004, Sabato 1991, Wolfsfeld 2004). This tendency makes the news hole much harder to enter because it contains fewer distinct stories. While specialized publications cover more diverse stories and encourage a "marketplace of ideas" (Baker 2007, Page 1996), the push for profit still encourages reporters for many mainstream outlets to follow a similar decision-making process and cover similar topics.[4]

[3] The following sections focus on selected aspects of news production that appear most relevant for coverage of the promotional campaigns analyzed in previous chapters. See Graber (2006) for a more comprehensive review of the many complexities of news production.

[4] Not all newsworthy stories enhance an outlet's immediate profit. Investigative journalism, for example, may produce attention-grabbing headlines, but only after consuming extensive time and resources. The growing importance of profit in the news industry makes that goal increasingly instrumental for journalists' public service activities such as investigative journalism (Underwood 2001). In a similar manner, elected officials must first meet the goal of reelection before pursuing others such as power or policy (Mayhew 1974).

The shrinking news holes certainly challenge members of Congress, as new outlets gradually reduce their coverage of congressional debates (Cook 1989, Sellers and Schaffner 2007, Underwood 1998). The limited congressional coverage in some outlets makes it difficult for their audiences to evaluate local members of Congress (Arnold 2004). This evidence suggests a scenario in which legislators' promotional efforts yield little news coverage, and by extension, their strategic communication has little effect on the legislative agenda or policy outcomes. Journalists may choose their news stories in other ways, however, which open the door to more effective public relations campaigns by politicians.

5.1.2. Mirroring Events

As a second approach to covering political debates, journalists may craft their news coverage to "mirror" those debates (Gans 2004, Graber 2006). This "straight news" describes just the facts of a story, "setting down information with a minimum of explicit interpretation. Any interpretive material that does appear in the news columns must be attributable to a news source" (Sigal 1973, 66). Even these elementary descriptions of politicians' messages are important, as they shape the audience's prioritizing of political issues and the attributes associated with those issues (Aday 2006, Chyi and McCombs 2004, McCombs and Ghanem 2001, McCombs and Shaw 1972, Miller 1997). Notably, this approach to coverage can limit journalists' independence. By narrowly following the facts of a story, reporters may rely upon official sources and devote little attention to viewpoints not promoted by those sources.[5]

[5] Such a reliance upon official sources underlies the theory of indexing, a widely shared and important theory often applied to news coverage of foreign policy issues. Under this theory, "Mass media news professionals, from the boardroom to the beat, tend to 'index' the range of voices and viewpoints in both news and editorials according to the range of views expressed in mainstream government debate about a given topic" (Bennett 1990, 106; see also Alexseev and Bennett 1995, Bennett 2007, Lawrence 1996, Schiffer 2006). As a result, their coverage mirrors elected officials' arguments. If the officials disagree, then coverage is diverse and reflects that disagreement. Agreement among the officials leads to no diversity of viewpoints reported. The extent of diversity in news coverage depends upon how frequently competing official voices promote their viewpoints. Analysts of indexing originally employed detailed measures of official and unofficial voices in the news coverage, while providing only general descriptions of the range of both types of voices actually making public statements in a debate (e.g., Bennett 1990). More recent studies of indexing increasingly use more detailed measures of the frequency of political actors' public statements, as opposed to coverage of those statements (Luther and Miller 2005, Schiffer 2006). The analysis in this book continues the trend toward more detailed and precise measures of actual public statements.

Nonetheless, mirrored coverage can enable journalists to realize goals from providing quality journalism to retaining their audience and avoiding chargers of bias (Entman 2004, Graber 2006, Niven 2005). After learning to mirror events in school or early training, individual reporters often view this type of coverage as good journalism (Bennett and Klockner 1996, Cook 1996, Entman 2004, Gamson and Modigliani 1989, Niven 2003, Patterson and Donsbach 1996, Sigal 1973). From editors' directions to socializing in the newsroom, the dynamics of news organizations further emphasize the desirability of this type of coverage (Aday 2006, Breed 1955, Cassidy 2005, Cohen and Young 1973, Craft and Wanta 2004, Gans 2004, King and Lester 2005, Lawrence 2006, Niven 2003, Sigal 1973, Singer 2004, Tuchman 1972, White 1950, Sumpter 2000). The environment outside the newsroom also reinforces this straight news strategy (Tuchman 1978), via competition from other journalists (Coulson and Lacy 1996, Entman 2004, Gans 2004, Graber 2006, Singer 2004, White 1950) or socialization on news beats (Alexseev and Bennett 1995, Lim 2006, Reinemann 2004, Schattschneider 1960, Sigal 1973). Thus, mirrored coverage offers journalists a way to provide quality journalism.

In addition, politicians and the public often criticize coverage deviating from the mirror approach. Illustrating the "hostile media effect," many individuals, particularly partisans, may view news through the lens of their own ideology. They consider an individual outlet or the overall news media as biased against them if the slant of its coverage differs from their own ideological viewpoint (Dalton et al. 1998, Gunther 1992, Schmitt et al. 2004, Vallone et al. 1985). This alleged bias has a strong impact – on "other" people. Both politicians and members of the public demonstrate the "third-person effect," in which they view the (biased) news media has having little influence over their own beliefs but extensive influence over the general public (Gunther and Mundy 1993, Watts et al. 1999). The public's susceptibility thereby enables "self-interested media to brainwash the masses" (Davison 1983, Niven 2001, 31; 2002, Perloff 1996). These pressures and criticisms further encourage journalists to embrace the objectivity of mirrored coverage (Tuchman 1972).[6]

[6] Notably, journalists may find it impossible to provide this type of coverage for some of their audience, due to the hostile media effect described above. Opposing partisans may disagree about whether the same piece of news supports their own viewpoint (Schmitt et al. 2004).

If journalists respond to these incentives and provide mirrored coverage of congressional debates, the political "tilt" of their news stories (Niven 2002) is likely reflect the competing promotional efforts. Journalists would devote more coverage to the messages with greater potential to impact that debate. Put simply, debate participants receive more coverage for their statements if they have more influence over policy outcomes (Bennett et al. 2007, Gans 2004, Entman 2004, Sheafer and Wolfsfeld 2004, Wolfsfeld and Sheafer 2006). This influence as an authoritative source can stem from institutional leadership. Sigal (1973) provided an early explanation of the link: "As the press increasingly organized its newsgathering around governmental institutions, authoritativeness began to vary with distance from positions of formal responsibility for public policy. Today, the higher up in government a man is, the better his prospects to make news.... On the White House beat, it means 'covering the body,' following the President's every movement." (69) The president and congressional party leaders possess more individual influence over the policy process than rank-and-file legislators do.

But by grouping together, these rank-and-file legislators can form a significant voting block and thereby claim influence in a legislative debate. Their frequent promotion of a message signals intense preferences about the issues and arguments in the message.[7] The intense preferences may lead the legislators to work harder to influence the legislative process, via filibuster, lobbying colleagues, or other strategies. These ideas lead to a specific expectation about mirrored coverage of the congressional debates: Journalists will give more coverage to a party's message if more rank-and-file members and more institutional leaders initiate events promoting that message (Kernell 1997, King and Lester 2005, Kuklinksi and Sigelman 1992).[8]

[7] The repetition of a message may also reduce its newsworthiness, due to reporters' preference for novelty (Gans 2004, Graber 2006). Politicians respond to this need to novelty, however, by frequently varying the issues and arguments in their message in a particular debate (Chyi and McCombs 2004). Evidence of such intentional variation exists in Appendix 3.C, which lists the content of the parties' messages in the four debates. Note the diverse issues, arguments, and words that each party used in its message in each debate.

[8] Event-driven news (Lawrence 1996, Lawrence and Birkland 2004, Wolfsfeld and Sheafer 2006) often reflects dramatic, unexpected events that "embolden the news media to bring challenging questions into mainstream discourse" (Bennett et al. 2007, 76). Examples of such events include the 9/11 attacks in the United States and the Abu Ghraib prison scandal in Iraq. While these events often occur outside official Washington, members of Congress and the president can also initiate such events and thereby shape news coverage to their advantage.

5.1.3. Balancing Arguments

A third approach to reporting assigns more independence to journalists. Instead of automatically basing coverage on how frequently politicians promote competing messages, reporters independently frame their stories to give equal attention to competing messages, regardless of the frequency of promotion (Gans 2004, Graber 2006, Kovach and Rosenstiel 2001, Kurtz 2001). This striving for balance means that journalists sometimes frame debates in a manner inconsistent with competing sides' promotion of their messages and influence over the final policy outcomes (Kernell 1997, Miller 1997). In the case of the partial birth abortion debate, reporters devote equal coverage to both sides' messages, instead of focusing coverage on the majority's issues and arguments in favor of the ban.

Creating balanced news accounts also helps emphasize conflict, another aspect of newsworthiness. Recounting the two parties' disagreements about partial birth abortion creates a more engaging narrative than a clinical listing of policy details about the procedure, or a one-sided review of the majority's arguments in favor of the ban. But, a balanced account of competing arguments in the debate does not accurately reflect the legislative importance of the two sides' messages in the debate. Such inaccuracy is perhaps greatest when journalists focus their coverage on conflict within a party (Groeling 2005). Even though such conflict may involve only a small minority's disagreement with the party majority, news stories may give similar attention to both sides.[9]

Journalists add balance to their stories for many of the same reasons that they mirror events when reporting. Journalistic training, newsroom dynamics, and public pressure may all encourage reporters to give equal attention to competing perspectives in their stories. While mirroring and balancing thus share common origins, they produce different versions of objectivity in coverage. A narrow focus on one type of coverage can in fact violate the other and lead away from objectivity (Gamson and Modigliani 1989, Miller 1997, Niven 2002). As described at the start of this chapter, the news media's early coverage of the Iraq War mirrored

[9] It is important to note, however, that the narrow partisan majorities of recent congresses may make even a small party minority influential in policy debates. In the 2003 debate over tax cuts, for example, a small minority of moderate Republican senators capitalized on the narrow GOP majority in the Senate and forced substantial changes in Bush's original tax cut.

the widespread support for that conflict among U.S. politicians. But, that coverage lacked balance and omitted arguments and evidence that proved important in later debates about the war. Conversely, balanced coverage of an election campaign may provide extensive but unjustified attention for a weak candidate offering little competition (Hofstetter 1976, Niven 2002). How might journalists resolve this tension between mirrored and balanced coverage?

Mirrored coverage arguably requires less effort by journalists, who must only report the public statements that politicians actually make. For balanced coverage, in contrast, reporters must describe the competing sides in a debate even if one side is providing little or no promotion of its message. Collecting evidence of the weaker side's message requires greater effort by reporters. This logic suggests a specific expectation about how journalists use mirroring and balancing when covering a congressional debate. During the debate's early stages, it may receive little public attention. Journalists are more likely to rely on the mirroring approach to coverage during these early stages, because that approach requires less effort. When the debate reaches later, more important stages, reporters work to add more balance to their coverage. These stages of the debate receive greater public interest and attention, and unbalanced coverage may lead to charges of bias from the disadvantaged side in the debate. Journalists may also be willing to expend more effort to produce coverage of high quality when that coverage is most important to the public, politicians, and the policy process.

5.1.4. Adding Partisan Bias

In a fourth approach to news coverage, reporters produce stories to fit a particular partisan viewpoint or bias (Graber 2006). The news coverage favors one side in a debate, regardless of underlying events, issue details, or promotional efforts. This presentation of a one-sided or biased narrative contrasts significantly with the objectivity of two previous approaches. Whenever reporters engage in partisan bias, they are exercising more independence than with mirrored or balanced coverage. The partisan slant[10] of their coverage likely limits the

[10] Entman (2007) distinguishes between slant (news stories "in which the framing favors one side over the other in a current or potential dispute" (165)) and content bias ("consistent patterns in the framing of mediated communication that promote the influence of one side in conflicts over the use of government power" (166)).

effectiveness of politicians' strategic communication. These promotional efforts work more effectively when reporters act as dependent conduits for politicians' messages, than as independent interpreters of those messages and creators of different messages (Reinemann 2004).[11]

Providing partisan coverage can conceivably help journalists further their goals. Surveys routinely find more liberal than conservative views across all journalists (Niven 2003, Patterson and Donsbach 1996, but see Saunders 2000). Thus, the liberal majority among journalists could further their policy preferences by favoring Democrats in their news stories (Groseclose and Milyo 2005). A similar logic can apply to a specific news outlet, in which management may directly push for slanted coverage by rewarding reporters with additional salary or advancement. The management may accomplish the same goal indirectly by hiring like-minded reporters (Aronoff 2006, Hart 2003, Niven 2003, Page 1995, 1996, Verner 2006). Finally, audience preferences may encourage reporters and their outlets to provide coverage slanted to reflect those preferences. Driven by maintaining market share and profit, outlets may alter the amount and political slant of their coverage, depending on the size and political leanings of their audiences (Breed 1955, Belt and Just 2008, McQuail 1994, Singer 2004).[12] FOX News, for example, has developed a conservative alternative to other outlets and thereby built a competitive and profitable niche in the marketplace (Hamilton 2004). More broadly, at the onset of the Iraq War in 2003, news coverage in the United States strongly favored the position of the Bush administration in the conflict, while displaying less attention to critics of the war effort outside the United States (Dimitrova et al. 2005). This ideologically unbalanced coverage

[11] Even greater journalistic independence is certainly possible, through investigative journalism and civic or public journalism (Bennett et al. 2007, Cassidy 2005, Graber 2006, Weaver and Wilhoit 1986). In both approaches, reporters initiate stories and debates independently of politicians' efforts. Compared to the approaches to reporting described in the text, investigative and public journalism require greater resources and often offer less profit. While these approaches of reporting are important, they remain beyond the scope of my analysis.

[12] The content and slant of coverage may also vary by the type of medium, particularly print versus television (Gans 2004, King and Lester 2005, McCombs and Shaw 1972). Druckman (2005), however, found different levels of newspaper and television coverage of U.S. Senate race, but little difference in the content of that coverage.

reflected the widespread public support for the war in the United States.[13] Reporters and news outlets can scarcely afford to ignore the partisan leanings of their audiences.

Despite these potential benefits of partisan bias in coverage, other concerns may discourage reporters' from providing this type of coverage. While partisan coverage was widespread during the early nineteenth century in the United States, news outlets increasingly embraced greater objectivity and balance over the next century (Davis 1996, Hamilton 2004). The growing professionalization of journalism also encouraged journalists to move away from partisan politics and present more thorough and accurate accounts in their news coverage (Cook 1998, West 2001). Contemporary surveys of journalists often find little connection between their personal beliefs and reporting (Niven 2001, Pew Research Center For the People and Press 2004, Weaver and Wilhoit 1986). In addition, both reporters and editors have a strong incentive to avoid biased coverage, because such stories could turn away portions of their audience (Gans 2004). Reflecting this concern, a strong separation often exists between a newspaper's news content and endorsements in election campaigns (Dalton et al. 1998). The head of the *Washington Post* editorial page describes one example of this insulation:

> the editorial page [staff and] our colleagues who report and edit the news ... operate totally independently from each other. Leonard Downie, the executive editor, has no input into our endorsements – he doesn't even know when they are coming – and our editorial endorsements have no influence on how Downie and his staff cover campaigns. Downie oversees the news staff. I oversee the editorial and op-ed pages, and neither of us reports to the other. (Hiatt 2006)

These obstacles to partisan coverage appear effective. Systematic analyses have only sometimes found evidence of liberal bias (Groseclose and Milyo 2005, Lichter and Rothman 1983, Schulman 1982), while at other times suggesting a conservative bias (Cohen and Young 1973, Herman and Chomsky 1988). Reviews of the overall body of evidence suggest that the news media do not consistently give one party

[13] See Domke et al. (2006) for another example of ideologically slanted coverage reflecting the ideological preferences of the American public.

more extensive or favorable coverage (Cook 2001, D'Allessio and Allen 2000).[14]

Given the obstacles to partisan coverage, overall coverage of congressional debates is unlikely to reveal a consistent bias favoring

[14] See Niven (2003) and Patterson and Donsbach (1996) for additional reviews of recent research on partisan bias in news coverage. Organizations evaluating liberal and conservative media bias include:

- Accuracy in Media (AIM) http://www.aim.org/ (last accessed June 24, 2008). AIM focuses on combating liberal bias in the news media.
- Center for Media and Democracy (CMD) http://www.prwatch.org/ (last accessed June 24, 2008). CMD calls itself "a non-profit, non-partisan, public interest organization that strengthens participatory democracy by investigating and exposing public relations spin and propaganda, and by promoting media literacy and citizen journalism."
- Committee of Concerned Journalists (CCJ) http://www.concernedjournalists.org/ (last accessed June 25, 2008). CCJ is composed of journalists, academics, and publishers working to improve the journalism profession and remind journalists about the core principles and responsibilities associated with journalism.
- Fairness & Accuracy in Reporting (FAIR) http://www.fair.org/ (last accessed June 24, 2008). A progressive and national organization, FAIR works to oppose censorship and to encourage greater balance in news coverage.
- Media Matters http://mediamatters.org/ (last accessed June 24, 2008). Media Matters is a nonprofit organization aimed at monitoring conservative biases that misinform news sources.
- Media Research Center (MRC) http://www.mediaresearch.org/ (last accessed June 24, 2008). Founded in 1987, this conservative watchdog organization documents liberal bias in the news media.
- NewsBusters http://www.newsbusters.org/ (last accessed June 25, 2008). This online blog provide evidence of liberal bias in news coverage.
- Reporting Wars http://www.reportingwars.com/ (last accessed June 24, 2008). Reporting Wars compares coverage of current events by mainstream news outlets.
- The Statistical Assessment Service (STATS) http://stats.org/ (last accessed June 25, 2008). STATS works to correct flawed science or statistical information that biases news coverage.

Political bias can also focus on specific policy issues:

- The Committee for Accuracy in Middle East Reporting in America (CAMERA) http://www.camera.org/ (last accessed June 25, 2008).
- Honest Reporting http://www.honestreporting.com/ (last accessed June 24, 2008).
- The Memory Hole http://www.thememoryhole.org/ (last accessed June 25, 2008).

The following indexes provide more extensive listings of organizations concerned with bias in news coverage:

- "News Bias Explored" University of Michigan http://www.umich.edu/~newsbias/links.html (last accessed June 25, 2008).
- "Bias and Balance" Google Directory http://www.google.com/Top/Society/Issues/Business/Media/Bias_and_balance/ (last accessed June 25, 2008).
- "What's Wrong With the News" FAIR http://www.fair/org/index.php?page=101 (last accessed June 25, 2008).

Democrats or Republicans. The greater incentives to provide mirrored or balanced coverage suggest that these types of stories will prove more common. News coverage with a partisan slant, if it exists, will more likely emerge in individual outlets responding to either their editors' political leanings or the partisan preferences of their audiences.

5.1.5. Feedback

The discussion of news coverage thus far has attempted to explain how and why that coverage may vary. It is also important to consider how the coverage and its variations may feed back to influence the politicians who initially promoted their messages and the broader policy process. Members of Congress could conceivably ignore news coverage of a policy debate, choosing not to alter their promotional efforts in response to coverage. In this argument about the lack of feedback, legislators work to win coverage to further their own individual electoral interests, but news stories have no effect on the legislative process or policy outcomes. Legislators, not journalists, choose the legislative language emerging from congressional committees and the voting alternatives allowed on the floors of the House and Senate. In addition, legislators are ultimately responsible to their constituents, not to journalists. As a result, news coverage has little effect on agenda setting and policy decisions inside Congress.

Contrary to this argument, uncertainty about the effectiveness of public relations campaigns can lead politicians to respond more directly to news coverage (Bennett and Mannheim 2001, Graber 2006, Kingdon 2003, Miller and Riechert 2001, Wolfsfeld 2001, 2004). If such a campaign is successful, the extensive coverage of a message encourages its proponents to promote it more frequently. If a message does not appear in news coverage, its proponents may promote that message less frequently. Eventually, they may grow silent, concede the debate, and hope that public attention soon shifts to a more favorable issue (Miller and Riechert 2001, Noelle-Neumann 1984).

In this cycle of promotion and coverage, the news stories become part of the policy-making agenda. Coverage of a particular message encourages legislators to pay more attention to the issue and arguments making up the message. Greater attention to these considerations encourages legislators to support the message's policy recommendation, which then becomes a more likely outcome of the policy process. Evidence of these patterns supports the argument that strategic communication campaigns effectively shape news coverage and thereby affect policy outcomes. These dynamics of feedback create strategic interaction between parties in their attempts to shape the legislative agenda. If one party wins substantially more coverage of its message, its members in Congress continue to promote that message, and the party can more effectively shape the legislative agenda. By winning less coverage for its message, the disadvantaged party loses influence over that agenda. The parties' competition over promoting messages thus translates, via coverage, into influence over the legislative agenda.

5.1.6. Patterns of Coverage and Feedback

To summarize, this chapter's arguments suggest a number of specific expectations about coverage of congressional debates and feedback from that coverage:

- The overall coverage is more likely to be mirrored and balanced than to have a consistent partisan bias.
  - → Mirrored coverage is likely to reflect the policy influence of politicians promoting messages, including their institutional position and the frequency of their promotional efforts.
  - → The frequency of mirrored and balanced coverage depends on the stage of the debate. Earlier, less important stages are likely to receive mirrored coverage, while balanced coverage is more likely during later, more important stages.
  - → Individual news outlets provide partisan coverage, with the particular slant reflecting the editorial leaning of the outlet and the political preferences of the outlet's market.
- Coverage of a party's message will encourage party members to promote that message more frequently. Conversely, a lack of coverage of a message discourages subsequent promotion of that message.

The remainder of this chapter illustrates how these patterns largely characterize news coverage of the four specific debates described in previous chapters. The next section compares legislators' promotional efforts to overall news coverage from across the United States. The third part of the chapter examines how coverage of the debates varies across individual outlets.

5.2. COVERAGE AND FEEDBACK

Unpacking the interaction between promotion and coverage requires detailed measures of both. To capture politicians' statements, I use the same evidence from previous chapters, organized differently. For this chapter I calculate the number of times each day that each congressional party and the president promote their party message in each of the four debates. Consequently, each debate has three measures of promotion, one for each congressional party and a third for the president.[15]

The measures of news coverage come from Lexis-Nexis, specifically twelve national outlets and a local newspaper from forty-three different states. Content analysis of these stories produced a measure of daily coverage for each party and its message in a debate: the number of stories each day mentioning the particular message and at least one member of the particular congressional party (or the president). Thus, one measure captures the daily number of stories mentioning Democrats and their message in the supplemental debate, while another measure focuses on Republicans and their messages in the debate. A third measure captures coverage of the president and his party's message.[16] The composition of these measures reflects the goal of the promotional strategies outlined in previous chapters: winning coverage for ones party and message. Overall, each debate's evidence includes six measures: the Democrats', the Republicans', and the president's promotion of their own party messages each day, and the daily news coverage of each of the three and its message.

For each of the four debates, I first review politicians' promotional efforts and journalists' news coverage across different stages of the debate, showing how reporters varied in their use of politicians' statements to produce news stories. I then use statistical analysis, specifically

[15] Earlier chapters focused largely on promotional efforts by members of Congress, and devoted relatively little attention to those of the president or to coordination among the president and his fellow partisans in Congress. This relative emphasis reflects the relatively limited coordination of promotion between Clinton and congressional Democrats that I witnessed while working in Daschle's office. In addition, we know relatively little about the promotional efforts of legislators, while those of the president have received extensive attention and analysis (Bichard 2006, Kernell 1997, Page 1995, Peake and Eshbaugh-Soha 2008, Rottinghaus 2008). In this chapter's analysis of news coverage, the president will receive more equal emphasis, reflecting the effectiveness of the presidential bully pulpit.

[16] See Appendix 3.B for more details on creating the measures of coverage.

vector autoregression (VAR), to estimate for each debate whether promotional efforts and news coverage influenced each other.[17]

5.2.1. The Supplemental

I first consider the promotional efforts of the congressional parties and the president in each stage of the supplemental debate. After establishing the relative frequency of the promotional efforts, I then examine the politicians' actual coverage in these same stages. If the news media's coverage mirrors politicians' actual statements, the relative frequency of the promotional efforts will correspond to the relative frequency of the coverage. But if the journalists independently add balance or partisan bias to the coverage (Althaus 2003, Entman 2003, Jerit 2005), that coverage will reflect the politicians' statements less closely.

Across the seven months of analysis in 1997, congressional Democrats averaged 1.33 mentions per day of their party's message in the supplemental debate (see the top portion of Table 5.1). President Clinton had a daily average of .09 mentions of the Democratic message, or 7% of the congressional Democrats' average.[18] Congressional Republicans averaged .90 mentions of their party message, or 67% of the Democratic daily average.

[17] Another dimension of this relationship involves legislators' pursuit of individual over collective party interests, and reporters' interest in such defection. As Chapter 4 explains, if members of Congress are more concerned with furthering their own individual interests, they may promote their disagreements with their party. Such conflict may yield more individual coverage for the legislator than joining with fellow partisans to promote the party message. In the debate over the Iraq War, for example, Senator Joseph Lieberman won extensive attention and coverage by opposing his fellow Democrats and reaching across party lines to support President Bush. Examining whether the collective or individual strategies more effectively win coverage requires more detailed content analysis than was possible for this project. In addition to measuring the tone of legislators' statements (which Chapter 4 discusses), this analysis would require measures of the tone of legislators' statements in news coverage. For a single debate, the appropriate VAR would include sixteen variables: the number of positive and negative mentions of each party's message by each party's members in their statements and news coverage.

[18] Note the method of calculating percentages in Table 5.1. If the mean for congressional Republicans is 10, and if the mean for congressional Democrats is 10, the corresponding calculation is 10/10 = 1.00, or 100%. In this case, the Republican mean is 100% of the Democratic mean, or 0% greater. But if the Republican mean changes to 13 while the Democratic mean remains 10, the corresponding calculation is now 13/10 = 1.30, or 130%. Here, the Republican mean is 130% of the Democratic mean, or 30% greater. Finally, if the Republican mean changes to 7 while the Democratic mean remains 10, the corresponding calculation is now 7/10 = .70, or 70%. Now, the Republican mean is 70% of the Democratic mean, or 30% less.

TABLE 5.1. *Promotion and Coverage in Congressional Debates, by Stage of Debate*

	Statements					Stories				
	Cong. Dems.	Cong. Reps.		Pres.		Cong. Dems.	Cong. Reps.		Pres.	
	Mean	Mean	Percent	Mean	Percent	Mean	Mean	Percent	Mean	Percent
The Supplemental										
Stage 1 (Jan. 1–Apr. 6)	.23	.06	27%	0	0%	1.51	.53	35%	1.50	99%
Stage 2 (Apr. 7–May 23)	2.09	1.85	89%	.05	2%	5.74	5.40	94%	6.57	114%
Stage 3 (May 24–Jun. 1)	.22	.11	50%	.22	100%	7.00	3.44	49%	7.11	102%
Stage 4 (Jun. 2–Jun. 15)	10.43	6.50	63%	.93	9%	24.50	29.07	119%	34.36	140%
Stage 5 (Jun. 16–Aug. 1)	.32	.13	40%	.04	13%	3.45	1.53	44%	4.47	130%
Overall	1.33	.90	67%	.09	7%	4.62	3.83	83%	5.67	123%
Partial Birth Abortion										
Periods of non-debate	.09	.12	124%	0	0%	.50	.58	114%	.61	122%
House debate (Mar. 3–Mar. 23)	.30	2.15	717%	0	0%	3.30	5.35	162%	5.20	158%
Senate debate (May 12–May 25)	1.71	3.86	225%	.07	4%	13.64	11.86	87%	13.71	101%
Overall	.22	.55	251%	.01	2%	1.63	1.77	108%	1.91	117%

(continued)

TABLE 5.1. (*continued*)

	Statements					Stories				
	Cong. Dems.	Cong. Reps.		Pres.		Cong. Dems.	Cong. Reps.		Pres.	
	Mean	Mean	Percent	Mean	Percent	Mean	Mean	Percent	Mean	Percent
1997 Budget										
Stage 1 (Jan. 1–Apr. 6)	2.54	8.45	332%	.50	20%	18.75	65.57	350%	14.50	77%
Stage 2 (Apr. 7–Jun. 8)	5.19	19.65	379%	.75	14%	24.67	75.25	305%	18.98	77%
Stage 3 (Jun. 9–Aug. 1)	6.17	27.31	443%	.91	15%	34.57	96.93	280%	32.85	95%
Overall	4.24	16.54	390%	.68	16%	24.51	76.38	312%	20.48	84%
2003 Budget										
Stage 1 (Jan. 1–Mar. 9)	5.97	1.49	25%	.31	5%	44.74	30.50	68%	41.54	93%
Stage 2 (Mar. 10–Apr. 13)	5.14	.56	11%	.08	2%	27.97	19.42	69%	22.11	79%
Stage 3 (Apr. 14–May 25)	4.33	1.52	35%	.29	7%	40.64	36.81	91%	34.14	84%
Stage 4 (May 26–Aug. 1)	3.42	1.38	40%	.42	12%	32.83	20.09	61%	28.18	86%
Overall	4.71	1.30	27%	.30	6%	37.37	26.63	71%	32.62	87%

Note: Each number, unless accompanied by a "%" sign, is the average number of statements or stories per day during the particular stage of the debate by congressional Democrats, congressional Republicans, or the president. Each "Percent" column presents the corresponding mean of statements or stories as a percentage of the congressional Democrats' relevant mean (i.e., the mean for congressional Republicans or the president, divided by the mean for congressional Democrats).

News coverage of the debate produced a different pattern of means and percentages. The combined outlets produced an average of 4.62 stories per day that mentioned the Democratic message and a Democratic legislator. President Clinton's average coverage per day (5.67 stories) was 23% greater than the congressional Democrats' average. While the president was much less active in promoting the Democratic message, he received substantially more coverage. The president's public statements appeared much more effective in winning coverage, reflecting the bully pulpit traditionally associated with his office and the legislative importance of the president's veto (Canes-Wrone 2006, Edwards and Wood 1999, Kernell 1997, Neustadt 1990). The news media give more coverage to each presidential statement than to each statement by a congressional Democrat. This difference is the first of many pieces of evidence that the news media incorporate institutional position and influence into their coverage of politicians' promotional efforts.

Evidence of balanced coverage emerges from a comparison of congressional Democrats and Republicans. In daily news coverage, congressional Republicans averaged 83% (i.e., 3.83 stories) of the number of stories of congressional Democrats. This deficit in coverage is actually smaller than the GOP deficit in promotion. Congressional Republicans lagged far behind (67%) in promoting their party's message, but they were only somewhat behind (83%) in the coverage that they received for that message. The news media covering Congress appear to have provided more balanced coverage of competing arguments than merited by promotional efforts of the two parties. Journalists appear to have gone beyond the relative frequency of legislators' statements to equalize the attention to competing partisan messages in news stories.

Equally remarkable is how the news media's own framing of congressional events varied over the four stages of the supplemental debate. Table 5.1 presents the average levels of promotion and coverage over the four stages. The first stage lasted from the beginning of the analysis, January 1, up to the beginning of congressional committee consideration of the actual supplemental legislation on April 6. Members of Congress were just beginning to discuss the need for a supplemental. The natural disasters (and congressional awareness of them) were only starting to develop during the late winter. Republican members had begun to promote the controversial riders later attached to the bill. During this initial stage of the debate, neither congressional Democrats, congressional Republicans, nor the President made many mentions of their respective party messages (with daily averages of .23, .06, and 0 mentions, respectively). Reflecting the limited public statements, news coverage was also low (1.51, .53, and 1.50 stories per day). The *relative* frequency of promotion and coverage is important. Republican legislators averaged only 27% of their congressional opposition's promotional efforts and 35% of their news coverage. During this period, news coverage largely mirrors the balance of debate in Congress. President Clinton made no public statements of the Democrats' message, but his news coverage was 99% of that of congressional Democrats. Again demonstrating the power of institutional position, journalists included the President and his arguments even though he did not publicly promote them.

The second stage of debate began on April 7 with committee consideration of the supplemental legislation, and lasted until May 23, the start of the Memorial Day congressional recess. During the week of April 21, the House Appropriations Committee marked up and approved a version of the supplemental legislation. The committee's counterpart in the Senate approved its own version during the following week. The entire Senate debated and passed this version during the week of May 5. During the next week the House passed its own version of the legislation. One week then remained before the Memorial Day recess. While a conference committee began meeting this week, the conferees faced little immediate pressure to produce a compromise. Congressional Republicans expected President Clinton to veto the bill, but did not want to be away from Washington when the veto occurred. Thus, Congress entered the recess without approving a final bill.

Promotional events and news coverage increased during this period, reflecting the supplemental's progress through the legislative process. Congressional Democrats, congressional Republicans, and the President all made more public statements of their party messages. Congressional Republicans increased their promotional efforts substantially, now averaging 89% of their Democratic colleagues. President Clinton again only made a fraction (2%) of congressional Democrats' public statements. News coverage of those statements also increased, albeit unevenly. Congressional Republicans now averaged 94% of their Democratic colleagues' coverage, while President Clinton actually won 14% more coverage than congressional Democrats. Both congressional parties increased their promotional efforts, which are mirrored in more extensive coverage. And the President again proves most effective in winning news coverage.

The third stage of the debate occurred during the Memorial Day recess, from May 24 to June 1. Most legislators went home; in Washington, there were only a total of five public statements of either party's message during the recess. But despite the limited promotional efforts in Washington, coverage of the debate was high nationwide, particularly for the Democrats and their message. Members of Congress appear to have promoted their party's message in their home states and districts, with those efforts producing coverage. Congressional Democrats apparently were particularly effective in these local public relations efforts. News coverage of GOP congressmen and their message was only 49% of that of congressional Democrats. President Clinton won levels of coverage similar to his Democratic colleagues in Congress.

The debate over the supplemental reached its peak during the fourth stage, which lasted from June 2 to June 13. During this stage, both the legislative and executive branches significantly increased their promotional efforts. But, congressional Republicans still averaged only 63% of their Democratic colleagues' public statements. The President averaged only 9%. The news coverage of this stage did not reflect the relative frequency of politicians' public statements. GOP legislators actually won 19% more stories than congressional Democrats did. The President won 40% more stories. These frequencies indicate that the news media gave more attention and coverage to the individuals who made relatively fewer public statements (i.e., congressional Republicans and the President). Reviewing the daily events of this fourth stage of the debate can help explain why.

After returning from the Memorial Day recess, the Republican-dominated conference committee produced its report on Wednesday, June 4. Both chambers passed the bill the next day. But, congressional Republicans waited to send the conference report to the White House until after the following weekend, again fearing that Clinton would veto the bill while congressional Republicans were home in their states or districts. During this week (June 2 – June 8), the Republican strategic disadvantage on this issue grew more evident. The Democrats promoted their arguments more frequently each day than the Republicans did, except on June 5 when the conference report passed Congress. On each of the seven days in the week, the news media gave more coverage to Democratic arguments than Republican ones.

On the following Monday afternoon (June 9), congressional Republicans sent the bill to the White House. Acting on his party's growing strategic advantage in the debate, Clinton confidently vetoed the supplemental and immediately sent the bill back to Congress. Clinton's veto statement echoed a number of arguments in the congressional Democrats' message:

> The congressional majority – despite the obvious and urgent need to speed critical relief to people in the Dakotas, Minnesota, California and 29 other states ravaged by flooding and other natural disasters – has chosen to weigh down this legislation with a series of unacceptable provisions that it knows will draw my veto. The time has come to stop playing politics with the lives of Americans in need. (*CQ Almanac* 1997, 9–90)

After Clinton's veto, the Republicans' troubles mushroomed. Hours after the veto announcement, Senate Majority Leader Lott began exploring possible compromises on census sampling, the most important issue in the debate for House Republicans. News coverage of the debate fanned disagreement about strategy among congressional Republicans. While public statements about the debate split equally between the two parties on that Monday, the day's news coverage favored the Democrats by more than 3-to-1 (thirteen, eleven, and twenty-one stories mentioning congressional Democrats, congressional Republicans, and the President, respectively).

On the next day (Tuesday, June 10), House Republicans returned Lott's favor, by signaling a willingness to compromise on the automatic CR, an important provision for Senate Republicans. That day's news stories increased coverage of the debate (twenty-three, seventy-six, and eighty-three stories), particularly of the Republican arguments, because those arguments were the central reason why Clinton had vetoed the bill one day earlier. On the evening of June 10, Democrats held their all-night vigil outside the Senate chamber, to focus media and public attention even more strongly on the Republicans and their alleged stalling tactics surrounding the supplemental.

Reflecting the Democrats' outreach to the media, news coverage on Wednesday, June 11, swung back in favor of the Democrats, mentioning their messages much more frequently than those of the Republicans (fifty-four, thirty-nine, and sixty-six stories). While Democrats remained unyielding in their demand for a "clean" supplemental, congressional Republicans moved closer to compromise and indeed collapse. In the House twenty Republican moderates wrote a letter to Gingrich, asking for a "clean, unencumbered" bill. These moderates' defection would deprive House Republicans of a working majority.

In the face of this internal party pressure, Republicans leaders soon reached a compromise with Democrats. Congress would pass a "clean" disaster relief supplemental. The Senate would consider the automatic CR provision as separate, stand-alone legislation. The House would address the census issue in negotiations with the administration. Many observers described the outcome as a complete loss for congressional Republicans (*CQ Almanac* 1997, 9–90). Earlier in the debate, Lott had described his interpretation of Clinton's veto threat: "Sometimes you threaten things you don't actually do. Sometimes you are bluffing." (*CQ Almanac* 1997, 9–90) The collapse of the Republicans' strategy suggested that Lott's quote more accurately described the GOP.

During the fourth stage of the supplemental debate, congressional Republicans faced a clear strategic disadvantage. Rank-and-file GOP legislators were unwilling to promote the party message, particularly compared to their counterparts across the aisle. Congressional Republicans more effectively won media coverage than congressional Democrats did, while President Clinton overshadowed both groups. Unfortunately for the Republicans, their newsworthiness appeared to stem from their controversial actions and disarray, not from coordinated and focused promotion of their preferred party message.

5.2.1.1. *The Interaction of Promotion and Coverage*

The previous descriptions illustrated how politicians' promotional efforts and journalists' news stories varied across the stages of the debate. The coverage sometimes reflected the relative frequency of politicians' competing statements, and sometimes presented a mix of messages unreflective of the politicians' statements. This account only begins to suggest the overall effectiveness of the parties' efforts to win coverage, as well as whether the parties reacted to changes in that coverage. Were the politicians driving or responding to stories?

To understand more clearly the interaction between public statements and news stories, I turn to VAR. This method of statistical analysis regresses each variable in an interrelated system on lagged values of the other variables in the system (Edwards and Wood 1999, Freeman et al. 1989). The resulting estimates indicate "the dynamic responses of each variable to the other variables in the system" (Bartels 1996). VAR can thus indicate whether and how the measures of promotion and coverage influence each other. Thus, this type of statistical estimation is most appropriate for estimating the relationships among promotion and coverage.

VAR hinges on a particular definition of causality: Prior values of one variable are correlated with, and therefore cause, current values of another variable. If this type of causality exists in a particular model, VAR can also suggest the cumulative magnitude of the causal effect, that is, the total amount of change in one variable over a period of time that is caused by a one-unit change or "shock" in another variable. This causal effect can be contemporaneous, occurring at the same time period as the shock. The effect can also extend over time. The same shock can have a delayed effect; for example, news organizations may not report about a politician's event until several days after the event occurred. In addition, the shock could affect another variable in the model, which could in turn affect the variable that we are trying to understand. VAR captures all these dynamic effects, showing the total amount of change in a variable over a period of time after the shock occurs in another variable.[19]

I use VAR to estimate the relationships among six measures of the supplemental debate: the daily promotional efforts of congressional Democrats, congressional Republicans, and President, and the daily news coverage of the three. The model also included six exogenous dummy variables capturing the days of the week and thereby controlling for the cyclical nature of the legislative and news cycles. These factors are less important for interpretation since the analysis focuses on the dynamic interaction between promotion and coverage. I estimated the VAR model and calculated the cumulative effect of each variable on the others. The upper left corner of Figure 5.1 presents the cumulative effects that were consistently significant in the debate over the supplemental. Arrows connect the variables where significant cumulative effects emerged. The direction of the arrow indicates the direction of the effect, with the magnitude of that effect reported at the point of each arrow. The lack of an arrow between two measures means that a variable did not significantly affect the second variable.

The cumulative effects suggest several important conclusions about the interaction among politicians and journalists in the battle over the supplemental. First, the politicians' promotional efforts appeared to generate news coverage on a day-to-day basis. Public statements by GOP

[19] See Appendix 5.A for more details on the estimation of the VAR models. As the appendix notes, the period of time for calculating the cumulative effect varies across the models. My goal is to determine whether one variable exerts a significant impact on a second variable, regardless of the time period of that effect. Consequently, each cumulative effect reported from the VAR models represents the longest period for which the particular effect is significant. If the significant effect involves only short-term dynamics, the period of time is only several days. But if the significant effect accumulates over the long term, the period may extend up to twenty days. Space limitations prevent more in-depth analysis and interpretation of these differing short- and long-term effects across the eight different VAR models in this book.

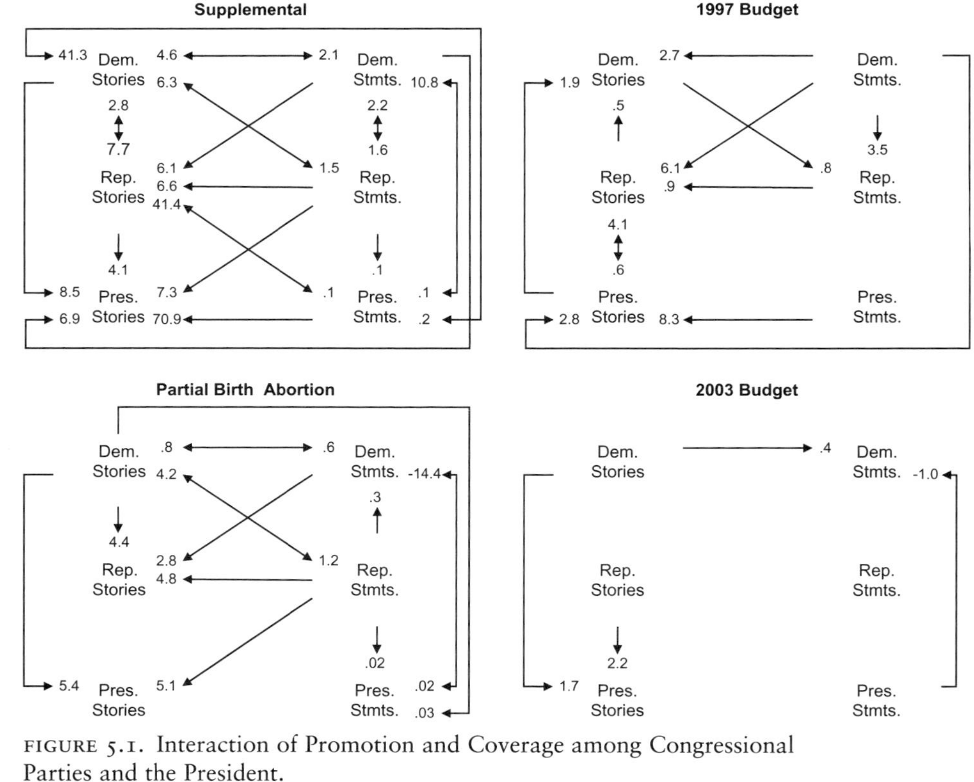

FIGURE 5.1. Interaction of Promotion and Coverage among Congressional Parties and the President.

legislators were slightly more effective than those of the Democrats in winning coverage. At congressional Democrats' press events, each mention of the Democratic message led to an estimated 4.6 news stories mentioning Democrats and that message. For each mention of the GOP message by congressional Republicans, the model estimates that 6.6 stories of that party and message would follow. Each of Clinton's mentions of the Democratic message results in 70.9 stories referring to him and the message. Again, the institutional power of the presidency helped Clinton win coverage much more effectively than members of Congress.

Similar evidence emerges from the broader effects of the politicians' promotional efforts. The VAR model estimates that each congressional Democratic mention of the Democratic message led to 6.1 stories mentioning Republicans and their message, as well as 6.9 stories mentioning Clinton and the Democratic message. The press events of congressional Republicans also affected coverage of the other two participants in the debate, leading to 6.3 stories about congressional Democrats and 7.3 stories about Clinton. The president's events gave equal boosts (41.3 and 41.4 stories) to coverage of the two congressional parties. Overall, the congressional Republicans' promotional efforts appeared slightly more effective than those of congressional Democrats. But as Table 5.1 indicated, the latter party promoted its message much more frequently, which helped produce the Democratic advantage in news coverage of the debate.

The coverage of this debate also fed back to shape the politicians' promotional efforts. Specifically, the legislators' promotional efforts appeared responsive to news stories mentioning congressional Democrats and their party message. Each such story led to 2.1 more mentions of the Democratic message by congressional Democrats, 1.5 more mentions of the GOP message by Republican legislators, and .2 mentions of the Democratic message by Clinton. Curiously, the other two types of stories provided no feedback. The impact of the Democratic coverage appears to be part of the party's strategic advantage in the debate, but the patterns in other debates suggest a more complicated interpretation.

News coverage of the supplemental debate also appeared to influence the debate's outcome. Across the various stages of the debate, nothing changed in the partisan distribution of power in Congress. The various natural disasters certainly grew in severity over the course of the spring, but they had already reached extremely high levels when members of Congress left Washington for the Memorial Day recess. At this point Republican leaders continued to express public confidence in their strategy in the debate. Within weeks, this confidence had completely dissipated. The most likely cause of the GOP defeat was the Democratic advantage in news coverage, which increased pressure on rank-and-file Republicans and their leaders to agree to a clean disaster relief bill.

The overall evidence in this section illustrates the components of the Democrats' strategic advantage in the supplemental debate. While congressional Republicans won news coverage somewhat more effectively, the Democrats promoted their message more frequently and won more coverage. This advantage certainly varied over the course of the debate. During the final weeks, Republicans actually won more coverage, but these stories presented the conflict and disarray among GOP legislators, rather than focusing on the Republicans' preferred message. Stories about congressional Democrats and their message also exerted a feedback effect on all the politicians' promotional efforts.

These patterns also provide insight into whether journalists tend to mirror politicians' varying promotional efforts in their press coverage, or to frame that coverage in a balanced light or in one favoring a particular party. Over the four stages of the supplemental debate, congressional Republicans consistently promoted their party's message less frequently than Democratic legislators discussed their own message. At the same time, each stage saw journalists giving more coverage to Republicans and their message than one would expect from the GOP's promotional efforts. As a result, coverage of the Republican message more evenly balanced that of the Democratic message. Additional evidence of journalists balancing coverage emerged from the VAR model. Instead of mirroring politicians' statements and producing similar numbers of stories for each party's statement, reporters gave widely varying levels of coverage to different politicians' statements. Most notably, Clinton won many more stories per public statement than members of Congress did.

The patterns of promotion and coverage suggested that reporters' coverage gave congressional Republicans more coverage than one would expect from their promotional efforts. Such a boost in coverage could indicate a partisan bias by reporters, in favor of Republicans. In this single debate, however, it is difficult to distinguish this explanation of partisan bias from an alternative: reporters were merely balancing their coverage during important stages of the debate. For leverage in sorting out these explanations, I next examine the partial birth abortion debate. In this debate favoring Republicans, reporters trying to slant their coverage in favor of the GOP will produce stories widening the

Republican advantage in promotion. Democrats would receive less coverage than their promotional efforts would suggest, while Republicans would win more coverage. In contrast, reporters concerned about balance will use their coverage to narrow the Republican advantage in promotional efforts.

5.2.2. The Partial Birth Abortion Ban

In the 1997 debate over partial birth abortion, politicians and journalists concentrated their statements and coverage in three periods, two of which occurred during my period of analysis. The House first took up legislation implementing a ban during the first three weeks of March. Then, the Senate debated its own version of the ban during two weeks in middle of May. Finally, in early October the House agreed to the Senate version of the ban, and President Clinton vetoed the bill on October 10.

My evidence of promotional efforts and news coverage includes the House and Senate debates during March and May. Outside these debates, senators, representatives, and journalists appeared to pay little attention to the issue during the seven months of evidence, as Table 5.1 suggests. From January 1 to August 1 (and excluding the two periods of debate), daily mentions of party messages averaged .12 or less for congressional Democrats, congressional Republicans, and President Clinton. The GOP mean was 24% greater than the Democratic legislators' average.

News coverage during these periods presented a slightly more balanced picture of the debate and the parties' messages. Here, the mean for GOP legislators was only 14% greater than that of congressional Democrats. The coverage of congressmen and their competing messages is more balanced than one would expect from their promotional efforts. In a similar vein, President Clinton averaged 22% more stories than congressional Democrats, despite making no public statements of his party message. Again, this coverage likely resulted from the President's prominent role in the legislative process, notably his expected veto of the ban.

Both the partisan advantage and the journalists' framing grew even more pronounced during the House debate of the partial birth abortion ban. This debate began during the week of March 3, with a week-long series of press events by Republican representatives. The following week saw the House and Senate Judiciary committees hold a joint hearing on the proposed ban. Republican members highlighted recent statements by Ron Fitzsimmons, acknowledging that he had understated the frequency of partial birth abortions. One day after the hearing, the House

Judiciary Committee approved its version of the ban. During the third week of March, the House approved legislation banning partial birth abortion.

As suggested by these events, the Republicans engaged in much more promotion than Democrats did during this period. Republicans legislators averaged 617% more mentions than congressional Democrats. Compared to this substantial GOP advantage in promotion, news stories about the debate were more balanced. Coverage of GOP members of Congress was only 62% more than that of congressional Democrats. Despite making no public statements about the debate, President Clinton averaged 58% more than his fellow Democrats in Congress. While congressional Republicans still maintained an advantage in news coverage of the debate, that advantage was much smaller than one would expect from their promotional efforts. Journalists do not appear to have engaged in partisan bias. Instead, they framed news coverage to give more balanced attention to the two congressional parties, and more extensive coverage to President Clinton.

The Senate debate over the partial birth abortion ban produced even more balance in promotional efforts and news coverage. During the week of May 12, the Senate began debating the GOP ban, as well as the alternatives proposed by Daschle and by Boxer and Feinstein. A bipartisan coalition turned back both alternatives and passed the Republican bill. During this stage, congressional Republicans' promotional average was only 125% more than that of their Democratic colleagues. This advantage turned into a disadvantage in news coverage. Republican legislators won 13% fewer stories than congressional Democrats did. President Clinton enjoyed the highest average coverage, despite making many fewer public statements than members of Congress made.

During the Senate debate, the difference between promotion and coverage partially resulted from the same considerations driving the House debate. Journalists appeared to balance coverage of the parties' message in news stories, thus reducing the GOP's ability to translate their promotional advantage into favorable coverage. But, the Republicans' relatively weaker strategic position in the Senate debate may also result from an important difference between the two chambers. In the House the minority party holds substantially fewer powers in the legislative process. During the partial birth abortion debate, the minority thus lacked an effective mechanism for altering debate inside and outside the chamber about an unfavorable issue. In contrast, Senate Democrats could force votes on their own proposals involving partial birth abortion. This opportunity helped the senators present their position on an unfavorable issue in a more politically appealing manner, in hopes of neutralizing the issue. Although the Democratic proposals failed, they appeared to encourage the Senate Democratic caucus to become more involved in the legislative debate.

Despite the Democrats' press efforts and news coverage in the Senate, congressional Republicans still enjoyed significant advantages at every stage of the partial birth abortion debate. The VAR model of the debate illustrates other aspects of these advantages. As presented in the lower-left portion of Figure 5.1, this model includes the same six variables as the previous model, created this time to capture promotion and coverage in the partial birth abortion debate. The cumulative effects indicate several ways in which congressional Republicans held an advantage in the debate. Republican promotional efforts appear to drive those of their Democratic counterparts. Each GOP statement of their party message leads to .3 Democratic statements of their own message on the issue. Significantly, the Democrats' statements do not exert a similar effect on Republicans' promotional efforts.

The politicians' statements also affected news coverage of the debate. Here, the Republicans again enjoyed an advantage. Each mention of the GOP message by a Republican legislator led to an estimated 4.8 stories mentioning the party's message and members. In contrast, each Democratic legislator's mention of the party message yielded only .8 stories about the party and message. Even the presidential bully pulpit appeared less effective in this debate, with President Clinton's statements not affecting his news coverage.

The politicians' statements also had broader effects on news coverage, and the GOP enjoyed another advantage in these effects. Each GOP legislator's mention of the party message led to 4.2 stories about Democrats and their message, as well as 5.1 stories about the President and his message. Each public statement by congressional Democrats was much less effective, producing only 2.8 stories about the Republicans and none about the President. Finally, statements by President Clinton appeared unrelated to stories about congressional Republicans and Democrats. Overall, the GOP's public statements more effectively drove news coverage than the Democrats' press efforts did.

The final aspect of the VAR model, involving feedback from press coverage, is surprising in that these results do not mirror those from the supplemental debate. In that debate, members of both congressional parties appeared more responsive to Democratic stories than Republican ones, perhaps reflecting the Democratic advantage in the supplemental debate. By extension, one would expect congressional parties to respond more to Republican stories in the partial birth abortion debate. Yet, Figure 5.1 indicates that Democratic stories in this debate shaped promotional efforts by both congressional parties and Clinton. Republican stories did not affect any promotional efforts. Even in a debate favoring Republicans overall, coverage of congressional Democrats and their message provided the strongest feedback to politicians promoting their message. The continued influence of these Democratic stories across the two debates suggests that the parties' strategic advantage is not the cause.

Instead, congressional Democrats' coverage may affect promotional efforts because of the party's status as a congressional minority. Unlike the Republican majority, congressional Democrats lacked extensive formal powers to shape the congressional agenda and thereby use the legislative process to win media coverage of preferred issues and arguments. Accordingly, the Democrats had to promote their messages directly to the news media, with varying degrees of success. The extent of their success helped determine whether the flow of coverage focused largely on the GOP majority's message, or presented a more balanced mix of Republican and Democratic messages. Since the minority's varying success in winning coverage helped determine the balance of that coverage, legislators from both parties used the minority's coverage when making subsequent decisions about whether to promote the party message. In both debates, coverage of congressional Democrats and their message encouraged both GOP and Democratic legislators to promote their message more frequently. Of course, this feedback did not continue indefinitely. In the supplemental debate, Republicans eventually gave up on their message and conceded victory to the Democrats. In the debate over the partial birth abortion ban, the Senate defeat of the Democratic alternatives led many in the party to concede victory to the Republicans.

The feedback from press coverage had less effect on the outcome of the partial birth abortion debate. Unlike in the supplemental debate, passage of a partial birth abortion ban was very likely; roll call votes from previous years indicated majority support for a ban in both chambers of Congress. Uncertainty in the partial birth abortion debate arose from two factors: which version of a ban would pass, and whether coalition supporting the ban was large enough to overturn a likely veto by Clinton. Senate Democrats hoped that Daschle's alternative ban would win majority support and replace the version proposed by Santorum. Senate Republicans hoped to win a veto-proof majority for Santorum's ban. During the

Senate debate, both sides pursued these goals both by publicly promoting their messages and by privately lobbying individual senators. But, news coverage of the debate failed to provide a sufficient boost to either side. Daschle's alternative failed, and the Republicans fell three votes shy of a veto-proof margin.

Overall, the partial birth abortion debate favored congressional Republicans in a number of ways. The party made more public statements of their message and received more news coverage during much of the debate. The Republicans' public statements appeared to drive Democrats' promotional efforts, as well as win press coverage more effectively. All these effects helped strengthen the Republicans' preexisting advantage in the debate. Notably, reporters appeared to narrow this advantage by providing more balanced coverage than one would expect from politicians' public statements. The combined coverage of this debate and of the supplemental debate suggests that reporters are more concerned with balancing their coverage than with biasing that coverage in favor of one party.

The Republicans' overall advantage in the partial birth abortion debate does not emerge in debates over other issues in Congress. In particular, the annual debates about the federal budget offer neither party a consistently clear advantage. Instead, the budget debates provide opportunities for each party to focus media and public attention on aspects of the budget that favor their electoral and policy interests. To illustrate these opportunities and how politicians take advantage of them, the next two sections investigate the budget debates in 1997 and 2003.

5.2.3. The 1997 Budget Debate

As described in previous chapters, budgetary politics in 1997 offered both parties numerous opportunities to promote their priorities, issues, and arguments, thereby furthering broader electoral and policy goals. The actual promotion and corresponding coverage suggest that congressional Republicans seized advantage most effectively. Their advantage appears closely tied to the partisan alignment of the legislative and executive branches in 1997.

That year's budget debate fell into three stages. First, the preliminary negotiations over the budget began with the start of the congressional session in January and extended through the first week in April. During this period, politicians from both parties submitted a number of proposals related to the budget, many of which became part of the eventual budget agreement. Most notably, President Clinton released his proposal for the federal budget on February 6. Republicans in Congress declared the President's budget "alive on arrival," a particularly noteworthy assessment given the intense budget disagreements of the preceding two years. As noted above, GOP legislators wished to reach agreement on a federal budget in 1997, which encouraged them to be more receptive to Clinton's budget. In addition, that budget contained fiscal proposals, such as tax and spending cuts, that congressional Republicans could support. On the other hand, Democrats in Congress responded warily to the President's budget, out of concern that Clinton would sacrifice Democratic principles in order to reach a budget agreement with Republicans.

These varied responses find illustration in the politicians' promotion of their messages, as summarized in Table 5.1. Congressional Republicans were much more vocal, averaging 232% more statements than Democratic legislators. The Republicans in Congress actively discussed the President's budget, emphasizing the issues and arguments in the GOP message. Their Democratic colleagues less actively engaged in the debate at this stage. The content of the President's budget made it harder for Democratic legislators to promote their message. As a congressional minority, Democratic legislators could and had to rely on the highest-ranking member of their party (President Clinton) to further their interests in budget negotiations. But, the President made relatively few public mentions of those interests, averaging only 20% of the congressional Democrats' mentions.

News coverage during this stage reflected and magnified the GOP's promotional advantage. GOP legislators averaged 250% more coverage than their Democratic counterparts. In contrast, President Clinton actually averaged 23% fewer stories than congressional Democrats did. At this initial stage of the budget debate, congressional Republicans enjoyed substantial advantages in promotion and coverage, while Democrats in Congress and the White House failed to mount an equivalent effort furthering their own issues and arguments. Notably, journalists' coverage mirrored the Republicans' promotional advantage; the news stories did not frame the debate as more balanced than the competing politicians' public statements suggested. During this stage of the budget debate, politicians appeared less seriously engaged in negotiations. In an implicit acknowledgement of the preliminary nature of the negotiations, journalists made less of an effort to balance the competing messages in their coverage. This explanation finds additional support during subsequent stages of the debate, as politicians engaged in more serious negotiations, and reporters changed their coverage.

The second stage of the debate began on April 7, when leaders from both parties and branches began high-level negotiations in hopes of reaching a budget deal by April 15, the statutory deadline for congressional passage of a budget resolution. Negotiators failed to meet the deadline, and discussions continued throughout April. On May 2 Democrats and Republicans announced the outlines of an agreement to balance the federal budget within five years. Specifying the details of that agreement required two more weeks of negotiations, and Congress did not pass a final budget resolution until June 5.

Throughout these developments, congressional Democrats expressed increasing concern about the sacrifices of Democratic principles required to reach an agreement with Republicans, and the general exclusion of congressional Democrats from the most important aspects of the negotiations. More than half the Democratic caucus in the House wrote the President to argue for adding cuts in defense spending to those proposed for domestic programs. As Representative Barney Frank (D-MA4) argued, "The president is making a fundamental mistake. You can't leave the military off the table." (*CQ Almanac* 1997, 2–22) To assuage these concerns, Clinton met with House and Senate Democratic leaders in late April. But, the Democratic legislators remained less committed than Clinton to reaching a deal. After an April 24 meeting with the President, Senator Frank Lautenberg (D-NJ) expressed little concern about missing the April 15 deadline: "Deadlines here come and go. The discussion can go on for a while" (*CQ Almanac* 1997, 2–22). And on the eve of the initial May 1 announcement of the budget deal, Senate Minority Leader Tom Daschle (D-SD) voiced frustration shared by many in his caucus:

> It's atrocious that deals would be cut and that decisions would be made behind closed doors with very, very few, if anybody, knowing what this whole package looks like. It's going to take several weeks before I can persuade my colleagues that this is a budget that they ought to support. I'm not going to sell it if I don't believe in it. (*CQ Almanac* 1997, 2–22)

On the next day, the two parties' separate events announcing the budget deal provided more evidence of the varying enthusiasm for the agreement. At the Republican event in the Capitol rotunda, enthusiastic cheering and applause greeted party leaders, who jubilantly described how the deal furthered basic Republican principles of a balanced budget in five years, significant and permanent tax cuts, and an extension of Medicare solvency. As House GOP Conference chairman John Boehner

(R-OH8) put it, "To our base, to our folks, those three issues are paramount." (*CQ Almanac* 1997, 2–22). The Democratic event, held in the midst of a party retreat in Maryland, was much more restrained. President Clinton's glowing description of the budget agreement generated only polite and restrained clapping; several commentators described the event as somber. (*CQ Almanac* 1997, 2–22). On May 2, the day when negotiators announced the agreement, the measures of message promotion contain 49 public mentions of the Republican message by GOP legislators. Democratic legislators only made five mentions of their party's budget message.

During this second stage of the budget debate, both parties increased their promotional efforts, reflecting the more intense negotiations and actual agreements of this stage. Congressional Republicans' public statements were now 279% greater than those of Democratic legislators, while President Clinton averaged only 14%. Reflecting the more intense negotiations and greater promotional efforts, news coverage also rose. The Republican mean was 205% greater than that of congressional Democrats; the President's average was 77%. While congressional Democrats still faced substantial disadvantages in promotion, they faced a smaller disadvantage in coverage. President Clinton also won more coverage for himself and the Democratic message than one would expect from his promotional efforts. These patterns provide further evidence of journalists providing more balanced accounts of politicians' statements than the politicians' promotional efforts would suggest.

After passing the budget resolution on June 5, Congress and the President entered a third stage of negotiations. The resolution provided for two reconciliation resolutions, one to implement tax cuts and a second to implement spending cuts. Congress and the president spent June and July working out the details of these bills, with Congress passing the final versions at the end of July. The negotiations often pitted the leaders in each party against ideologically extreme legislators. Democrats appeared particularly split about whether to support legislation implementing the budget deal. In House deliberations about tax cuts, no Democrats voted for the legislation in committee. In the Senate the Finance Committee reported a tax bill with the support of all Democratic and Republican members except conservative senators Don Nickles (R-OK) and Phil Gramm (R-TX). But outside the committee, liberal Democrats attacked their more conservative party colleagues on the committee. Senator Paul Wellstone (D-MN) charged that "[i]f Democrats don't stand for tax breaks for working families more than for the wealthy, then what do Democrats stand for?" (*CQ Almanac* 1997, 2–22). The passage of the spending reconciliation bill revealed similar misgivings among Democrats. In the House vote on the bill, 154 Democrats voted against the bill and their party leaders. Only seven Republicans opposed the bill. The final Senate vote produced a similar split. Twenty-one Democrats voted for the bill, while 24 voted "no." Only three GOP senators voted against the bill.

Additional evidence of the varying partisan responses to the budget deal emerges from the patterns of promotion during this third stage of budget deliberations. Democratic legislators were only slightly more active than during the previous stage. Such a small increase, occurring despite the greater importance of the later stage in the legislative process, provides another indication of the congressional Democrats' lack of enthusiasm for the budget agreement. Congressional Republicans, in contrast, substantially increased their promotional efforts, reaching 343% of the congressional Democrats' average. These more numerous statements reflect the Republicans' greater enthusiasm for the budget deal and greater involvement in writing the details of that deal. President Clinton only slightly increased his public statements of the Democratic message, thus doing little to help Democrats overcome their promotional disadvantage.

Fortunately for the Democrats, congressional Republicans held a smaller advantage in news coverage. GOP members won much more coverage, but their mean was only 180% greater than that of congressional Democrats. The smaller Republican advantage in coverage further indicates that the news media was attempting to provide more balanced coverage than the promotional efforts would suggest. In addition, President Clinton drew on average 95% of the congressional Democrats' stories, which also helped the Democrats in the battle over news coverage.

The patterns of promotion and coverage thus far paint a picture of Republicans dominating the budget debate in 1997. A similar picture emerges from the VAR model of this debate. The upper-right portion of Figure 5.1 presents the estimated cumulative effects from this model. Congressional Democrats, GOP legislators, and the President each were able to turn mentions of their party message into news stories. The impact of a single mention was strongest for the President (8.3 stories) and weakest for congressional Republicans (.9 stories). If congressional Democrats made one mention of their party message, they won 2.7 stories mentioning that message and at least one Democratic legislator. The same Democratic mention also boosted stories referring to congressional

Republicans and their message (6.1 stories), and stories mentioning President Clinton and the Democratic message (2.8).

Congressional Democrats' promotional efforts may have been more broadly effective for two reasons. First, the patterns are consistent with reporters giving relatively more coverage to Democratic statements in an effort to provide a more balanced account of the budget debate. Second, the congressional Democrats sometimes went beyond their party message to express concern about President Clinton and his efforts to reach agreement with Republicans. This expression of intra-party conflict likely made the statements of congressional Democrats more newsworthy and effective in generating coverage. Both reasons assign the Democrats' greater effectiveness to causes other than their own careful focus on a well-crafted message.

The VAR model for the 1997 budget debate again revealed evidence of Democratic news coverage feeding back to influence politicians' promotional efforts. Each mention of congressional Democrats and their message led Republicans to mention their message .8 more times. The Republicans' responsiveness again may result from concern about whether coverage of the debate would feature both sides equally. The Republicans' majority status and corresponding formal powers helped them win coverage of their own message. Stories about the Democratic message threatened the GOP's dominance of coverage, and the Republicans responded by promoting their own message.

The news coverage of the budget debate also fed back to influence the policy process, but in more subtle ways than occurred in the supplemental debate. One example of this feedback occurred after the two parties responded to the early May budget deal, as described above. A Democratic staffer summarized the two parties' contrasting responses at press conferences after the announcement: "The Democrats looked like they had gone to a funeral, and the Republicans were proclaiming all these greater victories" (Personal notes, May 13, 1997). The contrasting responses were central to many news accounts of the budget agreement.

Democratic leaders feared that such coverage would weaken their influence in future negotiations about implementing the agreement. The same staffer described the party leaders' reaction: "The Democratic leadership doesn't want this spin on the budget, so they're setting up budget events to give us ownership over the Democratic parts of the budget agreement" (Personal notes, May 13, 1997). At a subsequent meeting between Senate Democrats and executive branch officials, a White House staff member explained how this ownership would strengthen the

Democrats' negotiating position: "We can define the tax cut if we take strong ownership of all the tax cuts going to middle class families. Rather than the Democrats being boxed into being for or against a tax cut, we can frame it as being for a middle class tax cut, or one that explodes the deficit for years to come" (Personal notes, May 14, 1997). In hopes of neutralizing their unenthusiastic initial response to the budget agreement, the Democrats planned a series of press events designed to emphasize their own achievements in the agreement. Establishing this "ownership" would help the Democrats define the terms of subsequent budget negotiations, as well as their outcome.

Overall, the 1997 budget debate revealed evidence of both parties shaping news coverage. Congressional Republicans promoted their budget message more frequently and received relatively more coverage of that message. At the same time, Democrats, particularly in Congress, appeared more adept at converting mentions of their party message into news coverage. This greater effectiveness, however, may have resulted from journalists' efforts to present balanced accounts of the debate, and from the Democrats' intraparty conflict.

These dynamics of promotion and coverage appear linked to partisan alignments in Congress and the White House. Congressional Republicans could not rely on their control of both chambers to dominate the legislative process, because the Democrats controlled the White House. To counter Clinton's use of the presidential bully pulpit, Republicans had to promote their own arguments and issues publicly and frequently. While the minority Democrats also had an incentive to promote their party message aggressively, President Clinton's compromises with Republicans appear to have discouraged Democratic legislators and lowered their support for the balanced budget deal.

5.2.4. The 2003 Budget Debate

The budget debate in 2003 offered a different alignment of political power than existed in 1997. While the Republicans still controlled both chambers of Congress in 2003, the GOP had also gained the White House after George Bush's victory in the 2000 presidential race. This different alignment appeared to encourage different patterns of message promotion and coverage by members of Congress.

Despite the more extensive Republican control in 2003, the budget debate that year followed a path similar to that of 1997: Congress first approved a budget resolution in late spring, followed by the passage of a tax cut in early summer. Compared to their pronouncements in 1997, Republicans in 2003 appeared less concerned about reducing the federal budget deficit and more concerned about passing a tax cut and reducing the size of government. The new focus worked to their favor.

The first stage of the budget debate lasted from January 1 until the week of March 3, when budget committees in both chambers passed a budget resolution. During this initial period, congressional Democrats dominated message promotion and coverage. Congressional Republicans averaged only 25% of the Democratic average. President Bush's average was only 5% of that of the Democrats. The Democratic advantage in promotion narrowed somewhat in news coverage. Here, the mean for the congressional GOP was 68% of the Democratic average; President Bush averaged 93%. Overall, the stories mentioning congressional Republicans and their president came closer in number to those of the Democrats, particularly in comparison to their public statements. This narrowing provides further evidence of the news media's effort to present balanced news accounts.

These patterns continued during the remainder of the 2003 budget debate. During the second stage in which Congress debated and passed a budget resolution (March 10 through April 13), Democrats still promoted their party message much more frequently than congressional Republicans or Bush did. News coverage was again more balanced. The Democrats' daily average was only somewhat greater than those of GOP legislators and President Bush (69% and 79% of the Democratic mean, respectively).

The third stage of the budget debate focused on President Bush's tax cut proposal. After approving a budget resolution on April 11, Congress turned its attention to filling in the details of Bush's tax cut proposal. GOP senators and representatives disagreed about whether the tax cuts were limited to $350 billion or could expand up to $550 billion. While the House reconciliation bill cut taxes by a total of $550 billion, both houses eventually approved a $350 billion bill on May 23. As each chamber moved the reconciliation bill through committee and floor consideration, Democrats continued to dominate promotion and coverage of the issue, although their edge over Republicans narrowed. The promotional mean for congressional Republicans increased to 35% of the Democratic average. President Bush also spoke out more frequently on budgetary matters (7% of the Democrats' mean). In news coverage, Democrats enjoyed a continued but still smaller advantage over congressional Republicans. President Bush's coverage was 84% of that of the Democrats.

These continued Democratic advantages may have proved more influential in the Senate than the House. In the latter chamber, the majority's tighter control over the legislative process made it easier to resist short-term pressures from outside the chamber, such as news coverage and corresponding contacts by interest groups and constituents. The greater autonomy of individual senators reduces the majority party's control of the Senate legislative process, making that process more susceptible to short-term influences such as public relations and media coverage. During the final days of deliberation of the tax cut bill, senators defied House pressure to raise the total amount of tax cuts to $550 billion. News coverage of Democratic arguments about "reckless tax cuts" may have encouraged senators to insist on the smaller amount of tax cuts. This encouragement is another example of how news coverage feeds back to influence the policy process.

After passing Bush's tax cut bill, Congress immediately moved to a fourth stage of the budget debate. The Center on Budget and Policy Priorities (a liberal think tank) charged that the new tax bill excluded millions of low-income families from receiving a child tax credit that the bill created. Democrats immediately pounced, charging that the omission confirmed their strongest arguments against the Republican tax bill. In response, the Senate passed corrective legislation on June 5. The House followed suit on June 12 but added a number of additional tax breaks to the legislation. House Democrats offered numerous motions to instruct House conferees to agree to Senate language on the child tax credit. But, Republicans leaders never named a conference committee to resolve differences between the two bills, despite continuing Democratic attacks on the issue (*CQ Almanac* 2003, 17–11).

In public relations during this stage (May 26 to August 1), Democrats focused on the child tax credit and again enjoyed a promotional advantage. Congressional Republicans' average was only 40% of that of Democrats; President Bush only reached 12%. News coverage again gave Democrats a smaller advantage. GOP legislators won on average 61% of the Democrats' coverage, while President Bush won 86%. During this stage of the debate, public pressure by congressional Democrats forced Republicans to address the child tax credit. With control of the legislative and executive branches, the GOP could conceivably have ignored the Democrats' demands. But, the Democrats won extensive coverage of the inequity of the tax credit provision, intensifying pressure on the

Republicans and forcing them to act. The narrower Democratic advantage in promotion and coverage (compared to earlier stages) certainly helped the GOP resist the Democratic pressure. But, congressional Republicans still responded to news coverage of the Democrats' attacks.

These patterns create an overall picture of a budget debate in which Democrats promoted their party message much more frequently than the Republican discussed their own. Unlike six years earlier, the Republicans in 2003 controlled both the legislative and executive branches. As a result, the party's office holders controlled all stages of the legislative process and could avoid public disputes about control of that process. In fact, such public disputes would arguably enhance the minority Democrats' influence. Reflecting this partisan alignment between the two branches, congressional Republicans promoted their budget message much less frequently than the Democrats did.

Despite this disparity in public relations, the news media provided coverage that was more evenly balanced between the two parties' issues and arguments. If Republicans made fewer public statements, and if both parties won similar levels of coverage, one might conclude that the Republicans more effectively turned their public statements into news stories. Curiously, the VAR model of this debate (presented in the lower-right corner of Figure 5.1) suggests a different conclusion. The cumulative effects in this model indicate few links between promotion and coverage in the 2003 debate.

Each of the President's mentions of his party's message produces a decline in Democrats' promotion of their message. Coverage of both congressional parties and their messages lead to more stories mentioning President Bush and his message. Democratic stories also encourage congressional Democrats to mention their party message more frequently. The limited links between promotion and coverage contrast sharply with the results from the other three debates. In the VAR models for those debates, a mention of a party message by a legislative party or president always leads to more news stories mentioning that party or president and their message. In the 2003 budget debate, such a link does not exist for either congressional party or President Bush. Because the news media still produced stories containing both parties' messages, why is there no direct causal link between the promotional efforts and the news coverage?

The lack of such a link appears tied to the outbreak of the Iraq War. This conflict seized the attention of elected officials, journalists, and the public, often relegating other issues to insignificance. The budget appeared to be one such issue. The top portion of Table 5.2 presents

TABLE 5.2. *Average Daily Promotion and Coverage in the 2003 Budget Debate, by Month*

	Average					
	Events			Stories		
	Cong. Dems.	Cong. Reps.	Pres.	Cong. Dems.	Cong. Reps.	Pres.
January	10.65	1.97	0.29	54.58	42.10	53.48
February	2.21	0.82	0.36	38.79	22.43	34.82
March	2.10	0.94	0.16	29.68	19.97	23.77
April	5.07	0.40	0.13	29.53	24.20	22.07
May	5.39	2.00	0.26	43.23	37.48	38.45
June	4.83	0.97	0.50	38.90	22.90	34.20
July	2.52	1.94	0.42	26.84	16.71	21.45
	Standard Deviation/Average					
	Events			Stories		
	Cong. Dems.	Cong. Reps.	Pres.	Cong. Dems.	Cong. Reps.	Pres.
January	2.28	2.58	2.98	0.46	0.70	0.65
February	1.94	2.07	3.34	0.45	0.51	0.54
March	1.69	2.66	3.95	0.35	0.53	0.42
April	2.54	2.75	3.81	0.37	0.48	0.47
May	2.25	2.37	2.82	0.36	0.37	0.33
June	1.71	1.81	2.77	0.25	0.39	0.32
July	3.00	3.25	2.87	0.38	0.38	0.47

the average number (by month) of budget-related statements and news stories for congressional Democrats, congressional Republicans, and President Bush. After a high in January, both statements and stories dropped off significantly in subsequent months, particularly during March when the conflict in Iraq reached full intensity. The promotion and coverage increased somewhat during May when Congress and President Bush passed the tax cuts.

The outbreak of the Iraq War thus brought lower levels of public statements and news stories about the budget debate. The lower levels of activity could make it harder to link promotion and coverage in the VAR model. But, such a link should conceivably exist even with fewer public statements and news stories. The lack of a link appears to result from a change in news coverage: after the war broke out, politicians appeared to continue promoting their public statements, albeit at a lower level, and the news media appeared to grow less responsive to those statements.

Consider the extent of variation in statements and stories, presented in the lower portion of Table 5.2. This part of the table presents for each month the standard deviation of each measure of statements or stories, divided by its respective mean. The standard deviation captures how much the measure varies from day to day. Dividing the standard deviation by the mean controls for the magnitude of the measure in a particular month. If a measure lists a relatively large number of stories during a particular month, the standard deviation of that measure is likely to be relatively larger, regardless of the actual variation in the measure.

As Table 5.2 indicates, politicians' statements varied at similar levels before and after the outbreak of the Iraq War. From January to March, the variation in congressional Democrats' statements fell from 2.28 to 1.69, a decline of 26%. But, congressional Republicans increased the variation in their statements, from 2.58 to 2.66 (an increase of 3%). President Bush increased even more, from 2.98 to 3.95 (an increase of 33%). These patterns suggest that even after the war's outbreak the politicians continued to promote their party messages on some days while not mentioning those messages on other days. The overall level of promotion declined after January, but the politicians still appeared to be following a normal pattern of promoting their messages more frequently on some days than others.

The news coverage of the budget debate followed a different pattern. The variation in stories about congressional Democrats fell from its January high of .46 to .35 in March (a decline of 24%). For congressional Republicans, the variation in coverage fell from .70 to .53 between January and March (a decline of 24%). The stories about President Bush also declined in variation during this period, from .65 to .42 (a decline of 35%). In January the news coverage about both parties and their budget messages varied a great deal, with lots of stories on one day and fewer stories on the next. Such variation in coverage is more likely to reflect variation in the politicians' promotional efforts, as the reporters time their stories to cover politicians' newsworthy public statements on a particular day. When the war broke out in March, the variation in coverage declined substantially and remained relatively low for the duration of the analysis. Reporters' stories about the budget debate appeared at a more constant and less varied rate, which made them less responsive to the continued variation in politicians' public statements about the debate. Emerging as the Iraq War broke out, the lower variation in coverage suggests that the lack of a link in the VAR model between promotion and coverage appears tied to this conflict. With public attention focused on the war, journalists appeared to move to a more constant and less responsive mode of reporting about the budget debate.

This section has examined overall patterns of promotion and coverage in the four specific debates. The evidence above supports many of the expectations developed in the first part of the chapter. When covering the debates, reporters' stories mirrored the ebb and flow of the politicians' public statements. The coverage reflected both the frequency of public statements and the politicians' institutional influence, particularly that of the president.

In addition, the overall coverage across the debates displayed no consistent bias in favor of one party. Instead, reporters always added balanced to their coverage during important stages of debate, beyond what one would expect on the basis of promotion. This periodic balancing of coverage makes sense. Reporters often bring to their coverage narrative structures containing "clear chronological markers" of important, newsworthy points or periods (Lawrence 2000, 97). Important periods of debate, such as floor votes, exemplify such markers and may attract greater coverage. These stages of the policy process often contain predictable, clear structures, which allow clearer and more efficient reporting. Such qualities are lacking in earlier stages, such bill introduction or committee deliberation, or in later stages, such as policy implementation. As a result, the reporters may use different news frames across the stages of policy making (Cook 1996, Lawrence 2000, Lawrence and Birkland 2004).

Finally, news coverage of the debates fed back to shape politicians' promotional efforts. In the supplemental debate, the Democratic advantage in news coverage effectively undermined Republican opposition to a clean disaster relief bill. In the 1997 budget debate, news coverage accurately captured Democrats' lukewarm response to the balanced budget deal; in response, the Democrats recalibrated their party message to take stronger ownership of the agreement. The VAR models also revealed feedback, almost exclusively from coverage of congressional Democrats and their message. Politicians from both parties may have used the minority party's coverage as an indicator of the balance of coverage of a debate, which can in turn guide subsequent decisions about whether to promote the party message.

To uncover these patterns of coverage and promotion, I combined news stories from 55 different outlets. As the first part of this chapter suggests, coverage of the parties' messages could vary across these outlets, depending on the political leanings of their editors and audiences. The next section explores these links.

5.3. PARTISAN BIAS ACROSS NEWS OUTLETS

As the first step in this exploration, I calculated how frequently individual news outlets covered the two congressional parties and their messages in the four debates. The top portion of Table 5.3 summarizes that coverage in the twelve national outlets included in my analysis. For each debate and outlet, the table presents the average number of stories mentioning each congressional party and message per day, as well as the Democratic percentage or share of the sum of both party averages. Observers often argue that the *New York Times* and the *Washington Post* provide more liberal coverage (Aronoff 2006, Page 1996, Pew Research Center for the People and the Press 2004, Verner 2006), while FOX News and the *Washington Times* display a conservative tilt (Hart 2003, Pew Research Center for the People and the Press 2004, Sellers 2000). The results in Table 5.3 provide little support for such partisan reputations.

The *New York Times* provided the most Democratic coverage in the 1997 budget debate (33%), but nearly the least Democratic coverage in the debate over the supplemental (46%). The *Washington Post* gave the most attention to the Democratic message in the 2003 budget debate (65%), but the least attention to Democratic arguments in the supplemental debate (44%). Across the six papers' coverage of the supplemental debate, the *Washington Times* ranked second in the proportion of coverage mentioning congressional Democrats and their message. In the partial birth abortion debate, the paper's ranking was dead last. Regardless of reputation, no individual print outlet provided uniformly greater coverage of either party across the four debates.

In the budget debates, four television outlets (ABC, CBS, CNN, and NBC) provided similar coverage to that of the print outlets and *NPR*. A notable exception was FOX News in 2003, whose coverage paid the least attention to the Democratic message of all twelve outlets. This pattern was consistent with the outlet's conservative reputation. In the other two more specific debates, the first four television outlets diverged in their coverage. When Congress was debating the partial birth abortion ban, the four television outlets provided less Democratic coverage (a mean of 31%) than the seven other outlets did (a mean of 54%). The difference in coverage may have resulted from congressional Republicans' use of

TABLE 5.3. *Average Daily Coverage of Congressional Democrats and Republicans, by Outlet and Debate*

	1997 Budget			Partial Birth Abortion			Supplemental			2003 Budget		
	Dem.	Rep.	Dem. Share	Dem.	Rep.	Dem. Share	Dem.	Rep.	Dem. Share	Dem.	Rep.	Dem. Share
Individual national outlets												
ABC	.41	1.14	26%	.04	.05	44%	.12	.06	67%	.43	.59	42%
CBS	.64	2.92	18%	0	.01	0%	.19	.16	54%	.40	.48	45%
CNN	2.81	7.22	28%	.22	.17	56%	.54	.23	70%	3.65	3.66	50%
FOX										1.09	1.72	39%
NBC	.55	1.84	23%	.02	.07	22%	.24	.05	83%	.53	.62	46%
NPR	1.31	2.29	36%	.12	.10	55%	.23	.15	61%	1.41	.98	59%
Los Angeles Times	.99	2.34	30%	.05	.04	56%	.15	.08	65%	1.64	1.41	54%
New York Times	1.24	2.54	33%	.16	.13	55%	.11	.13	46%	2.86	2.32	55%
Roll Call	.62	1.38	31%	.03	.01	75%	.20	.18	53%	.84	.84	50%
USA Today	.62	1.86	25%	.04	.05	44%	.05	.06	45%	.69	.77	47%
Washington Post	1.56	4.90	24%	.08	.07	53%	.24	.30	44%	.60	.32	65%
Washington Times	1.00	4.00	20%	.11	.19	37%	.23	.17	58%	1.66	1.56	52%
Local outlets with												
Dem.-leaning endorsements	8.94	25.42	26%	.65	.61	52%	1.19	1.16	51%	20.79	13.08	61%
Rep.-leaning endorsements	4.82	15.92	23%	.39	.43	48%	.72	.56	56%	11.16	5.94	65%
Local outlets in												
Dem.-leaning markets	10.76	32.26	25%	.71	.63	53%	1.73	1.47	54%	15.88	8.32	66%
Rep.-leaning markets	5.26	19.28	21%	.30	.36	45%	1.10	1.02	52%	6.08	3.23	65%

Note: For each debate, the "Dem." column contains the average daily number of stories in each outlet (or group of outlets) that mentioned congressional Democrats and their message in the particular debate. The "Rep." column contains the corresponding number for congressional Republicans and their message. The "Dem. Share" column is the "Dem." value divided by the sum of the "Dem." and "Rep." values.

graphic and visually engaging images of fetuses or the actual abortion procedure. Democrats could not employ similarly graphic images in promoting their message in the debate, which apparently made it harder for that message to win coverage. Democrats won relatively more coverage for their message in the print outlets and on National Public Radio. In these outlets, visual images appear to play a less important role in determining coverage.

The fortunes of the parties and their messages switched during the debate over the supplemental. Here, the television outlets provided substantially more Democratic coverage (a mean of 69%) than their competitors in print and radio did (a mean of 53%). Television editors and reporters may have found the Democratic message in the supplemental debate more attractive because of its compelling visual images. Unlike the relatively dry budget debates about levels of taxing and spending, the supplemental debate brought gripping images of flooding and fires to local and national news coverage. Congressional Democrats encouraged the focus on these images, because these images helped emphasize the need to pass the disaster relief as soon as possible. The emphasis also brought into question why congressional Republicans were attaching unrelated provisions to the supplemental and slowing its passage. The visual aspects of the Democrats' message appear to have won greater coverage of that message in television news, compared to coverage in the other national outlets. Thus, the television outlets devoted more attention visually engaging messages (Graber 2006).

Overall, the twelve national outlets' varying coverage largely failed to follow any liberal or conservative patterns. This lack of partisan bias among national media is consistent with the overall body of research on this topic (Cook 2001, D'Allessio and Allen 2000, Erikson and Tedin 2007). It is also important, however, to explore whether local newspapers vary in their partisan bias.[20] Their greater number creates the potential for more variation in the structure of outlets and their local context (Shaw and Sparrow 1999). Each of the four debates offers the opportunity to assess whether Democratic- and Republican-leaning local papers offered similar or different coverage of the same events in the debate.

[20] The local newspapers in this analysis often appear to use the national outlets as guides in creating news stories (Page 1995, Shaw and Sparrow 1999). In VAR models, national outlets' coverage of party messages consistently drove or "caused" coverage of those messages in local outlets.

It can be difficult to determine the political leaning of an outlet. Employees and owners often hesitate to reveal their own political leanings, hoping to avoid (or at least minimize) charges of bias against their news coverage. But, many newspapers regularly make political statements on editorial pages. To capture the political leaning of newspapers in this analysis, I examined each outlet's endorsements in recent statewide elections in its state. As noted earlier, such pronouncements may reflect the political preferences of only the outlet's editors, who make up only one part of the overall news organization. The outlet may consequently claim that the endorsements in no way influence its coverage of elections and other issues. Nonetheless, the endorsements provide concrete evidence of an outlet's editorial leanings, which one can compare to its coverage to assess whether the two are truly separate (Dalton et al. 1998, Kahn and Kenney 2002).

I calculated levels of news coverage in local outlets endorsing Democratic candidates, and in those endorsing Republican ones.[21] The middle section of Table 5.3 summarizes the coverage in the two types of outlets. For each party's message in each debate, the average level of coverage is higher in outlets with Democratic-leaning endorsements. These outlets appear to provide more stories about congressional debates, regardless of issue or party. This difference could simply be a result of Democratic-leaning papers being more numerous, but that is not the case. Of the eighty-two local outlets included in the analysis (forty-three from 1997 and thirty-nine from 2003), the number of Democratic-leaning papers (twenty-eight) equals the number of Republican-leaning ones (twenty-eight). The difference in coverage could also result from the Democratic-leaning papers being larger (i.e., publishing more stories on a daily basis), which turns out to be the case. The Democratic-leaning papers averaged a total of 14,030 news stories during the seven-month period of analysis; the mean for the Republican-leaning outlets was 10,965 stories ($p = .04$).

[21] For each outlet, coauthors for another paper (Masi et al. 2006) reviewed election-related articles during October of 1994, 1996, 2000, and 2004. They recorded each endorsement by the outlet of a candidate in a presidential, gubernatorial, or senatorial race in the outlet's state. They then summed the endorsements for the outlet, with each endorsement of a Democratic candidate assigned a -1, and each endorsement of a Republican candidate receiving a 1. The resulting sums ranged from -3 to 3 across the outlets. If an outlet had a negative sum, they categorized that outlet as having made Democratic-leaning endorsements. A positive sum indicated an outlet making Republican-leaning endorsements. Some outlets did not fall into either category because they made no endorsements or an equal number of Democratic and Republican endorsements.

Beyond size, the outlets have a more fundamental difference in their coverage. If one controls for the total number of stories in the outlets (by dividing each day's number of stories mentioning a particular message by the total number of stories appearing that day), the Democratic-leaning outlets provide more coverage of seven of the eight party messages across the four debates. In other words, the Democratic-leaning outlets devote a greater proportion of their coverage to congressional affairs; outlets with more Republican endorsements assign a smaller proportion of their coverage to Congress.

The two groups of outlets displayed greater similarity in their balance of stories mentioning Democratic and Republican messages. If one calculated the Democratic "share" of coverage in each debate and group of outlets,[22] both groups of outlets devoted about one fourth of their 1997 budget coverage to the Democrats and their message (26% and 23%). Six years later the two groups of outlets both gave nearly two thirds of their coverage to the Democrats and their budget message (61% and 65%). In the other two debates, Democrats received about half the coverage in each group of outlets (53%, 45%, 54%, and 52%). The similar patterns of coverage between the two groups suggest that the local papers effectively separate their production of news stories from any endorsements or political leanings of their editorial staff (Dalton et al. 1998, Patterson and Donsbach 1996).

Overall, the Democratic- and Republican-leaning outlets offered different types of coverage, but the difference was not the political bias often charged by critics of the news media. The two groups of outlets provided a similar balance of Democratic and Republican messages in their coverage of each of the four debates. Instead, the quantity of coverage provided the main difference between the two groups. The outlets with more Democratic endorsements produced substantially more stories about both parties' messages in each debate; the Republican-leaning outlets generated fewer such stories.

5.3.1. Markets and Coverage

Characteristics of the news organizations themselves may not be the only cause of variation in coverage. The outlets may also structure

[22] For each debate and group of outlets, the Democratic share is the daily average number of mentions of the Democratic message, divided by the sum of the daily averages of the Democratic and Republican messages.

their coverage in response to their audiences. Democratic voters may prefer to read more about Democratic issues and arguments than those of Republicans. Markets dominated by these voters could reject more balanced or Republican-leaning coverage as politically biased, and could turn to another outlet (see the discussion above of the "hostile media effect"). Conversely, Republican audiences might prefer more coverage of GOP politicians and their messages. These characteristics of audiences could thereby influence coverage, independently of the political leanings of the outlets' owners and employees. The need to attract and maintain an audience creates a separate and distinct influence on outlets' coverage.

To investigate how markets' political leanings shape coverage, I categorized the local outlet's market as Democratic-leaning or Republican-leaning, based on the market's voting in presidential elections.[23] With each group of outlets and markets, I again calculated the number of stories mentioning each message on average each day. The bottom portion of Table 5.3 presents the results of these calculations. Across all four

[23] Calculating each market's presidential vote required defining the market of each outlet and that market's political leaning. Doing so posed several challenges: the market for an outlet often crosses county and state lines. In addition, subscribers to an outlet are not evenly distributed across counties; some counties have lots of readers, while others have only a few. To address these problems, I turned to Audit Bureau of Circulation (ABC) surveys, which indicate the number of subscribers to a particular outlet in each county, across state lines. With the survey capturing which counties are in an outlet's market, I collected for each county the number of Democratic and Republican votes in the 2000 and 2004 presidential elections. I then added up the total votes for each party across the counties in the outlet's market. But before adding the counties' vote totals, I weighted each county's votes by its importance to the outlet's overall audience, as indicated by the percentage of the outlet's total subscribers in that county. Thus, if a county makes up only a small percentage of the outlet's audience, that county's political leanings are relatively less important to the outlet's management attempting to match its coverage to its audience's political leaning. The Democratic and Republican votes in this county will contribute relatively little to the sums of votes for the entire market. On the other hand, the outlet's management will pay more attention to the political leanings of a county with a majority of the outlet's subscribers. Dominating the market, the subscribers in this county will be most likely to notice a balance in coverage that does not fit their political perceptions. Accordingly, the Democratic and Republican votes from this county contribute a relatively largely amount to the vote totals for the overall market. After combining the weighted vote totals for all counties in the outlet's market, I calculated the Republican percentage of the overall vote in each market. Using these vote percentages, I categorized each outlet's market as Republican (with Republican vote percentage greater than 50%) or Democratic (with Republican vote percentage less than 50%). Note that these measures apply only to local outlets and their markets. Consequently, coverage in national outlets is not part of the calculations in the bottom of Table 5.3.

debates, the outlets in Democratic-leaning markets devoted a greater proportion of coverage to the Democratic politicians and messages than outlets in Republican-leaning markets did. The largest difference occurred in the debate over partial birth abortion, where Democratic legislators and their message won 53% of the coverage in outlets in Democratic-leaning markets but only 45% of coverage in outlets in Republican-leaning markets.

A larger and more consistent difference emerges in the amount of coverage that politicians and messages received. In each of the four debates, outlets in Democratic-leaning markets provided substantially more coverage of both parties; newspapers in more Republican markets produced substantially less. To explain the different levels of coverage between the two groups of markets, we can consider other parallel differences between the two groups of markets. Most notably, the Democratic markets tend to be more urban than the GOP markets are. The percentage of population living in urban areas was 91% in the 43 Democratic markets and 84% in the 39 Republican markets ($p = .02$). With greater density of population, urban areas may have greater demand for news. Indeed, the outlets in the Democratic markets averaged a total of 14,790 stories over the seven-month period of analysis; the corresponding mean for Republican markets was 10,054 ($p = .003$). Thus, the differences in coverage between the groups of markets stem at least partially from the larger outlets in the more urban Democratic markets. These outlets produce more stories, both overall and in each of the four debates that are the center of this analysis.

The differences between groups of markets go beyond size, however. After controlling for the size of each outlet in the calculation of daily averages,[24] the differences in coverage still exist. For seven of the eight messages in Table 5.3, outlets in Democratic-leaning markets devote a greater proportion of their coverage to a particular message than outlets in Republican-leaning markets do. More urban outlets appear to provide more news overall, and to devote a greater portion of their coverage to congressional debates. Individuals in urban areas tend to be more educated and read the newspaper more frequently (Erikson and Tedin 2007).

[24] For the Democratic measure, the calculation divides each day's number of stories mentioning the Democratic message by the total number of news stories on any topic appearing on that day in the outlets in Democratic-leaning markets. Averaging the resulting percentages over the seven months of analysis indicates the daily proportion of all stories that mentioned the Democratic message. The corresponding Republican measure has a similar calculation.

The news outlets in these areas appear to be responding to their audience's demand. Conversely, outlets in less urban areas also respond to their audience, but by providing less coverage of congressional affairs. It is important to add that these differences between markets do not appear to encourage a partisan bias in coverage. The partisan balance of coverage substantially differed between Democratic- and Republican-leaning outlets only in the partial birth abortion debate.

So, what leads certain outlets to provide more coverage of both parties' messages, the characteristics of the outlets or those of the outlet's market? The measures of the outlets' editorial leanings and their markets are largely but not perfectly correlated. Of the thirty-two outlets in Democratic-leaning markets, twenty made Democratic-leaning endorsements. Of the twenty-four outlets in Republican-leaning markets, eight made Democratic-leaning endorsements.[25] This lack of perfect correlation provides leverage to assess whether outlet or market characteristics more strongly influence coverage. For six of the eight messages in Table 5.3, splitting the outlets by markets produces a greater difference in coverage between the two categories of outlets. Regression analysis further suggests that market characteristics are more important than outlet characteristics in explaining the coverage. In regression models explaining variation in the outlets' coverage of each message, the measure of each market's presidential vote is significant for seven of the eight messages. The measure of endorsements never reaches significance in the models.[26] While the outlets certainly vary in the coverage they provide, this

[25] The measures of outlets' editorial leanings and their markets' presidential voting are correlated at $r = .29$. It is difficult to determine which factor drives the other, particularly over the short time period of my data. The political leanings of a market are likely to influence the editorial leanings and endorsements of a newspaper in that market; as argued above, the paper can attract more readers by reflecting the ideological leanings of its audience. But over the short term, the editorial endorsements of a paper may influence the voting of its audience (Coombs 1981, Erikson 1976, Robinson 1974). This voting is also subject to influence by many other factors, particularly campaigns.

[26] For each of the eight messages, I estimated a negative binomial regression model. The dependent variables in the models are counts of stories in each outlet, and none of measures are normally distributed (each variable's mean minus two standard deviations produces a negative number). In addition, the counts displayed evidence of over dispersion. The negative binomial model was therefore appropriate. The independent variables in the models included the original endorsement measure, as well as the presidential vote measure and the same vote measure squared. The latter variable is part of the models because the presidential vote measure appeared to have a nonlinear relationship with the measures of coverage. See Masi et al. (2006) for more details.

variation appears to be in response to the market that each outlet is trying to reach.[27]

Overall, this chapter has presented a variety of evidence that undermines charges of politically biased news coverage consistently favoring one party over the other. First, neither party dominated coverage of all four congressional debates. In Table 5.1 the overall patterns of coverage reveal greater news attention for congressional Democrats' messages in the supplemental and 2003 budget debates; congressional Republicans won relatively more coverage for their messages in the debates over partial birth abortion and the 1997 budget.[28] The coverage sometimes favored Democrats and sometimes favored Republicans. Second, the partisan balance of each debate's coverage appeared fairly uniform across outlets, both national and local. For each debate, that balance varied little between outlets and markets favoring each party. Third, the news coverage varied more significantly and consistently in quantity. Markets with more Democratic voters appeared to encourage outlets to provide more coverage of congressional debates, including both parties' messages.

Across the outlets and debates, journalists do not appear to adopt a consistent political bias. But if observers ignore the combined evidence and only consider the coverage of an individual debate in only one outlet, they could easily reach the opposite conclusion. In the 2003 budget debate, for example, congressional Democrats' advantage in news coverage was particularly large in outlets serving Democratic-leaning markets. Readers in these markets could react to the unbalanced coverage by charging these newspapers with a liberal bias. Such a criticism would not be valid. While these papers did provide substantially more coverage of Democratic messages than Republican ones, the causes of the imbalance do not appear to result from the political leanings of the outlets' owners or employees. Instead, an imbalance in the parties' promotional

[27] Another possible influence on media coverage is the supply of political information from the members of Congress representing the area and market in which an outlet is located. Urban areas are more populated and therefore elect more members of Congress, who may in turn promote partisan messages to news outlets in these areas. The local supply of political information does not appear to influence the measures of local coverage in this analysis. In the regression models mentioned immediately above, the number of U.S. House members in an outlet's state is never significantly related to the outlet's coverage of partisan messages. After adding the measure of House members, the market's presidential vote remains significant in seven of the eight models.

[28] If each president's coverage is added to that of his fellow partisans in Congress, each party still holds an advantage in coverage in two of the four debates.

efforts encouraged the disparity in coverage of the parties' messages. In the Democratic-leaning markets, that disparity grew even larger because of those markets' preference for more extensive coverage of congressional debates. Most importantly, the disparity in coverage does not consistently reoccur in other congressional debates. The combined evidence reveals important differences in coverage but no consistent partisan bias.

5.3.2. Sources of News

The analysis in this chapter has focused on explaining the content of the news coverage. Missing from the explanations of coverage and bias is consideration of how different outlets respond to the parties' promotional efforts. These decisions by reporters and editors create another potential avenue for bias, beyond the influence of outlets' political leanings or audiences on overall levels of coverage. Democratic-leaning outlets may respond more favorably to Democratic promotional efforts by providing more coverage of those efforts. Any feedback from news coverage may also vary across outlets, as these same Democratic legislators may pay more attention to coverage in Democratic-leaning outlets.

To investigate these patterns, I estimated (for each debate) a VAR model with six variables: each congressional party's daily number of mentions of its message, and the daily number of stories mentioning each party's legislators and message in outlets in Democratic-leaning and Republican-leaning markets. Figure 5.2 presents the estimated effects that proved significant in each debate's model.

The figure provides mixed evidence of partisan news coverage. Promotional events by members of both parties appear to have greater impact on news coverage in Democratic outlets than in Republican outlets. In three of the four debates, an increase in Democratic events produced a greater surge in the party's coverage in Democratic outlets than in Republican ones. While not large, the differences are consistent across the three debates. The sole exception was the 2003 budget debate, where the Iraq War appeared to sever the link between Democrats' promotional efforts and news coverage. Republican events also produced coverage more effectively in Democratic outlets than Republican ones. In three of four debates, each mention of the GOP message by congressional Republicans led to a greater increase in coverage in Democratic outlets than in Republican ones.

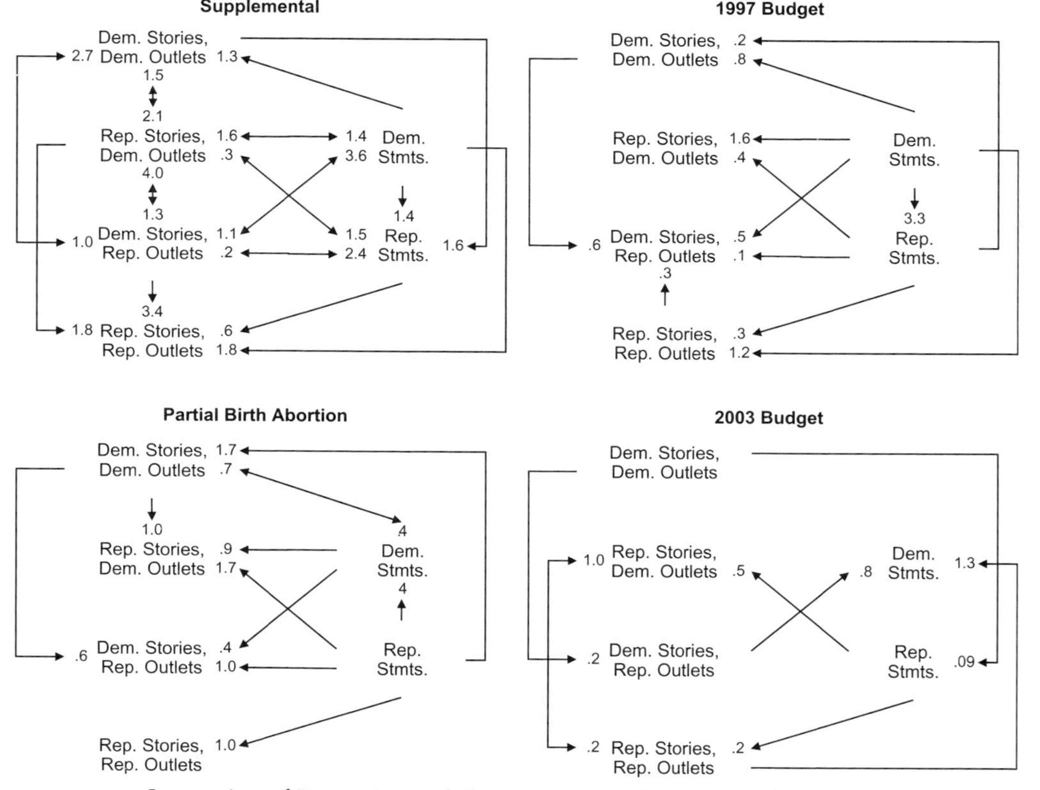

FIGURE 5.2. Interaction of Promotion and Coverage among Partisan Outlets (Markets).

These patterns provide further evidence that Democratic-leaning outlets crafted their news coverage in a manner different from that followed by Republican outlets. Specifically, the Democratic outlets were more responsive than Republican outlets to legislators' events. This finding goes beyond the results in Table 5.3, because the VAR models underlying Figure 5.2 directly measure the outlets' responsiveness to legislators' promotional efforts. The greater congressional coverage in Democratic-leaning outlets is not solely the result of these outlets always covering Congress more frequently and providing more congressional coverage regardless of what Congress does. Instead of framing stories about Congress independently of legislators' actual statements (which is a possible interpretation of the results above), the coverage in Democratic outlets more closely reflects legislators' day-to-day promotional efforts. In turn, Republican outlets are less responsive to these efforts. Thus, Democratic outlets do more than provide more congressional coverage all the time; these outlets are also more responsive to varying public statements in congressional debates. Republican outlets display less responsiveness to variations in those debates.

The importance of Figure 5.2 goes beyond its evidence of newspapers' varying responsiveness to statements and events in Congress. The figure also suggests how the papers may exert their own influence. The initial impact may occur among the outlets themselves, as news stories in one outlet may encourage coverage in another outlet. Figure 5.2 suggests that of the four types of coverage (Democratic and Republican messages in Democratic-leaning and Republican-leaning outlets), the most influential were stories about Democrats and their party message in Democratic-leaning outlets.

This type of story significantly influenced several other types of coverage. Most notably, an increase in Democratic stories in Democratic outlets produced a subsequent increase in this type of story in Republican outlets, during all four debates. The same increase in Democratic stories in Democratic outlets also led to the same outlets producing more stories mentioning the Republican message (in two debates). Each of the other types of coverage exerted little or no influence in this manner.

These patterns suggest that the diffusion of party messages in congressional debates may not be uniform. Readers of Democratic-leaning publications may first encounter the Democratic message in news coverage of a congressional debate. These readers subsequently learn of the Republican message in the debate, but the initial exposure to the Democratic message may shape their perception of the debate and make them more skeptical of the Republican message. In addition, Republican outlets may create their coverage of congressional debates in response to Democratic outlets' stories about the Democratic message in those debates. This influence of Democratic outlets may again allow them to influence news coverage of Congress, by drawing attention to certain debates while ignoring others.

As noted earlier, Democratic outlets provide more coverage than Republican outlets of both parties' messages in congressional debates. In this respect, coverage in the Democratic and Republican outlets differs in a nonpartisan manner. But, the dynamic interaction among the types of coverage indicates a more partisan difference in coverage. Democratic outlets' stories about the Democrats' messages appear to influence other types of coverage, and this influence may allow the Democrats' messages to set initial public perceptions of congressional debates and thereby shape the progression of those debates.

In addition to the interaction among outlets, news coverage may also feed back to influence the promotional efforts of members of Congress. Stories mentioning congressional Democrats and their messages appear particularly influential. Across the four debates in Figure 5.2, six of the nine instances of feedback come from Democratic coverage. Democratic and Republican outlets produce these effects with similar frequency and no discernable difference between the types of outlets. As suggested earlier, it makes sense to focus on coverage of the congressional minority if one is concerned with the balance of messages flowing to the public. Given the majority's relative ease of winning coverage, the extent of the minority party's coverage can indicate which congressional party is winning a public debate.

Figures 5.1 and 5.2 thus show how members of Congress altered their promotional efforts in response to news coverage. To gauge which side was ahead in a public debate, legislators appeared to focus on the minority Democrats' success in winning coverage. If congressional Democrats were able to win coverage, they could counteract the GOP majority's message and create a two-sided flow of information through the news media.

5.4. LESSONS FROM THE FOUR DEBATES

The four debates in 1997 and 2003 produced a range of outcomes, from the standpoint of both policy and public relations. In the debate over the supplemental appropriations bill, Democrats forced Republicans to pass a clean version of the legislation. The strategic advantage switched in the debate over partial birth abortion, where GOP legislators won majority support for the ban (although President Clinton eventually vetoed the bill). In the 1997 budget debate, both parties claimed victory in the final budget agreement, although the GOP successes in the agreement appeared to encourage greater unity and excitement in their party. In a similar debate six years later, Republicans eventually passed a substantial tax cut, but congressional Democrats (and moderate Republicans) succeeded in cutting President Bush's original tax proposal by more than half.

This chapter investigated how politicians' strategic communications influenced these debates and outcomes, and how journalists responded to the promotional campaigns. The politicians' public statements certainly appeared to shape news coverage. In this chapter's debates, politicians' public relations campaigns led to subsequent increases in coverage of their messages. Across the various stages of the debates, differences in the parties' promotional efforts often corresponded to similar differences in their coverage. In three of the four debates, the VAR results yielded evidence of this link on a day-to-day basis. In the one debate without such a link, the onset of the Iraq War appeared responsible for reducing journalists' responsiveness to politicians' messages.

In producing the news stories, reporters appeared to mirror and balance the politicians' statements, instead of covering those statements with a consistent bias favoring one party. The news coverage of competing messages often reflected disparities in the promotion of those messages. The most frequently promoted message usually won the most coverage (institutional influence also helped presidents win more coverage for their messages). In the debates over the supplemental and partial birth abortion, the advantaged party's more frequent promotion of its message appeared to account for its advantage in news coverage. At the same time, the journalists appeared to limit any such advantage, by providing more balanced coverage of competing messages. Regardless of which party held a promotional advantage, the news media always gave more coverage to the disadvantaged party than their promotional efforts would suggest. This tendency toward balanced coverage was greatest during important stages of policy making in Congress. At other times of lower legislative activity in a debate, the news coverage more closely reflected the relative frequency of politicians' public statements. During periods of intense negotiation and deliberation, it is arguably more important to give attention to politicians' competing messages, so that these issues and arguments receive full consideration inside and outside Congress. Journalists appear to respond to this need, by adding a more independent, balanced frame to their coverage.

The four debates thus revealed little evidence of a consistent partisan bias in news coverage. Instead, partisanship influences coverage in two ways. First, the partisan balance of news stories reflected the balance of the two parties' public statements and events. Coverage and promotion varied together across congressional debates, with both sometimes favoring Democrats and sometimes Republicans. Second, news markets with more Democratic voters provided more coverage of both parties' promotional efforts, while more Republican markets produced less such coverage. The two groups of markets differed in terms of numbers of stories, proportion of overall coverage, and responsiveness to politicians' promotional efforts. In addition to these partisan components of coverage, the outlets also appeared to influence politicians' promotional efforts, although not uniformly. Legislators from both parties mainly responded to news coverage of the Democratic congressional minority. Using evidence collected across multiple outlets, politicians, and debates, this chapter argues powerfully against the existence of news coverage consistently biased in favor of Democrats or Republicans. Instead, journalists incorporate partisanship into their news coverage in understandable and predictable ways, with the exact manner depending on each debate's particular alignment of politicians, messages, and markets.

Finally, this chapter's analysis suggested that journalists' news coverage feeds back to influence subsequent promotional efforts, albeit in a particular manner. In the VAR models, the feedback to politicians' public statements emerged from coverage of congressional Democrats and their message. These stories encouraged legislators from both parties to promote their parties' issues and arguments, whereas coverage of congressional Republicans and their messages provided little feedback. The impact of the Democrats' stories appears linked to their status as a congressional minority.

The congressional majority can use its formal powers to direct events inside Congress and thereby win attention and coverage for desired issues and arguments. The minority party lacks such options for winning coverage, so Democratic legislators had to turn to press conferences and other less formal strategies for attracting media attention to their message. If the majority party can often win coverage of its message, an important indicator of which side is winning a public debate is whether the minority party succeeds in winning coverage of its own message. If the majority party and its message dominate coverage of a debate, the information will be largely one-sided with little attention to the opposition's issues and arguments. But if the minority's message wins as much or more coverage than that of the majority, the two-sided coverage suggests much greater success for the minority party in the public debate. In this manner, the minority party's coverage can provide useful feedback about which congressional party is winning a public debate. Ironically, the congressional Democrats' minority status gave their stories more influence over both parties' public relations campaigns.

In addition to influencing politicians' promotional efforts, journalists' news coverage also affected the policy process. The nature of this effect varied across the debates. Neither press conferences nor news coverage appeared to affect the outcome of the partial birth abortion debate. In the 1997 budget debate, Democrats struggled to gain "ownership" of the deficit reduction agreement and thereby influence its details. In the debate over the supplemental, a barrage of critical comments by Democrats and unfavorable news coverage forced congressional Republicans into an embarrassing surrender. These diverse outcomes demonstrate the variety of ways in which strategic communication and news coverage can influence the policy process.

Overall, this chapter's combined evidence provides strong evidence of the importance of politicians' public relations campaigns. Those campaigns often influence news coverage, although journalists' attempts to balance coverage may reduce a party's advantage from promoting its message more frequently. The news coverage, in turn, feeds back to the policy process, influencing both subsequent promotional efforts and policy outcomes.

APPENDIX 5.A. ESTIMATION OF VAR MODELS

The estimated cumulative effects in Figures 5.1 and 5.2 emerged from an extensive set of VAR models. This appendix reviews the steps required to estimate those models and calculate the cumulative effects. The analysis relied heavily upon Brandt and Williams (2006). Many details of the estimation process (from lag-specification tests to impulse-response functions) are available at http://cyclesofspin.davidson.edu.

The figures in Chapter 5 present the results of 8 separate VAR models, all estimated using *Stata 9.0*. For each model, I followed several steps. The first involved specifying the correct number of lags to include in the model. The *varsoc* command in *Stata* calculates the final prediction error (FPE), Akaike's information criterion (AIC), Schwarz's Bayesian information criterion (SBIC), and the Hannan and Quinn information criterion (HQIC) lag-order selection statistics. Using these statistics, I began specification tests with a small number of lags and gradually increased the lags until the tests recommended an appropriate number of lags. This selection process yielded models ranging from one to eighteen lags.

In two of the eight models, the specification tests did not produce a clear recommendation for the number of lags. For the model of the supplemental debate in Figure 5.2, the AIC test never produced a recommended number of lags, up to the maximum number of lags testable with available computing resources. Across the tests for varying numbers of lags, the FPE test always recommended more lags than the HQIC or SBIC tests. I therefore used the minimum number of lags recommended by the FPE test for each model.

In the model of the supplemental debate in Figure 5.1, the four specification tests never produced a recommended number of lags, again up to the maximum number of lags testable with available computing resources. To address this problem, I estimated eight versions of this model. The first version had only two lags, and each additional version increased the number of lags by two, up to a total of 16 lags in the eighth version. I then compared the estimated cumulative effects across the eight versions. For many of the relationships in the model, the estimated cumulative effects were remarkably constant across the eight versions. Figure 5.1 (and my analysis in the text) use the cumulative effects from a fourteen-lag model (chosen to capture as much of the model's dynamics as possible), but only those effects that were similar in magnitude and sign in at least seven of the eight versions of the model. If two or more versions produced an estimated effect substantially different from that of the other versions, I excluded that estimated effect from the results reported for this model of the supplemental debate. The results of all eight versions of the model are available on the book's website.

With the number of lags specified for each model, the next step involved estimating the coefficients of each VAR. I used the *var* command in *Stata* for this estimation. The estimated results form the basis of the third step: calculating the impact of each variable on the other variables in the model. VAR analysis commonly uses a variety of approaches to assess each variable's impact, including Granger causality tests, forecast error variance decomposition (FEVD), and impulse response functions (IRF's). Space considerations prevent reporting these tests and values for all eight models in the text, although these details are available on the book's website.

Instead, the figures and my analysis only employ a version of the impulse response functions. Each such function calculates how a shock in one variable affects the expected value of another variable in each succeeding time period, up to a specified number of periods. It is possible to calculate a confidence interval around each expected value, making it possible to assess for each period whether the first variable impacts the second with an effect significantly different from 0 (i.e., the confidence interval around the expected value does not overlap with 0). Impulse response functions present these effects, with the confidence intervals often separating from 0 for early periods but eventually moving to overlap as the expected value approaches 0.

The impulse response functions present an additional complication: the assumed causal ordering of the model's variables can affect whether the impulse response function yields a statistically significant impact. If some of a model's variables are contemporaneously correlated (i.e., the residuals from the regressions are correlated), the order in which the variables are put into the calculation of the impulse response function can affect the results in that function. For example, each model in Figure 5.1 contains measures of the daily number of statements by congressional Democrats, congressional Republicans, and the president. For these variables, their residuals from the regressions in each VAR model are highly correlated. In the model for the 1997 budget debate, the correlations range from .14 to .52 and are all significant. These significant correlations suggest that the president and the two groups of congressmen tended to make public statements in the debate on the same days.

As a result, the assumed causal ordering of the measures of promotion could affect calculations of their effect on each other. We could assume, for example, that congressional Democrats' statements are causally prior to those of congressional Republicans, that is, that the Democrats' statements cause those of their opposition. Under this assumption, the impulse response function would provide evidence that the Democrats' statements cause those of their opposition, and that the opposite causal influence does not occur. Assuming that the Republicans' statements are causally prior would produce the opposite results. Either assumption (and corresponding result) is invalid, since neither party's statements always cause those of the opposite party.

When this type of contemporaneous correlation exists in a VAR model, the analyst may calculate the impulse response function under each assumed causal ordering that is possible. The differences in results may prove instructive for assessing which assumed ordering is most accurate (Williams and McGinnis 1988). In this book's analysis, it is not feasible to analyze in detail the variation in IRFs under different assumptions of causal orderings. In Figure 5.1, for example, each VAR model contains six variables. Bursts of legislator and journalist activity often occur on the same day; in the model of the 1997 budget debate, ten of the fifteen possible correlations (among the six variables) are significant. As a result, the possible assumed causal orderings can number in the hundreds.

To avoid the cumbersome interpretation of hundreds of IRF graphs, I simplified the calculation and presentation of results in several ways. First, I focused on the cumulative impulse response function (CIRF), which captures the total impact of a shock over a specific period of days. Each CIRF has a corresponding confidence interval and can therefore suggest whether the shock has a statistically significant impact. This single number more concisely presents the impact than an IRF graph does (although the latter certainly presents a more detailed picture of dynamics over time). Since each model contains six variables, there are thirty possible pairings or relationships among those variables[29] and therefore thirty CIRFs that could be significant.[30]

Given the extensive contemporaneous correlation in the measures of promotion and coverage, for each model I estimated CIRFs for a subset of the possible causal orderings. I made the assumption that on a particular day, the stories about the various politicians appear before and therefore

[29] For example, congressional Democrats' statements could influence congressional Republicans' statements, the president's statements, congressional Democrats' stories, congressional Republicans' stories, and the president's stories. In this manner, each variable could influence each of the other five variables.

[30] The period used to calculate the CIRF varies across the models and causal orderings. For some models and orderings, the CIRF remained significant at the end of a twenty-day period, suggesting long-term dynamics among the variables. For other models and orderings, the CIRF was significant after four to five days but became insignificant after twenty days. Here, the effect of the impulse variable appears more short-term and direct, and the lack of a significant impact during the latter days appears to cancel out the significant impact during the first four to five days. I am concerned with identifying whether a variable exerts a significant impact, regardless of whether that impact is over the short or long term. To capture these potentially diverse effects, I report for each model and causal ordering the CIRF over the longest period in which it is significant (up to a maximum of twenty days). If I calculated the CIRF for the same time period across all models and causal orderings, selecting the particular time period would be arbitrary but would make some CIRFs significant and others insignificant. Choosing different time periods would lead to different patterns of results.

are causally prior to the politicians' actual statements.[31] After making this assumption, I calculated CIRFs for all possible orderings of congressional Democrats, congressional Republicans, and the president.

Each possible ordering thus has thirty CIRFs, with one CIRF for each of the thirty possible relationships in the model. I then examined each relationship, looking at all the CIRFs calculated for that relationship across the possible causal orderings. If all the CIRFs for the individual relationship were positive and significant, I calculated their average and reported it as the estimated effect in Figure 5.1. If all the CIRFs for the relationship were negative and significant, I again calculated their average and reported it in Figure 5.1. But if the CIRFs for the relationship varied in sign or were not all significant, I reported nothing for that relationship in Figure 5.1 and concluded that the relationship was insignificant.

This method for determining significant results is conservative. Some models produced large and significant CIRFs for a particular causal ordering, yet that result is not reported in the figures if it is not robust across the causal orderings. This approach ensures that the figures only report results that are relatively unaffected by the assumed causal ordering of variables. It is important to add that the results for all causal orderings are available on the book's website.

One additional aspect of the calculations is relevant for interpreting the figures. VAR analysis often estimates the amount of change in one variable resulting from a one-standard-deviation change in the relevant residuals of the VAR model (Brandt and Williams 2006). The analysis in this book calculates the effects of one-unit changes (by dividing the CIRF by the standard deviation of the residual of the "impulse" variable), in order to present more precisely the varying effectiveness of public relations strategies. In each debate I discuss how a single statement by a congressional Democrat or Republican is estimated to produce a certain number of news stories. Calculating the effects of one-standard-deviation changes makes such a comparison harder, because congressional Democrats and Republicans may produce different numbers of statements, and the corresponding measures of promotion (and their residuals) therefore have standard deviations of different sizes.

[31] Approximately 90% of the news stories come from newspapers. While broadcast outlets usually produce stories after politicians make statements, adjusting for this difference does not substantially alter the results. But, the adjustment substantially complicates the reporting of results.

6

Completing the Cycle

Cycles of spin bring diverse actors and strategies into policy debates that extend far beyond the halls of Congress. This book unpacks the strategic communication campaigns that create these cycles of spin. By combining theories of agenda setting and collective action with diverse evidence from a variety of congressional debates, I have developed arguments about how politicians and journalists jointly shape the policy agenda and legislative outcomes. To summarize these arguments, this concluding chapter first reviews the four stages of promotional campaigns and how these stages interact. In the chapter's second section, I discuss four broader insights emerging from my arguments and findings: the strengths of multimethod research, the sticky yet malleable reputations of political parties, reporters' struggle for independence, and the diverse influence of institutional rules on promotion and coverage. The final section discusses the book's broadest implication: whether strategic communication helps or hinders the functioning of our democracy.

6.1. FUNDAMENTALS OF CYCLES OF SPIN

In the congressional debates in this book, two central concerns motivated the parties' strategic communication campaigns: agenda setting and collective action. Each congressional party wished to concentrate the legislative agenda on favorable issues, which unify the party while dividing the opposition. Partial birth abortion offered a favorable issue for Republicans, while the supplemental debate favored congressional Democrats. Focusing the policy process on these issues helped steer Congress toward producing outcomes that furthered the reelection and policy interests of each party's members. Promotional campaigns offered a useful tool for this agenda setting, but the campaigns had to overcome a collective action problem: A party member could benefit from the agenda setting without helping provide it. Each congressional party had to limit this free riding in order for their promotional campaign to succeed.

These dynamics of agenda setting and collective action flowed throughout each debate's cycle of spin. In the first stage of each cycle, a party's leaders initiated a promotional campaign. Each of these campaigns enlisted the participation of party members as well as furthered further their interests. To discourage free riding in the campaign, the leaders created a message that focused on a favorable issue. Because rank-and-file members were likely to support the arguments and position in this message, the members could receive individual policy and electoral benefits from promoting the message. The party leaders hoped that these individual benefits would help counteract the temptation to free ride and thereby increase the effectiveness of the promotional campaign.

The party leaders' hopes were realized, at least in their promotional campaigns on favorable issues. In the second stage of each promotional campaign, rank-and-file members had to decide whether to participate in the campaign and to promote the party message. Legislators promoted their party's message more frequently when they supported the position in the party message, which was more likely on favorable issues. In the legislators' decisions about whether to promote their party's message, individual benefits seemed paramount, an important consideration in party leaders' efforts to minimize free riding.

Unfortunately for party leaders, legislators could not always focus on favorable issues. External events, as well as the opposing party's promotional efforts, sometimes forced each party to address unfavorable issues, which divided its members. On these issues, the decision to promote the party's message was still a function of individual benefits; disagreement with the position in that message discouraged a legislator from promoting it. Such disagreement sometimes meant that the legislator in turn agreed with the position in the opposing party's message. Torn between party loyalty and issue positions, the legislator had to balance the individual benefits (from promoting an agreeable message) and the collective costs (to the legislator's party when he defects to promote the opposing party's message). Resolving this tension depended on the relative importance of individual and collective considerations, which varied by member and issue. In the partial birth abortion debate, moderate Democrats voted for the Republican ban but remained silent and did not promote the

Republican message. These Democrats did not want to hurt their own party, and collective considerations outweighed individual ones. But in the supplemental debate, Republicans from disaster-stricken states publicly called for passage of a clean disaster relief bill. For these legislators, individual concerns about meeting their constituents' need outweighed any collective costs from defecting from the GOP and helping promote the Democratic message.

The varying advantages across the four debates had their roots in the legislators' issue positions on those debates. Legislators' preferences guided their promotional efforts. It is important to note, however, that the promotional efforts often reinforced and expanded any advantage stemming from members' issue positions in a debate. The mechanism driving this reinforcement was a positive link between promotion and coverage. In this third stage of promotional campaigns, legislators' promotion of their party message yielded greater attention to that message in news coverage. Across the four debates, coverage of the competing messages largely mirrored changes in the promotion of those messages. Reporters also demonstrated some independence from the promotional campaigns during important stages of the debates, when the news coverage gave more balanced attention to the competing messages than the relative promotion of those messages would suggest.

The journalists' coverage displayed little evidence of a second type of independence: adding a consistent partisan bias to news stories. The coverage favored each party at different times. In each debate, news coverage provided more mentions of the disadvantaged party than one would expect from the promotional efforts, regardless of whether the debate favored Democrats or Republicans. Local newspapers adjusted their coverage to fit their respective audiences, but not by adding a partisan bias to their balance of Democratic and Republican messages in news stories. Instead, the papers adjusted the amount of their coverage of Congress. Democratic audiences appeared to desire more such coverage. Newspapers in these markets provided more coverage and were also more responsive to the promotional efforts of politicians from both parties.

The variations in news coverage proved important. In the final stage of promotional campaigns, the coverage fed back to influence promotional efforts and the policy process. During the promotional campaigns in the four debates, legislators from both parties paid more attention to coverage of the Democratic minority's message. The Republican majority's influence over the legislative process made coverage of its messages very likely. As a result, the extent of the minority's coverage could have indicated whether parties' promotional campaigns were evenly matched, or the majority's campaign would dominate coverage and the debate.

The news coverage also fed back to influence more specific aspects of the debates. In the 1997 budget debate, unfavorable news coverage forced congressional Democrats to struggle to maintain ownership of the budget deal. Democratic legislators were more successful in the supplemental debate. Their vigorous promotion of the party message yielded favorable news coverage, which increased public pressure on congressional Republicans and eventually forced the collapse of the GOP strategy.

Overall, this book provides strong evidence of how legislators' promotional campaigns produce cycles of spin. The stages of the cycles are interrelated. Party leaders create messages that encourage rank-and-file members to promote them. Ebbs and flows in those promotional efforts yield corresponding changes in coverage. The varying coverage feeds back to shape legislators' promotional efforts. These linkages combine to produce cycles of spin.

6.2. BROADER LESSONS

In the opening chapter of this book, I outlined three reasons why it is important to investigate these dynamics of the cycles of spin. We need to understand how strategic communication helps parties build legislative coalitions, how reporters create news stories to help set legislative agendas, and how the interaction of politicians and journalists shapes the quality of political information that voters receive. The remainder of this chapter links these three questions to the arguments and evidence in this book. The resulting insights are relevant for students of political science, Congress, the news media, and the broader democratic process.

6.2.1. Multimethod Research

Cycles of spin involve complex interactions among politicians and journalists. Understanding such complexity requires investigating it from multiple angles. This book serves as a useful example for students of political science investigating problems of similar complexity. I employ an unusual diversity of analytical techniques and evidence, from participant observation (during my work in Daschle's office) and structured interviews (of Senate press secretaries), to computerized content analysis (of politicians' statements and reporters' stories) and vector auto regression (analyzing the interaction between promotion and coverage). It is rare to combine the methods of scholars as different as Fenno (1978), Tuchman (1972), and Williams (1990). But, the diverse evidence and analysis makes the book's arguments more complete and compelling (King, Keohane, and Verba 1994).

For example, Chapter 4 asks the important question of how variation in the alignment of policy preferences affects legislators' promotional activities. To address this question, I turned to the four specific debates, chosen intentionally for their variation in alignment of legislators' policy preferences. In the debate over partial birth abortion, the Republicans were largely unified in support of a ban, while the Democrats were more divided. The supplemental produced the opposite alignment, with unified Democrats facing a split Republican Party. In contrast to these issues with a clear advantage, the budget debates were too complex to yield a single alignment of policy preferences or a clear partisan advantage. The analysis then examined legislators' public relations efforts across these four diverse cases. Contextual insights from the press secretary interviews helped confirm interpretations of the quantitative analysis of legislators' public statements. In turn, this quantitative analysis established the generalizability of the insights emerging from the forty-one press secretary interviews. Such diversity of evidence and methods is particularly useful when trying to understand difficult topics like legislators' beliefs and motivations, which they often hesitate to reveal completely (Fenno 1978, Sinclair 2006).

6.2.2. The Reputations of Parties

A second insight addresses the role of political parties in Congress. Many observers of congressional parties focus on the parties' agenda setting powers, examining static cross sections of individual congresses and explaining how congressional majorities and minorities fight over the short-term policy agenda (Aldrich and Rohde 1995, 1996, Cox and McCubbins 2004, Krehbiel 1998). The assumption is that legislators' preferences about policy proposals and the most important issues are exogenous and unresponsive to the legislative conflicts (Harris 2005).

This work demonstrates that those preferences are endogenous, at least in part. The goal of strategic communication campaigns is to influence the policy agenda and thereby reshape politicians' preferences about what issues Congress should address and how to address them. A campaign may not be able to change politicians' fundamental ideological preferences (Jacobs and Shapiro 2000), but the campaign can shape how the politicians link those fundamental preferences to policy proposals and debates. During the supplemental debate, for example, congressional Democrats' public relations campaign forced many Republicans to focus on the need for immediate disaster relief, regardless of their beliefs about sampling in the census or other concerns that the GOP leadership attempted to link to the supplemental. The GOP rank-and-file's focus on immediate disaster relief forced their leaders to retreat and allow passage of a clean supplemental bill. The Democrats' reshaping of the policy agenda forced Republican legislators to support a policy proposal that they might otherwise resisted.

The reshaping of legislators' preferences about policy proposals opens the door to reshaping parties' reputations and the broader political landscape (Aldrich 2003; Baumgartner and Jones 1993, 2002; Carmines and Stimson 1986). In its strategic communication, the majority party in Congress works to focus on favorable issues that unify its members around a publicly popular position, while creating divisions among the opposition. The party can link new, uncertain issues to existing ones where it already enjoys an advantage. The congressional minority hopes to follow a similar strategy, focusing the policy agenda on a similar set of issues favoring its members. If a party can focus public attention on favorable issues over a long period of time, the party can win a stable electoral majority and realign the political system to its advantage.

In recent elections, President Bush and his advisors hoped to rebrand the Republican Party and foster such a realignment. The themes of "compassionate conservatism" and "opportunity society" provided a coherent framework for promoting positions on issues from taxes to education reform. As a result, many Americans came to support Republican messages containing these issues and arguments (Luntz 2007). While compelling in the 2000, 2002, and 2004 elections, the GOP messages foundered two years later, disrupted by the Iraq War and ethics scandals. Riding the wave of these external events (Ansolabehere et al. 1993), minority Democrats in Congress refocused attention on messages such as foreign policy mismanagement and congressional corruption, which criticized Republicans and which many constituents accepted. As a result, many congressional Republicans struggled in the 2006 midterm elections, and the Democratic Party won congressional majorities for the first time since 1994. This progression of campaigns and messages illustrates the difficulty of successfully maintaining public relations campaigns over the long term, and of converting short-term political gains into a lasting realignment.

6.2.3. The Independence of the Press

The success of promotional campaigns depends on how reporters cover those campaigns.[1] If journalists are more independent, they will resist a party's framing of a debate and cover the debate using their own terms. But if the journalists are highly dependent upon the party for information about a story, the reporters are more likely to include the party's issues and arguments without interpretation or change. This book has provided mixed evidence of journalistic independence. Reporters' stories often mirrored the ebb and flow of the parties' promotional campaigns, suggesting a lack of independence. Reflecting the varying partisan advantages in the debates, news coverage sometimes favored Democrats, while providing more attention to Republicans at other times. The contrasting patterns across debates provided strong evidence against claims of a widespread pro-Democratic or pro-Republican bias in overall news coverage (Schattschneider 1960).

Evidence of greater independence from politicians emerged in other aspects of the coverage. One was the relative quantity of local coverage across outlets. The journalists appeared to respond to the preferences of their audiences for more political coverage (in Democratic-leaning markets) or less such coverage (in Republican-leaning ones). Journalists' independence also was evident in their tendency to balance coverage of politicians' competing messages. At crucial junctions in debates where one party promoted its message much more frequently than the opposition did, the news coverage gave more equal attention to competing messages than the promotional efforts would suggest. This balancing occurred across issues, regardless of which party held a promotional advantage. Occurring most extensively during important periods of a debate, the balancing increased the likelihood of audiences receiving both sides' messages in the debate. While this goal is desirable (Althaus 2003, Simon 2002), balanced coverage can also create problems. Equal coverage of competing messages may give attention to a party's message that few members of the party support. This outcome occurred during the

[1] This book examines cycles of spin initiated by members of Congress. A different set of cycles may emerge through investigative journalism. Reporters initiate stories, and politicians then respond, which in turn encourages additional coverage. The growing concern with profit in journalism threatens the continuation of investigative journalism, as news organizations reduce news room staff (Graber 2006 and Underwood 2001). Opposing this trend, some observers argue that investigative journalism can actually increase a news outlet's profitability (Chen et al. 2005, Heider et al. 2005).

latter stages of the debate over the supplemental. GOP leaders insisted on continuing the same communication strategy and message, while many rank-and-file Republicans offered little support. Despite this lack of support among Republican legislators, the news coverage balanced the two parties' competing argument. Eventually, the Republican leaders eventually had to back down and concede the debate.

Reporters' attempts to frame a balanced story may also encourage their audience to perceive that coverage as biased, due to the "hostile media effect" described in Chapter 5. Upon receiving the finished product of the politicians' promotional efforts and journalists' coverage of those efforts, an audience evaluates the accuracy of the news account through the lens of personal partisan leanings (Druckman 2001, Iyengar 1991). If the account fits the audience's perception of the broader political debate, the audience will view the account as accurate. But if a journalist's balanced account diverges from that perception, the audience may evaluate the account as inaccurate and biased (Hamilton 2004).

While this potential criticism may discourage journalists from providing balanced accounts, reporters appeared to resist discouragement in the outlets and types of coverage examined in this book. Chapter Five found that outlets in Democratic- and Republican-leaning markets differed little in the balance of partisan messages that they presented to their audiences. But, the pursuit of market share can lead new outlets to attract more narrowly partisan audiences by providing less balanced news accounts (Gentzkow and Shapiro 2007, Hamilton 2004). Table 5.3 presented evidence of a pro-Republican bias in FOX News' coverage of the 2003 budget debate. Partisan news coverage is extremely common on the Internet, with numerous blogs and other web sites strongly promoting each party's issues and arguments in any debate.

The growth of these partisan outlets creates a very different media environment for contemporary audiences. As recently as the 1980s, many Americans relied on the three major networks for their news coverage. Coverage from these networks provided diverse political viewpoints on many political issues (Graber 2006). News coverage exposed individuals to dissimilar opinions more extensively than interpersonal discussions did, partly because of the difficulty of limiting ones news coverage to similar opinions only (Mutz and Martin 2001). The growing partisanship and fragmentation of news coverage in the last decade has made it much easier for individuals to restrict their news exposure to stories and outlets that fit their own perspective. Reflecting the patterns in Table 5.3, conservative Republicans, for example, increasingly rely upon FOX News for coverage. At the same time, audiences for other major news outlets appear more balanced ideologically (Pew Research Center 2005), so many Americans still receive exposure to diverse political viewpoints (Horrigan et al. 2004).

But, the continued growth in partisan news coverage and selective exposure to that coverage threatens our political process. Receiving only one side of a debate makes an audience more susceptible to framing and manipulation (Zaller 1992). The audience members develop less understanding and appreciation of viewpoints contrary to their own. While encouraging individuals' political participation and interest, this selective exposure also harms our political deliberation (Mutz 2006).

6.2.4. Institutional Rules

In the four congressional debates, institutional rules played an important role in legislators' promotional activities and reporters' coverage of those activities. During debates in both chambers, rules of the legislative process allowed the majority party to set the policy agenda, particularly the specific alternatives considered on the floor. With fewer such powers, the minority engaged more frequently in promotional campaigns, in hopes of broadening debates beyond Congress and thereby influencing the policy agenda (Schattschneider 1960).

Institutional differences between chambers also impacted the congressional debates. The less tightly controlled floor agenda in the Senate enabled the minority Democrats to introduce their own proposals during the partial birth abortion ban. The opportunity to promote and defend Democratic proposals likely increased rank-and-file participation in the Democrats' promotional efforts during the Senate debate. Lacking such opportunities, Democratic representatives were nearly silent during the corresponding House debate. The opportunity to defend a party's own proposal during floor debate may encourage the party's legislators to promote that proposal and the corresponding message.

Politicians' effectiveness in winning news coverage was also tied to institutional considerations, specifically politicians' varying influence in the policy process. Representatives, senators, and the president each possess different levels of individual influence, due to the rules outlined in the U.S. Constitution. These differences in influence affect the politicians' ability to win news coverage. Each of the president's public statements proves extremely effective in winning coverage; statements by members of Congress are less effective. These less influential politicians, particularly representatives, can minimize their disadvantage and win coverage by combining together in promotional campaigns. Their unified efforts suggest a larger voting bloc, greater policy influence, and therefore greater newsworthiness.

These consequences of institutional rules continue to apply, regardless of which party controls the branches of government. After the 2006 congressional elections, the new Democratic congressional majorities used their new agenda-setting powers to focus on issues favoring their party, much as congressional Republicans did after winning control of Congress in 1994 (Nather 2007a). In 2008, the last year of Bush's presidency, each of his public statements still received more coverage than that of any member of Congress. At the same time, almost all press conferences on Capitol Hill included multiple members. Rare are the press briefings by individual legislators other than party leaders.[2] As these examples illustrate, the institutional rules of our government guide both the promotion and coverage of policy debates.

6.3. THE VIRTUES OF SPIN

Beyond these insights about specific components of cycles of spin, it is also important to consider how politicians' reliance on strategic communication impacts our broader democratic process. Cycles of spin were not always a central part of the interaction among politicians and the public. During the decades after World War II, relatively stable partisan attitudes and coalitions dominated American politics (Campbell et al. 1960, Erikson and Tedin 2007). As political elites engaged in substantive debates, the content of those debates received coverage in relatively limited news outlets of the time. But, voters appeared to pay little attention to that substantive coverage, instead basing their evaluations of politicians and policies on partisan and other group loyalties (Blumler and Kavanagh 1999, 212). As a result, observers commonly concluded that news coverage during the period exerted minimal effects on public attitudes (Iyengar and McGrady 2007).

In the 1960s and 1970s, the mass media, particularly national television news, expanded their offerings and audiences. Newscasts increasingly emphasized objective accounts of political debates (Blumler and Kavanagh 1999, West 2001a). In addition, candidates and parties could pay for broadcast time to reach potential voters directly, offering more direct communication between political elites and the public (Smith et al.

[2] See http://ebbs.senate.gov/ for a daily listing of press events on Capitol Hill.

1998). Politicians and journalists could now reach citizens who had not received political messages and news in earlier decades. With less political interest and weaker political attitudes, these individuals offered more attractive targets for a persuasive message. But, they were also more volatile in their voting patterns (Blumler and Kavanagh 1999).

During the same period, the partisan and institutional ties among the president and members of Congress grew weaker (Kernell 1997). As described in Chapter 1, individual politicians grew more independent and less reliant upon each other for winning reelection. At the same time, politicians in both branches of government represented more people than their predecessors did in previous decades. The larger constituencies made it harder to communicate with individual voters, particularly using more traditional approaches like town meetings or franked letters. These combined developments made the policy agenda in Washington more volatile. The addition of any issue to that agenda depended more heavily upon the ability of its promoters and their promotional campaign (Kernell 1997).

The start of the twenty-first century has brought continued expansion of the media outlets, as well as their fragmentation. Most newspapers have added websites for distributing their new stories, as well as video clips to accompany those stories. Despite the growing concentration of outlet ownership and accompanying reduction in diversity of coverage (Baker 2007), the Internet offers nearly endless opportunities for diverse coverage, from millions of blogs to exclusively on-line news outlets such as Salon.com and Politico.com. Radio has grown significantly more flexible in presenting news stories, by offering podcasts and broadcasting live programs over the Internet. Video offerings have expanded dramatically through the growth of cable, satellite television, and websites such as YouTube. These developments have created a much more fragmented media environment, offering many more paths to reach voters and many more competitors taking those paths.

The fragmentation of media outlets has altered preexisting patterns of control over that communication, among both politicians and journalists (Carpini and Williams 2001, Popkin 2006). The changes in media outlets have made it harder for members of Congress to win news coverage. In addition to the national media paying less attention to Congress (Cook 1989, Sellers and Schaffner 2007, Underwood 1998), politicians' messages must now cut through the "data smog" of information flowing to the public (Baker 1996, Shenk 1997). These challenges have pushed politicians to rely more heavily on strategic communication (Blumler and Kavanagh 1999, Crozier 2007). The coordinated efforts of promotional campaigns may yield more attention for their messages. Politicians also adopt a more "shot-gun" approach to distributing their messages, going beyond traditional tactics, such as press conferences, to include websites, blogs, and email campaigns (Blumler and Kavanagh 1999).

The fragmentation of media outlets also affects journalists by reducing their original gatekeeping authority over the flow of news (Ben-Porath 2007). With more ways for stories and ideas to enter public debate, the "cascade of information" from elites to the public grows flatter. Elites have less control over that flow of information (Entman 2004, Entman and Herbst 2001). This fragmented environment may reduce the diversity of coverage, because many journalists share common views about newsworthiness and therefore cover the same stories (Bennett 1996). The result is pack journalism and similar coverage across outlets (Cook 2001, 189). But, the advent of blogs creates opportunity for input from millions of new voices, which can diversify coverage beyond the messages of public officials (Blumler and Kavanagh 1999). One observer described the potential for blogs to influence coverage of the Iraq War:

> In the present case, in which the issue involved whether to examine the rationale for entering a war two years after entering it, elite conflict was minimal. Though liberal activists obviously wanted the story covered, only relatively small players within the Democratic Party's conventional hierarchy pushed the story. Thus an elite consensus – albeit an imperfect one – formed around silence. One potential of the Internet is to expand the range of voices to which coverage is indexed. Can activists – amplified by the new cyber-megaphone – replace squeamish minority-party officials in breaking down the consensus and serving as one side of a conflict? (Schiffer 2006, 496)

Finally, the expansion of communication via cable television and the Internet has increased the speed of promotional campaigns. The news media outlets offer many more paths for news stories to feed back and influence the policy process. These same paths offer more opportunities for the public, after watching news coverage, to contact their elected officials and express opinions based on that coverage. The on-line world contains many of these paths, while also encouraging faster and more immediate communication (Cassidy 2005, Crozier 2007). As a result, politicians must respond to such feedback more quickly. The pressure for instant response reduces the time available for deliberation and in-depth analysis (Blumler and Kavanagh 1999).

In response to these many changes, politicians must adopt new promotional strategies in order to remain effective in shaping news coverage and policy agendas. Strategic communication increasingly requires targeting many more outlets and audiences. Elected officials also need to promote their messages more frequently, while developing greater agility to respond to new developments or critical messages. The Senate "war" and "peace" rooms described in Chapter 3 are only the most recent examples of politicians institutionalizing promotional and rapid response capabilities.

Perhaps most importantly, politicians are changing how they create the messages of promotional campaigns. This process has traditionally operated in a top-down fashion, with party leaders formulating and distributing campaign messages. Chapter 3 described how congressional parties are gradually decentralizing this creative process to include more members of Congress. If elected officials continue this decentralization beyond Congress, they can take advantage of the social networking potential of the Internet, often described as Web 2.0. If the officials allow activists and voters to contribute to the creation of campaign messages, those individuals add innovative ideas as well as take greater ownership of the messages that they helped create. As a result, these individuals will help promote the messages and can become stronger advocates for the party (Ansley and Sellers 2009).[3] The increasingly complex and fragmented media outlets are likely to encourage politicians to embrace these new techniques of strategic communication. Extending this book's analysis to examine the new promotional campaigns can further our understanding of how politicians, journalists, and voters interact in the new media environment.

6.3.1. Simplicity Over Substance

Politicians' growing reliance on strategic communication is likely to draw criticism. Many observers have expressed worry that promotional campaigns harm our democratic process by hindering the exchange of information between voters and politicians. In the eyes of these critics, politicians create messages for strategic communication not to stimulate

[3] See http://www.barackobama.com/index.php and http://www.johnmccain.com/ for recent examples of this type of social networking in a campaign. Some observers advocate the extension of social networking to governing, i.e., "Governing 2.0" (Ansley 2008). OpenCongress aims to "provide a comprehensive snapshot of every bill and Member of Congress [by] bringing together official Congressional information with the social wisdom and valuable context created by people in news and blog posts" (http://www.opencongress.org/, last accessed July 28, 008). PublicMarkup.org offers the opportunity to post legislation that Congress is considering and to solicit public comments on individual components of that legislation (http://publicmarkup.org/, last accessed July 28, 2008).

independent thinking, but to use framing "to draw out the audience's pretested, preexisting emotional concerns" (Bennett and Entman 2001, 7; see also Cook 2001). The framed messages often emphasize simple, short, and snappy phrases instead of detailed discussion of policy alternatives and their proponents (Belt and Just 2008, Entman and Herbst 2001). Evaluating messages grows even harder when sponsors of promotional campaigns conceal their identity behind generic titles or industry-wide coalitions. The lack of transparency makes it harder to evaluate the message and underlying motivations (Bennett and Mannheim 2001). In addition, strategic communication campaigns may simply repackage old policies in new, more attractive terms, for the sole goal of winning more support for those policies. In the 2005 debate over Social Security reform, President Bush changed the name of his most important proposal from "private accounts" to "personal accounts," with no change in the underlying policy recommendation (Bai 2005, 13).

An observer of the White House Press Room aptly summarized these concerns about the content of promotional campaigns: "Style is substituted for substance. Complicated issues are transformed into simple slogans and slick sound-bites" (Maltese 1994, 265, as quoted in Graber 2006). The arguments listed in Appendix 3.C provided many examples of such phrases. The simplicity, brevity, and novelty of promotional messages often make them more newsworthy in the eyes of reporters. The resulting coverage further encourages politicians to engage in strategic communication. This self-reinforcing spiral feeds public's cynicism about politics and journalism (Bennett and Mannheim 2001, Blumler and Kavanagh 1999, Cappella and Jamieson 1997). Ironically, such cynicism may encourage voters to discount all politicians' messages (Tsfati 2004). This discounting forces politicians to work even harder to communicate with the public. As a result, the politicians may rely even more heavily upon strategic communication, in hopes of providing more effective and persuasive public communication.[4]

[4] Another common concern about strategic communication is the selective targeting of promotional campaigns. These campaigns may exclude many parts of the electorate, by focusing narrowly on certain legislators' constituents or other subsets of citizens in order to influence policy outcomes (Bennett and Entman 2001, Gandy 2001). This targeting can result in different voters possessing different levels of information about policy issues. Such differences are important; voters with contrasting levels of information about a policy issue tend to have different opinions about that issue (Althaus 1998). These problems grow worse if the "digital divide" in Internet access leads some citizens to learn less about policy debates (Brants 2005, Bennett and Entman 2001).

Counterbalancing these concerns are arguments and evidence that voters can use the simplified messages from competing strategic communication campaigns to assess political debates effectively. A variety of heuristics and other mechanisms can help voters sort through complex and voluminous information to reach substantively grounded decisions (Lupia 1994, Lupia and McCubbins 1998, Popkin 1994). Longer-term, more stable heuristics such as partisan identification may prove more accurate and less susceptible to distortion (Kuklinski and Quirk 2000). But, even short-term considerations such as economic performance can help voters make decisions and evaluations. For example, voters were able to cut through the hype and sensationalism of the Monica Lewinsky scandal and make substantive evaluations of Clinton, using the economy as a guide (Zaller 2001). In a similar manner, voters may be able to use the simplified messages of promotional campaigns to reach substantive evaluations of politicians and policies. If so, the more extensive message promotion of strategic communication campaigns leads to greater public involvement in policy debates as well as improved understanding of those debates. As previous chapters have demonstrated, the messages in these campaigns have their origins in policy debates on Capitol Hill; legislators' own policy preferences guide the creation of these messages. With such substantive origins, the messages can help voters evaluate politicians' priorities and policies.

These disagreements about the impact of strategic communication boil down to contrasting beliefs about voters' competence in evaluating messages, politicians, and policies (Lippmann 1920/2008). When assessing the competing arguments in this debate, it is important to consider the broader information environment in which political elites produce messages and the public may use those messages to evaluate the elites (Bennett and Entman 2001). To assess voters' competence, observers sometimes focus on highly salient issues. This narrow focus creates a potential problem, because the salience of these issues may result from strategic communication (Entman and Bennett 2001). While voters may exhibit competence in evaluating the salient issues, the competence may in fact result from politicians' promotional campaigns. The voters may be less competent on less salient issues outside the promotional campaigns and messages. Thus, the focus on salient issues may exaggerate the level of voter competence. Avoiding such a selective focus and corresponding bias in conclusions requires considering how political elites may attempt to shape the salience of issues and how this competitive agenda setting impacts voters.

This book places politicians' promotional messages within the broader information environment of congressional debates. The politicians' strategic communication does influence the salience of issues, often in a competitive manner (Druckman and Chong 2007). In this respect, the promotional campaigns provide useful signals of the parties' competing priorities in congressional debates, which can help the public with decision making and evaluations. These more understandable and accessible signals inform citizens about policy debates that previously took place only inside Congress. As a result, the promotional campaigns can encourage citizens to participate in politics because they think they understand it better (Baker 1996, Gamson 2001b).

6.3.2. Distortion and Dialogue

Beyond the simplification of issues and arguments, another criticism of the public relations campaigns concerns their frequent distortions of issue positions and lack of direct dialogue on common issues (Bennett and Mannheim 2001, Gandy 2001, Ornstein and Mann 2000). In many public debates, politicians often portray their opponents' issues and arguments unfavorably, often in the worst possible way. In 2003, the Democrats described the Republican budget plans as "a sham, wrapped in spin, shrouded in deception" (Daschle 2003f). In the partial birth abortion debate six years earlier, GOP legislators accused Democrats of defending "abortionists" who practiced "infanticide" and "violence and cruelty to baby girls and boys." (Canady 1997c, Smith 1997) The distortions of strategic communications can extend to the broader legislative process, when congressional parties use that process to promote messages and partisan goals, instead of policy agreements (Evans and Oleszek 2001). Through all these public maneuverings, each party promotes its own favorable issues and arguments, while trying to avoid discussing those of the opposition. As a result, the parties may talk past each other, instead of directly engaging the same topics (Bennett et al. 2007, Graber 1996, Simon 2002). Instead of deliberating about policy issues, the politicians use their messages to maneuver for political advantage (Iyengar and McGrady 2007).

Blatant lies and distortions are certainly bad from a normative standpoint. But, most statements by politicians contain an element of truth, and a message considered a lie by one side may be an accepted fact for the opposition. In the 2004 presidential election, Republicans attacked Democratic nominee John Kerry for voting ninety-eight times to raise taxes.

Kerry's fellow Democrats charged that the attack distorted his record. Many of the votes involved relatively minor procedural questions, and Kerry voted against the 1990 tax increase promoted by President Bush's father to reduce the budget deficit. Republicans stood by their charge, however, arguing that Kerry's votes did move the Senate toward increasing taxes (Rosenbaum 2004). In a debate covered in this book, congressional Democrats and Republicans argued in 1997 about whether disaster relief funding was already "in the pipeline" and flowing to disaster-stricken communities. Some assistance was certainly reaching the communities, but the disagreement was over how much and whether that amount was sufficient.

In both these examples, each competing argument was based on at least some portion of truthful evidence. A message lacking such evidence risks exposure, often by the news media, which can lead to embarrassment for the promoters of the message. While politicians do sometimes make outright lies in their public statements[5], the potential for embarrassment more often discourages these lies. Politicians usually seek to support their messages with at least some truthful, accurate information.

More generally, these tactics of distortion and selective emphasis of favorable arguments and evidence are common rhetorical strategies (Riker 1986). In the past, politicians often used these strategies in less public settings inside Congress, such as committee meetings or floor discussions. Recent decades have brought expanded television coverage and public attention to all aspects of Congress. Many debates that formerly took place inside the institution have expanded outward into the broader public arena, especially in the news media. Policy making has become closely linked to news making (Cook 1989). Thus, the public relations campaigns are extending into the public arena the rhetorical strategies previously employed inside Congress. As one knowledgeable observer of Congress put it, "In a democracy, politicians attempt to persuade citizens; they are advocates, so expecting total objectivity in how they present their case is unrealistic" (Sinclair 2006, 347). Even if competing politicians are not providing "dialogue" by discussing the same issue, their emphasis of different messages can suggest which issue(s) that each politician prioritizes (Druckman and

[5] In a 2006 congressional race in New York, the National Republican Campaign Committee charged a Democratic candidate with using taxpayer dollars for phone sex. In actuality, a staff member for the Democrat had tried to call the state Division of Criminal Justice, whose phone number closely resembled that of a pornography telephone line. The staffer's misdial cost $1.25 (Grunwald 2006).

Chong 2007, Miller and Riechert 2001, Riker 1986). Such an indication of priorities can help voters evaluate those politicians. In sum, the policy agenda and the efforts to shape it have grown more public, extending far beyond politicians' personal interactions within the confines of institutions like Congress. The public can benefit because the more public discussions provide more extensive and accessible information about policy debates.

While the public relations battles now extend into the news media and the Internet, the goal of such battles remains the same: Set the terms of debate in order to win. This self-interested pursuit of victory differs substantially from the goal of providing quality dialogue, a goal that underlies many criticisms of the public relations campaigns. Yet, the pursuit of self-interest is a fundamental part of our political system. When defending the U.S. Constitution, the authors of *The Federalist Papers* argued that "[a]mbition must be made to counteract ambition" (Hamilton et al. 1961, 322). Public relations campaigns emerge from the self-interested conflict encouraged by the Constitution, and extend that conflict into a broader public arena. The maneuvering of public relations campaigns may encourage greater partisanship and policy gridlock in the short term. But, even the most partisan floor votes or messages have a long-term goal: to shift the overall partisan balance in Congress and the overall country, and thereby affect policy outcomes. While a public relations campaign "may seem unedifying and the media are likely to label it grandstanding and to interpret it entirely as posturing for the next election, it is often directly focused on policy, and it has the virtue of involving the public – at least the attentive public – in the process" (Sinclair 2006, 354).

6.3.3. The Nature of Public Opinion

A final criticism of politicians' promotional efforts charges that campaigns of strategic communication manipulate the public's issue positions (Bartels 2003, Lippman 1920/2008). If these campaigns are successful, they must shape and influence public opinion. As a result, public opinion on an issue may depend on how politicians frame that issue and the surrounding debate. In the debate over the supplemental, for example, support for quickly passing the supplemental depended on whether the American public believed that political games by Republicans were delaying much-needed assistance for disaster-stricken states, or that such aid was already in the pipeline and that it was more important to prevent future government shutdowns. The public's opinion about passing the supplemental would depend on which argument the public accepted. In this manner, the politicians often craft competing messages to bring public opinion closer to their preferred position (Jacobs and Shapiro 2000, Tversky and Kahneman 1974). If so, what is the public's true opinion? What position should politicians support if they are attempting to represent the public's opinion as closely as possible? If politicians can determine the public's opinion, what stops politicians from shaping that opinion to further their own self-interest?

Fortunately, politicians face limits when trying to manipulate public opinion by framing issues and arguments (Druckman 2001). The elected officials find it difficult to use framing to move the public from its issue preferences and preferred issues too far or too long (Jacobs and Shapiro 2000, Rottinghaus 2008). Framing effects tend to be more temporary than long lasting. In addition, the extent of manipulation may depend on whether the intended frame faces any competition. The effects of framing decrease if the target audience also receives information countering the intended frame (Zaller 1992). The relative quality of competing frames also mediates their impact (Druckman and Chong 2007).

In turn, the existence of competitive frames may depend upon equal access to relevant policy details for both sides in a debate. If one side lacks such information, it may prove harder for that party to create a competitive message and mount a strong promotional campaign (Pan and Kosicki 2001). Thus, in 2003 the Republicans' control of the White House and U.S. intelligence agencies provided an advantage in the congressional debate over the Iraq War (Aday 2006, Bennett and Klockner 1996). Congressional Democrats had to rely upon the Republican administration for substantive information about the debate. That reliance made it harder for the Democrats to create and coalesce around a unified competitive message in opposition to the Republicans' war effort. The GOP lacked such an advantage in many domestic debates, where Democrats could acquire more extensive and independent information for mounting an opposing promotional campaign.

Such countervalent information and messages are central themes in this book. The evidence from previous chapters suggests that the effectiveness of a party's public relations campaign may depend on how much the opposing party promotes a competing message. Across the four debates, the promotion of competing messages varied substantially. The flow of messages was sometimes one-sided, with one side's message dominating, and sometimes two-sided, with both sides winning equal attention. But even when the promotion of messages was extremely one-sided, journalists independently balanced news coverage to give the parties' messages more equal attention.

Overall, these arguments highlight the benefits of politicians' public relations campaigns. Most fundamentally, these campaigns help structure and communicate policy debates. As one political observer noted, "It's not just spin. It's the construction of meaning" (Bates 1997; see also Bichard 2006, Crozier 2007, Crigler 1996, Tuchman 1978). Promotional campaigns are "a way to discursively organize public deliberation, allowing political actors to present their arguments and for others to understand and evaluate these arguments. That is the essence of public deliberation." (Pan and Kosicki 2001, 60) Politicians and parties use the campaigns to extend policy debates beyond the confines of Congress, and thereby shape the policy-making agenda. Many journalists use the politicians' messages to present the debates to the public in balanced, meaningful terms, although new outlets, particularly on the Internet, often offer more partisan, less balanced accounts of the debates. If all outlets, both new and old, made a greater attempt to balance competing messages, the public would better understand how complicated policy debates affect their lives. The parties often offer sharply divergent messages about those effects, but such differences help the public understand what each party would do. The public better understands the meaning of policy debates for their lives, which can help them evaluate politicians. Improved evaluations can help the public hold politicians accountable. So while acknowledging the problems of strategic communication campaigns, we also need to recognize the campaigns' contributions to contemporary political debates. Unpacking the cycles of spin can help us better understand and evaluate how politicians, journalists, and the public interact in the political and media environments of the twenty-first century.

References

ABC News, *September 4–September 7, 2003*. Retrieved May 26, 2008 from the iPOLL Databank, The Roper Center for Public Opinion Research, University of Connecticut < http://www.ropercenter.uconn.edu/ipoll.html >.

Aday, Sean. 2006. "The Framesetting Effects of News: An Experimental Test of Advocacy Versus Objectivist Frames." *J&MC Quarterly* 83(4): 767–784.

Aldrich, John. 1995. *Why Parties?* University of Chicago Press: Chicago, Illinois.

Aldrich, John. 2003. "Electoral Democracy during Politics as Usual – and Unusual." In Michael MacKuen and George Rabinowitz, editors, *Electoral Democracy*. University of Michigan Press: Ann Arbor, Michigan.

Aldrich, John and Michael McGinnis. 1989. "A Model of Party Constraints on Optimal Candidate Positions." *Mathematical and Computer Modeling* 12(4–5): 437–450.

Aldrich, John and David Rohde. 1995. "Theories of the Party in the Legislature and the Transition to Republican Rule in the House." *Political Institutions and Public Choice Working Paper 95–05*. Institute for Public Policy and Social Research, Michigan State University: East Lansing, Michigan.

Aldrich, John and David Rohde. 1996. "A Tale of Two Speakers: A Comparison of Policy Making in the 100th and 104th Congresses." *Political Institutions and Public Choice Working Paper 96–04*. Institute for Public Policy and Social Research, Michigan State University: East Lansing, Michigan.

Alexseev, Mikhail and W. Lance Bennett. 1995. "For Whom the Gates Open: News Reporting and Government Source Patterns in the United States, Great Britain, and Russia." *Political Communication* 12: 395–412.

Allen, Mike. 2005. "Congressional Republicans Agree to Launch Social Security Campaign." *The Washington Post* January 31. Section A, A04. http://www.lexisnexis.com/academic/ (last accessed September 10, 2006).

Althaus, Scott. 1998. "Information Effects in Collective Preferences." *American Political Science Review* 92(3): 545–558.

Althaus, Scott. 2003. "When News Norms Collide, Follow the Lead: New Evidence for Press Independence." *Political Communication* 20: 381–414.

Andsager, Julie. 2000. "How Interest Groups Attempt to Shape Public Opinion with Competing News Frames." *Journalism and Mass Communications Quarterly* 77(3): 577–592.

Ansley, Taylor. 2008. "Next Up: Collaborative Governance?" Posting on http://tropophilia.com/, April 23 (last accessed July 28, 2008).

Ansley, Taylor and Patrick Sellers. 2009. "Mobilizing to Frame the Agenda in Election Campaigns." In Brian Schaffner and Patrick Sellers editors. *Winning With Words: The Origins and Impact of Framing*. Routledge: New York, New York.

Ansolabehere, Stephen, Roy Behr, and Shanto Iyengar. 1993. *The Media Game: American Politics in the Television Age*. Macmillan: New York, New York.

Arnold, R. Douglas. 1990. *The Logic of Congressional Action*. Yale University Press; New Haven, Connecticut.

Arnold, R. Douglas. 2004. *Congress, the Press, and Political Accountability*. Princeton University Press, Princeton, New Jersey.

Aronoff, Roger. 2006. "The Greenhouse Effect." *Media Monitor*. Accuracy in Media. www.aim.org. November 13 (last accessed November 16, 2006).

Austin, Jan. 1998. *Congressional Quarterly Almanac, 105th Congress, 1st Session, 1997*. Congressional Quarterly Inc.: Washington, DC.

Bachrach, Peter and Morton Baratz. 1962. "Two Faces of Power." *American Political Science Review*. 56(4): 947–952.

Bader, John B. 1996. *Taking the Initiative: Leadership Agendas in Congress and the "Contract with America."* Georgetown University Press: Washington, DC.

Bai, Matt. 2005. "The Framing Wars." *New York Times*. www.nytimes.com (last accessed July 19, 2005).

Baker, C. Edwin. 2007. *Media Concentration and Democracy: Why Ownership Matters*. Cambridge University Press: New York, New York.

Baker, Ross. 1996. "Congress – Boom Box and Black Box." *Media Studies Journal* 10(1): 1–11.

Barshay, Jill. 2003 "Democrats Splinter on Stimulus Alternative As Daschle's Plan Fails to Unite Caucus." *CQ Weekly Online* (January 25, 2003): 199–201. http://library.cqpress.com/cqweekly/weeklyreport108-000000579131 (last accessed May 22, 2009).

Bartels, Larry. 1996. "Politicians and the Press: Who Leads, Who Follows?" Paper presented at the annual meeting of the American Political Science Association, San Francisco, California.

Bartels, Larry. 2003. "Democracy with Attitudes." In Michael MacKuen and George Rabinowitz, editors. *Electoral Democracy*. University of Michigan Press: Ann Arbor, Michigan.

Bates, Robert. 1997. Panel on "Rational Choice and Interpretative Approaches to Studying Politics." Presented at the annual meeting of the Midwest Political Science Association, Chicago, Illinois.

Baumgartner, Frank and Bryan D. Jones. 1993. *Agendas and Instability in American Politics*. University of Chicago Press: Chicago, Illinois.

Baumgartner, Frank and Bryan D. Jones. 2002. *Policy Dynamics*. University of Chicago Press: Chicago, Illinois.

Baumgartner, Frank, and Beth Leech. 2001. *Basic Interests: The Importance of Groups in Politics and Political Science*. Princeton University Press: Princeton, New Jersey.

Belt, Todd and Marion Just. 2008. "The Local News Story: Is Quality a Choice?" *Political Communication* 25(2): 194–215.

Ben-Porath, Eran. 2007. "Internal Fragmentation of the News: Television News in Dialogical Format and its Consequences for Journalism." *Journalism Studies* 8(3): 414–431.

Bennett, W. Lance. 1990. "Toward a Theory of Press-State Relations in the United States." *Journal of Communication* 40: 103–124.

Bennett, W. Lance. 1996. "An Introduction to Journalism Norms and Representations of Politics." *Political Communication* 13: 373–384.

Bennett, W. Lance. 2007. *News: The Politics of Illusion. Seventh edition*. Pearson Longman: New York, New York.

Bennett, W. Lance and Robert Entman. 2001. "Mediated Politics: An Introduction." In W. Lance Bennett and Robert Entman editors. *Mediated Politics: Communication in the Future of Democracy*. Cambridge University Press: New York, New York.

Bennett, W. Lance and John Klockner. 1996. "The Psychology of Mass-Mediated Publics." In Ann Crigler editor. *The Psychology of Political Communication*. University of Michigan Press: Ann Arbor, Michigan.

Bennett, W. Lance, Regina Lawrence, and Steven Livingston. 2007. *When the Press Fails: Political Power and the News Media from Iraq to Katrina*. University of Chicago Press: Chicago, Illinois.

Bennett, W. Lance and Jarol Mannheim. 2001. "The Big Spin: Strategic Communication and the Transformation of Pluralist Democracy." In W. Lance Bennett and Robert Entman editors. *Mediated Politics: Communication in the Future of Democracy*. Cambridge University Press: New York, New York.

Bichard, Shannon. 2006. "Building Blogs: A Multi-Dimensional Analysis of the Distribution of Frames on the 2004 Presidential Candidate Web Sites." *J&MC Quarterly* 83(2): 329–345.

Billings, Erin. 2005b. "House Democrats Become iPod People." *Roll Call* July 14. http://www.lexisnexis.com/academic/ (last accessed September 19, 2006).

Billings, Erin. 2006. "Democrats Kick Off Five-Point Message Strategy." *Roll Call* July 13. http://www.lexisnexis.com/academic/ (last accessed September 19, 2006).

Billings, Erin. 2006b. "Lack of Messenger Bedevils Democrats." *Roll Call* June 28. http://www.lexisnexis.com/academic/ (last Accessed September 19, 2006).

Billings, Erin and Mark Preston. 2003. "Focus on 'Home Front': Democrats Mount Push on Domestic Issues." *Roll Call* October 22. http://www.lexisnexis.com/academic/ (last accessed September 10, 2006).

Blumenthal, Sidney. 2008. "Afterword." In Walter Lippmann editor. *Liberty and the News*. Princeton University Press: Princeton, New Jersey.

Blumler, Jay and Dennis Kavanagh. 1999. "The Third Age of Political Communication: Influences and Features." *Political Communication* 16(3): 209–230.

Bond, Jon and Richard Fleisher. 1990. *The President in the Legislative Arena*. University of Chicago Press: Chicago, Illinois.

Brandt, Patrick and John Williams. 2006. *Modeling Multiple Time Series*. Sage Publications: Beverly Hills, California.

Brants, Kee. 2005. "Guest Editor's Introduction: The Internet and the Public Sphere." *Political Communication* 22: 143–146.

Breed, Warren. 1955. "Social Control in the Newsroom: A Functional Analysis." *Social Forces* 33(4): 326–335.

Broder, Jonathan. 2005. "Taking 'As Long As It Takes' No Longer." *CQ Weekly Online* (November 21, 2005): 3114–3121. http://library.cqpress.com/cqweekly/weeklyreport109–000001975394 (last accessed July 2, 2008).

Bumiller, Elisabeth. 2004. "White House Letter; A Democratic Rallying Cry: Vote Bush Out of Rove's Office." *The New York Times* January 19, 2004. www.nytimes.com (last accessed September 25, 2006).

Campbell, Angus, Philip Converse, Warren Miller, and Donald Stokes. 1960. *The American Voter.* Wiley: New York, New York.

Canady, Charles. 1997a. "Canady To Introduce Partial-Birth Abortion Ban." Press Release, January 22.

Canady, Charles. 1997b. "House Passes Ban On Partial-Birth Abortion." Press Release, March 20.

Canady, Charles. 1997c. *Congressional Record* March 20: Page 1202.

Canes-Wrone, Brandice. 2006. *Who Leads Whom? Presidents, Policy, and the Public*. University of Chicago Press: Chicago, Illinois.

Cappella, Joseph and Kathleen Hall Jamieson. 1997. *Spiral of Cynicism: The Press and the Public Good.* Oxford University Press: New York, New York.

Carey, Mary Agnes. 1997. "Senate Heads for Showdown On Controversial Procedure." *CQ Weekly*. May 17. 1137.

Carmines, Edward and James Stimson. 1986. "On the Structure and Sequence of Issue Evolution." *American Political Science Review* 80(3): 901–920.

Carmines, Edward and James Woods. 2002. "The Role of Party Activists in the Evolution of the Abortion Issue." *Political Behavior* 24(4): 361–377.

Caro, Robert. 2003. *Master of the Senate: The Years of Lyndon Johnson*. Random House: New York, New York.

Carpini, Michael X. and Bruce Williams. 2001. "Let Us Infotain You: Politics in the New Media Environment." In W. Lance Bennett and Robert Entman editors. *Mediated Politics: Communication in the Future of Democracy.* Cambridge University Press: New York, New York.

Cassidy, William. "Variations on a Theme: The Professional Role Conceptions of Print and Online Newspaper Journalists." *J&MC Quarterly* 82(2): 264–280.

Chen, Rene, Esther Thorson, and Stephen Lacy. 2005. "The Impact of Newsroom Investment on Newspaper Revenues and Profits: Small and Medium Newspapers, 1998–2002. *J&MC Quarterly* 82(3): 516–532.

Chyi, Hsiang Iris and Maxwell McCombs. 2004. "Media Salience and the Process of Framing: Coverage of the Columbine School Shootings." *J&MC Quarterly* 81(1): 22–35.

Cobb, Roger and Charles Elder. 1983. *Participation in American Politics: The Dynamics of Agenda-Building*. Johns Hopkins University Press: Baltimore, Maryland.

Cochran, John. 2003. "Management by Objective: How Frist Deals in 51–49 Senate." *CQ Weekly*. August 30. 2062. http://www.lexisnexis.com/academic/ (last accessed September 10, 2006).

Cohen, Stanley and Jock Young. 1973. *The Manufacture of News: A Reader.* Sage Publications: Beverly Hills, California.

Congressional Quarterly. 2005. Patriot Act Reauthorization – Cloture. (in Sen.) HR3199. (2005). In *CQ Weekly Online*: Retrieved September 13, 2006, from CQ Electronic Library, CQ Congress Collection, http://library.cqpress.com/congress/wklyoe-245–15559–864025. Document ID: wklyoe-245–15559–864025.

Congressional Quarterly. 2006. War in Iraq and U.S. Troops/Adoption (in H.R.) H Res 557. (2005). In Congressional Roll Call 2004. : Retrieved September 13, 2006, from CQ Electronic Library, CQ Congress Collection, http://library.cqpress.com/congress/rc2004–235-10325–662427. Document ID: rc2004–235–10325–662427.

Cook, Timothy. 1989. *Making Laws and Making News: Media Strategies in the U.S. House of Representatives*. The Brookings Institution: Washington, DC.

Cook, Timothy. 1996. "The Negotiation of Newsworthiness." In Ann Crigler editor. *The Psychology of Political Communication*. University of Michigan Press: Ann Arbor, Michigan.

Cook, Timothy E. 1998. *Governing with the News*. University of Chicago Press: Chicago, Illinois.

Cook, Timothy. 2001. "The Future of the Institutional Media." In W. Lance Bennett and Robert Entman editors. *Mediated Politics: Communication in the Future of Democracy*. Cambridge University Press: New York, New York.

Cook, Timothy. 2006. "The News Media as a Political Institution: Looking Backward and Looking Forward." *Political Communication* 23(2): 159–171.

Coombs, Steven. 1981. "Editorial Endorsements and Electoral Outcomes." In Michael MacKuen and Steven Coombs editors. *More Than News*. Sage Publications: Beverly Hills, California.

Coulson, David and Stephen Lacy. 1996. "Journalists' Perceptions of How Newspaper and Broadcast News Competition Affects Newspaper Content." *J&MC Quarterly* 73(2): 354–363.

Cox, Gary and Mathew McCubbins. 1993. *Legislative Leviathan: Party Government in the House*. University of California Press: Berkeley, California.

Cox, Gary and Mathew McCubbins. 2004. *Setting the Agenda: Responsible Party Government in the U.S. House of Representatives*. Unpublished typescript. Department of Political Science, University of California at San Diego: San Diego, California.

CQ Almanac 1997. Washington: Congressional Quarterly, Inc.

CQ Almanac 2003. Washington: Congressional Quarterly, Inc.

CQ Almanac Online Edition. 1970. "Federal Disaster Assistance." CQ Electronic Library, CQ Almanac Online Edition, cqal70–1294923. Originally published in *CQ Almanac 1970* (Washington: Congressional Quarterly, 1971). http://library.cqpress.com/cqalmanac/cqal70–1294923 (last accessed May 29, 2008).

CQ *Almanac Online Edition*. 1981. "Congress Enacts President Reagan's Tax Plan." CQ Electronic Library, cqal81–1171841. Originally published in *CQ Almanac 1981* (Washington: Congressional Quarterly, 1982). http://library.cqpress.com/cqalmanac/cqal81–1171841 (last accessed May 28, 2008).

CQ *Almanac Online Edition*. 1992. "Fiscal 1992 Natural Disasters Bill Signed." CQ Electronic Library, CQ Almanac Online Edition, cqal91–1109870. Originally published in *CQ Almanac 1991* (Washington: Congressional Quarterly, 1992). http://library.cqpress.com/cqalmanac/cqal91–1109870 (last accessed May 29, 2008).

CQ *Almanac Online Edition*. 1993. "Deficit-Reduction Bill Narrowly Passes." CQ Electronic Library, CQ Almanac Online Edition, cqal93–1105159. Originally published in *CQ Almanac 1993* (Washington: Congressional Quarterly, 1994). http://library.cqpress.com/cqalmanac/cqal93–1105159 (last accessed May 28, 2008).

CQ *Almanac Online Edition*. 1996. "104th Congress Ushers in New Era of GOP Rule." CQ Electronic Library, CQ Almanac Online Edition, cqal95–1099419. Originally published in *CQ Almanac 1995* (Washington: Congressional Quarterly, 1996). http://library.cqpress.com/cqalmanac/cqal95–1099419 (last accessed June 3, 2008).

CQ *Almanac Online Edition*. 1999. "GOP Offers Party-Defining Tax Cut Proposal; Clinton Responds With Veto." CQ Electronic Library, CQ *Almanac Online Edition*, cqal99–0000201210. Originally published in CQ Almanac 1999 (Washington: Congressional Quarterly, 2000). http://library.cqpress.com/cqalmanac/cqal99–0000201210 (last accessed May 28, 2008).

CQ *Weekly*. 1997. "President Details Rejection of Supplemental Bill." June 14. 1393.

CQ *Weekly Online*. 1996a. "Social Policy: Welfare." (November 2): 3148–3149. http://library.cqpress.com/cqweekly/WR403228 (last accessed May 28, 2008).

CQ *Weekly Online*. 1996b. "Special Report: Appropriations." (January 6): 11–18. http://library.cqpress.com/cqweekly/WR409722 (last accessed June 4, 2008).

CQ *Weekly Online*. 2001. "2001 Legislative Summary: Tax Cut Reconciliation." (December 22): 3049–3050. http://library.cqpress.com/cqweekly/weeklyreport107–000000358973 (last accessed May 28, 2008).

CQ *Weekly Online*. 2003a. "Fiscal 2004 Intelligence Authorization – Intelligence Communications." (June 26). http://library.cqpress.com/cqweekly/floorvote108–80140000 (last accessed May 26, 2008).

CQ *Weekly Online*. 2003b. "Fiscal 2004 Defense Appropriations – Intelligence Funding." (July 17). http://library.cqpress.com/cqweekly/floorvote108–84631000 (last accessed May 26, 2008).

CQ *Weekly Online*. 2003c. "Fiscal 2004 Supplemental for Iraq and Afghanistan – Conference Report." (October 30). http://library.cqpress.com/cqweekly/floorvote108–97120000 (last accessed May 26, 2008).

Crabtree, Susan. 2003. "DeLay Will Deliver a 'Speech of the Week.'" *Roll Call* January 29. http://www.lexisnexis.com/academic/ (last accessed September 10, 2006).

Craft, Stephanie and Wayne Wanta. 2004. "Women in the Newsroom: Influence of Female Editors and Reporters on the News Agenda." *J&MC Quarterly* 81(1): 124–138.

Crane, Phil. 1997. "Crane Scores Win on Tax Reform." Press Release, June 10.

Crigler, Ann. 1996. "Introduction: Making Sense of Politics; Constructing Political Messages and Meanings." In Ann Crigler editor. *The Psychology of Political Communication*. University of Michigan Press: Ann Arbor, Michigan.

Crozier, Michael. 2007. "Recursive Governance: Contemporary Political Communication and Public Policy." *Political Communication* 24: 1–18.

D'Alessio, D. and M. Allen. 2000. "Media Bias in Presidential Elections: A Meta-Analysis." *Journal of Communication* 50(4): 133–156.

Dalton, Russell, Paul Beck, and Robert Huckfeldt. 1998. "Partisan Cues and the Media: Information Flows in the 1992 Presidential Election." *The American Political Science Review* 92(1): 111–126.

Daschle, Tom. 1997a. "Children's Health Coverage Act of 1997 Summary." Press Release, January 16.

Daschle, Tom. 1997b. "Daschle on Medicare Trustees Report." Press Release, April 24.

Daschle, Tom. 1997c. "Democrats to Hold All Night Vigil Unless Senate Acts on Disaster-Relief Conference Report." Press Release, June 9.

Daschle, Tom. 1997d. "House and Senate Democrats to Join Secretary Riley and the National Teacher of the Year to Talk About Lifetime Learning Provisions." Press Release, July 15.

Daschle, Tom. 1997e. "News Conference on Children's Health Care Initiative." Press Release, January 14.

Daschle, Tom. 1997f. "Principles of a Balanced Budget: Putting Families First." Press Release, January 24.

Daschle, Tom. 1997g. "Republican Budget Unmasked - A One-Third Cut in Federal Programs." Press Release, March 19.

Daschle, Tom. 1997h. Press Conference. June 12. Washington, DC. www.nexis.com (last accessed November 1, 2006).

Daschle, Tom. 1997i. *The Congressional Record*. May 20. Page S4715.

Daschle, Tom. 2003a. "Adminstration Plan to Cut LIHEAP to Fund More Tax Breaks for the Wealthy a 'Brazen Demonstration of Misplaced Priorities' – Democrates will Force Vote." Press Release, January 6.

Daschle, Tom. 2003b. "Daschle Calls for No New Tax Cuts or New Spending Until the Cost of War is Determined." Press Release, March 18.

Daschle, Tom. 2003c. "Daschle Calls on White House and Republican Leaders to Support Extension of Unemployment Benefits. Says Extending Unemployment Benefits Will Provide Potent Economic Stimulus." Press Release, May 21.

Daschle, Tom. 2003d. "Senator Tom Daschle Unveils Plan to Improve South Dakota's Economy by Creating Jobs and Restoring Growth." Press Release, January 24.

Daschle, Tom. 2003e. "Statement by Senator Tom Daschle on the Impact to Seniors of the President's Tax Plan." Press Release, February 27.

Daschle, Tom. 2003f. "Statement by Senator Tom Daschle on the President's Proposed Budget for Fiscal Year 2004." Press Release, February 3.

Daschle, Tom. 2003g. "Statement by Senator Tom Daschle." Press Release, January 13.

Daschle, Tom. 2003h. "Statement of Senator Daschle in Response to President Bush's Economic Speech in Georgia." Press Release, February 20.

Daschle, Tom. 2003i. "Statement of Senator Tom Daschle on the President's Proposed Budget for Fiscal Year 2004." Press Release, February 3.

Daschle, Tom and Mary Landrieu. 1997. Press Conference. May 15. Washington, DC. http://www.nexis.com (last accessed November 1, 2006).

Davis, Richard. 1996. *The Press and American Politics: The New Mediator. Second edition*. Prentice Hall: Englewood Cliffs, New Jersey.

Davidson, Roger and Walter Oleszek. 1998. *Congress and Its Members. Sixth edition*. Congressional Quarterly Press: Washington, DC.

Davison, W. Philliops. 1983. "The Third-Person Effect in Communication." *Public Opinion Quarterly* 47: 1–15.

Denzau, Arthur, William Riker, and Kenneth Shepsle. 1985. "Farauharson and Fenno: Sophisticated Voting and Home Style." *American Political Science Review* 79(4): 1117–1134.

Dimitrova, Daniela, Lynda Lee Kaid, Andrew Paul Williams, and Kaye Trammell. 2005. "War on the Web: The Immediate News Framing of Gulf War II." *The Harvard International Journal of Press/Politics* 10(1): 22–44.

Domke, David, Erica Graham, Kevin Coe, Sue Lockett John, and Ted Coopman. 2006. "Going Public as Political Strategy: The Bush Administration, an Echoing Press, and Passage of the Patriot Act." *Political Communication* 23: 291–312.

Downie, Leonard, Jr. and Robert Kaiser. 2002. *The News About the News: American Journalism in Peril*. Vintage Books: New York, New York.

Downs, Anthony. 1957. *An Economic Theory of Democracy*. Harper and Row: New York, New York.

Drucker, David. 2006. "Dean: Mayors To Provide Boost." *Roll Call* May 24. http://www.lexisnexis.com/academic/ (last accessed September 19, 2006).

Druckman, James. 2001. "The Implications of Framing Effects for Citizen Competence." *Political Behavior* 23, 3, Special Issue: Citizen Competence Revisited (September): 225–256.

Druckman, James. 2005. "Media Matter: How Newspapers and Television News Cover Campaigns and Influence Voters." *Political Communication* 22: 463–481.

Druckman, James and Dennis Chong. 2007. "Framing Public Opinion in Competitive Democracies." *American Political Science Review* 101: 637–655.

The Economist. 2006. "More Media, Less News." U.S. Edition. 52–54.

Edsall, Thomas. 2006. *Building Red America: The New Conservative Coalition and the Drive for Permanent Power*. Basic Books: New York, New York.

Edwards, George and B. Dan Wood. 1999. "Who Influences Whom? The President, Congress, and the Media." *American Political Science Review* 93(2): 327–344.

Elving, Ronald and Andrew Taylor. 1997. "A Balanced-Budget Deal Won, a Defining Issue Lost." *CQ Weekly* August 2. 1831.
Entman, Robert. 1993. "Framing: Toward Clarification of a Fractured Paradigm." *Journal of Communication* 43, 4: 51–58.
Entman, Robert. 2003. "Cascading Activation: Contesting the White House's Frame after 9/11." *Political Communication* 20: 415–432.
Entman, Robert. 2004. *Projections of Power: Framing News, Public Opinion, and U.S. Foreign Policy.* University of Chicago Press: Chicago, Illinois.
Entman, Robert. 2007. "Framing Bias: Media in the Distribution of Power." *Journal of Communication* 57: 163–173.
Entman, Robert and W. Lance Bennett. 2001. "Communication in the Future of Democracy: A Conclusion." In W. Lance Bennett and Robert Entman editors. *Mediated Politics: Communication in the Future of Democracy.* Cambridge University Press: New York, New York.
Entman, Robert and Susan Herbst. 2001. "Reframing Public Opinion as We Have Known It." In W. Lance Bennett and Robert Entman editors. *Mediated Politics: Communication in the Future of Democracy.* Cambridge University Press: New York, New York.
Epstein, Edward. "Her Key to the House." *CQ Weekly Online.* (October 29, 2007): 3158–3165. http://library.cqpress.com/cqweekly/weeklyreport110–000002614662 (last accessed June 3, 2008).
Erikson, Robert. 1976. "The Influence of Newspaper Endorsements in Presidential Elections." *American Journal of Political Science.* 20(May): 207–234.
Erikson, Robert and Kent Tedin. 2007. *American Public Opinion. Seventh edition.* Allyn and Bacon: Boston, Massachusetts.
Evans, C. Lawrence and Walter J. Oleszek. 2001. "Message Politics and Senate Procedure." In Colton Campbell and Nicol Rae, editors. *The Contentious Senate.* Rowman & Littlefield Publishers, Inc.: New York, New York.
Fenno, Richard F., Jr. 1978. *Homestyle.* Little, Brown: Boston, Massachusetts.
Fessenden, Helen and John Cochran. 2003. "Congress Seeks to Find Its Voice as Iraq War Rages." March 22. Page 676. http://www.cqweekly.com (last accessed on September 14, 2006).
Finocchiaro, Charles and David Rohde. 2002. "War for the Floor: Agenda Control and the Relationship Between Conditional Party Government and Cartel Theory." Unpublished typescript, Department of Political Science, Michigan State University: East Lansing, Michigan.
Firestone, David. 2003. "Democrats Pulling Together United Front Against G.O.P." *The New York Times* March 3. http://www.lexisnexis.com/academic/ (last accessed September 10, 2006).
Foerstel, Karen. 2002. "Campaign Finance Bill Wins Its Day on the House Floor." *CQ Weekly* January 26. P.221. www.cqweekly.com (last accessed September 26, 2006).
Fox, Julia, James Angelini, and Christopher Goble. 2005. "Hype Versus Substance in Network Television Coverage of Presidential Election Campaigns." *J&MC Quarterly* 82(1): 97–109.

Franklin, Charles. 1991. "Eschewing Obfuscation: Campaigns and Perceptions of U.S. Senate Incumbents." *American Political Science Review* 85(4): 1193–1214.

Freeman, John, John Williams, and Tse-min Lin. 1989. "Vector Autoregression and the Study of Politics." *American Journal of Political Science* 33(4): 842–877.

Frisch, Scott and Sean Kelly. 2008. "Leading the Senate in the 110th Congress." *PS: Political Science and Politics* XLI(1): 69–76.

Frist, Bill. 2003a. "Frist Comments on Senate Passage of the Tax Relief Reconciliation Act." Press Release, May 23.

Frist, Bill. 2003b. "Frist Reacts to Budget Passage." Press Release, April 11.

Gamson, William. 1996. "Media Discourse as a Framing Resource." In Ann Crigler editor. *The Psychology of Political Communication*. University of Michigan Press, Ann Arbor, Michigan.

Gamson, William. 2001. "Foreword." In Stephen Reese, Oscar Gandy, and August Grant editors. *Framing Public Life: Perspectives on Media and Our Understanding of the Social World*. Lawrence Erlbaum Associates, Publishers: Mahwah, New Jersey.

Gamson, William. 2001b. "Promoting Political Engagement." In W. Lance Bennett and Robert Entman editors. *Mediated Politics: Communication in the Future of Democracy*. Cambridge University Press: New York, New York.

Gamson, William and Andre Modigliani. 1989. "Media Discourse and Public Opinion on Nuclear Power: A Constructionist Approach." *The American Journal of Sociology* 95(1): 1–37.

Gandy, Oscar. 2001. "Dividing Practices: Segmentation and Targeting in the Emerging Public Sphere." In W. Lance Bennett and Robert Entman editors. *Mediated Politics: Communication in the Future of Democracy*. Cambridge University Press: New York, New York.

Gans, Herbert. 2004. *Deciding What's News: A Study of CBS Evening News, NBC Nightly News, Newsweek and Time, 25th Anniversary Edition*. Northwestern University Press: Evanston, Illinois.

Gentzkow, Matthew and Jesse Shapiro. 2007. "What Drives Media Slant? Evidence from U.S. Daily Newspapers." NBER Working Paper 12707. University of Chicago, Chicago, Illinois.

Gephardt, Richard. 1997a. "Dear Colleague Letter on Children's Health Care and Campaign Finance Reform." Press Release, February 26.

Gephardt, Richard. 1997b. "Dear Colleague Urging Immediate Action on Disaster Aid Bill." Press Release, June 3.

Gephardt, Richard. 1997c. "Democratic Leaders to Join Freshman to Decry 'Do-Nothing' Congress." Press Release, April 8.

Gephardt, Richard. 1997d. "Gephardt Calls GOP Tax Cuts 'Anti-Family.'" Press Release, June 19.

Gephardt, Richard. 1997e. "Gephardt Comments on Gingrich Tax Giveaway." Press Release, April 10.

Gephardt, Richard. 1997f. "Gephardt Criticizes Gingrich Tax Cut Proposal." Press Release, April 9.

Gephardt, Richard. 1997g. "Gephardt Opposes Budget Agreement." Press Release, May 20.

Gephardt, Richard. 1997h. "Gephardt Statement Regarding Bipartisan Budget Agreement." Press Release, July 29.

Gephardt, Richard. 1997i. "Medicare Budget Cuts." Press Release, July 11.

Gephardt, Richard. 1997j. "Remarks Before the Economic Policy Institute." Press Release, January 24.

Gephardt, Richard. 1997k. "Statement on GOP Cuts in Children's Nutrition Programs." Press Release, April 30.

Gephardt, Richard. 1997l. "Statement Regarding President's State of the Union Address." Press Release, February 4.

Gephardt, Richard. 1997m. Press Conference. July 24. Washington, DC. www.nexis.com (last accessed November 1, 2006).

Gerrity, Jessica. 2007. "Winning a Framing War?: Interest Group Framing and Media Coverage of the Partial-Birth Abortion Debate." In Brian Schaffner and Patrick Sellers editors. *Winning With Words: The Origins and Impact of Framing*. Routledge: New York, New York.

Gimpel, James. 1996. *Fulfilling the Contract: The First 100 Days*. Allyn & Bacon: Boston, Massachusetts.

Gingrich, Newt. 1997a. "Letter to Clinton Urging Clinton to Begin Bipartisan Talks with Congress about 105th Congress Agenda." Press Release, February 3.

Gingrich, Newt. 1997b. "Letter to Gephardt, Daschle, Urging Bipartisan Approach to Balancing Budget." Press Release, March 6.

Gingrich, Newt. 1997c. "Letter to President Clinton Confirming Important Aspects of the Balanced Budget Agreement." Press Release, May 15.

Gingrich, Newt. 1997d. "Speaker Gingrich Applauds Debt Repayment Act as Road Map for Smaller, Smarter Government." Press Release, July 17.

Gingrich, Newt. 1997e. "Speaker Statement on Cost of Government Day." Press Release, July 3.

Gingrich, Newt. 1997f. "Speaker's Statement on Veto of Disaster Relief." Press Release, June 9.

Gingrich, Newt. 1997g. Press Conference. July 29. Washington, DC. www.nexis.com (last accessed November 1, 2006).

Gingrich, Newt and Bill Archer. 1997. Press Conference. June 19. Washington, DC. www.nexis.com (last accessed November 1, 2006).

Graber, Doris. 1996. "Whither Research on the Psychology of Political Communication." In Ann Crigler editor. *The Psychology of Political Communication*. University of Michigan Press: Ann Arbor, Michigan.

Graber, Doris. 2006. *Mass Media & American Politics*. CQ Press: Washington, DC.

Graham, Bradley. 2004. "Generals See Gains from Iraq Offensives." *The Washington Post* December 6: Page A01. www.nexis.com (last accessed November 30, 2006).

Groeling, Tim. 2005. "Man Bites President: The Mediation of Partisan Communication." Typescript. Department of Communication Studies, UCLA: Los Angeles. California.

Groeling, Tim and Samuel Kernell. 2000. "Congress, the President, and Party Competition via Network News." In Jon Bond and Richard Fleisher editors. *Polarized Politics: Congress and the President in a Partisan Era*. CQ Press: Washington, DC.

Groseclose, Tim and Jeffrey Milyo. 2005. "A Measure of Media Bias." *The Quarterly Journal of Economics* CXX(4): 1191–1237.

Grunwald, Michael. 2006. "The Year of Playing Dirtier; Negative Ads Get Positively Surreal." *Washington Post* October 27: Page A01. www.nexis.com (last accessed November 30, 2006).

Gunther, Albert. 1992. "Biased Press or Biased Public? Attitudes Toward Media Coverage of Social Groups." *The Public Opinion Quarterly* 56(2): 147–167.

Gunther, Albert and Paul Mundy. 1993. "Biased Optimism and the Third-Person Effect." *Journalism Quarterly* 70(1): 58–67.

Hager, George. 1997a. "Hill OKs Fiscal '98 Resolution, But Trouble Spots Abound." *CQ Weekly* June 7. 1304.

Hager, George. 1997b. "For GOP, a New Song – Same Ending." *CQ Weekly* June 14. 1406.

Hager, George. 1997c. "Clinton Budget 'Alive on Arrival' But GOP Wary of Fine Print." *CQ Weekly* February 8. 327.

Hager, George. 1997e. "Clinton, GOP Congress Strike Historic Budget Agreement." *CQ Weekly* May 3. 993.

Hall, Richard. 1996. *Participation in Congress*. Yale University Press: New Haven, Connecticut.

Hamburger, Tom and Peter Wallsten. 2006. *One Party Country: The Republican Plan for Dominance in the 21st Century*. Wiley: New York, New York.

Hamilton, Alexander, James Madison, and John Jay. 1961. *The Federalist Papers, Number 51*. Signet: New York, New York.

Hamilton, James. 2004. *All the News That's Fit to Sell*. Princeton University Press: Princeton, New Jersey.

Hardin, Russell. 1982. *Collective Action*. The Johns Hopkins University Press: Baltimore, Maryland.

Harris, Douglas. 1998. "The Rise of the Public Speakership." *Political Science Quarterly* 113(2): 193–212.

Harris, Douglas. 2005. "House Majority Party Leaders' Uses of Public Opinion Information." Paper presented at the annual meeting of the American Political Science Association, Washington, DC, September 1–4.

Hart, Peter. 2003. *The Oh Really? Factor: Unspinning Fox News Channel's Bill O'Reilly*. Seven Stories Press: New York, New York.

Hastert, Dennis. 2003a. "Hastert: This Tax Cut Will Grow the Economy and Create More Jobs." Press Release, May 22.

Hastert, Dennis. 2003b. "Regarding the President's Budget." Press Release, March 24.

Hastert, Dennis. 2003c. "Speaker Calls for Better Access to Quality Health Care." Press Release, March 12.

Hastert, Dennis. 2003d. "Speaker Hastert Strongly Supports President Bush's Economic Growth and Creation Package." Press Release, February 13.

Hastert, Dennis. 2003e. "Speaker Hastert's Speech at the American Medical Association's 2003 Advocacy Conference." Press Release, March 4.

Healey, Jon. "Provisions: Emergency Disaster Supplemental." *CQ Weekly Online* (February 19, 1994): 438–444. http://library.cqpress.com/cqweekly/WR103403642 (last accessed May 29, 2008).

Hearn, Josephine. 2005. "Dems Test New Slogan: 'Can Do Better' Message Aims for Big '06 Theme." *The Hill*. October 25. http://www.lexisnexis.com/academic/ (last accessed September 19, 2006).

Heath, Diane. 1998. "Staffing the White House Public Opinion Apparatus: 1969–1988." *Public Opinion Quarterly* 62: 165–189.

Heider, Don, Maxwell McCombs, and Paula Poindexter. 2005. "What the Public Expects of Local News: Views on Public and Traditional Journalism." *J&MC Quarterly* 82(4): 952–967.

Herman, Edward and Noam Chomsky. 1988. *Manufacturing Consent: The Political Economy of the Mass Media*. Pantheon: New York, New York.

Herrnson, Paul. 2004. *Congressional Elections: Campaigning at Home and in Washington*. CQ Press: Washington, DC.

Hess, Stephen. 1986. *The Ultimate Insiders: U.S. Senators in the National Media*. The Brookings Institution: Washington, DC.

Hess, Stephen. 1991. *Live From Capitol Hill! Studies of Congress and the Media*. The Brookings Institution: Washington, DC.

Hiatt, Fred. 2006. "How We Endorse, and Why." *Washington Post*. September 11. Page A17. www.washingtonpost.com (last accessed September 12, 2006).

Hilgartner, James and Charles Bosk. 1988. "The Rise and Fall of Social Problems: A Public Arenas Model." *American Journal of Sociology* 94(1): 53–78.

Hoffman, Lindsay. 2006. "Is Internet Content Different After All? A Content Analysis of Mobilizing Information in Online and Print Newspapers." *J&MC Quarterly* 83(1): 58–76.

Hofstetter, C. Richard. 1976. *Bias in the News: Network Television Coverage of the 1972 Election Campaign*. Ohio State University Press: Columbus, Ohio.

Hopkins, Daniel and Gary King. 2007. "Extracting Systematic Social Science Meaning from Text." Paper presented at the annual meeting of the Society for Political Methodology. http://gking.harvard.edu/files/words.pdf (last accessed July 28, 2008).

Horrigan, John, Kelly Garrett, and Paul Resnick. 2004. *"The Internet and Democratic Debate."* Washington, DC: Pew Internet and American Life Project. http://www.pewinternet.org/pdfs/PIP_Political_Info_Report.pdf (last accessed July 28, 2008).

Iyengar, Shanto. 1991. *Is Anyone Responsible?: How Television Frames Political Issues*. University of Chicago Press: Chicago, Illinois.

Iyengar, Shanto and Donald Kinder. 1987. *News that Matters: Television and American Opinion*. University of Chicago Press: Chicago, Illinois.

Iyengar, Shanto and Jennifer McGrady. 2007. *Media Politics: A Citizen's Guide*. W.W. Norton & Company: New York, New York.

Jacobs, Lawrence and Robert Shapiro. 2000. *Politicians Don't Pander: Political Manipulation and the Loss of Democratic Responsiveness*. University of Chicago Press: Chicago, Illinois.

Jacobs, Lawrence, Eric Lawrence, Robert Shapiro, and Steven Smith. 2002. "Congressional Leadership of Public Opinion." *Political Science Quarterly* 113(1): 21–41.

Jacobson, Gary. 2004. *The Politics of Congressional Elections*. Pearson Longman: New York, New York.

Jacoby, William. 2000. "Issue Framing and Public Opinion on Government Spending." *American Journal of Political Science* 44: 750–767.

Jasperson, Amy, Dhavan Shah, Mark Watts, Ronald Faber, and David Fan. 1998. "Framing and the Public Agenda: Media Effects on the Importance of the Federal Budget Deficit." *Political Communication* 15: 205–224.

Jerit, Jennifer. 2005. "Reform, Rescue, or Run Out of Money? Problem Definition in the Social Security Reform Debate." Paper presented at the annual meeting of the American Political Science Association, Washington, DC, September 1–4.

Kady, Martin. 2006. "Party Unity: Learning to Stick Together." *CQ Weekly*. January 6. Page 92. www.cqweekly.com (last accessed September 14, 2006).

Kahn, Kim Fridkin, and Patrick Kenney. 2002. "The Slant of the News: How Editorial Endorsements Influence Campaign Coverage and Citizens' View of Candidates." *American Political Science Review* 96(2): 381–394.

Katz, Jeffrey. 1997. "Studios beam members from Hill to hometown." *Congressional Quarterly Weekly Report*. November 29. 55(47): 2946–2947. www.epnet.com (last accessed January 19, 2005).

Kedrowski, Karen. 1996. *Media Entrepreneurs and the Media Enterprise in the U.S. Congress*. Hampton Press: Cresskill, New Jersey.

Kernell, Samuel. 1997. *Going Public: New Strategies of Presidential Leadership. Third edition*. CQ Press: Washington, DC.

Kieweit, D.Roderick and Mathew McCubbins. 1991. *The Logic of Delegation: Congressional Parties and the Appropriations Process*. University of Chicago Press: Chicago, Illinois.

King, Cynthia and Paul Martin Lester. 2005. "Photographic Coverage During the Persian Gulf War and Iraqi Wars in Three U.S. Newspapers." *J&MC Quarterly* 82(3): 623–637

King, Gary, Robert Keohane, and Sidney Verba. 1994. *Designing Social Inquiry: Scientific Inference in Qualitative Research*. Princeton: Princeton University Press.

King, Gary, Michael Tomz, and Jason Wittenberg. 2000. "Making the Most of Statistical Analyses: Improving Interpretation and Presentation." *American Journal of Political Science* 44(2): 347–361.

Kingdon, John. 2003. *Agendas, Alternatives, and Public Policies. Second edition*. Longman Press: New York, New York.

Kirkpatrick, David and Adam Nagourney. 2006. "In an Election Year, a Shift in Public Opinion on the War." *The New York Times* March 27: Page A12. www.nexis.com (last accessed November 30, 2006).

Klein, Rick. 2005b. "Senate Democrats Coordinate Message, Attack on Bush." *The Boston Globe* January 25. www.boston.com (last accessed September 21, 2006).

Koch, Jeffrey. 2001. "When Parties and Candidates Collide: Citizen Perception of House Candidates' Positions on Abortion." *Public Opinion Quarterly* 65: 1–21.

Kornacki, Steve. 2005. "House Democrats Initiate Morning Issue Calls." *Roll Call* December 14. http://www.lexisnexis.com/academic/ (last accessed September 19, 2006).

Koszczuk, Jackie. 1995. "Gingrich's Abortion Strategies." *CQ Weekly Online* (November 4): 3376–3376. http://library.cqpress.com/cqweekly/WR409312 (last accessed June 4, 2008).

Koszczuk, Jackie. 1997. "Republicans Set the Stage: Try 104th Agenda Again." *CQ Weekly.* March 8. 575.

Kovach, Bill and Tom Rosenstiel. 2001. *The Elements of Journalism.* Crown Publishers: New York, New York.

Krehbiel, Keith. 1991. *Information and Legislative Organization.* University of Michigan Press: Ann Arbor, Michigan.

Krehbiel, Keith. 1998. *Pivotal Politics: A Theory of U.S. Lawmaking.* University of Chicago Press: Chicago, Illinois.

Krosnick, Jon and Donald Kinder. 1990. "Altering the Foundations of Support for the President Through Priming." *American Political Science Review* 84(2): 497–512.

Kuklinski, James and Paul Quirk. 2000. "Reconsidering the Rational Public: Cognition, Heuristics, and Mass Opinion." In Arthur Lupia, Mathew McCubbins, and Samuel Popkin editors. *Elements of Reason: Cognition, Choice, and the Bounds of Rationality.* Cambridge University Press: New York, New York.

Kuklinski, James, and Lee Sigelman. 1992. "When Objectivity is Not Objective: Network Television News Coverage of U.S. Senators and the 'Paradox of Objectivity.'" *The Journal of Politics* 54(3): 810–833.

Kurtz, Howard. 2001. "CNN Chief Orders 'Balance' in War News." *The Washington Post.* October 31. C01.

Lacy, Dean. 2001. "A Theory of Nonseparable Preferences in Survey Responses." *American Journal of Political Science* 45(2): 239–258.

Lake, Celinda, Daniel Gotoff, and Erica Prosser. 2005. "The Battleground 2006." *Typescript* (last accessed July 8, 2008).

Lakoff, George. 2004. *Don't Think of An Elephant.* Chelsea Green Publishing: White River Junction, Vermont.

Lawrence, Regina. 1996. "Accidents, Icons, and Indexing: The Dynamics of News Coverage of Police Use of Force." *Political Communication* 13: 437–454.

Lawrence, Regina. 2000. "Game-Framing the Issues: Tracking the Strategy Frame in Public Policy News." *Political Communication* 17: 93–114.

Lawrence, Regina. 2006. "Seeing the Whole Board: New Institutional Analysis of News Content." *Political Communication* 23: 225–230.

Lawrence, Regina and Thomas Birkland. 2004. "Guns, Hollywood, and School Safety: Defining the School-Shooting Problem Across Public Arenas." *Social Science Quarterly* 85(5): 1193–1207.

Lichter, Robert and Stanley Rothman. 1983. *The Media Elite: America's New Power Brokers.* Adler and Adler: Bethesda, Maryland.

Lim, Jeongsub. 2006. "A Cross-Lagged Analysis of Agenda Setting Among Online News Media." *J&MC Quarterly* 83(2): 298–312.

Lipinski, Daniel. 2004. *Congressional Communication: Content and Consequences*. University of Michigan Press: Ann Arbor, Michigan.

Lippmann, Walter. 1920/2008. *Liberty and the News*. Princeton University Press: Princeton, New Jersey.

Loomis, Burdett. 2001. "Senate Leaders, Minority Voices: From Dirksen to Daschle." In Colton Campbell and Nicol Rae editors. *The Contentious Senate: Partisanship, Ideology, and the Myth of Cool Judgment*. Rowman & Littlefield: New York, New York.

Lott, Trent. 1997a. "Trent Lott's remarks at National Association of Counties Annual Legislative Conference." March 3. www.nexis.com (last accessed November 1, 2006).

Lott, Trent. 1997b. "Letter to President Clinton about the Pictures of Devastation on the Great Plains." Press Release, May 22.

Lott, Trent. 1997c. "Senate Majority Leader Trent Lott Gives Republican Radio Address." Press Release, June 14.

Lott, Trent. 1997d. Press Conference. June 3. Washington, DC. www.nexis.com (last accessed November 1, 2006).

Lott, Trent. 1997e. Press Conference. June 5. Washington, DC. www.nexis.com (last accessed November 1, 2006).

Lott, Trent. 1997g. "Remarks of U.S. Senator Trent Lott of Mississippi, the Senate Majority Leader, The Economic Club of Chicago." Press Release, May 5.

Luntz, Frank. 2007. *Words That Work: It's Not What You Say, It's What People Hear.* Hyperion: New York, New York.

Lupia, Arthur. 1994. "Shortcuts versus Encyclopedias: Information and Voting Behavior in California Insurance Reform Elections." *American Political Science Review* 88: 63–76.

Lupia, Arthur and Mathew McCubbins. 1998. *The Democratic Dilemma: Can Citizens Learn What They Need to Know?* Cambridge University Press: New York, New York.

Luther, Catherine and M. Mark Miller. "Framing of the 2003 U.S.-Iraq War Demonstrations: An Analysis of News and Partisan Texts." *J&MC Quarterly* 82(1): 78–96.

Maltese, John Anthony. 1994. *Spin Control: The White House Office of Communications and the Management of Presidential News. Second edition.* University of North Carolina Press: Chapel Hill, North Carolina.

Manheim, Jarol. 1991. *All of the People, All the Time: Strategic Communication and American Politics.* M.E. Sharpe: Armonk, New York.

Manheim, Jarol. 1994. "Strategic Public Diplomacy." In W. Lance Bennett and David Paletz editors. *Taken By Storm.* University of Chicago Press: Chicago, Illinois.

Manheim, Jarol. 2008. "The News Shapers: Strategic Communication as a Third Force in Newsmaking." In Doris Graber, Denis McQuail, and Pippa Norris editors. *The Politics of News, The News of Politics.* CQ Press: Washington, DC.

Masi, Paul, Joe Reed, Patrick Sellers, and Lauren Woodall. 2006. "Capturing Partisan Bias in News Coverage." Typescript. Davidson College: Davidson, North Carolina.

Mason, Julie. 2004. "Kerry Slams Bush War Policy." *The Houston Chronicle* September 25: Page A23. www.nexis.com (last accessed November 30, 2006).

Matthews, Donald. 1959. "The Folkways of the United States Senate: Conformity to Group Norms and Legislative Effectiveness." *The American Political Science Review* 53(4): 1064–1089.

Mayhew, David. 1974. *Congress: The Electoral Connection*. Yale University Press: New Haven, Connecticut.

McCombs, Maxwell and Salma Ghanem. 2001. "The Convergence of Agenda Setting and Framing." In Stephen Reese, Oscar Gandy, and August Grant editors. *Framing Public Life: Perspectives on Media and Our Understanding of the Social World*. Lawrence Erlbaum Associates, Publishers: Mahwah, New Jersey.

McCombs, Maxwell and Donald Shaw. 1972. "The Agenda-Setting Function of Mass Media." *The Public Opinion Quarterly* 36(2): 176–187.

McCombs, Maxwell and Donald Shaw. 1993. "The Evolution of Agenda-Setting Research: Twenty-Five Years in the Marketplace of Ideas." *Journal of Communication* 43(2): 58–67.

McQuail, Denis. 1994. *Mass Communication Theory: An Introduction. Third edition*. Sage: London, England.

Media Research Center. 2005. "TV's Bad News Brigade: ABC, CBS and NBC's Defeatist Coverage of the War in Iraq." October 13. Special Report. Alexandria, VA. http://www.mrc.org/specialreports/2005/pdf/TVs_Depressing_Iraq_News.pdf (last accessed July 2, 2008).

Milbank, Dana and Claudia Deane. 2005. "Poll Finds Dimmer View of Iraq War." *The Washington Post* June 8: Page A01. www.nexis.com (last accessed November 30, 2006).

Miller, M.Mark. 1997. "Frame Mapping and Analysis of News Coverage of Contentious Issues." *Social Science Computer Review* 15(4): 367–378.

Miller, M.Mark and Bonnie Parnell Riechert. 2001. "The Spiral of Opportunity and Frame Resonance: Mapping the Issue Cycle in News and Public Discourse." In Stephen Reese, Oscar Gandy, and August Grant editors. *Framing Public Life: Perspectives on Media and Our Understanding of the Social World*. Lawrence Erlbaum Associates, Publishers: Mahwah, New Jersey.

Miller, Susan. 1977. "News Coverage of Congress: The Search for the Ultimate Spokesman." *Journalism Quarterly* 54(Autumn) 459–465.

Mutz, Diana. 2006. *Hearing the Other Side*. Cambridge University Press: New York, New York.

Mutz, Diana and Paul Martin. 2001. "Facilitating Communication Across Lines of Difference: The Role of Mass Media." *American Political Science Review* 95(1): 97–114.

Nagourney, Adam. 2006. "Lost Horizons." *The New York Times* September 24. www.nytimes.com (last accessed September 25, 2006).

NARAL. 2006. "2005 Congressional Record on Choice." http://www.prochoiceamerica.org/assets/files/CAC-cong-record-on-choice-2005.pdf (last accessed September 8, 2006).

Nather, David. 2006a. "Does 'Majority of the Majority' Have a Future?" *CQ Weekly* August 14. 2229. www.cqweekly.com (last accessed September 14, 2006).

Nather, David. 2006b. "Dems Strike Out Haltingly in 'New Direction.'" *CQ Weekly Online* July 31. 2086–2086. http://library.cqpress.com/cqweekly/weeklyreport109-000002350491 (last accessed June 3, 2008).

Nather, David. 2007a. "A Waning Season for Making Law." *CQ Weekly Online* July 9. 2008–2016. http://library.cqpress.com/cqweekly/weeklyreport110-000002546501 (last accessed June 3, 2008).

Nather, David. 2007b. "A Crisis of Confidence in Congress." *CQ Weekly Online* October 22. 3060–3066. http://library.cqpress.com/cqweekly/weeklyreport110-000002609420 (last accessed June 3, 2008).

Nather, David. 2007d. "Democrats' Turn at Immigration Split." *CQ Weekly Online* March 5. 636–637. http://library.cqpress.com/cqweekly/weeklyreport110-000002461937 (last accessed June 4, 2008).

Neuendorf, Kimberly. 2002. *The Content Analysis Guidebook*. Sage Publications, Inc.: Thousand Oaks, California.

Neustadt, Richard. 1990. *Presidential Power and the Modern Presidents*. Free Press: New York, New York.

Niven, David. 2001. "Bias in the News: Partisanship and Negativity in Media Coverage of Presidents George Bush and Bill Clinton." *Harvard International Journal of Press/Politics* 6(3): 31–46.

Niven, David. 2002. *Tilt? The Search for Media Bias*. Praeger Publishers: Westport, Connecticut.

Niven, David. 2003. "Objective Evidence on Media Bias: Newspaper Coverage of Congressional Party Switchers." *J&MC Quarterly* 80(2): 311–326.

Niven, David. 2005. "An Economic Theory of Political Journalism." *J&MC Quarterly* 82(2): 247–263.

Noelle-Neumann, E. 1984. *Spiral of Silence: Our Social Skin*. University of Chicago Press: Chicago, Illinois.

O'Connor, Patrick. 2006. "GOP Brass Enlists Help on Message." *The Hill*. April 19. http://www.lexisnexis.com/academic/ (last accessed September 19, 2006).

Olson, Mancur. 1965. *The Logic of Collective Action*. Harvard University Press: Cambridge, Massachusetts.

Ornstein, Norman. 2003. "To Boost Power, Unity Is Key for Both Parties." *Roll Call* September 8. http://www.lexisnexis.com/academic/ (last accessed September 10, 2006).

Ornstein, Norman and Thomas Mann. 2000. *The Permanent Campaign and Its Future*. American Enterprise Institute and Brookings Institution: Washington, DC.

Ornstein, Norman, Thomas Mann, and Michael Malbin. 2002. *Vital Statistics on Congress, 2001–2002*. AEI Press: Washington, DC.

Ota, Alan. 2003a. "Uncertain Future in Conference Awaits Bush Tax Cut Package." *CQ Weekly* April 19. 935.

Ota, Alan. 2003b. "Tax Cut Package Clears Amid Bicameral Rancor." *CQ Weekly* May 24. 1245.

Page, Benjamin. 1995. "Speedy Deliberation: Rejecting '1960s Programs' as Causes of the Los Angeles Riots." *Political Communication* 12(July): 245–261.

Page, Benjamin. 1996. *Who Deliberates? Mass Media in Modern Democracy.* University of Chicago Press: Chicago, Illinois.

Palazzolo, Dan. 1999. *Done Deal? The Politics of the 1997 Budget Agreement.* Chatham House Publishers: New York, New York.

Paletz, David and Robert Entman. 1981. *The Mass Media Election.* Free Press: New York, New York.

Pan, Zhongdang and Gerald Kosicki. 2001. "Framing as a Strategic Action in Public Deliberation." In Stephen Reese, Oscar Gandy, and August Grant editors. *Framing Public Life: Perspectives on Media and Our Understanding of the Social World.* Lawrence Erlbaum Associates, Publishers: Mahwah, New Jersey.

Patterson, Thomas. 1994. *Out of Order.* Vintage Books: New York, New York.

Patterson, Thomas and Wolfgang Donsbach. 1996. "News Decisions: Journalists as Partisan Actors." *Political Communication* 13: 455–468.

Peake, Jeffrey and Matthew Eshbaugh-Soha. 2008. "The Agenda-Setting Impact of Major Presidential TV Addresses." *Political Communication* 25(2): 113–137.

Pearson, Kathryn. 2005. "Party Discipline in the Contemporary Congress: Rewarding Loyalty in Theory and in Practice." Ph.D. dissertation. Department of Political Science. University of California: Berkeley, California.

Pelosi, Nancy. 2003a. "House Republicans Buckle Under Pressure from Democrats to Restore Veterans' Funding." Press Release, April 1.

Pelosi, Nancy. 2003b. "Pelosi Statement on New Job Loss Numbers." Press Release, January 10.

Pelosi, Nancy. 2003c. "Pelosi: 'It is Simply Wrong to Pass a Budget that Fails Veterans, Students, Seniors, Children, and the Disabled.'" Press Release, March 31.

Pelosi, Nancy. 2003d. "Daschle, Pelosi: 'President Must Take Immediate Action to Expand Child Tax Credit.'" Press Release, June 9.

Pelosi, Nancy. 2003e. "Pelosi Republican Budget 'Reckless and Irresponsible.'" Press Release, March 13.

Pelosi, Nancy. 2003f. "Pelosi Statement on Bush Administration's Promotional Economic Tour." Press Release, February 12.

Pelosi, Nancy. 2003g. "Pelosi Statement on Covering the Uninsured." Press Release, March 12.

Pelosi, Nancy. 2003h. "Pelosi Statement on House Democratic Economic Stimulus Plan." Press Release, January 6.

Pelosi, Nancy. 2003i. "Pelosi Statement on Impact on Seniors of Bush Economic Plan." Press Release, February 27.

Pelosi, Nancy. 2003j. "Pelosi to GOP Leadership: 'Let Us Vote This Week to Extend Unemployment Insurance.'" Press Release, May 21.

Pelosi, Nancy. 2003k. "Pelosi: 'Irresponsible GOP Tax Cut for Millionaires Leaves Working Families Out In the Cold.'" Press Release, May 9.

Pelosi, Nancy. 2003l. "Pelosi: On Economic Tour, Administration Should Listen to Families – Job Losses are Taking a Real Toll." Press Release, July 29.

Pelosi, Nancy. 2003m. "Pelosi: 'Republican Budget is a National Disgrace.'" Press Release, April 10.

Pelosi, Nancy. 2003n. "Pelosi: 'Tax Bill President Signed is Oblivious to the Needs of Real Families.'" Press Release, May 28.

Pelosi, Nancy. 2003o. "Pelosi: 'Tax Cut Will Not Grow the Economy, Only the Deficit." Press Release, May 23.

Pelosi, Nancy. 2003p. Press Conference. July 24. Washington, DC. www.nexis.com (last accessed November 1, 2006).

Perloff, Richard. 1996. "Perceptions and Conceptions of Political Media Impact: The Third-Person Effect and Beyond." In Ann Crigler editor. *The Psychology of Political Communication*. University of Michigan Press: Ann Arbor, Michigan.

Pershing, Ben. 2005. "GOP Tries to Find Voice." *Roll Call* September 26. http://www.lexisnexis.com/academic/ (last accessed September 19, 2006).

Pershing, Ben. 2006. "GOP Hopes to Tout Economy; Aides to WH: No Surprises." *Roll Call* March 1. http://www.lexisnexis.com/academic/ (last accessed September 19, 2006).

Petrocik, John R. 1996. "Issue Ownership in Presidential Elections, with a 1980 Case Study." *American Journal of Political Science* 40(August):825–850.

Pew Research Center. 2005. *Trends 2005*. Pew Research Center: Washington, DC. http://pewresearch.org/assets/files/trends2005.pdf (last accessed July 28, 2008).

Pew Research Center For The People and Press. 2004. "Press Going Too Easy on Bush: Bottom-Line Pressures Now Hurting Coverage, Say Journalists." Washington, DC. News Release, May 23.

Poole, Keith. 2005. http://voteview.com/dwnl.htm (last accessed July 25, 2005).

Pope, Jeremy and Jonathan Woon. 2005. "The Dynamics of Party Reputation." Paper presented at the annual meeting of the American Political Science Association. September 3. Washington, DC.

Popkin, Samuel. 1994. *The Reasoning Voter: Communication and Persuasion in Presidential Campaigns. Second edition*. University of Chicago Press: Chicago, Illinois.

Popkin, Samuel. 2006. "Changing Media, Changing Politics." *Perspectives on Politics* 4, (2): 327–341.

Preston, Mark and Erin Billings. 2004. "Democrats Tout '80 Reagan Line." *Roll Call* May 18. http://www.lexisnexis.com/academic/ (last accessed September 10, 2006).

Preston, Mark and Susan Crabtree. 2002. "Parties Vie for Edge on Education." *Roll Call* May 6. http://www.lexisnexis.com/academic/ (last accessed September 10, 2006).

Price, David E. 1978. "Policy Making in Congressional Committees: The Impact of 'Environmental' Factors." *American Political Science Review* 72(2): 548–574.

Quinn, Kevin, Burt Monroe, Michael Colaresi, Michael Crespin, and Dragomir Radev. 2006. "An Automated Method of Topic-Coding Legislative Speech Over Time with Application to the 105th-108th U.S. Senate." Paper presented at the annual meeting of the American Political Science Association: Philadelphia, Pennsylvania.

Reese, Stephen. 2001. "Prologue – Framing Public Life: A Bridging Model for Media Research." In Stephen Reese, Oscar Gandy, and August Grant editors. *Framing Public Life: Perspectives on Media and Our Understanding of the Social World.* Lawrence Erlbaum Associates, Publishers: Mahwah, New Jersey.

Reinemann, Carsten. 2004. "Routine Reliance Revisited: Exploring Media Importance for German Political Journalists." *J&MC Quarterly* 81(4): 857–876.

Riffe, Daniel, Stephen Lacy, and Frederick Fico. 2005. *Analyzing Media Messages: Using Quantitative Content Analysis in Research.* Lawrence Erlbaum Associates Publishers: Mahway, New Jersey.

Riker, William. 1986. *The Art of Political Manipulation.* Yale University Press: New Haven, Connecticut.

Riker, William. 1982. *Liberalism Against Populism: A Confrontation Between the Theory of Democracy and the Theory of Social Choice.* Waveland Press: Prospect Heights, Illinois.

Riker, William H. and Peter Ordeshook. 1968. "A Theory of the Calculus of Voting." *American Political Science Review* 62(1): 25–42.

Robinson, John. 1974. "Perceived Media Bias and the 1968 Vote." *Journalism Quarterly* 49(Summer): 239–246.

Rojecki, Answer. 2008. "Rhetorical Alchemy: American Exceptionalism and the War on Terror." *Political Communication* 25: 67–88.

Rosenbaum, David. 2004. "Fact Check." *New York Times* October 26: Page 8. www.nexis.com (last accessed November 30, 2006).

Rosenbaum, David. 2005. "Bush to Return to 'Ownership Society' Theme in Push for Social Security Changes." *New York Times* January 16, section 1, page 20.

Rosenthal, Cindy Simon and Ronald Peters. 2008. "Who is Nancy Pelosi?" *PS: Political Science and Politics XLI* 1(January): 57–62.

Rottinghaus, Brandon. 2008. "Presidential Leadership on Foreign Policy, Opinion Polling, and the Possible Limits of 'Crafted Talk.'" *Political Communication* 25(2): 138–157.

Rubin, Alissa. 1997. "GOP, White House Show Willingness To Move Toward Middle Ground." *CQ Weekly*: April 19. 896.

Rutenberg, Jim. 2006. "White House Memo: For White House, War of Words, at Least, Is Battle Where It Excels." *The New York Times* September 26, 2006. www.nytimes.com (last accessed September 26, 2006).

Ryan, Charlotte, Kevin Carragee, and William Meinhofer. "Framing, the News Media, and Collective Action." *Journal of Broadcasting & Electronic Media* 45(Winter): 175–182.

Sabato, Larry. 1991. *Feeding Frenzy: How Attack Journalism Has Transformed American Politics.* Free Press: New York, New York.

Sandler, Michael. 2006. "Chambers Still at Odds on Immigration." *CQ Weekly* July 7. 1880. www.cqweekly.com (last accessed September 14, 2006).

Santorum, Rick. 1997a. "AMA Report Renders Partial-Birth Abortion Unnecessary." Press Release, May 14.

Santorum, Rick. 1997b. "Debate On Partial-Birth Abortion to Begin In Senate." Press Release, May 13.

Saunders, Dusty. 2000. "The Nation's Radio and Television News Directors Prefer NBC Nightly News, Peter Jennings, and George W. Bush." *Rocky Mountain News* September 26.

Schaffner, Brian. 2006. "Local News Coverage and the Incumbency Advantage in the U.S. House." *Legislative Studies Quarterly XXXI*, 4(November): 491–512.

Schattschneider, E.E. 1960. *The Semisovereign People*. The Dryden Press: Hinsdale, Illinois.

Schiffer, Adam. 2006. "Blogswarms and Press Norms: News Coverage of the Downing Street Memo Controversy." *J&MC Quarterly* 83(3): 494–510.

Schiller, Wendy. 2000. *Partners and Rivals*. Princeton University Press, Princeton, New Jersey.

Schmitt, Gary. 2003. "American Power Inspires Dreams of Liberation." *Pittsburgh Post-Gazette* March 30: E-1. www.nexis.com (last accessed November 30, 2006).

Schmitt, Kathleen, Albert Gunther, and Janice Liebhart. 2004. "Why Partisans See Mass Media as Biased." *Communication Research* 31(6): 623–641.

Schulman, Bob. 1982. "The Liberal Tilt of Our Newsrooms." *Bulletin of the American Society of Newspaper Editors* 654: 3–7.

Sellers, Patrick. 1998. "Strategy and Background in Congressional Campaigns." *American Political Science Review* 92(1): 159–172.

Sellers, Patrick. 2000. "Manipulating the Message in the U.S. Congress." *Harvard International Journal of Press and Politics* 5(1): 22–31.

Sellers, Patrick and Brian Schaffner. 2007. "Winning Coverage in the U.S. Senate." *Political Communication* 24: 377–391.

Shaw, Daron, and Bartholomew Sparrow. 1999. "From the Inner Ring Out: News Congruence, Cue-Taking, and Campaign Coverage." *Political Research Quarterly* 52(2): 323–351.

Sheafer, Tamir. 2001. "Charismatic Skill and Media Legitimacy." *Communication Research* 28(6): 711–736.

Sheafer, Tamir and Gadi Wolfsfeld. 2004. "Production Assets, News Opportunities, and Publicity for Legislators: A Study of Israeli Knesset Members." *Legislative Studies Quarterly* XXIX(4): 611–630.

Shenk, David. 1997. *Data Smog: Surviving the Information Glut*. Harper Edge: San Francisco, California.

Shepsle, Kenneth and Barry Weingast. 1994. "Positive Theories of Congressional Institutions." *Legislative Studies Quarterly* 19(2): 149–179.

Shin, Jae-Hwa and Glen Cameron. 2005. "Different Sides of the Same Coin: Mixed Views of Public Relations Practitioners and Journalists for Strategic Conflict Management." *J&MC Quarterly* 82(2): 318–338.

Sigal, Leon. 1973. *Reporters and Officials: The Organization and Politics of Newsmaking*. D.C. Heath and Company: Lexington, Massachusetts.

Simon, Adam. 2002. *The Winning Message: Candidate Behavior, Campaign Discourse, and Democracy*. Cambridge University Press: New York, New York.

Sinclair, Barbara. 1997. *Unorthodox Lawmaking: New Legislative Processes in the U.S. Congress*. Congressional Quarterly Press: Washington, DC.

Sinclair, Barbara. 2006. *Party Wars: Polarization and the Politics of National Policy Making*. University of Oklahoma Press: Norman, Oklahoma.

Singer, Jane. 2004. "More Than Ink-Stained Wretches: The Resocialization of Print Journalists in Converged Newsrooms." *J&MC Quarterly* 81(4): 838–856.

Skorneck, Carolyn. 2003. "Iraq Supplemental Will Pass, But Many Say Well Is Going Dry." *CQ Weekly Online* (September 27): 2369–2372. http://library.cqpress.com/cqweekly/weeklyreport108–000000841704 (last accessed July 2, 2008).

Smith, Christopher. 1997. *Congressional Record* March 20. H1210.

Smith, Steven, Jason Roberts, and Ryan Vander Wielen. 1998. *The American Congress*. Houghlin Mifflin: New York, New York.

Sparrow, Bartholomew. 1999. *Uncertain Guardians: The News Media as a Political Institution*. Johns Hopkins University Press: Baltimore, Maryland.

Sparrow, Bartholomew. 2006. "A Research Agenda for an Institutional Media." *Political Communication* 23(2): 145–157.

Stanton, John. 2005b. "Reid Seeks to Keep Caucus on Same Page." *Roll Call* December 8. http://www.lexisnexis.com/academic/ (last accessed September 19, 2006).

Stanton, John. 2006. "Democrats Plan Aggressive Recess." *Roll Call* March 15. http://www.lexisnexis.com/academic/ (last accessed September 19, 2006).

Stanton, John. 2006b. "Frist Launches Message Shop." *Roll Call* January 19. http://www.lexisnexis.com/academic/ (last accessed September 19, 2006).

State of the American Newspaper. 2006. *American Journalism Review.* <http://www.ajr.org/Article.asp?id=3269>.

Sulkin, Tracy. 2005. *Issue Politics in Congress*. Cambridge University Press: New York, New York.

Sumpter, Randall. 2000. "Daily Newspaper Editors' Audience Construction Routines: A Case Study." *Critical Studies in Media Communication* 17(September): 334–346.

Tankard, James. 2001. "The Empirical Approach to the Study of Media Framing." In Stephen Reese, Oscar Gandy, and August Grant editors. *Framing Public Life: Perspectives on Media and Our Understanding of the Social World*. Lawrence Erlbaum Associates, Publishers: Mahwah, New Jersey.

Taylor, Andrew. 1997. "Clinton Signs 'Clean' Disaster Aid After Flailing GOP Yields to Veto." *Congressional Quarterly Weekly Report*. June 14, 1362. CQ Press: Washington, DC.

Taylor, Andrew. 1997a. "House Panel Quickly Approves Disaster Relief, Bosnia Bill." *CQ Weekly* April 26. 950.

Taylor, Andrew. 1997b. "Veto-Bait Provisions Ensnarl Emergency Spending Bill." *CQ Weekly* May 3. 1009.

Taylor, Andrew. 1997c. "Divided Republicans Go Home without Passing Disaster Aid." *CQ Weekly* May 24. 1188.

Taylor, Andrew. 1997d. "Clinton Signs 'Clean' Disaster Aid After Flailing GOP Yields to Veto." *CQ Weekly* June 14. 1362.

Taylor, Andrew. 1997f. "House Panel Quickly Approves Disaster Relief, Bosnia Bill." *CQ Weekly* April 26. 950.

Taylor, Andrew. 1997g. "Veto-Bait Provisions Ensnarl Emergency Spending Bill." *CQ Weekly* May 3. 1009.

Taylor, Andrew. 2003a. "Hang-Tough GOP Moderates Still Key to Budget Resolution." *CQ Weekly* April 5. 816.

Taylor, Andrew. 2003b. "Concessions to Moderates Imperil Early GOP Tax Cutting Accord." *CQ Weekly* April 12. 866.

Time, Cable News Network and Harris Interactive, April 8, 2004. Retrieved May 26, 2008 from the iPOLL Databank, The Roper Center for Public Opinion Research, University of Connecticut <http://www.ropercenter.uconn.edu/ipoll.html>.

Tomz, Michael, Jason Wittenberg, and Gary King. 2003. *CLARIFY: Software for Interpreting and Presenting Statistical Results*. Version 2.1. Stanford University, University of Wisconsin, and Harvard University. January 5. Available at http://gking.harvard.edu/.

Toner, Robin. 2005. "Bush on Social Security and Clinton on Health Care: Oh, Those Devilish Details." *New York Times* February 1. www.nytimes.com (last accessed July 8, 2008).

Tsfati, Yariv. 2004. "Exploring Possible Correlates of Journalists' Perceptions of Audience Trust". *J&MC Quarterly* 81(2): 274–291.

Tuchman, Gaye. 1972. "Objectivity as Strategic Ritual: An Examination of Newsmen's Notions of Objectivity." *The American Journal of Sociology* 77(4): 660–679.

Tuchman, Gaye. 1978. *Making News: A Study in the Construction of Reality*. The Free Press: New York, New York.

Tversky, Amos and Daniel Kahneman. 1974. "Judgment under Uncertainty: Heuristics and Biases." *Science* 185, (4157): 1124–1131.

Underwood, D. 1998. "Market Research and the Audience for Political News." In Doris Graber, Denis McQuail, and Pippa Norris editors. *The Politics of News*. CQ Press: Washington, DC.

Underwood, Doug. 2001. "Reporting the Push for Market-Oriented Journalism: Media Organizations as Businesses." In W. Lance Bennett and Robert Entman editors. *Mediated Politics: Communication in the Future of Democracy*. Cambridge University Press: New York, New York.

Vallone, Robert, Less Ross, and Mark Lepper. 1985. "The Hostile Media Phenomenon: Biased Perception and Perceptions of Media Bias in Coverage of the Beirut Massacre." *Journal of Personality and Social Psychology* 49(September): 577–588.

Verner, Jennifer. 2006. "Post Reporter Dana Priest's Troubling Connections." Special Report. *Accuracy in Media*. May 9. 2006. www.aim.org (last accessed November 16,2006).

Vinson, C. Danielle. 2003. *Local Media Coverage of Congress and its Members: Through Local Eyes*. Hampton Press: Creskill, New Jersey.

Von Zielbauer, Paul. 2006. "Bomber Attacks Baghdad Paper on Day when 52 Are Killed." *The New York Times* August 28: Page A6. www.nexis.com (last accessed November 30, 2006).

Walsh, Edward. 2003. "At Local Government Level, Opposition to Iraq War Rises." *The Washington Post* February 14: A26. www.nexis.com (last accessed November 30, 2006).

Wanta, Wayne, Guy Golan, and Cheolhan Lee. 2004. "Agenda Setting and International News: Media Influence on Public Perceptions of Foreign Nations." *J&MC Quarterly* 81(2): 364–477.

Watts, Mark, David Domke, Dhavan Shah and David Fan. 1999. "Elite Cutes and Media Bias in Presidential Campaigns: Explaining Public Perceptions of a Liberal Press." *Communication Research*. 26(2): 144–175.

Weaver, David and Cleveland Wilhoit. 1986. *The American Journalist: A Portrait of U.S. News People and Their Work*. Indiana University Press: Bloomington, Indiana.

Wellstone, Paul. 1997. "Statement by Senator Paul Wellstone, the Budget Agreement." Press Release, May 5.

West, Darrell. 2001. *The Rise and Fall of the Media Establishment*. Bedford/St. Martin's: Boston, Massachusetts.

West, Mark, Ed. 2001. *Theory, Method, and Practice in Computer Content Analysis*. Ablex Publishing: Westport, Connecticut.

White, David Manning. 1950. "The 'Gate Keeper': A Case Study in the Selection of News." *Journalism Quarterly* 68(Fall): 383–396.

Williams, John. 1990. "The Political Manipulation of Macroeconomic Policy." *American Political Science Review* 84(3): 767–795.

Williams, John and Michael McGinnis. 1988. "Sophisticated Reaction in the U.S. Soviet Arms Race: Evidence of Rational Expectations." *American Journal of Political Science* 32(4): 968–995.

Wolfsfeld, Gadi. 2001. "Political Waves and Democratic Discourse: Terrorism Waves During the Oslo Peace Process." In W. Lance Bennett and Robert Entman editors. *Mediated Politics: Communication in the Future of Democracy*. Cambridge University Press: New York, New York.

Wolfsfeld, Gadi. 2004. *Media and the Path to Peace*. Cambridge University Press: New York, New York.

Wolfsfeld, Gadi and Tamir Sheafer. 2006. "Competing Actors and the Construction of Political News: The Contest Over Waves in Israel." *Political Communication* 23: 333–354.

Zachary, Pascal. 2001. "Give Hope a Headline." *Foreign Policy* 122(Jan.-Feb.): 78–79.

Zaller, John. 1992. *The Nature and Origins of Mass Opinion*. Cambridge University Press: New York, New York.

Zaller, John. 2001. "Monica Lewinsky and the Mainsprings of American Politics." In W. Lance Bennett and Robert Entman editors. *Mediated Politics: Communication in the Future of Democracy*. Cambridge University Press: New York, New York.

Zilber, Jeremy and David Niven. 2000. *Racialized Coverage of Congress: The News in Black and White*. Praeger Publishing: Westport, Connecticut.

Index

Titles in the Series *(continued from page iii)*:

Bruce Bimber, *Information and American Democracy: Technology in the Evolution of Political Power*
Murray Edelman, *The Politics of Misinformation*
Frank Esser and Barbara Pfetsch, eds., *Comparing Political Communication: Theories, Cases, and Challenges*
Hernan Galperin, *New Television, Old Politics: The Transition to Digital TV in the United States and Britain*
Myra Marx Ferree, William Anthony Gamson, Jürgen Gerhards, and Dieter Rucht, *Shaping Abortion Discourse: Democracy and the Public Sphere in Germany and the United States*
Daniel C. Hallin and Paolo Mancini, *Comparing Media Systems: Three Models of Media and Politics*
Robert B. Horwitz, *Communication and Democratic Reform in South Africa*
Philip N. Howard, *New Media Campaigns and the Managed Citizen*
Richard Gunther and Anthony Mughan, eds., *Democracy and the Media: A Comparative Perspective*
L. Sandy Maisel, Darrell M. West, and Brett M. Clifton, *Evaluating Campaign Quality: Can the Electoral Process be Improved?*
Pippa Norris, *A Virtuous Circle: Political Communications in Postindustrial Society*
Pippa Norris, *Digital Divide: Civic Engagement, Information Poverty, and the Internet Worldwide*
Adam F. Simon, *The Winning Message: Candidate Behavior, Campaign Discourse*
Gadi Wolfsfeld, *Media and the Path to Peace*

Crafts Galore!

The Ultimate Guide for Girlfriends

Loveland, Colorado
www.group.com

Crafts Galore!

The Ultimate Guide for Girlfriends

Copyright © 2008 Group Publishing, Inc.

Visit our Web site: **www.group.com/women**

All rights reserved. No part of this book may be reproduced in any manner whatsoever without prior written permission from the publisher, except where noted in the text and in the case of brief quotations embodied in critical articles and reviews. For information, e-mail Permissions at inforights@group.com, or write Permissions, Group Publishing, Inc., Ministry Essentials, P.O. Box 481, Loveland, CO 80539.

Credits

Crafty Contributors: Jody Brolsma, Pamela Clifford, Andrea Filer, Linda Jordan, Veronica Lucas, Samantha Wranosky, and Jill Wuellner
Editor and Cake Decorator Extraordinaire: Jill Wuellner
Project Manager and Creative Genius: Amber Van Schooneveld
Executive Developer and Expert Beader: Amy Nappa
Chief Creative Officer: Joani Schultz
Copy Editor and Crafter Wanna-be: Ann Jahns
Cover Art Director/Designer and Art Director: Artsy Andrea Filer, Samantha Wranosky
Book Designer and Print Production Artist: YaYe Design
Production Manager: DeAnne "All-Thumbs" Lear

Unless otherwise indicated, all Scripture quotations are taken from the *Holy Bible*, New Living Translation, copyright © 1996, 2004. Used by permission of Tyndale House Publishers, Inc., Carol Stream, Illinois 60188. All rights reserved.

Library of Congress Cataloging-in-Publication Data
Crafts galore! : the ultimate guide for girlfriends.
p. cm.
ISBN 978-0-7644-3657-4 (pbk. : alk. paper)
1. Women in church work. 2. Handicraft--Religious aspects--Christianity. I. Group Publishing.
BV4415.C73 2007
246--dc22

2007029595

ISBN 978-0-7644-3657-4
10 9 8 7 6 5 4 3 2 1   17 16 15 14 13 12 11 10 09 08
Printed in the United States of America.

Table of Contents

Introduction

No More Refrigerator Magnets!

Is your fridge cluttered with the magnets you've made at the past four women's ministry events? Are you tired of making bookmarks, placemats, and anything that can be formed from Popsicle sticks and glue? Are you ready to quit making crafts that get tossed into the trash as soon as you get home? Or are you simply intimidated by those "crafty" women who can make a lamp out of three toilet paper tubes and an empty mayonnaise jar—and then tell you how easy it is?

If you can relate to any of these questions, *Crafts Galore!* is for you! This book is packed with crafts that truly *are* easy—and that are so attractive that you'll want them in your home and can delight your friends with them as gifts. Imagine that!

Using This Book

For simplicity, we've placed the crafts into five chapters: Service Projects, Gifts, Seasonal Crafts, Crafts With Devotions, and Food Crafts. However, all the crafts can be done for a variety of reasons, such as for fundraisers, gifts for the women in your church, wedding showers, anniversaries, Christmas, the end or beginning of a Bible study, or any kind of special event.

All of the supplies listed for each craft will make one item, unless otherwise noted. General supplies that women will share (such as scissors or glue) are listed under the "Supplies per table" heading. As we've tried to make this a user-friendly book, all supplies can be purchased at your local craft or hobby store, and some craft kits, where noted, can be purchased directly from Group at **www.group.com/women.**

With each craft, you'll see a photo of the finished project (and these were made by real women—not professional craft stylists!) and information on about how long it takes to make the craft. You'll also see a dollar symbol ($) that helps you know about how much this craft will cost to make. Here's the key:

$ = under $2.50 per woman

$$ = under $5 per woman

$$$ = more than $5 per woman

Perhaps your budget will allow you to provide the supplies for a smaller craft. For higher-priced projects, you can add that into the cost of your event or charge a fee for making the items. If you have a sample craft already made, and women see how adorable the craft is, they'll quickly chip in for the cost of the supplies!

And to make doing these projects super easy for you and the women in your group, each craft also includes a reproducible handout with the instructions on it. This means you can photocopy the step-by-step instructions and set these on each table where women will be working, making it easy for them to work at their own pace.

So invite some women over, share in laughter and deepening friendships, relax, and enjoy the process of making something beautiful with your own hands.

Service Projects

Ribbon Cards

Service Projects

- $
- Takes about 30 minutes
- An eye-catching (and useful) item for new moms, high school grads, or a bride-to-be

Supplies per woman:

- 8 to 10 blank notecards and envelopes
- a variety of grosgrain or satin ribbon, approximately 1½ yards per woman

Supplies per table:

- glue sticks or rubber cement
- waxed paper
- scissors

New moms, graduates, and brides-to-be will appreciate having these pretty cards on hand for instant thank-you notes. You may want to provide themed ribbon to match the occasion. For example, pink and blue ribbons for new moms, high school colors for graduates, or ivory ribbons for brides. Women can make the cards as elaborate or simple as they wish—the craft is so easy that even one line of ribbon looks tasteful.

Prior to your event, make a few Ribbon Cards to show as an example. To prepare your room for this craft, set up tables and chairs. On each table, place enough cards, ribbon, and other supplies so every woman can make four to five cards.

Tip

Be sure to provide sharp scissors so women can easily trim the edges of the ribbon from the cards. Dull scissors are not only hard to use, but they leave lots of frayed edges.

Rubber cement dries more nicely than regular glue with the ribbon and paper, but it may have fumes that are irritating to some women.

While women work, encourage them to talk about people who helped them during transitional times of their lives.

You can also collect these cards and send them to a missionary your church supports as the beginning of a pen pal relationship. Everyone loves to get "real" mail!

Ribbon Cards

1. Choose the Ribbon

Select a few coordinating colors to use on a batch of cards.

2. Create

Determine a pattern for each card. For example, a line of ribbon on the left-hand side with a coordinating line along the bottom, or a simple line of ribbon across the top.

3. Measure

Lay the ribbon on the card and cut the ribbon, allowing about ¼ inch to extend off of the edge of the card.

4. Get Gluey

Lay the ribbon facedown on a sheet of waxed paper. Spread glue or rubber cement on the ribbon, and then position the ribbon on the card. Press down firmly to secure the ribbon in place.

5. Trim the Edges

Use sharp scissors to trim the edges of the ribbon. When the cards are complete and dry, use a piece of ribbon in a coordinating color to tie the stack of cards and envelopes together.

Permission to photocopy this page from *Crafts Galore!* granted for local church use. Copyright © Group Publishing, Inc., P.O. Box 481, Loveland, CO 80539. www.group.com

Blanket of Love

- $$
- Takes about 30 minutes
- A soft and practical gift to remind others of God's love

Supplies per table:

- 2 pieces of fleece, measuring 2 yards, edges cut into strips 4 inches deep and 1 inch wide
- scissors
- one 4x6-inch piece of red felt

Have you ever been to a quilting bee? They're not as common anymore, but these gatherings provided a way for women to share their hearts while they work on a blanket together.

The Blanket of Love encourages that same feeling of community as women work on an easy gift that will blanket someone else with God's love. In groups of four, women will create a soft fleece blanket and give it to a woman in need who can wrap her child in its warmth. Or the blankets can be donated to a nearby homeless shelter, children's hospital, crisis pregnancy center, clothing bank, or mission group that your church supports.

Prior to your event, make a Blanket of Love to show as an example. To prepare your room for this craft, set up tables and chairs. Make sure each table is set up for four women to complete a blanket.

Tip

Don't have time to adequately prepare for this craft? Make it easy by ordering the "Jesus Loves Me" Blankets at www.group.com/women. Each kit includes two pieces of precut fleece that is custom printed with the message "Jesus Loves Me" in both English and Spanish.

If you have enough time before your event, gather brochures or pictures from the place where the blankets will be given as gifts. It personalizes the giving when women can see the faces of women or children who are likely to receive these comforting gifts.

Blanket of Love

1. Blanket on Blanket

Lay one sheet of fleece on top of the other, so the wrong sides are on the inside. If you are using fleece that has not been precut, make cuts into both layers of fabric, so that the cuts are 4 inches deep and 1 inch wide.

2. Fringe

Line up the fringes that are closest to the corners. Beginning at the corners, tie one piece of fringe from the top piece of fleece to one piece of fringe on the bottom piece of fleece. Tie tight knots, but try not to stretch out the fringe pieces. Tie edges until you have about 1 foot left on one side of the blanket.

3. Hearts

Cut one heart shape from the felt, and insert this inside the layers of fleece. Take a moment and pray for the child who will receive this blanket. Even though he or she won't know of this secret message of love you've tucked inside, pray that this child will know God's love when using this blanket.

Continue tying until you run out of fringe.

Permission to photocopy this page from *Crafts Galore!* granted for local church use. Copyright © Group Publishing, Inc., P.O. Box 481, Loveland, CO 80539. www.group.com

Giggle Jars

Service Projects

- $
- Takes about 30 minutes
- Sure to make you laugh!

Supplies per woman:

- small glass jar with a lid
- 20 empty gelatin capsules (find these at your local pharmacy)
- photocopies of the "Giggle Sheet" on page 14 (For added fun, copy these on brightly colored paper!)

Supplies per table:

- toothpicks
- pens
- scissors

Tip

For added fun, decorate your Giggle Jars with stickers, ribbons, feathers, or permanent markers.

Don't have time to gather all the supplies needed for this craft? Make it easy by ordering Giggle Jar kits that include the capsules, jars with lids, and preprinted paper slips at www.group.com/women.

The old adage "laughter is the best medicine" may be more true than we realize. In addition to just making you feel happier, some studies suggest that a good hearty laugh can help reduce stress, lower blood pressure, boost the immune system, protect the heart, and improve brain function.

So now it's time to record and share funny clips from your own lives! For this craft everyone will join together in creating jars of laughs-to-go called "Giggle Jars." These are containers of tiny capsules for women to open up and chuckle at when they're in need of a good laugh! These jars are great to have on hand to give as a gift to encourage women in your congregation, to pass along to ladies who need a laugh every day, or to give to anyone who needs a reason to smile.

When setting up for your event, make one or two Giggle Jars to show as samples. Make sure to place enough supplies at each table so every woman can make a Giggle Jar. These can be collected at the end of your event to give away to those in need of a smile. Just open up a Giggle and have a laugh!

Giggle Jars

1. Fill Out the Giggle Sheet

Look at the "Giggle Sheet" (that fun handout on your table). Before you start your craft, choose one of the unfinished sentences on the "Giggle Sheet" to answer aloud with those sitting near you. When everyone has had a turn and the laughter slows for a moment, go ahead and complete one "Giggle Sheet."

2. Cut and Roll

After you finish your "Giggle Sheet," cut it into smaller slips as indicated. Choose your favorite 20 slips from your own collection, and make these into Giggles.

Take one slip of paper, and roll it tightly around the end of a toothpick. Then insert the rolled slip into an opened gelatin capsule, and replace the other half of the capsule to make one Giggle.

3. Mix and Fill

When a few other women around you have finished making their 20 Giggles, mix your Giggles with theirs. Then count out 20 Giggles from that mixed pile to put into your own Giggle Jar. This will give you a mixture of Giggles created by yourself and others.

Permission to photocopy this page from *Crafts Galore!* granted for local church use. Copyright © Group Publishing, Inc., P.O. Box 481, Loveland, CO 80539. www.group.com

Giggle Sheet

Finish the sentences or fill in the blanks to make someone giggle.

The movie that always makes me laugh is …	The name Isaac means "he laughs." What's a name that makes you laugh?
If the shoe fits…	Roses are red, violets are blue…
When the going gets tough…	I was embarrassed when…
Too many cooks…	The funniest outfit I ever wore was…
A penny saved…	My favorite game to play for laughs is __________ . Try it today!
A stitch in time…	The funniest question I've heard a child ask is…
I once laughed so hard I…	To be funny I once wore…
The goofiest way I ever wore my hair was…	The TV show that makes me laugh the most is…

Use these if you run out of ideas, or make up your own.

"He will once again fill your mouth with laughter and your lips with shouts of joy" (Job 8:21).	Proverbs 17:22 says, "A cheerful heart is good medicine." To whom can you give a dose of laughter today?
Need a smile? Blow soap bubbles out your window!	Need a chuckle? Whistle while you work…or play
Need a giggle? Jump in the snow, in a pile of leaves, or into a mound of pillows!	Spin around until you get dizzy.
Tickle your funny bone by singing in the shower. Loud!	Make up a silly poem, and read it to a friend.
Amuse yourself—talk to everyone in "pig Latin" for 10 minutes	______________________________
______________________________	______________________________

Permission to photocopy this page from *Crafts Galore!* granted for local church use. Copyright © Group Publishing, Inc., P.O. Box 481, Loveland, CO 80539. www.group.com

Personalized Book Bag

- $
- Takes about 30 minutes
- Great for outreach as a bag to carry donated books, or for a gift bag filled with other donated items

Supplies per woman:

- brown paper grocery bag
- three 12x12-inch sheets of craft/scrap-book paper
- ready-made tags (found at any craft store)
- 6 feet of ribbon

Supplies per table:

- pens or markers
- hot-glue gun
- glue sticks
- scissors
- hole punch (optional)

Reach out to students by creating a book bag that can be filled with donated books. Instead of just holding a book drive, this craft allows the opportunity to create a fun tote bag to deliver the books to the students, and each bag can be personalized! Before your event, contact a school with a low-income classroom, and retrieve a roster of students' names. Gather a group of volunteers, a woman's ministry group, or students from a youth group, and divide the names of the students between your volunteers. Each person can create a Personalized Book Bag.

Tip

Choose a simple area of the decorated bag to write words on. For example: Write "read," "learn," and "share" with an inch between each word. Then punch holes of colored paper, and glue the circles between each of the words.

If your church has a toy drive at Christmas, these bags can be made into Christmas gift bags and used to deliver those special gifts. This craft can also be created as a home-made gift bag for any occasion. Instead of purchasing a gift bag in the store, add a personal touch by creating it with themed papers and ribbon.

Prior to your event, create a Personalized Book Bag to show as an example. To prepare your room for this craft, set up tables and chairs. On each table, place enough brown bags, scrapbook paper, ribbon, tags, and other supplies so every woman can make a bag.

Personalized Book Bag

1. Prepare Paper Bag

Set the brown paper bag upright. Measure about 5 inches down from the top, and cut off straight across, creating a smaller bag. Use the discarded paper to cover any branding or logos that may be on the bag, using a hot-glue gun to secure the paper.

2. Decorate the Bag

Cut strips of scrapbook paper the width of the paper bag with various heights of 2 to 3 inches. Glue horizontally with the hot-glue gun. Line the strips of paper with ribbon for added decoration.

3. Create Handles

Punch four holes on the top of the bag for handles, two for each side. Cut six lengths of ribbon, 18 inches each. Thread three lengths of ribbon through one of the holes. Tie a knot, making sure to place the knot on the outside of the paper bag. Braid into a ribbon. Before tying off, thread the braid through the second hole on the same side of the bag, and then tie a knot. Repeat these steps for the opposite handle.

4. Create the Tag

Cut two rectangles of craft paper, approximately 2½ x 4 inches. Glue the paper on each side of the tags. For extra decoration, punch circles out of paper and glue down. Then write the student's name on one side and words related to reading on the other. For example: read • learn • share.

5. Tie Tag to Bag

Punch a third hole in the top of the bag. Cut one length of ribbon approximately 6 inches. Thread the ribbon through the hole and tie a knot, placing the knot on the inside of the paper bag. Thread the other end of the ribbon through the hole of the tag, and tie a knot.

6. Prepare and Deliver Book Bags to Students

Hold a mini book drive to gather books to place into book bags. Disperse the books among all the student bags. Contact the teacher of the classroom, and schedule a time to deliver the new book bags filled with books.

Permission to photocopy this page from *Crafts Galore!* granted for local church use. Copyright © Group Publishing, Inc., P.O. Box 481, Loveland, CO 80539. www.group.com

Creative Clipboard

- $
- Takes about 20 minutes
- Reach out to students in a classroom, use as a fundraiser, or give as a gift to help with organizing

Supplies per woman:

- blank clipboard
- one 12x12-inch sheet of craft/scrapbook paper
- 4 feet of ribbon

Supplies per table:

- pens or markers
- hot-glue gun
- glue sticks
- scissors
- hole punch (optional)
- strips of magnetic material (optional)

This craft is an opportunity to give a twist to an ordinary object. Whenever there is a need for organization, this is a great and easy way to share a decorated clipboard that can be personalized. Whether created for a student or as a way to spice up a grocery list, it is wonderful to share.

For a service-oriented craft, find a local school that will allow you to retrieve a roster of a classroom, and then gather a group of volunteers to decorate one clipboard per student.

Prior to your event, create a Creative Clipboard to show as an example. To prepare your room for this craft, set up tables and chairs. On each table, place enough clipboards, scrapbook paper, ribbon, and other supplies so every woman can make a Creative Clipboard.

Tip

Die-cuts are an easy way to add some flair.

Creative Clipboard

1. Decorate the Clipboard
Cut craft paper into the size of the clipboard, leaving a little extra space for a border. Glue down with a glue gun. Cut another strip of paper, and write the name of the student or a fun title for the clipboard, such as "Pesky Papers" or "Homework Holder." Glue in one corner of the clipboard. For a fun decorating idea, punch holes out of paper and glue around words or around the border for more decoration.

2. Decorate the Handle
Cut 10 lengths of ribbon, 4 inches each, and tie them onto the clip of the clipboard, making sure to spread them evenly on the clip. Tie twice to reinforce.

3. Magnetize the Clipboard
If this clipboard was created for a grocery list or homework holder, cut strips of magnetic material and press to the back of the clipboard to hang on the refrigerator or the side of a filing cabinet.

4. Deliver the Clipboards
If your clipboard was created for a student, contact the teacher of the class, and schedule a good time for your group to deliver these fun clipboards.

Permission to photocopy this page from *Crafts Galore!* granted for local church use. Copyright © Group Publishing, Inc., P.O. Box 481, Loveland, CO 80539. www.group.com

Door Delights

- $$
- Takes about 30 minutes
- These are created to be a gift that can be delivered anonymously: a surprise for a new neighbor, for a friend with a birthday, for residents in a nursing home, or for any special occasion.

Supplies per woman:

- wooden door hanger (found at any craft store)
- three 12x12-inch sheets of craft/scrapbook paper
- ready-made tags (found at any craft store)
- 12 inches of ribbon

Supplies per table:

- pens/markers
- hot-glue gun
- glue sticks
- scissors
- hole punch (optional)

Have you ever wanted to encourage someone but just didn't know the right words to say? Or maybe you've wanted to give a gift anonymously and needed a fresh, new idea. This project is the perfect fix for both of these dilemmas, as it uses God's Word, which is always perfect, and can be left on a door. It is a simple way to lift someone's spirit or say "Welcome to the neighborhood."

If using as a service project, gather a group of women or youth students to make these Door Delights. These can be used to hang on the doorknobs of residents in a nursing home, or disperse them throughout your neighborhood to those who may have just moved in. It is also a unique gift that you can hand-deliver to a friend.

Prior to your event, create a Door Delight to show as an example. To prepare your room for this craft, set up tables and chairs. On each table, place enough door hangers, scrapbook paper, ribbon, tags, and other supplies so every woman can make a Door Delight.

Door Delights

1. Wrap the Door Hanger With Paper

Take a piece of scrapbook paper, and wrap the wooden door hanger lengthwise, using hot glue to secure the paper. Notice that the hole of the hanger is covered with paper. Take a pair of scissors, and cut the paper out of the circle.

2. Line the Circle With Ribbon

To seal any of the jagged edges of paper, use a short piece of ribbon and hot glue to line the inside of the circle. Disperse glue generously on the inside of the circle, center the ribbon, and press it firmly, continuing around the circle until the wood is covered.

3. Create the Envelope

Take a piece of the craft paper to make the pocket that will be glued to the front of the door hanger. Measure and cut a rectangle of paper that is 4x5½ inches, cutting off the corners at an angle. Fold in ½-inch flaps on three sides of the rectangle. Place glue on the folded flaps and press them, centered and flush with the bottom of the door hanger. See the illustration as a guide.

4. Decorate Tags

Cut six rectangles approximately 2½x4 inches, using a variety of craft paper. It's a good idea to choose the most simply decorated paper for this. Glue the paper on each side of the tags. For extra decoration, use the hole punch to punch circles out of paper and glue down. Then write encouraging notes on each side of the tags. Here are some examples to get started:

Tag 1:

Side 1: "I have told you these things so that you will be filled with my joy." John 15:11

Side 2: "Lord, your joy is unending and wonderful. May I embrace each day and each moment. Thank you for filling my heart so graciously."

Tag 2:

Side 1: "The Lord is my rock, my fortress, and my savior; my God is my rock, in whom I find protection." Psalm 18:2

Side 2: "Lord, no matter what I am going through in this moment, you pour out your comfort. Thank you, Lord."

Tag 3:

Side 1: "Thank God for this gift too wonderful for words." 2 Corinthians 9:15

Side 2: "Lord, your blessings overwhelm my life every day. May I always have a thankful heart."

Permission to photocopy this page from *Crafts Galore!* granted for local church use. Copyright © Group Publishing, Inc., P.O. Box 481, Loveland, CO 80539. www.group.com

Door Delights page 2

5. Tie Tags Together With Ribbon and Place Into Pocket

6. Deliver Door Delights

Call a local nursing home, and find out a good time to deliver these encouraging door hangers. Or choose a neighborhood to brighten each door with this anonymous gift.

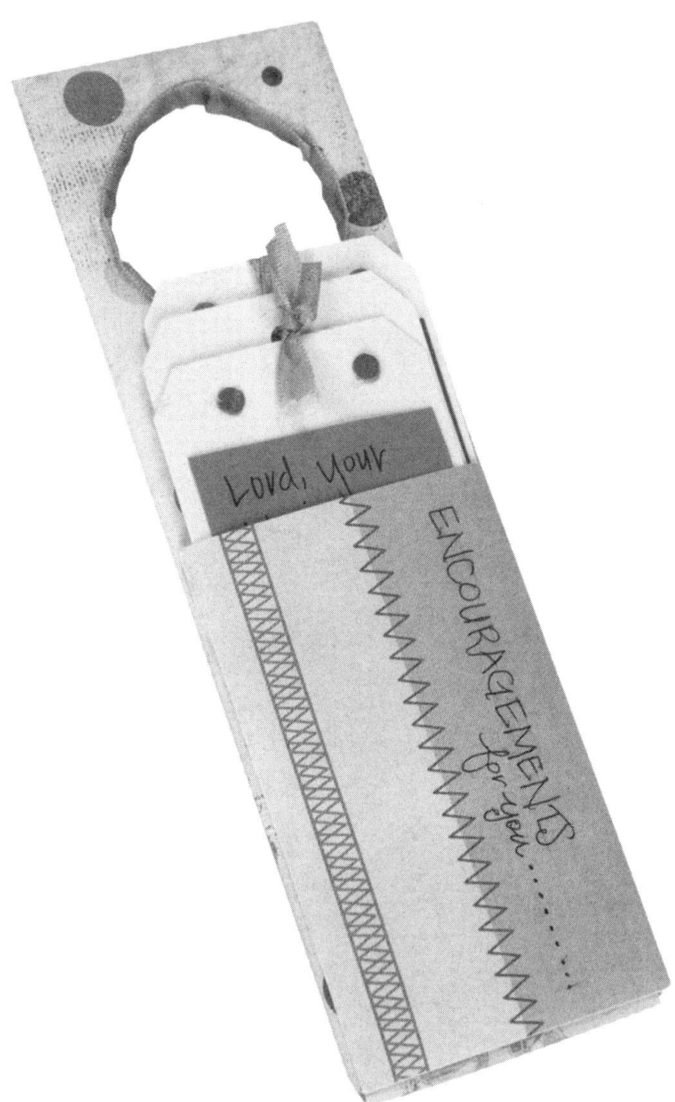

Permission to photocopy this page from *Crafts Galore!* granted for local church use. Copyright © Group Publishing, Inc., P.O. Box 481, Loveland, CO 80539. www.group.com

Gifts

Earth laughs in flowers.
-Ralph Waldo Emerson
SNAPDRAGON
Dwarf Magic Carpet
99¢
100

Bath Sundaes

- $$
- Takes about 20 minutes
- Great for a fundraiser, a gift, or a fun craft for any meeting

Supplies per woman:

- ice cream parfait glass
- ⅔ cup bath salts
- resealable small plastic bag
- nylon net bath pouf
- bath-oil ball
- cellophane or clear plastic gift wrap
- 18 inches of colorful ribbon

Gifts

Who doesn't like to be pampered, especially on days when you're tired and stressed? Most women love the thought of a quiet bath at the end of a hectic day, and one that's filled with soothing smells and skin-softening oils is even better. Which is why this craft is such a hit as a fundraiser or gift; women not only like to give it as a gift, but they love to receive it as well.

Before your event, make a Bath Sundae for an example for women to see. Then prepare your area by setting up tables and chairs. On each table, place the parfait glass, bath salts, plastic bags, bath pouf, bath-oil ball, cellophane, and a ribbon for each woman.

Tip

You may want to put the bath salts into a larger bowl on each table, and let women scoop out the amount they'll need. If you do this, be sure to have a 2/3 cup measuring cup handy for each table.

Bath Sundaes

1. Measure Bath Salts
Put 2/3 cup bath salts into the plastic bag. Squish out the air, and seal the bag. Place the bag at the bottom of the parfait glass.

2. Place the Bath Pouf
Place the bath pouf on top of the bath salts so the string is on the underside. Place the bath-oil ball on top of the bath pouf (to represent the cherry).

3. Place the Glass
Place the glass on a sheet of cellophane. Bring the cellophane up around the bath sundae, and wrap the sundae tightly enough that the pouf and the bath-oil ball don't fall off.

4. Tie With a Pretty Ribbon
Tie the cellophane together with piece of ribbon to finish off the project.

Permission to photocopy this page from *Crafts Galore!* granted for local church use. Copyright © Group Publishing, Inc., P.O. Box 481, Loveland, CO 80539. www.group.com

Journal in a Jar

Gifts

• $$
• Takes about 30 minutes
• Perfect gift for the women in your small group or congregation

Supplies per woman:

• quart-size canning jar with lid
• blank journal
• pretty pen
• square of calico fabric at least 3 inches bigger than the lid of your jar
• pretty ribbon that coordinates with the fabric
• 1 photocopy of the handout (you can make this prettier by using colored paper)

Supplies per table:

• scissors
• pinking shears

Women love relationships, but not just any relationships. We want meaningful friendships that touch our hearts. And what friendship is more important than our relationship with God?

Create these journals to give as gifts to the women in your Bible study or to new women who visit your church. They're inexpensive, quick to make, suitable for any occasion, and will help women in your church grow to love God more.

Before your event, make a Journal in a Jar for an example for women to see. Set up tables and chairs. On each table, place enough supplies for every woman to make a craft.

Tip

If your journal cannot be tied to the jar, you can wrap the journal and jar together in cellophane or clear gift wrap, and tie that with a bow.

Also, if you'd like to make this gift extra special, include wrapped candies or packaged tea bags in each jar.

Journal in a Jar

1. Photocopy and Cut

Cut the photocopied page with journaling questions on it into strips. Cut out the gift tag, below, and set that aside. Fold each strip in half, and place all the folded strips in the jar along with a pretty pen.

2. Cover the Jar

Use pinking shears to cut a square of fabric slightly bigger than the diameter of the jar mouth. Put the fabric over the lid of the jar, and screw on the ring.

3. Tie With Ribbon

Use the ribbon to tie the blank journal to the jar. Also use the ribbon to attach the directions gift tag to the jar.

Gift tag

Journal in a Jar

Use this journal to *explore your relationship with God in a very personal way. Take out one slip of paper, and read the question. Pray about the question. Then write your answer in the journal.*

Permission to photocopy this page from *Crafts Galore!* granted for local church use. Copyright © Group Publishing, Inc., P.O. Box 481, Loveland, CO 80539. www.group.com

Journal in a Jar

Why did God create me?

What is my God-given purpose in life?

How has God shown his love for me?

What would I like my non-Christian friends to understand about why I love God?

What do my trials help me to know about God?

What do I find delightful about God?

What are my secret doubts about God?

What are my deepest fears? How can I overcome those?

What in this world breaks God's heart? Does it break my heart, too?

How will I rejoice and be glad in this day that God has made?

How will I give myself as a living sacrifice to God?

Permission to photocopy this page from *Crafts Galore!* granted for local church use. Copyright © Group Publishing, Inc., P.O. Box 481, Loveland, CO 80539. www.group.com

What is worship? Describe a time of sweet worship that affected you deeply.

What are your favorite worship songs? Find a quiet place, and sing them to God. Explain why you love them.

What does it mean to "be still and know that I am God"? What do you know about God when you're still?

What are my biggest questions about life, God, and faith?

What does God's creation tell me about him?

What does God look like?

How does God answer my prayers? How does he know what's best for me?

Do my prayers change what God plans to do?

Why has God made me the way I am, with my own particular strengths and weaknesses?

Why did God give me the family that I have?

What does it mean to do justice, to love mercy, and to walk humbly with God?

How can I pray without ceasing?

Permission to photocopy this page from *Crafts Galore!* granted for local church use. Copyright © Group Publishing, Inc., P.O. Box 481, Loveland, CO 80539. www.group.com

Culinary Queen Apron

- $$$
- Takes about 30 minutes
- Fun and creative craft for a retreat, a cooking group, a new homemaker, or a recent graduate

Supplies per woman:

- plain solid-colored apron (these are available in a variety of colors at most craft or hobby stores)

Supplies per table:

- fabric paints
- fabric pens and markers
- stencils
- appliqués
- iron-on transfers
- beads and sequins
- fabric glue
- anything else you can think of to put on those aprons!

Gifts

It's easy to get discouraged about household chores, but when women put on these aprons at home, they won't be able to help but smile and remember that they're Culinary Queens. The point is to look good, no, *beautiful*, even in the kitchen.

Before your event, you'll want to make your own Culinary Queen Apron to show as an example. When setting up for this craft, provide tables with a variety of decorating supplies. The more you can have to decorate with the better. Remember, each woman is unique, so the aprons will come out in every style from country to funky to bling-bling and everything in between.

Tip

If doing any type of iron-ons, make sure you have a few ironing boards and irons to be used for the event. (And be sure you have adequate electrical outlets, too!)

Empty any water out of the irons ahead of time as any amount of water will ruin an appliqué.

Culinary Queen Apron

1. Choose Your Apron

Pick your favorite color or one that you think the person you're making this for will enjoy.

2. Decorate!

Wander around to see what decorating supplies are available. Then use paints, marker, appliqués, fabric glue, and any other supplies you want to decorate your apron. If this is a gift, decorate this to reflect the interests and personality of your friend.

Permission to photocopy this page from *Crafts Galore!* granted for local church use. Copyright © Group Publishing, Inc., P.O. Box 481, Loveland, CO 80539. www.group.com

Scissor Savers

Gifts

- $$$
- Takes about 45 minutes
- Use as a fun gift idea for a girlfriend

Supplies per woman:

- 6-inch scissors
- decorative felt (you can use solid colors of felt, but printed felt is much more fun!)
- 10 inches of ¼-inch rickrack
- poster board
- Scissor Savers Template
- sticky-backed magnetic strips

Supplies per table:

- colorful permanent markers
- quick-drying craft glue
- pencil or ballpoint pen

Doesn't it seem that you can never keep track of a pair of scissors? No matter how many you have, they tend to "walk" away or disappear, seemingly all by themselves, whether you live alone or with a houseful of people. This Scissor Saver will help you keep track of your scissors and keep them in a handy spot.

You can make these for secret-sister gifts, stocking stuffers, bride-to-be gifts, or just something to save your sanity (because what non-female member of your household would want to use girly scissors?!).

Scissor Savers can be made alone or as a small group. If you are making them in a group setting, you'll want to make a Scissor Saver beforehand to show as an example. Make sure to have enough scissors for everyone, or ask each woman to bring her own (this is an especially good idea, as some women may be left-handed and need adapted scissors), and set out enough supplies for each woman. Photocopy the Scissor Savers Template from page 34 so each woman can have a copy of that as well.

Scissor Savers

1. Prepare Supplies

Trace the Scissor Savers Template onto a piece of poster board. Cut out the shape, and mark fold lines on the cut-out poster board. Measure the top edge of the template, and cut rickrack to match that length.

Score the fold lines on the poster board with the back side of your scissor blade, making sure the poster board is scored and not cut. Fold the poster board in, along the score lines, overlapping one side over the other. This will be the general shape of the Scissor Saver. Once folds are made in the poster board, unfold and lay flat.

2. Preparing the Felt

Trace the outline of the template onto the felt piece. Cut along the inside edge of tracing so it won't show on the finished piece.

3. Putting It Together

Put glue on the outside of the poster board, and place the *back* side of the felt on top of this. Immediately fold back into the previous shape.

Glue poster board together where it overlaps, so the Scissor Saver closes. This will be the back of the project.

Set the Scissor Saver aside so glue can dry. It helps to have a heavy item, such as a large book, to lay on top as it dries.

4. Decorate

Once the Scissor Saver glue is dry, attach the rickrack to the top edge with glue. Again place it under the heavy item and allow it to dry.

While glue is drying, use the permanent markers to decorate the light-colored handles of the scissors. Avoid smudging by waiting for ink to dry completely.

When the rickrack trim is dry, cut the magnetic strip to the length desired. The longer the strip, the more powerful adhesion it will have when hanging up the scissors. Peel off the backing from the magnetic strip and press firmly to the back of the Scissor Saver.

If you'd like to stick your Scissor Saver to a nonmetallic surface, cut a second piece of magnetic strip the same size as the first, and place the magnetic sides together. When you get home, the adhesive side can then be attached to a nonmetallic surface, such as the inside of your kitchen cabinet.

Permission to photocopy this page from *Crafts Galore!* granted for local church use. Copyright © Group Publishing, Inc., P.O. Box 481, Loveland, CO 80539. www.group.com

Scissor Savers Template

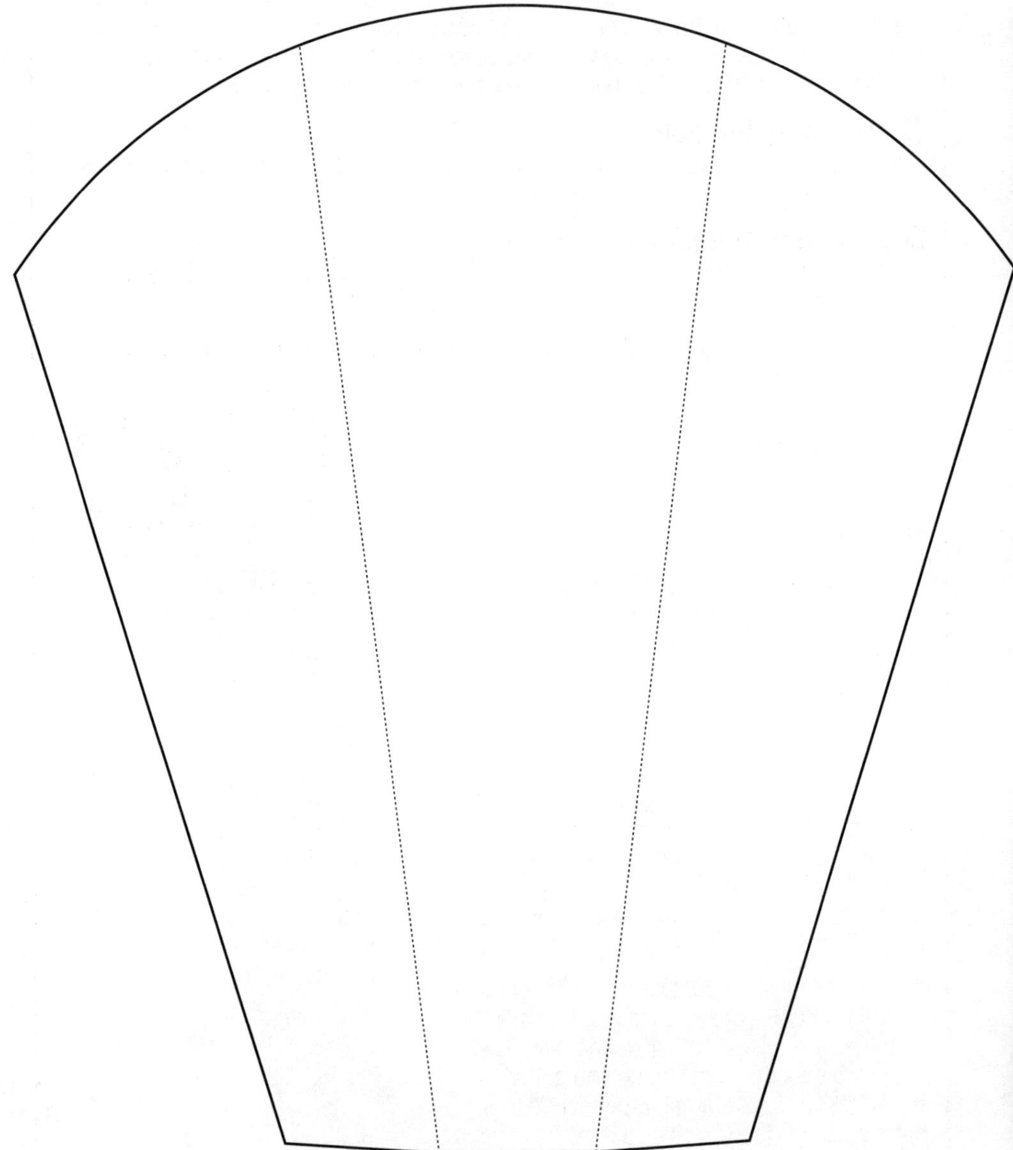

Permission to photocopy this page from *Crafts Galore!* granted for local church use. Copyright © Group Publishing, Inc., P.O. Box 481, Loveland, CO 80539. www.group.com

Bird Nest Jar Terrarium

- $$$
- Takes about 45 minutes
- Makes a beautiful gift or home decoration, or is perfect for fundraising

Supplies per woman:

- 4-inch clear glass jar with lid
- 2-inch craft bird nest
- 2-foot strands of raffia
- two 1-inch plastic or wooden bird eggs

Supplies per table:

- hot-glue gun
- paper towels
- 1 small bag of green super Spanish moss. Each woman will use about ½ cup to ¾ cup of moss.
- 1 small bag of mood moss. Each woman will use two torn pieces, approximately 1x2 inches.
- 1 stem silk hydrangea flowers. Use three blossoms for each woman.
- 1 small bunch of dried flowers with smaller flower heads
- 2 pairs of long tweezers so fingers won't be burned

Gifts

This is an easy craft that women can make together to decorate their homes or give as gifts. This project will bring in a touch of nature, and nature reminds us of God's love for us.

Before your event, make a Bird Nest Jar Terrarium to show as an example. When setting up, provide supplies at each table for every woman to make a jar. Depending on the size of your group, you might want to lay out the green super Spanish moss, mood moss, and silk and dried flowers on one table and have the women take what they need.

Tip

To eliminate burned fingers, use a pair of long tweezers to place the flowers into the jar.

Add a personal touch by attaching a small card or piece of colored paper. Write a favorite Scripture or saying on it. Make a hole in the side of the card using a hole punch, and then slip the card onto the raffia and tie into a bow.

Bird Nest Jar Terrarium

1. Remove Lid
Wipe out the inside of jar. If the jar lid has a rubber seal across the entire top of the jar, cut away the seal, leaving it only on the outside rim. You'll want to be able to see through the lid when looking from the top of the jar.

2. Moss Bed
Put a little hot glue onto the bottom of the jar, and carefully place the Spanish moss in the bottom. Push moss down around the edge of the glass.

3. Bird Nest
Hot-glue a sprig of the mood moss inside the bird nest. Add a few sprigs of dried flowers to the nest, and then hot-glue the two bird eggs inside the nest. Glue the nest on top of the moss bed. Tilt the nest slightly on its side when gluing.

4. Add Silk Flowers
Carefully hot-glue the three small blossoms on the left side of the nest, hiding the stem in the moss.

5. Finishing Touches
Place the jar lid back on the jar. Wrap two pieces of raffia around jar and tie into a bow.

Permission to photocopy this page from *Crafts Galore!* granted for local church use. Copyright © Group Publishing, Inc., P.O. Box 481, Loveland, CO 80539. www.group.com

Gardener's Friend Flowerpot

- $$
- Takes about 45 minutes
- Makes a nice spring gift for gardening friends, fundraisers, and women's groups

Supplies per woman:

- 4-inch terra cotta flowerpot
- pair of solid color garden gloves
- small garden tool such as a trowel with wood handle
- flower seed packet
- 9-inch length of $\frac{3}{16}$-inch wooden dowel
- small craft paintbrush
- 2-foot lengths of raffia
- 2x3-inch piece of floral foam

Supplies per table:

- bottled acrylic craft paint in dark yellow, light green, and purple
- waxed paper
- clear tape

At the end of those long winter months, some women love to put on the gardening gloves and dig in the soil. What better way to encourage those women than to give them a beautiful, handmade gift they can use? This is an easy craft that women can make together to give as gifts, use as a door prize, use for a fundraiser, or to even decorate their home.

Prior to your event, make a Gardener's Friend Flowerpot to use as an example. To prepare your room for this craft, set up tables and chairs. On each table, place enough supplies for every woman to make one pot.

To speed up the drying time, have a couple hair dryers to use.

We've suggested colors of paint that look nice together. You can choose to have more colors available and let women create their own color combinations.

Paint markers are quick drying and easy to control and use. Consider having both paint to use with brushes and paint markers on hand.

Waxed paper is good to use for setting items on for drying. The object won't stick, and your workspace will stay clean.

Use the dowel to help push the glove into the foam.

Gardener's Friend Flowerpot

1. Paint Your Pot

Using the handle end of the paintbrush (or a paint marker) and the dark yellow paint, make dots on the lip of the pot by dipping the handle tip into the paint and touching to the pot. Make these about 1/2 inch apart. Let dots dry.

With the purple paint, make six dots around every other yellow dot to make the petals of the flower. Set aside the pot to dry.]

2. Paint the Garden Gloves

Use the purple paint to make dots on the top of each one of the fingers of the gloves. Let dry.

3. Paint the Garden Tool Handle

Paint the handle of the garden tool with purple paint. Set aside and let dry.

4. Seed Packet

While the pot, gloves, and garden tool are drying, paint the 9-inch dowel light green. Set aside and let dry. When dry, tape the dowel to the back of the flower seed packet. Tie a raffia bow around the dowel right under the flower packet.

5. Decorate!

Push the florist foam into the bottom of the pot. Take the right-hand glove, turn up the wristband, and stick into the foam at the back of the pot. Take the left-hand glove and place in the front portion of the foam, making sure to leave about 1½ inches of foam showing in the front. Insert the seed packet on the dowel in between the gloves, tilting slightly to the left. Add the garden tool in front of the left-hand glove, tilting it slightly to the right.

6. Add Ribbon

Wrap raffia around the pot and tie into a bow. Use a small amount of glue to hold the raffia onto the rim of the pot. Add extra loops of raffia in front of the glove, next to the garden tool, by tying and sticking them into the foam.

Permission to photocopy this page from *Crafts Galore!* granted for local church use. Copyright © Group Publishing, Inc., P.O. Box 481, Loveland, CO 80539. www.group.com

Mailable Photo Frame

- $
- Takes 30 to 45 minutes
- A creative way to stay in touch with loved ones who are far away

Supplies per woman:

- 12x12-inch card stock paper
- string or ribbon
- photocopy of template
- patterned scrapbook paper

Supplies per table:

- scissors
- hole punch
- rulers
- scrapbooking embellishments
- glue sticks and/or photo mount squares
- pens and markers
- pencils

Gifts

Pictures are such a fun way to stay in touch with friends and family that are far away. Everyone loves to get an updated photo of a friend, grandchild, niece, or nephew. In this age of computers and the Internet, it's always meaningful to receive a picture in the mail, and even more so when the envelope and frame have been handcrafted.

Women will find that this project is a great way to share recent photos while sending an unexpected note of encouragement or thoughtfulness.

Prior to your event, make a Mailable Photo Frame to show as an example. To prepare your room for this craft, set up tables and chairs. On each table, have 12x12-inch card stock in various colors for women to use, patterned paper, and other supplies women will need to complete this project.

Suggest that women bring a horizontal photo to place in their frame so they can have it ready to mail on the way home!

In order for the frame to sit upright correctly, it will be important to make sure the picture is mounted so the shorter of the large flaps is on the bottom of the picture.

Mailable Photo Frame

1. Make the Envelope

Use the template to help you draw a 5x7-inch box in the center of 12x12-inch card stock. Cut the corners off of the card stock by cutting at an angle to the corners of the 5x7-inch box. Make sure to cut so that the flaps have room to fold onto the photo without creasing or bending the corners.

Lightly score the edges of the flaps so that the card stock folds without ripping. Trim about 1 inch off of the bottom of one of the larger flaps. This will be the bottom of the frame. Punch holes about an inch from the edge. Measure two lengths of string or ribbon, and string one piece through each hole.

2. Add the Frame and Picture

Now you'll work on the inside frame. Cut a 5x7-inch paper, and measure a rectangle about 1¼ inch in from the outer edge. Slightly fold the middle, and cut along the inside of the frame so the middle can be removed.

Glue the frame on top of the photo, and then glue, or use photo mount squares, to stick the photo and the frame in the 5x7 center of the envelope.

3. Decorate!

Using the embellishments and markers, personalize and decorate the interior of the envelope and frame.

4. Tie and Mail

Tie the flaps backwards as shown with the side flaps folded behind the larger flaps. The envelope turns into a frame that stands on its own, but when the flaps are closed and tied, it can be sent as an envelope.

Permission to photocopy this page from *Crafts Galore!* granted for local church use. Copyright © Group Publishing, Inc., P.O. Box 481, Loveland, CO 80539. www.group.com

Mailable Photo Frame Template

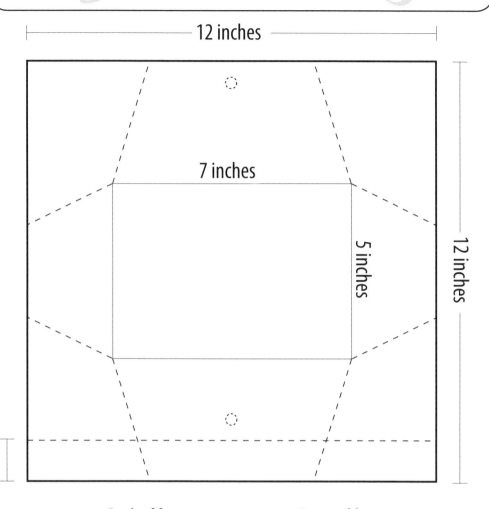

12 inches

7 inches

5 inches

12 inches

1 inch

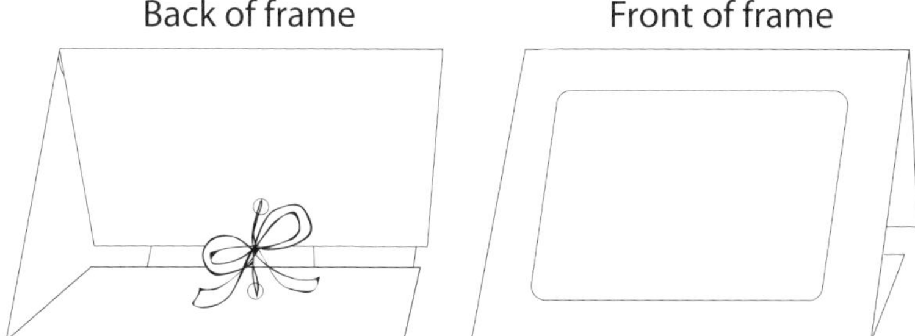

Fold the flaps of your frame backwards
and tie loosely to create a photo frame!

Permission to photocopy this page from *Crafts Galore!* granted for local church use. Copyright © Group Publishing, Inc., P.O. Box 481, Loveland, CO 80539. www.group.com

Travel Jewelry Box

- $
- Takes about 30 minutes
- A cute craft, yet simple enough to allow women to easily make more than one (so have extra supplies on hand!)

Supplies per woman:

- empty small matchbox
- scrapbook paper and/or map paper

Supplies per table:

- scrapbook embellishments like decorative brads, tag rims, buttons
- glue sticks
- hot-glue gun
- scissors
- pens and markers

Gifts

This is a perfect little gift for any woman in your life that you would like to encourage. We created it to store earrings or small jewelry while traveling, but it can also be used for storing small objects, such as buttons or pins; for a pill box; or for placing flower seeds inside with directions for planting and growing care.

These little gifts don't take long to make and don't take many supplies, which make them a great craft for just about any occasion or season. Depending on how much time you have, it may be nice for women to decorate more than one.

Prior to your event, make a Travel Jewelry Box to show as an example. To prepare your room for this craft, set up tables and chairs. On each table, place enough matchboxes, embellishments, glue, and other supplies for every woman to make at least one box.

Tip

Look for pads of scrapbook paper with coordinating patterned and solid paper at your local craft and hobby store.

Find scrapbook supplies or old maps at garage sales!

Make sure to glue to the edge of the flaps so they stay on the inside of the box.

Travel Jewelry Box

1. Wrap Box

Take the matchbox apart, and set the "drawer" aside. Use the matchbox as a quick template, and cut out paper to wrap around it, leaving about 1/4 of an inch that will tuck into the inside.

Before applying glue, wrap the outside of the matchbox with the paper, much like wrapping a gift. With the paper taut around the box, cut the paper at the corners of the box so the flaps can then fold into the inside of the box. Then take the paper off, apply glue (the glue sticks work nicely for this), and rewrap the paper onto the box.

2. Decorate!

Add other accents to the outside of the box, such as small buttons, accent paper, ribbon, or other embellishments. Use the hot-glue gun to add these decorations. Use the markers and pens to personalize the boxes, if you wish. When the glue is dry, put the "drawer" back in, and your gift is ready to go!

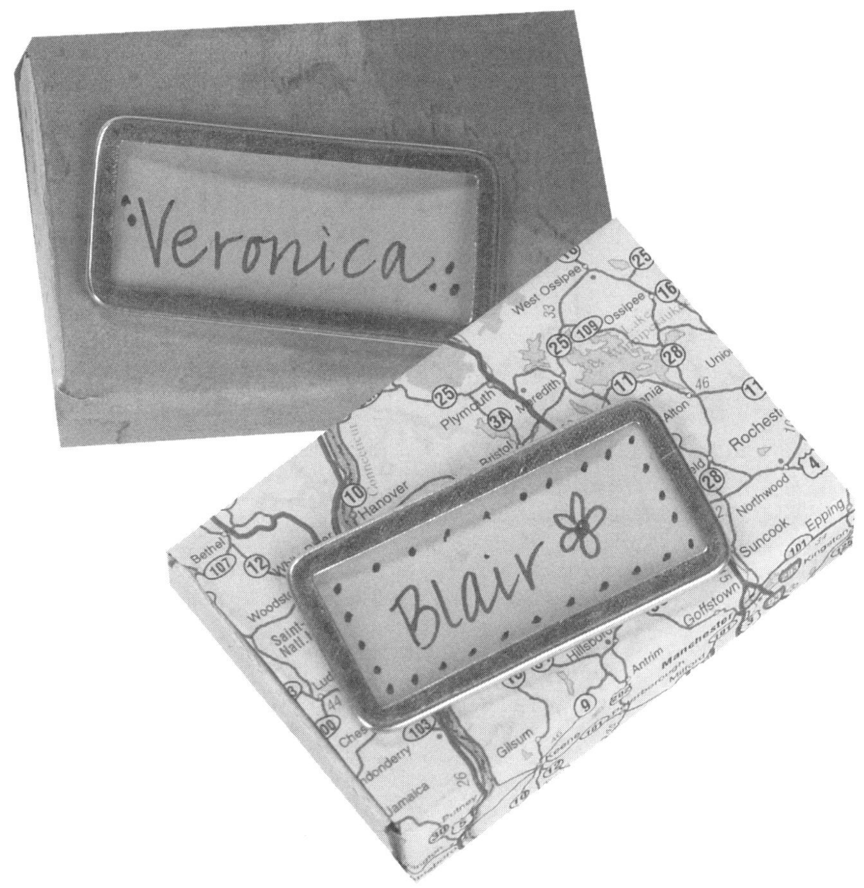

Permission to photocopy this page from *Crafts Galore!* granted for local church use. Copyright © Group Publishing, Inc., P.O. Box 481, Loveland, CO 80539. www.group.com

Mini Journal

Gifts

- $
- Takes about one hour
- Perfect use for those old greeting cards

Supplies per woman:
- brown paper sacks
- old greeting card
- string or ribbon

Supplies per table:
- scissors and a straight cutter
- pens and markers
- ruler
- glue
- large paper clips
- eyelet hole punch with hammer and/or hole punch

Have you ever received a beautiful card and wished you could use it again or frame it just to be able to look at it? Have you kept a card simply because it reminds you of the person who sent it? If you have, those cards are probably taking up valuable space in a drawer, and you really aren't enjoying them as you had hoped.

Well, this craft is the perfect use for those cards we just can't seem to throw away. In this project, you will use a greeting card for the cover of a journal. This journal can be used as a gift for a special friend, a coworker, or a neighbor. Give it to a mother-to-be to record thoughts and dreams she has for her child. Or make these journals and use them for the Journal in a Jar craft on page 26.

Prior to your event, make a Mini Journal to show as an example. To prepare your room for this craft, set up tables and chairs. On each table, place enough brown grocery bags, ribbon, glue, and other supplies for every woman to make at least one journal.

Tips

Have women bring their own greeting cards to use, but be sure to bring extras for women who may not have a greeting card on hand.

Save time by cutting and flattening the grocery sacks before your event. To get out the creases, iron the paper with your iron set to low/medium-low, spraying with a little water to get out those stubborn creases.

Using a paper clip can help with weaving ribbon through the binding holes. Simply flatten a paper clip so that one end is straight, like a needle, and attach the ribbon to the fold in the opposite end.

Mini Journal

1. Make the Pages

Open your greeting card, and cut pieces from the brown paper sacks to the same size as the unfolded card. Fold the brown paper in half, in the same direction as the greeting card, and then run the ruler over the crease to create a crisp fold. Once you have as many pages as you want, place these inside the greeting card. Note that too many pages will keep your journal from staying folded.

If it's necessary to cover signatures and messages on the inside page of the greeting card, glue a brown paper page to the inside cover and decorate it.

2. Bind the Pages Together

With the ruler, mark out even spaces along the "spine" of the journal. Then use a large hole punch, or eyelet punch with hammer and cutting board, to punch holes into the spine. Weave ribbon or string through the holes, and tie a bow on the outside of the spine to bind the pages together. Brads or staples can also be used for a more simplistic appearance.

3. Decorate!

Draw some lines or decorations onto the inside journal pages, or personalize it by signing the inside cover for a specific friend.

Earth laughs in flowers.
-Ralph Waldo Emerson

Permission to photocopy this page from *Crafts Galore!* granted for local church use. Copyright © Group Publishing, Inc., P.O. Box 481, Loveland, CO 80539. www.group.com

Seasonal Crafts

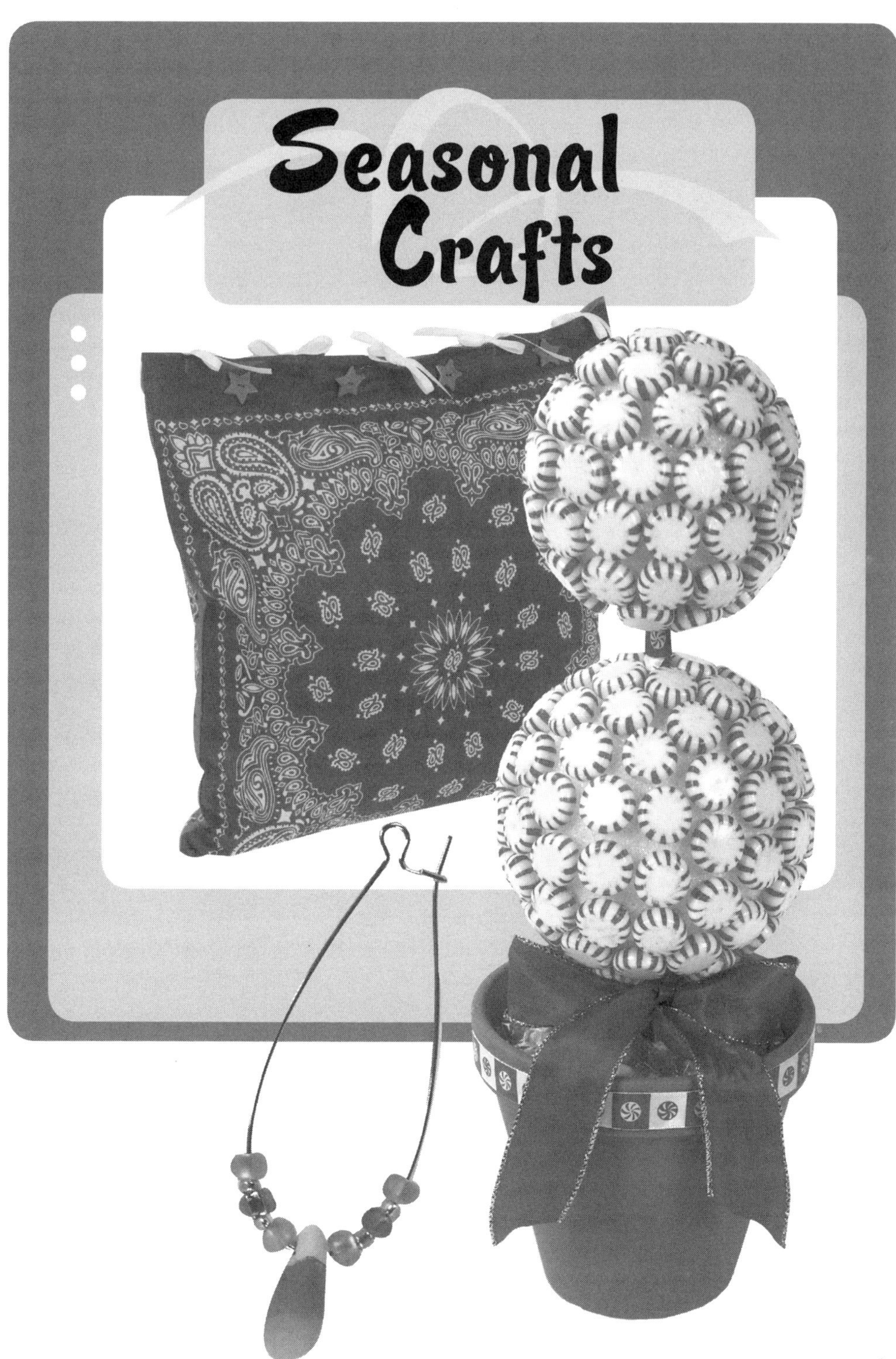

Christmas Candy Topiary

Seasonal Crafts

- $$
- Takes about 30 minutes
- Fun and versatile Christmas decoration for home or as a gift

Supplies per woman:
- bag of red and white mints, gumdrops, or hard candies
- hot-glue gun
- terra cotta pot
- foam ball (not to exceed the diameter of your pot)
- sturdy candy stick, such as a thick red and white candy cane or a dowel
- 2 cups of sugar (depending on the size of pots you buy, amount of sugar should be able to nearly fill the pot)
- 2 feet of ribbon

This is a fun, easy craft that women can make together to decorate their homes with or give as gifts. The topiaries don't take very long to make, but they will add a lot of color to a woman's home or your church. They can be used as centerpieces for a women's event, and they also make appealing gifts! If you'd like, choose one color as your theme. For example, create an all-blue and white topiary or an all-red and white topiary. Or mix it up with multicolored gumdrops and green ribbon, or gold or silver ribbon with blue candies.

Prior to your event, make a Christmas Candy Topiary to show as an example. When setting up your room, provide supplies at each table for each woman to make one. While women work to glue their candies on, encourage the women to discuss fun topics, such as favorite Christmas memories or what their favorite family tradition is.

You can also use sand to fill the pots instead of sugar.

Christmas Candy Topiary

1. Create Your Base

Glue the candy stick into the bottom of your pot with a glue gun so that it stands straight up. Use as much of the hot glue as you need.

2. Create Your Soil

Fill the pot with sugar, up to about 1 inch from the top. Cover this with a layer of red and white mints or gumdrops.

3. Place the Ball

Place the foam ball on the candy stick, pushing it onto the stick about 1 inch deep.

4. Decorate!

Starting at the top of the ball, glue your candy on. Cover the entire ball, alternating colors to create a pattern or design as desired.

When the foam ball is completely covered, add the final addition of a decorative bow on the topiary.

Permission to photocopy this page from *Crafts Galore!* granted for local church use. Copyright © Group Publishing, Inc., P.O. Box 481, Loveland, CO 80539. www.group.com

Spring Seeds of Friendship

Seasonal Crafts

- $$
- Takes about 30 minutes
- Fun, easy craft that can be given as a gift to a friend, child, or coworker

Supplies per woman:

- small, unprinted envelopes

Supplies per table:

- rubber stamps
- ink pads
- markers
- "seeds" (such as M&M'S candies, mints, bath crystals, potpourri, nuts, or flower seeds)

Why keep all the friendship in one house? Spend some time creating Spring Seeds of Friendship seed packets to give to other people you care about—friends, children, or spouses—whomever you wish to reach out to with love. These are envelopes made to look like seed packets, created to give away to someone special so love can flourish. Each woman can make five to six packets, all for different people in her life. For example, a mom might fill a packet with candy and tuck it in her child's lunch, a woman might fill packets with bath crystals and give them to friends, or a wife might fill a packet with nuts and hide it under her husband's pillow for a surprise.

Tip

We had custom rubber stamps made just for this craft, with springtime artwork and the phrases "Seeds of Friendship" and "Sweet Seeds" on them. You can order these at www.group.com/women.

For additional fun in decorating, use small terra cotta pots on tables, filled with the "seeds."

This is a perfect craft for a spring fling event, for the beginning or ending to a Bible study, as a way to celebrate spring, or even as a way to welcome back the school year. Whenever you choose to use this craft, women will not only love what they make, but they will find great joy in passing them on.

Prior to your event, make several Spring Seeds of Friendship packets to show as examples. When setting up your area, set out enough envelopes and "seeds" so each woman can make several packets for different people in her life.

Spring Seeds of Friendship

1. Stamping

You're going to make a "seed" packet filled with a treat to show your love for a friend or family member. Choose a blank envelope, and decorate it with the rubber stamps and markers. You might want to write or stamp "Seeds of Friendship" or "Sweet Seeds" on it to let the person who receives this know you're planting love in his or her heart with this gift.

2. Filling

You'll use small candies, stickers, bath salts, or other tiny items as the "seeds" for your gift. Place a small amount of your chosen "seeds" into each packet. Seal them well, then tuck into a lunch, under a pillow, inside a purse, or anywhere someone you love will find them.

Permission to photocopy this page from *Crafts Galore!* granted for local church use. Copyright © Group Publishing, Inc., P.O. Box 481, Loveland, CO 80539. www.group.com

Patriotic Pillows

- $$$
- Takes about one hour
- A decorative way to show your patriotic spirit

Supplies per woman:
- 2 bandannas (1 red, 1 blue)
- polyester fiberfill or pillow form
- 5 feet of red, white, or blue ½-inch ribbon
- four 1-inch (or larger) star-shaped buttons (either red, white, or blue)
- red or blue thread (contrasting color to buttons)
- hand-sewing needle

Supplies per table:
- scissors
- straight pins
- sewing machine
- ruler
- pencil
- iron and ironing board

Patriotic pillows are a fun way to decorate for summer months; to give as gifts to kids, teens, or friends with birthdays in the summer; or to give as gifts to new neighbors and share your patriotic spirit. They are easy to create and can be used as an easy way to teach your kids how to iron, sew by hand, and sew with a machine.

Prior to your event, make a Patriotic Pillow to show as an example. When setting up the room, set up tables and chairs. On each table provide enough supplies for women to make one pillow. Be sure to have your sewing machine thread and bobbin loaded and usable sewing machine needles ready before you begin. You'll also need to have plenty of scissors, needles, and thread to go around for each person.

Patriotic Pillows

1. Iron the Bandannas

Frequently bandannas come folded, so it makes a better finished product to iron them before you begin. If the fold lines are distinct, misting some water on them before ironing helps smooth them out quickly.

2. Place Bandannas Together

Place the bandannas directly on top of each other, with the most colorful sides of the bandannas facing each other so you see the wrong side of the fabric. Match corners where possible. Pin the bandannas together to hold them in place while sewing.

Bandannas may not be exactly the same size, so you'll want to decide where any overlap will land before you begin sewing.

3. Begin Sewing

Using the sewing machine, sew three sides of the bandannas together.

4. Add Ribbon

Cut the ribbon so that you have five pairs of 6-inch ribbons.

Use the ruler to measure the length of the open end of the pillow. Using a pencil (on the wrong side of the fabric), place five marks that are an equal distance apart (approximately 1 inch from either side), and then place marks for three ribbons evenly spaced between those. This is where the ribbons will be attached.

Begin with one color of ribbon and pin to the wrong side of the fabric, approximately ½ to 1 inch deep, at markings. Flip pillow over and repeat, using the other color of ribbon so each ribbon pair is together.

Using the sewing machine, sew back and forth vertically along the pinned end of the ribbon so that the end is solidly attached to the pillow.

Trim any ends of threads, and turn the pillow right-side out.

5. Fill the Pillow

Place the polyester fiberfill or pillow form into the open end of the pillow. Fill to the density you desire, making sure it doesn't show outside of the ribboned edge.

Permission to photocopy this page from *Crafts Galore!* granted for local church use. Copyright © Group Publishing, Inc., P.O. Box 481, Loveland, CO 80539. www.group.com

Patriotic Pillows page 2

6. Add the Buttons

Add the buttons in the spaces between the ribbons, placing them approximately 2 inches deep, being sure to use contrasting buttons and fabric (such as red buttons with a blue bandanna).

Tie the ribbons together into bows or decorative knots for your finished look.

Your pillow is now ready to toss onto the couch, onto your child's bed, or into a gift bag to present to your new neighbor as a nice "welcome to our neighborhood" gift.

Permission to photocopy this page from *Crafts Galore!* granted for local church use. Copyright © Group Publishing, Inc., P.O. Box 481, Loveland, CO 80539. www.group.com

Harvest Baubles

- $$
- Takes about one hour per pair
- Excellent to use as a craft fair project for fundraising

Supplies per woman:

- dangling kidney earring wires
- plastic teaspoon
- toothpick

Supplies per table:

- colored baking clay (such as Sculpey) in autumn colors such as brown, rust, and gold
- 6/0 Czech glass beads in autumn colors
- seed beads in autumn colors
- small bowls
- felt pieces
- baking sheet
- oven

Any woman with pierced ears is always looking for new earrings, which makes this project perfect for fundraisers or for gifts. The earrings in this craft are easily made with a small group or with a girlfriend. You don't have to have jewelry-making tools to make these…they're a simple type of earring to put together. And the more pairs of earrings you make with the baking clay, Czech glass beads, and seed beads, the less expensive each pair gets. Since the clay beads you'll make are small in size, you won't use much of the baking clay, and it lasts for years if packaged in a resealable plastic bag.

Prior to your event, make several pairs of earrings, using different kinds of beads, to show as an example. When setting up your room, set up tables and chairs, placing supplies women will need at each table, including bowls to place the beads in and felt pieces for each individual making earrings. This will prevent the beads from rolling off the creation surface.

As you get used to making these earrings, consider using a variety of bead types. And you don't have to limit your designs to autumn colors; feel free to add variety with your own color schemes.

Harvest Baubles

1. Create Autumn Beads

Using a variety of colors of baking clay, create small autumn-shaped beads. You'll want to make at least two of each bead in order to have a pair for each pair of earrings.

The baking clay will be stiff at first, but it easily becomes pliable from the warmth of your hand. See directions below for creating candy corn, leaves, and pumpkins. Feel free to create something that means "autumn" to you.

*Candy corn beads: Use white, orange, and gold baking clay. Warm each of the colors in your hand, then tear off small pieces of the clay. Flatten to 1/8 inch thick, and create the triangular-shaped candy corn beads.

*Leaves: Use any fall color—orange, gold, brown, deep red, and so on. Tear off small pieces of the clay, and warm the pieces in your hand. Create an oval shape, and flatten to 1/8 inch thick. Then using a plastic teaspoon, indent the top and sides for stem and leaf indentations. Pinch the bottom point of the oval shape into the pointed end of the leaf.

*Pumpkins: Use orange clay. Tear off small pieces of the clay, and warm the pieces in your hand. Create a round shape, and flatten to 1/8 inch thick. Using a plastic teaspoon, indent creases into both front and back sides of the pumpkin, making sure not to press too hard on the second side, as it will smooth the side already indented. Again, use the teaspoon to make indentations in the top to form pumpkin stems.

Use a toothpick to poke a hole from both front and back sides of the beads. This will allow you to thread them onto the earring wire.

2. Bake

Place beads on a baking sheet, and bake them in an oven set to the temperature suggested on baking clay packaging. Bake to length of time given on package, being careful not to burn the beads. As long as beads are not touching, and they are all the same general size and thickness, you can bake a sheet filled with them all at the same time.

After baking, allow the beads to cool on the baking sheet. If they're small and 1/4 inch thick, this will not take much time.

3. Choose Beads

As clay beads are cooling, begin sorting through the colored seed beads and Czech glass beads to decide what colors and how many to use on each earring. Make sure to choose all the beads for the pair of earrings to ensure they match.

4. Thread Beads Onto Wire

Once clay beads are cool, begin making the first earring by threading Czech glass beads and seed beads onto earring wire in the order chosen for your design. Thread half of the beads you want to use at this time.

Permission to photocopy this page from *Crafts Galore!* granted for local church use. Copyright © Group Publishing, Inc., P.O. Box 481, Loveland, CO 80539. www.group.com

Harvest Baubles page 2

Thread on clay bead so it will hang in the center of the earring.

Thread the other half of the Czech glass beads and seed beads onto the earring wire to match the design of the first half of the earring.

Close the earring wire, and make a matching earring from the remaining beads, earring wire, and clay bead.

Permission to photocopy this page from *Crafts Galore!* granted for local church use. Copyright © Group Publishing, Inc., P.O. Box 481, Loveland, CO 80539. www.group.com

Spring Flowerpot

- $$
- Takes about one hour
- Makes a pretty spring or Easter gift

Supplies per woman:

- 4-inch terra cotta pot and saucer
- 1-inch foam paint brush
- small craft paint brush
- pencil
- 24-inch piece of ribbon to complement paint colors

Supplies per table:

- bottled acrylic craft paint in white, pink, and light green
- waxed paper
- green Easter grass (optional)
- jelly beans (optional)

Spring and Easter are a time of renewal and new growth, which makes it a perfect time for this craft. It's enjoyable, easy, and women can make it together as a decoration or to give as a gift. You can fill these with plastic grass and jelly beans, or add a small plant from your local plant nursery. Either way, these make cheerful gifts for someone who needs a little encouragement, or they can brighten your own home during the spring months. These pots look great in groups of two or three, so sit them on a windowsill and enjoy the bright, cheery colors.

Prior to your spring or Easter event, make a Spring Flowerpot to use as a sample. When setting up for this project, set up tables and chairs, placing supplies at each table for each woman to use.

Tip

Some women are more comfortable using paint markers, so consider using paint markers to decorate the pots, or have both paint and paint markers available.

Hair dryers are excellent to have on hand to speed up the drying time of the paint.

Spring Flowerpot

1. Paint the Flowerpot

Paint the flowerpot with the color of your choice using the foam brush. White is recommended. Smooth out the paint, making sure there are no globs. Paint the inside of the pot with same color. Paint the saucer with a complementing color.

2. Let Dry

Set flowerpots aside on waxed paper and allow to dry.

3. Decorate

Using the skinny side of the foam brush, paint stripes with the same color used for the saucer. To make it easier, divide the top of the pot into eight equal segments, then paint the stripes. Make sure to carry the stripe inside the pot at least 1 inch. Paint a stripe around the center of the saucer by measuring down ⅜ inch from the top of the saucer, marking with a pencil, and painting the stripe.

4. Add Dots

Add dots to the pot and saucer using the handle end of the craft paintbrush. Dip the end of the brush into the paint, and apply dots. For smaller dots, use the end of a toothpick or ballpoint pen. The dots should be placed randomly, so have fun!

5. Add Ribbon

Wrap ribbon around pot and tie into a bow. You might want to use a small amount of glue to help hold the ribbon onto the rim of the pot.

6. Fill Pot

Fill the pot with Easter grass and jelly beans, or consider a small flowering plant, candies, or small lotions and soap.

Permission to photocopy this page from *Crafts Galore!* granted for local church use. Copyright © Group Publishing, Inc., P.O. Box 481, Loveland, CO 80539. www.group.com

Thanksgiving Blessings Box

- $$
- Takes about one hour
- Perfect to use as a Thanksgiving or fall gift

Supplies per woman:

- 4-inch papier-mâché box with top
- 1-inch foam paint brush
- 12-inch piece of plastic wrap, crumpled

Supplies per table:

- bottled acrylic craft paint in burnt or dark orange, dark yellow, and gold
- water
- 1 to 2 small rubber stamps with leaf designs
- fine-point black Sharpie pen
- gold paint pen
- black paint pen
- waxed paper
- 2x3-inch slips of paper cut from plain paper grocery bag

Thanksgiving is a time of remembering all God has blessed our lives with, especially our family and friends. What better way to celebrate Thanksgiving, then, than to use this Thanksgiving Blessings Box? Use this box to hold family blessings that can be read aloud all month long or at the table before your Thanksgiving dinner. These are memories that will be cherished for years to come.

This is an easy craft that women can make together to take home to bless their families, or it can be given as a gift.

Prior to your Thanksgiving event, make your own Thanksgiving Blessings Box to show as an example. When setting up for your event, set up tables and chairs, placing supplies at each table for every woman to make a box.

Tip

For a special touch, use pieces of colored card stock instead of the grocery bag paper.

Consider having a couple of hair dryers on hand to speed up the drying time of the paint.

You can decorate each blessing by adding pictures of family and friends, or add mementos with the cards.

Thanksgiving Blessings Box

1. Paint Box

Using the foam brush, paint the inside and outside of the box bottom and lid with burnt orange paint. Set aside on a piece of waxed paper and allow to dry.

Squeeze out a small amount of the yellow paint onto waxed paper. Add about four to five drops of water to the paint and mix together. Using the crumpled piece of plastic wrap, dab into the watered-down paint, making sure not to saturate the plastic wrap. Dab onto the box sides and the top of the box. Let dry.

2. Leaf Stamping

Take the foam brush and spread gold paint onto the first stamp, making sure to smooth out the paint. Stamp the inside bottom of the box and stamp several leaves on the top of the box. Let dry.

3. Outline the Leaves

Using a black fine-point Sharpie, outline the stamped edges of the leaves to help them stand out from the background.

4. Gold Edge

Outline the edges of the box top and the box bottom edge with a gold paint pen. If you wish, use gold and black paint pens to write "I am thankful" on the top of the box.

5. Write a Blessing

On each 2x3-inch piece of paper, write something that you are thankful for, or write your blessings. You may want to add a blessing for each day of the month.

Permission to photocopy this page from *Crafts Galore!* granted for local church use. Copyright © Group Publishing, Inc., P.O. Box 481, Loveland, CO 80539. www.group.com

Pretty Pretzel Hearts

- $
- Takes about 30 minutes
- A yummy Valentine's Day treat

Supplies per woman:

- 10 mini pretzels

Supplies per table:

- white chocolate chips or chocolate bark
- red sugar sprinkles
- nonstick aluminum foil
- white paper sacks or cardboard candy containers (found in the candy-making section of most craft and hobby stores)
- markers or rubber stamps and ink pads
- cellophane bags
- curling ribbon
- access to freezer or refrigerator
- microwave
- several microwaveable bowls
- spoons (for stirring the melted chocolate)
- forks

These simple treats make an eye-catching addition to a party table, picnic lunch, or gift bag. Follow the directions below for a Valentine-themed snack, or set out a variety of sprinkles, jimmies, or chocolate chips to make these an "any-day giveaway." Just provide coordinating markers or stickers for women to decorate the snack containers.

Prior to your event, make a batch of Pretty Pretzel Hearts to show (and sample) as an example. When setting up your room, set up tables and chairs, placing supplies on the tables that women will need to make their own pretzels. Microwave the chocolate according to package directions, just as women arrive. You may want to set the bowls of chocolate on heating pads to keep the chocolate melted. While the pretzels are freezing (to set up the chocolate), women can decorate paper sacks or other containers to hold their pretzels.

Pretty Pretzel Hearts

1. Dip Your Pretzels
Place the pretzels (a few at a time) into the bowl of melted chocolate. Use a fork to completely cover the pretzels with chocolate.

2. Decorate Your Pretzels
Set the pretzels on a sheet of nonstick aluminum foil. Shake red sugar sprinkles over the pretzels.

3. Freeze!
Place the pretzels in a freezer or refrigerator to set the chocolate.

4. Create a Container
Use stamps and markers on the white sacks or boxes to make a pretty container for the pretzels.

5. The Finishing Touches
When the chocolate has set (after about 10 minutes), place the pretzels in a cellophane bag. Tie a piece of curling ribbon around the bag, and set the bag inside the decorated container.

Permission to photocopy this page from *Crafts Galore!* granted for local church use. Copyright © Group Publishing, Inc., P.O. Box 481, Loveland, CO 80539. www.group.com

Crafts With Devotions

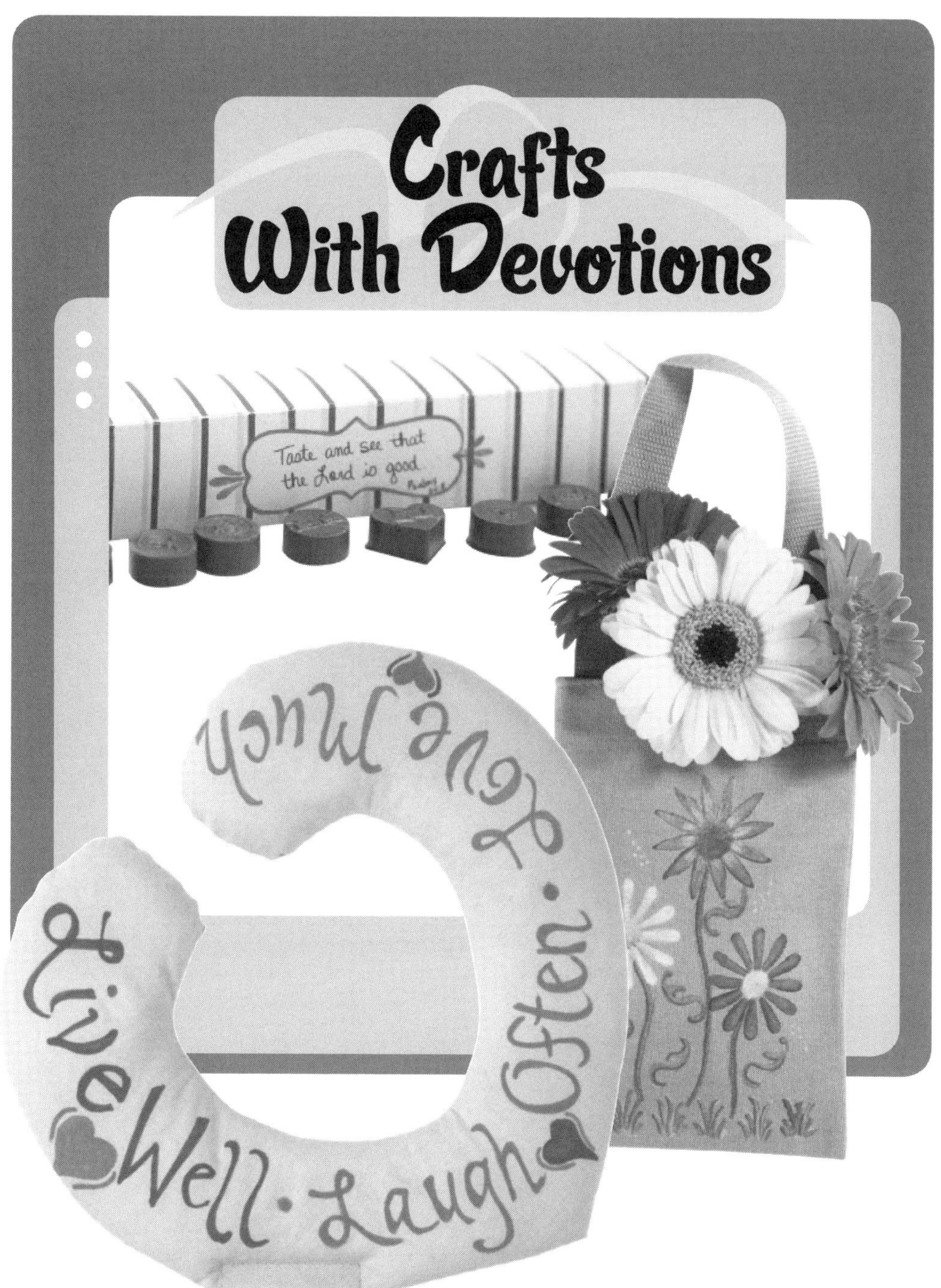
Taste and see that
the Lord is good
Live Well · Laugh Often · Love Much

Treasure Tin

Crafts With Devotions

- $
- Takes about 30 minutes
- A craft to be carried as a reminder to treasure what God treasures

Supplies per woman:

- empty small mint tin, such as an Altoids tin
- photocopies of the blank paper slips

Supplies per table:

- glue
- scissors
- additional decorating supplies such as ribbons, markers, card stock, stick-on gems, stamps, ink pads, and stickers
- photocopies of the "My Treasures" handout
- Bibles

This devotion and craft help women consider the things they treasure and what God treasures. They'll reflect on verses that remind us of what God treasures and add their own verses as well.

Before your event, make a Treasure Tin as an example for women to see.

Then prepare your area by setting up tables and chairs. On each table, place mint tins, decorating supplies, verse slips, and a handout for each woman.

Treasure Tin Devotion

Have each woman find a partner or two (no more than three per group). Have each small group take one of the "My Treasures" handouts and use this for a short time of discussion. Allow about 10 minutes for this.

After 10 minutes, gather women together again. Explain that they'll use the verse they discussed, and other verses that they like, to make a Treasure Tin, filled with papers with verses on them. These can be kept in a drawer, in a purse, on a table, or in any place women will find them occasionally and take out a verse to read for encouragement and a reminder of what is most important in life.

Have women make the Treasure Tins.

Treasure Tin

1. Decorate the Tin

This is your own little treasure box! Use the supplies provided to personalize your tin however you like.

2. Verse Slips

Cut apart the page with the blank slips to create a stack of papers with rounded corners that will fit inside your tin. Copy the text of Micah 6:8 onto one of the slips. Then work with the women around you to find other verses from the Bible that will remind you of what God treasures. Write these verses or other verses that are meaningful to you on the slips of paper, and tuck them into your tin. You can add colorful borders to these slips with markers or tiny stickers if you like.

Keep your Treasure Tin handy. Whenever you need a reminder of what's most important in life, read one of these verses, and reflect on what it means.

Permission to photocopy this page from *Crafts Galore!* granted for local church use. Copyright © Group Publishing, Inc., P.O. Box 481, Loveland, CO 80539. www.group.com

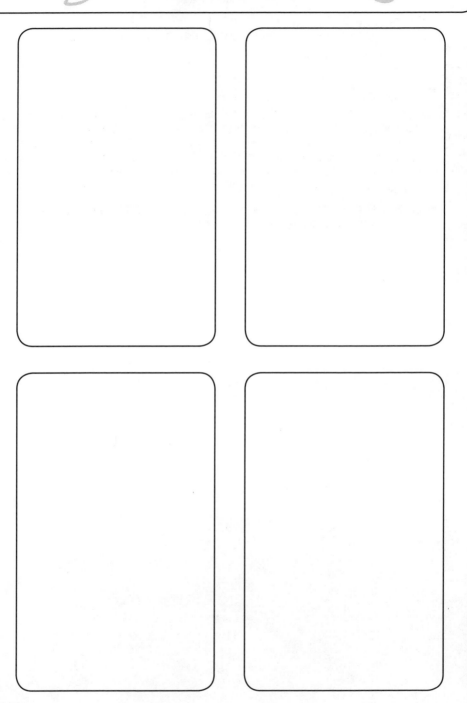

Permission to photocopy this page from *Crafts Galore!* granted for local church use. Copyright © Group Publishing, Inc., P.O. Box 481, Loveland, CO 80539. www.group.com

Memorial Candle

- $$
- Takes about 20 minutes
- A meditative devotion and craft

Supplies per woman:

- tube-shaped glass vase
- sand
- small seashells or stones
- funnel
- tea light candle
- slips of paper and pens

Supplies per table:

- scoops or large spoons for spooning the sand into the vases
- bowls for the sand
- paper to cover tables

Many of us spend time reading messages *from* God, but, unless you are a woman who journals, we don't often spend time writing our own messages *to* him. Many times the busyness of life keeps us from spending peaceful time in reflection. In this devotion, women will take time to ponder who God is and ways they have seen him active in their lives, and then write a message that they will place in a decorative candle. Each time they light the candle, they will be reminded to pray and continue communicating with God.

To prepare for this devotion and craft, make a Memorial Candle for women to see.

When setting up for your event, cover the tables with butcher paper for easy cleanup. Set out the vases, sand, funnels, shells, and/or stones, so all the supplies are readily available.

Memorial Candle Devotion

Have women form pairs to discuss this question: ***Tell about a time you saw God work in your life.*** *Allow about three minutes for women to share.*

After three minutes, say: ***In Joshua chapter 3, we read how God parted the waters of the Jordan River, allowing the Israelites to cross into the Promised Land. In Joshua chapter 4, God instructs the Israelites to gather 12 stones and place them as a memorial to what God did that day. Several books later, in 1 Chronicles 16:8-12 it says: "Give thanks to the Lord and proclaim his greatness. Let the whole world know what he has done. Sing to him...Exult in his holy name; rejoice, you who worship the Lord. Search for the Lord and for his strength; continually seek him. Remember the wonders he has performed."***

Today we are going to make a Memorial Candle to help us remember what God has done—and is doing—in our lives. Each time you light your candle, remember the good things God has done, and offer a praise of thanksgiving for who he is and what he has done.

Have women begin making the craft.

Memorial Candle

1. Write a Message

On a slip of paper, write a message to God. It might be a commitment, a prayer for his help, a praise to him, or the words of a verse that are especially meaningful. Roll up the paper, and place it in the bottom of the vase.

2. Pour Sand

Using a funnel, pour sand in the vase, filling it ⅔ full. Fill the remainder of the vase with small shells or stones, and then place a tea light candle in the center.

3. Light the Candle

Set this candle of remembrance in a place where you can enjoy its glow and be reminded of what God has done in your life.

Permission to photocopy this page from *Crafts Galore!* granted for local church use. Copyright © Group Publishing, Inc., P.O. Box 481, Loveland, CO 80539. www.group.com

Bead Bracelets

- $$
- Takes about 30 minutes
- A craft that will create deep conversation and lasting memories

Supplies per table:

- pieces of short-nap fabric such as velveteen or felt (you can cut up an old blanket for this)—these will serve as bead mats
- small bowls or containers for beads
- round needle-nose pliers
- 1 small pair of wire cutters
- beads of different colors, shapes, and sizes
- memory wire
- photocopies of the "Bead Bracelets" handout pages

In this jewelry-themed devotion, you and your friends will make your own bracelets with ease—and you'll have fun in the process! Each woman will take home a beaded bracelet that she made herself and will use that as a reminder to pray for others.

Tip

Make prep easier! Memory wire and an assortment of beads (enough for eight women) can be ordered from www.group.com/women.

Beads can be placed in several small bowls so everyone can reach them easily.

Bead Bracelets Devotion

This devotion is done as women work on their bracelets. Encourage women to use the handouts on their table and form small groups for discussion as they work on their jewelry.

You may want to assign group leaders to each table to be sure the discussions get started. Of course, once they're started, no one will want to stop talking!

Be sure to make one or two bead bracelets ahead of time to use as samples for women to see.

Bead Bracelets

First, choose a handful of beads and place these on one of the bead mats (those pieces of fabric on your table). This will help you sort the beads without them rolling off the table.

Sort through the beads and find several that you like. Before you begin putting the beads onto a wire, create the design or pattern you like on the bead mat. This will help you make sure there are enough of each color or bead to finish your pattern.

While you're sorting, take time to talk to a few women around you using this guide to get you started.

Let's Talk!

- Choose one bead you like from your bead pile and set it aside. Then go around the circle or your small group, giving each woman a turn to tell a short story about herself based on the color of the bead she's chosen:

RED: Tell about an embarrassing moment you can laugh about now.

BLUE: Tell about a time you won first place—or did something really, really well!

GREEN: Tell about a time you were jealous of someone else.

YELLOW: Tell about something that brings you great joy.

PINK: Tell about something that makes you most glad to be a girl.

PURPLE: Tell about a person or thing that makes you feel like royalty.

ORANGE: Tell your best spring or autumn memory.

CLEAR: Share a fact about life that you finally "figured out."

- When everyone has shared, consider this: Philippians 1:3 says, "Every time I think of you, I give thanks to my God."

- Discuss: How can your beads remind you of different friends that you're thankful for?

Go ahead and work on making your bracelets, and keep on sharing about friends you're thankful for. Then take a few minutes to pray together, thanking God for those friends.

Permission to photocopy this page from *Crafts Galore!* granted for local church use. Copyright © Group Publishing, Inc., P.O. Box 481, Loveland, CO 80539. www.group.com

Bead Bracelets page 2

Let's Make Our Bracelets!

1. Size the Wire
Wrap the memory wire once around your wrist, overlapping the ends about 1 or 2 inches. Cut wire to this size using wire cutters.

2. Close One End
Close up one end of your bracelet by forming a tiny loop in the wire. Using the tip of your needle-nose pliers, grip the wire about ¼ inch from the end and bend the wire until you've formed a tiny loop.

3. String the Beads
Starting at the opposite end of the wire, string your beads in any pattern you choose. Let imagination be your guide!

4. Close the Other End
Close the other end of the wire using the method described in step 2.

Permission to photocopy this page from *Crafts Galore!* granted for local church use. Copyright © Group Publishing, Inc., P.O. Box 481, Loveland, CO 80539. www.group.com

Hanging Garden

- $$
- Takes about 30 minutes
- A craft that women can keep, give as a gift, or make for a fundraiser

Supplies per table:

- 1 Hanging Garden Kit per five women
- paint markers

Women love to give and receive flowers. And why not? They're beautiful, full of color, and emit wonderful fragrances. Have you ever wanted to leave flowers on a friend's doorstep but were afraid the vase would get knocked over and break? Well, we've got the perfect solution for you!

These waterproof bags can be filled with cut flowers and water, then hung on a doorknob for a girlfriend to find later.

Make one or more Hanging Garden vases to use as samples. Go the extra mile and put flowers inside one of them so women can see how these are used. When setting up your room for making the Hanging Gardens, prepare by setting up tables and chairs. On each table, place several Hanging Garden Kits and an assortment of paint markers. You may want to provide scraps of paper for women to test the markers on before using them.

Tips

The waterproof cloth bags used in this craft are unique and are not available at craft or hobby stores. You can order a kit that includes waterproof cloth bags and stencils at www.group.com/women. These are available in three different colors—blue, green, and yellow. Each color comes with a different set of garden-themed stencils.

Paint markers are more colorful than permanent markers and dry faster than fabric paints. You can find them at craft and hobby supply stores.

Add color and fragrance to your area by placing vases of flowers around the room. These can later be used for filling the vases!

Hanging Garden Devotion

Say: ***Find a partner at your table, and tell her about a favorite gift you once received. It could be something expensive, or something tiny. What was the gift, and what made it memorable?***

Allow about three minutes for women to share.

After three minutes, say: ***The Bible tells us in James 1:17, "Whatever is good and perfect comes down to us from God our Father, who created all the lights in the heavens. He never changes or casts a shifting shadow." Share with your partner some of the good and perfect gifts you believe God has given you.***

After about three minutes, say: ***When we give gifts, we hope to delight the receiver and say to that person, "You're special!" God has shown us how special we are to him. Let's take the opportunity to show a friend how special she is to us with a gift of flowers. The vase we're making today is unique, unlike any you've seen before.***

Hold up one of the sample vases you created ahead of time.

Say: ***This little bag is lined with plastic and can be filled with a bouquet of flowers and water to keep those flowers fresh. It won't leak, and you can hang this gift on your friend's doorknob to greet her when she comes home! Let's make them!***

Have women make the craft.

Hanging Garden

1. Pick a Color

The Hanging Garden vases are available in three colors: Forget-Me-Not Blue, Garden Green, and Daffodil Yellow. Choose the one you like best! There are six different stencils available as well. Share the stencils for a wide variety of options.

2. Let the Decorating Begin

Use paint markers and stencils to personalize these gifts. You can also draw freehand if you are artistic, but the stencils will make things easier if you're not as crafty. Both sides of the vase can be decorated.

3. Give It Away!

Fill the vase with cut flowers and a little water. Hang it on the doorknob of a friend, knock…and run!

Permission to photocopy this page from *Crafts Galore!* granted for local church use. Copyright © Group Publishing, Inc., P.O. Box 481, Loveland, CO 80539. www.group.com

Memory Garden Picture Frame

- $
- Takes about 30 minutes
- A meaningful craft for a small group, retreat, gift, or any time you want to make something beautiful with your friends

Supplies per table:
- pressed flowers
- white glue on disposable plates
- cotton swabs
- scissors

Supplies per woman:
- acrylic frame (approximately 3x5 or 4x6)
- acetate sheets cut to the same size as the frames (you can use overhead transparencies for this)

There's no question that flowers are beautiful, and all of us like to stop and enjoy them. Sometimes flowers remind us of a person we love, and sometimes they remind us of an event that was significant, such as a birthday or wedding. Flowers are also beautiful reminders of God's creativity and care for even the most intricate details of our lives.

In this activity you'll lead women in a project that allows them to reflect on these memories every time they see their creation—a Memory Garden Picture Frame.

Prior to your event, take time to create a Memory Garden Picture Frame to use as an example. To prepare your room for making Memory Garden frames, set up tables and chairs. On each table, place several Memory Garden frames, acetate sheets, pressed flowers, plates of glue, handfuls of cotton swabs, and a few pairs of scissors to share.

Tip

Make your preparation super easy by ordering supply kits from Group. You can order a kit that includes the acrylic frames, acetate sheets, and an assortment of beautiful pressed flowers at www .group.com/women. Each kit has supplies for five women.

The flowers are very delicate! Remind women to use care when handling them.

A slightly dampened cotton swab can be used to easily pick up the delicate flowers.

Memory Garden Picture Frame Devotion

Say: ***Have you ever pressed a flower from a special occasion? If so, turn to a partner at your table and tell about one of those occasions and the flowers you pressed. If not, tell about a special occasion you remember that involved flowers.***

Allow about three minutes for women to share.

After three minutes, say: ***Sometimes flowers remind us of a person we love, and sometimes they remind us of an event that was significant. They're so beautiful and fragrant that we often associate them with special memories such as weddings, birthdays, anniversaries, the birth of a baby, and so on. Just seeing those pressed flowers we saved from those events or getting a whiff of a flower that we were given on a special day reminds us of the people and experiences surrounding that event.***

We're going to use flowers to make a miniature Memory Garden Picture Frame.

Show the samples that you made ahead of time.

Second Thessalonians 1:3 says, "We can't help but thank God for you, because your faith is flourishing and your love for one another is growing." These pressed flowers are beautiful reminders of God's creativity and care for even the most intricate details of our lives, and of the faith and love that God is growing in each of us.

Have women make the craft.

Memory Garden Picture Frame

1. Choose and Arrange

Choose several flowers and arrange them on one of the clear acetate sheets. Consider how the flowers will accent a picture when it is placed in the frame.

2. Affix the Flowers

When you have a nice arrangement, use the cotton swabs and dots of glue to affix the flowers to the clear acetate.

3. Wait and Chat

Let the glue dry for several minutes. While you're waiting, chat with the girlfriends around you about special memories related to flowers.

4. Place the Flowers in the Frame

Carefully place the acetate sheet of flowers inside your frame. Then you can easily slide a photograph behind it.

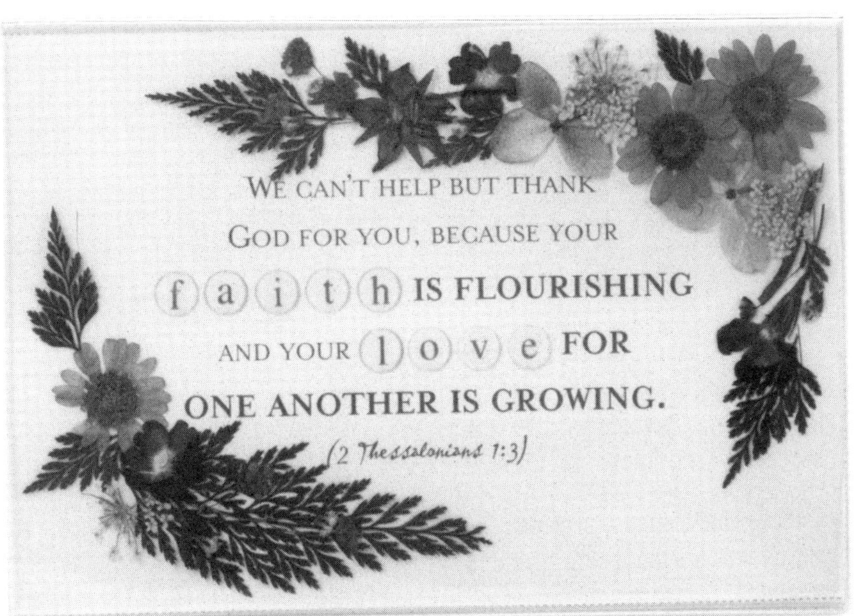
WE CAN'T HELP BUT THANK
GOD FOR YOU, BECAUSE YOUR
f a i t h IS FLOURISHING
AND YOUR l o v e FOR
ONE ANOTHER IS GROWING.
(2 Thessalonians 1:3)

Permission to photocopy this page from *Crafts Galore!* granted for local church use. Copyright © Group Publishing, Inc., P.O. Box 481, Loveland, CO 80539. www.group.com

Sweet Psalms Box of Chocolates

- $$
- Takes about 45 minutes
- A tasty gift that anyone would love to receive

Supplies per woman:

- white gift box
- chocolate candy mold
- plastic trays to fit inside gift box
- 2 ounces melted chocolate

Supplies per table:

- stencils
- chocolate melting supplies (see below for tips)
- plastic spoons
- paint markers

Women love chocolate. We enjoy tasting chocolate and sharing it with each other—which makes this the perfect craft! You'll lead women in a project that allows them to pass along the gift of friendship with a chocolatey version of Psalm 34:8.

For this activity, you will need access to a refrigerator or freezer.

Before your event, make a Sweet Psalms Box of Chocolates to use as an example.

Prepare the area you'll be using by setting up tables and chairs. Place one table near the front of the room for additional supplies. On each table, place several gift boxes, chocolate molds, trays, stencils, a few paint markers, and plastic spoons. You may also want to have paper towels handy for cleaning up drips and spills.

Melt the chocolate using the method that will work best for your facility. (See next page.) Just before women arrive, place the melted chocolate on the tables.

Tip

This project uses a chocolate mold where each chocolate spells out a portion of Psalm 34:8, "Taste and see that the Lord is good." You can order a kit that includes the custom chocolate molds, gift boxes, trays, and stencils for five women at www.group.com/women.

Women enjoy having a few options! Provide a variety of milk chocolate, dark chocolate, and white chocolate.

Be sure no water gets mixed into your chocolate, as this will cause the chocolate to stiffen and become unusable for molding. (However, it still tastes fine and can be eaten.)

Melting Options

You will need to choose the chocolate-melting option that will work best for your facility.

Electric Skillet

This option it is the easiest for cleanup afterward.

Place your chocolate bits into inexpensive plastic containers. The disposable kind commonly used for leftovers work great. Put these containers in an electric skillet that has a few inches of water in it. The water should be about halfway up the sides of the plastic containers so that it does not spill into the chocolate.

Turn your electric skillet to a low setting, and stir the chocolate every few minutes. Once the chocolate is melted, you can remove the plastic containers from the skillet and place them where women can use them. If chocolate begins to harden, simply return it to the warm water for a few minutes.

This method allows you to control the temperature of the chocolate so burning is less likely. However, remember to keep an eye on the chocolate and stir it often. When your activity is over, simply put the lids on the plastic containers.

Microwave Oven

Place the chocolate bits into microwave-safe bowls. Microwave about 30 seconds, and then stir the chocolate. Repeat this step until the chocolate is smooth. Place the bowls of melted chocolate on the tables where women can use them. If chocolate begins to set while women are working, you can pop the bowls back in the microwave and warm the chocolate for 30 seconds again.

Remember, chocolate burns easily, so don't cook for longer than 30 seconds at a time.

Sweet Psalms Devotion

Have women find partners and discuss:

- ***What's the most lavish gift anyone has given you?***

After about two minutes, say: ***Have you ever considered it a gift to be associated with someone? For example, if someone you admired introduced you as her best friend, would you consider that a gift?***

The Bible tells us in 1 John 3:1, "How great is the love the Father has lavished on us, that we should be called children of God! And that is what we are!" *(NIV).*

God has given us the lavish gift of being called his children. He wants to be associated with us! What an incredible gift—that God would say, "Hey! That's my daughter over there!"

We can give our friendship as a gift, too. We're going to make boxes of chocolate that we can give to friends to say, "Your gift of friendship is special to me." It's not as lavish as God's gift to us, but it's a start! And these chocolates are extra special because they share a sweet Psalm. When these are finished, you'll have chocolates that express Psalm 34:8, which says, "Taste and see that the Lord is good."

Let women make the craft.

Sweet Psalms Box of Chocolates

1. Fill Molds
Use a plastic spoon to put melted chocolate into each of the cavities in the mold.

2. Refrigerate
Place filled molds in a refrigerator or freezer, and leave them there for 15 to 20 minutes.

3. Decorate Boxes
While waiting for the chocolate to harden in the molds, personalize the gift boxes using the paint markers and stencils.

4. Place Chocolates in Boxes
When chocolates have set, pop them out of the molds. Place a plastic tray inside the gift box, and put the chocolates into the tray so the verse can be read when the box is opened.

Taste and see that
the Lord is good

Permission to photocopy this page from *Crafts Galore!* granted for local church use. Copyright © Group Publishing, Inc., P.O. Box 481, Loveland, CO 80539. www.group.com

Comfort Pillow

- $$
- Takes about 30 minutes
- Perfect idea to encourage relaxation and rest

Supplies per woman:

- Comfort Pillow shell
- 3 cups of uncooked white rice

Supplies per table:

- bowls
- disposable paper cups
- paint markers

Women enjoy a time of rest and refreshment, so why not send them home with a Comfort Pillow they created? Each heart-shaped pillow is filled with uncooked rice and scented beads and then closed with a Velcro fastener (so no sewing is required!).

After a long day or strenuous exercise, women can pop a Comfort Pillow into the microwave and warm it for a few minutes. The rice holds heat for a long time, and the heat releases the fragrance of the scented contents. The Comfort Pillow can then be placed around the neck to warm and relax muscles. Comfort Pillows can also be placed in the freezer and used as an ice pack when a cooling effect is preferred.

Tip

Due to the unique heart shape of this pillow, which is not available in stores, you will want to order the Comfort Pillow kit directly from www.group.com/women. Kits come in three different colors and scents (lavender, gardenia, and vanilla). Each kit includes five pillow shells and scented beads.

Before your event, you'll want to make a Comfort Pillow to use as a sample. Then prepare your area by setting up tables and chairs.

On each table, place several Comfort Pillow kits, a large bowl of rice, a stack of disposable paper cups, and paint markers in a variety of colors.

Comfort Pillow Devotion

Say: ***I'd like each person to find a partner nearby. Take turns giving each other a one-minute neck and shoulder massage. I'll let you know when a minute is up so you can switch places.***

Help everyone find partners. If there are an uneven number of women, you can partner with someone. Keep track of the time, and after one minute, indicate that women should switch places so everyone has a chance to have a brief massage. After another minute, have women finish their massages and return to their seats.

Say: ***I'm sure we all wish we could take our partners home to give us shoulder massages each time we've had a stressful day or worked out a little too hard at the gym. But since we can't do that, we're going to make the next best thing!***

Hold up the Comfort Pillow that you made as a sample.

Say: ***This is a Comfort Pillow. It's filled with rice and scented beads. When you need some warmth and relaxation, you can put this into your microwave and heat it for two to three minutes. The rice will hold the heat, and a soft fragrance will be released. Then you simply place the Comfort Pillow around your neck*** *(demonstrate this)* ***and enjoy a few moments of rest. You can also put it into the freezer if you prefer a cooling effect.***

Take the Comfort Pillow off your neck, and hold it so it forms a heart.

Say: ***And you can see that the heart shape will always remind you of God's love for you!***

Have women make the craft.

Comfort Pillow

1. Scent Packets

Open the scent packet and pour some of the contents into the pillow. You'll be sharing this packet with others, so only use about a fifth of the packet.

2. Fill Pillow With Rice

Using the paper cups (bend the edge to make a narrow spout), fill the pillow with rice. The pillows should be full but not packed too tightly. You will want to be able to move the pillows around so the pillows are comfortable on the neck.

As you fill your pillow, consider Psalm 139:17-18, which says, "How precious are your thoughts about me, O God. They cannot be numbered! I can't even count them; they outnumber the grains of sand! And when I wake up, you are still with me!"

We aren't working with grains of sand here, but we do have grains of rice. Consider that God's thoughts about you—you!—are precious. They are even greater in number than the grains of rice in your cup. Wow!

As you fill your Comfort Pillow with these grains of rice, tell one or two women around you what you hope God is thinking when he thinks of you. You might hope he's thinking, "Candace always brings joy to my heart!" or "Roxy's smile is so delightful!" What do you hope God thinks when he thinks of you? Tell someone!

3. Close and Decorate

Close the pillow using the Velcro fasteners.

Using paint markers and creativity, decorate the pillow in a way that reflects who you are, adding polka dots, swirls, or stripes, or write a verse or words that are meaningful to you.

Live Well. Laugh Often. Love Much

Permission to photocopy this page from *Crafts Galore!* granted for local church use. Copyright © Group Publishing, Inc., P.O. Box 481, Loveland, CO 80539. www.group.com

Sugar and Spice Spa Set

- $$$
- Takes about 45 minutes
- A project that's great as a gift, but one that women will want to keep for themselves

Supplies per woman:

- 2 plastic jars with lids
- rice bran oil or almond oil
- sea salts
- scented oils (such as lavender)
- organza "shimmer" bag with drawstring
- labels
- ½ cup brown sugar

Supplies per table:

- bowls
- plastic spoons
- paper towels
- paint markers or permanent markers

When it's complete, the Sugar and Spice Spa Set includes a brown sugar scrub and a soothing sea-salt soak. Women can use the brown sugar scrub to exfoliate and remove dead skin and then enjoy the salt soak in a warm bath. It's a perfect craft to do alongside the Comfort Pillow or Bath Cookies!

You'll guide women in making the Sugar and Spice Spa Set and in a devotional discussion that helps them consider God's constant presence.

Before your event, make a Sugar and Spice Spa Set to use as a sample.

Prepare your area by setting up tables and chairs. On each table, place the supplies each woman will need, including the jars, oils, a bowl of brown sugar, plastic spoons, paper towels, and paint markers in a variety of colors.

Tip

If you want an easy way to gather all the items needed for this project, order a kit from www.group.com/women. Each kit contains the supplies needed for five women, and includes jars and lids, rice bran oil, sea salts, lavender oil, water blossom ivy oil, shimmer bags, and a sheet of labels.

Sugar and Spice Spa Devotion

Say: ***Think about one of the first times you were away from home—perhaps when you went to an overnight camp, when you traveled abroad, or even when you spent the night with a friend for the first time. Join with one or two people sitting near you, and tell about those experiences.***

Allow several minutes for women to share about their away-from-home experiences. Then say: ***Let me read you Psalm 139 verses 7-12:***

"I can never escape from your Spirit! I can never get away from your presence! If I go up to heaven, you are there; if I go down to the grave, you are there. If I ride the wings of the morning, if I dwell by the farthest oceans, even there your hand will guide me, and your strength will support me. I could ask the darkness to hide me and the light around me to become night—but even in darkness I cannot hide from you. To you the night shines as bright as day. Darkness and light are the same to you."

Our feelings about being away from home may change with the circumstances, but one thing that never changes is the presence of God with us. He is always there!

We're often more aware of God's presence while we're participating in retreats, at church, or at Bible study. The craft we're going to make will allow us to take something home with us so we can regularly be reminded of God's refreshing and constant presence.

Hold up the sample Sugar and Spice Spa Set you made ahead of time, and indicate the items as you explain them.

Say: ***This is a brown sugar scrub. This mixture of rice bran oil and brown sugar can be rubbed onto your body to remove dead skin cells. You massage it in and then rinse off the excess. It's great on hands and feet, too!***

After you've used the brown sugar scrub, you might want to relax in a soothing sea-salt soak. Today we'll make a mixture of salts and scents to add to a bath. You'll be able to blend just the right amount of fragrance into your salt soak to suit your own preferences. Salt soaks are said to ease sore muscles and general body aches.

Let women make the craft.

Sugar and Spice Spa Set

1. Brown Sugar Scrub

Begin by spooning brown sugar into a jar. Fill the jar about halfway. Then open the rice bran oil, pour a little oil over the brown sugar, and mix with a spoon. Add more brown sugar as needed until the jar is nearly full and the mixture is very thick.

If there is too much sugar in the mixture, the mixture will appear dry and grainy. If there is too much oil, the oil will pool at the top of the mixture. Add sugar until the mixture is glossy and has a smooth appearance.

Tightly screw a lid onto the jar, wipe the sides with a paper towel to remove excess oils, and set the jar aside.

2. Salt Scrub

Begin by pouring sea salt into the second jar. Add a few drops of the scented oil to the salt, and stir them together. Then more drops can be added and stirred in until the desired scent has been reached. Put the lid on your jar, wipe down the sides with paper towels, and set it aside.

3. Personalize

Using labels and paint markers, create custom labels for the jars, giving fun names such as "Sue's Sweet Scrub" or "Psalm 139 Salt Soak." Let the ink dry for a minute or two before placing them on their jars.

Place both jars in one shimmer bag, take home, and enjoy!

Permission to photocopy this page from *Crafts Galore!* granted for local church use. Copyright © Group Publishing, Inc., P.O. Box 481, Loveland, CO 80539. www.group.com

Mended~Heart Valentine

- $
- Takes about one hour
- Good craft to lead into a discussion, or as a gift to ask or show forgiveness

Supplies per woman:

- four blank pre-scored cards
- 2 contrasting colors of construction paper or scrapbook paper
- 2 embroidery needles
- 2 contrasting colors of embroidery thread to match with contrasting papers
- T-pin
- photocopy of heart template

Supplies per table:

- glue sticks
- scissors
- pencil

Mended-Heart Valentines are unique expressions of love or as a request for forgiveness. Taking the time to create this gift card and including a few kind words inside will show someone just how special he or she is.

To prepare for this project, you'll want to make a sample Mended-Heart Valentine to use as an example. First, draw a heart that fits on your card. Then photocopy this heart template. Before your meeting begins, set each table with the supplies women will need to complete this craft, including copies of the heart template, plenty of scissors, embroidery needles, and contrasting thread and paper for each person.

Tip

These cards don't have to be made only in February—they're great for any time of year!

For variety, give each woman a specific color scheme to work with, and have her make several cards of that color. Then have ladies share their cards, and each will have several cards of different colors to take home.

Mended-Heart Valentine Devotion

Say: ***Find a partner at your table, and share a time when you were a child and you hurt someone. Tell your partner how you went about making amends.***

Allow about three minutes for discussion.

Ask: ***Do you remember the sadness of hurting a friend? And then how good it felt to receive forgiveness? Think about the ways you've asked others for forgiveness as an adult and how that differs from your apologies as a child.***

In Colossians 3:12-13, the Bible tells us that just as God forgives us, we should forgive others. Yet as adults it can often be harder to apologize than it was as a child, and we are also slower to forgive.

Thankfully, forgiveness is God's specialty. He requires only that we ask for forgiveness, and it's freely given. We as humans, however...that's a different story. Many times our stubbornness and pride get in the way of asking for forgiveness or even giving it.

Today we're going to create Valentines that can serve as "gifts" of forgiveness to people who have hurt us or as requests for forgiveness from those we have hurt. As you make the stitches in the card, use that time to ask God to help you forgive others and for others to forgive you.

Have women make the craft.

Mended-Heart Valentine

1. Cut and Trace

Make sure the heart template fits within your blank card, leaving a 1-inch border on the card. Cut out the heart template, and fold it in half lengthwise.

On the edge of one of the contrasting papers, trace the left side of the heart, using the straight edge of the paper as the center fold line. Flip the template and trace the right side of the heart on the second piece of contrasting paper, again using the straight edge of the paper as the center fold line.

Cut out both halves of the heart from the contrasting papers.

2. Glue

Glue each heart half to the front of the blank card, making sure to center the heart on the card.

3. Poke Holes

Using the T-pin, poke holes down the middle edge of each heart shape, making sure to stay ⅛ inch away (or more) from the edge of the paper, so that sewing does not create a tear in the edge of the paper. You will need to create an even and equal number of holes on each side, so that you have complete cross-stitches down the center of the heart. A complete cross-stitch will consist of four holes (two on each side of the heart).

4. Cross-Stitch

Load the two embroidery needles with contrasting colors of embroidery thread, using three strands in each needle. The light-colored thread will be used on the dark-colored paper, and the dark thread is for the light paper.

Beginning at the top, make cross-stitches down the middle of the heart. Just for these center stitches, you will be making half of the cross-stitch with the lighter color of thread, and the other half of the cross-stitch with the darker color of thread. Remember to keep all the stitches the same; if you make the first X with the first stitch crossing top right to bottom left, make sure to continue this pattern with all of the stitches.

Once the middle stitches are done, continue on to the sides of the heart. Again, use the T-pin to create the stitch holes, making sure to keep them evenly spaced on each side of the heart.

Using the light-colored thread, make complete cross-stitches on the darker paper heart. Then, using the darker-colored thread, make complete cross-stitches on the lighter paper heart.

When cross-stitches are completed, neatly tie off the thread on the back side of the

Permission to photocopy this page from *Crafts Galore!* granted for local church use. Copyright © Group Publishing, Inc., P.O. Box 481, Loveland, CO 80539. www.group.com

Mended-Heart Valentine page 2

front page of the card, so the inside of the card looks just as pretty as the outside.

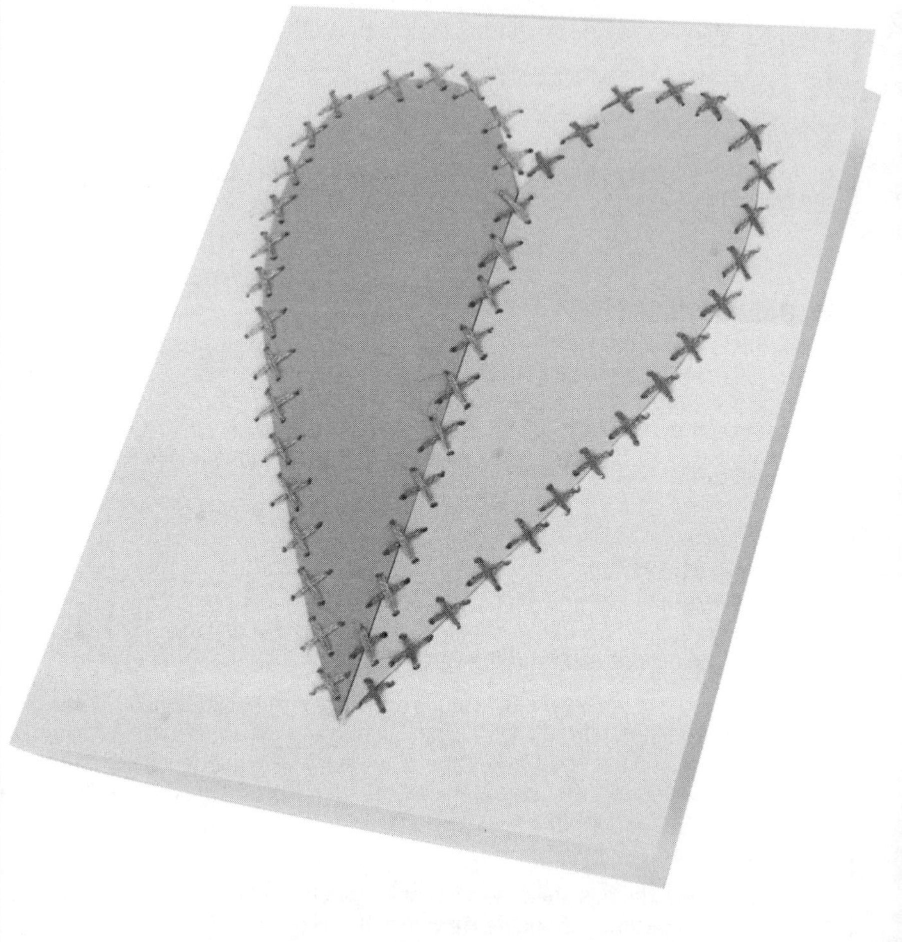

Permission to photocopy this page from *Crafts Galore!* granted for local church use. Copyright © Group Publishing, Inc., P.O. Box 481, Loveland, CO 80539. www.group.com

Food Crafts

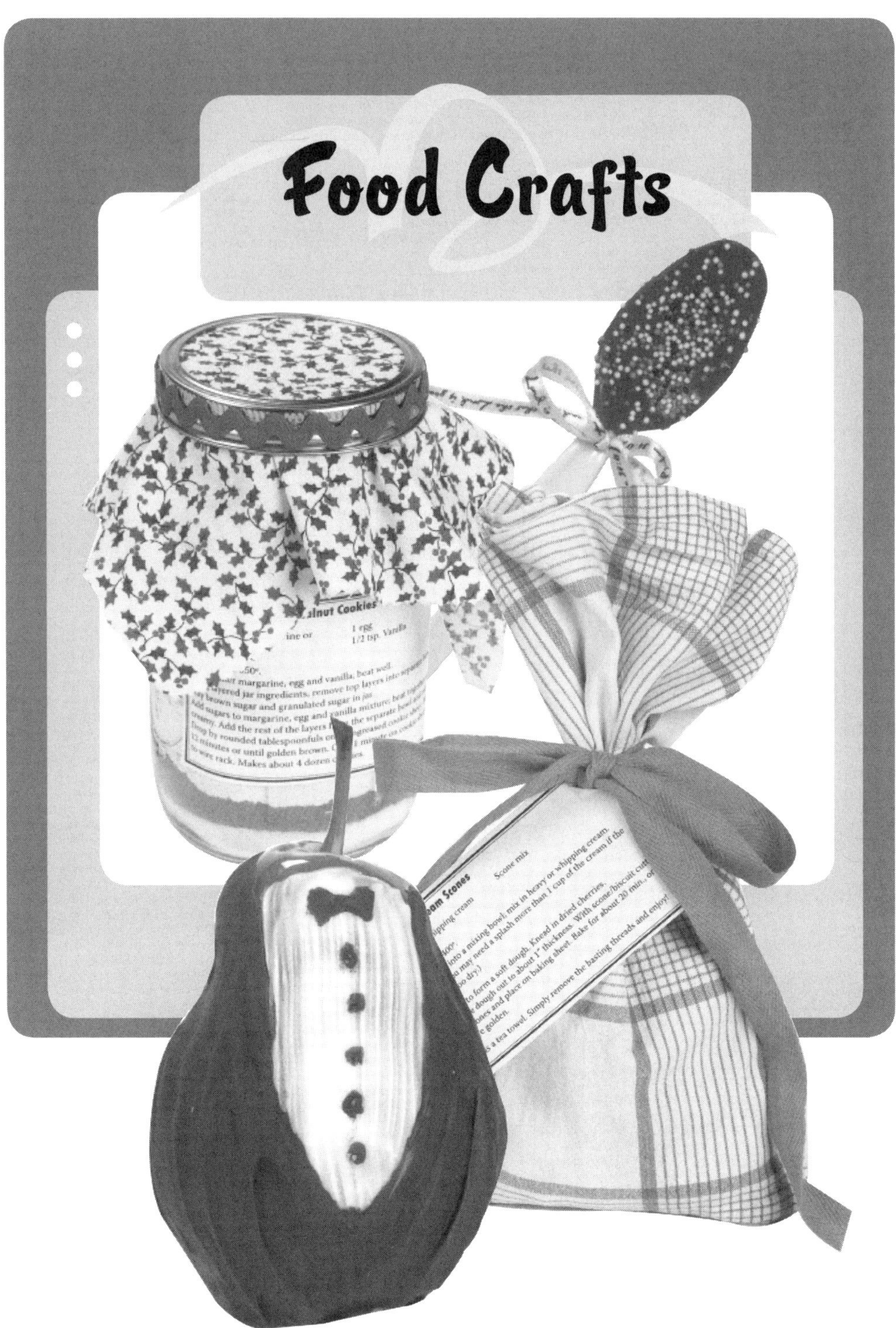

Soup Mixes

• $$
• Takes about 30 minutes
• These mixes can be used for many different purposes and events.

Supplies per jar:

• square of pretty fabric
• ribbon
• photocopy of directions
• small plastic sandwich bag

Supplies for Savory Bean Soup (makes 12 gifts):

• 12 pint-sized Mason jars and lids
• 4 cups dried black beans
• 4 cups dried great northern beans
• 4 cups dried red kidney beans
• 4 cups dried pinto beans
• 4 cups dried green split peas
• 4 cups dried yellow split peas
• 36 teaspoons beef bouillon granules
• 36 tablespoons dried chives
• 12 teaspoons dried savory
• 6 teaspoons black pepper
• 12 bay leaves

Supplies for Creamy Potato Soup (makes 4 gifts):

• 4 pint-sized Mason jars and lids
• 3⅓ cups dried potato flakes
• 2½ cups dried milk powder
• ½ cup powdered coffee creamer
• 4 tablespoons chicken bouillon granules
• 4 teaspoons dried minced onion
• 2 teaspoons dried parsley
• ½ teaspoon white pepper
• ½ teaspoon dried thyme
• 3 teaspoons salt
• large bowl and wire whisk

Food Crafts

Tip

You'll also want to have plenty of measuring spoons and cups on hand.

This is a gift everyone loves to get! Not only are they creative, but the soups they make are easy and delicious—two things any cook looks for in a good recipe.

You can use these soup mixes in a variety of ways. You might use them as fundraisers by selling the mixes at craft shows or festivals. You can give them away as gifts to visitors at your church or distribute them in your church's neighborhood as an outreach project. You can also have the women in your church make them as simple, inexpensive holiday gifts for their own family and friends.

Prior to your event, make up a couple jars of Soup Mixes to show as an example. When setting up the room, place all the Mason jars on one table, and allow women to take them as needed. A simple way of putting this craft together is in assembly-line fashion, where each woman completes one step and then passes the jar to the next woman.

Soup Directions

Savory Bean Soup

1. Layer
Layer ⅓ cup of *each kind of bean* in a wide-mouth pint jar to make pretty layers.

2. Spices
Put the following spices in a small plastic sandwich bag, one for each jar being made:

3 teaspoons beef bouillon

3 tablespoons dried chives

1 teaspoon dried savory

½ teaspoon pepper

1 bay leaf

Place spice bag inside the jar, on top of beans.

3. Attach Directions
Place lid on jar and screw on tightly. Attach the directions card to the piece of ribbon. Place fabric square evenly over the lid, and tie on using the ribbon.

Creamy Potato Soup

1. Mix
Mix all ingredients together in a large bowl with a wire whisk.

2. Divide and Fill
Divide the mix among four pint jars.

3. Attach Directions
Place lid on jar and screw on tightly. Attach the directions card to the piece of ribbon. Place fabric square evenly over the lid, and tie on using the ribbon.

Permission to photocopy this page from *Crafts Galore!* granted for local church use. Copyright © Group Publishing, Inc., P.O. Box 481, Loveland, CO 80539. www.group.com

Soup Recipes

Savory Bean Soup

Set aside the seasoning packet.

Put the beans in a large pot with 9 cups of water. Bring the beans and water to a boil, and boil for 3 minutes. Set aside for an hour.

Drain and rinse the beans. Add 5 cups of water and the seasoning packet to the beans and cook for 1½ hours. Add 1 can of diced tomatoes and a teaspoon of salt. Simmer for 20 minutes.

Enjoy!

Creamy Potato Soup

Mix ½ cup of the dry mix with 1 cup of boiling water. Stir until smooth and creamy. Yum!

Permission to photocopy this page from *Crafts Galore!* granted for local church use. Copyright © Group Publishing, Inc., P.O. Box 481, Loveland, CO 80539. www.group.com

Chocolate-Dipped Spoons

- $$
- Takes about 30 minutes
- A fun gift for women to give away

Supplies per woman:

- 4 plastic spoons
- 4 to 5 feet of ribbon
- 4 pieces of plastic wrap cut into 8x6-inch pieces

Supplies per table:

- dark, milk, semi-sweet, and white chocolate (you can use bark, baking bars, or chips)
- 4 microwaveable bowls
- waxed paper
- powdered chocolate and cinnamon (optional)

Food Crafts

Used for stirring chocolate into coffee or hot chocolate, these gifts are a great way to extend your outreach. Quick and easy to make, Chocolate-Dipped Spoons are sweet gifts (literally!) that the women at your event can give to others as tokens of friendship.

For this craft, you will need a microwave for melting the chocolate and a refrigerator or cooler nearby, as the spoons may need to be placed in the refrigerator for approximately 20 minutes to harden.

Prior to your event, make up a few Chocolate-Dipped Spoons to enjoy and show as an example. When setting up the room, place supplies women will need at each table, including four bowls, each for a different kind of chocolate.

Melt the chocolate just before starting. Find instructions for melting chocolate on page 81. Place the bowls of melted chocolate on the tables.

Tip

Chocolate bark tends to be the easiest and least expensive option for making the Chocolate-Dipped Spoons, but consider indulging in one expensive brand of chocolate just for fun!

For added color and fun, you can get colorful spoons at your local grocery or party store.

You can find custom chocolate-themed ribbon at www.group.com/women.

For extra indulgence, sprinkle coated spoons with powdered chocolate, colored sugar, or cinnamon.

Chocolate~Dipped Spoons

1. Dip Spoons

Dip a plastic spoon in melted chocolate to coat the bowl of the spoon. Let excess chocolate drip off, and place coated spoon facedown on a sheet of waxed paper. If you need to speed cooling and hardening of the chocolate, place the spoons in the refrigerator for about 20 minutes before wrapping in plastic.

While you're waiting for the chocolate to harden (and after everyone has finished dipping), dip graham crackers, marshmallows, or banana chunks into the melted chocolate and enjoy. Yum!

2. Wrap

Complete your chocolatey spoons by wrapping each one in a piece of clear or colored plastic wrap and tying with ribbon.

Permission to photocopy this page from *Crafts Galore!* granted for local church use. Copyright © Group Publishing, Inc., P.O. Box 481, Loveland, CO 80539. www.group.com

Brownie Bouquet

- $
- Takes about 15 minutes per flower (plus baking/cooling time)
- Fun, easy gifts for coworkers, spouses, children, neighbors—and it's so tasty!

Supplies per flower:

- 8- to 10-inch piece of clear plastic wrap
- green cloth-wrapped floral wire, 18 gauge
- 8-inch piece of ribbon, any width or style

Supplies per table:

- simple-shaped cookie cutters (heart, star, circle, flower), 1 to 2 inches deep
- flat spatulas
- scissors

Supplies for brownies:

- brownie mix (22.5 ounce size)
- ¼ cup water
- ⅓ cup applesauce
- 3 eggs
- spray cooking oil
- 13x9-inch pan

Food Crafts

Brownie Bouquets are easy to make. Prior to your event, make a Brownie Bouquet. When setting up your room, place on tables all supplies that women will need to make their own bouquets, including a pan of brownies, cookie cutters, plastic wrap, floral wire, and ribbon.

Tip

We've listed supplies per flower—but women will want to make several, so plan accordingly!

Make sure to use the cakelike recipe—fudgy brownies are too sticky for cutting.

Baking adds about 45 minutes and should be done *prior* to the group gathering. Brownies also need to cool at least three hours prior to cutting; overnight is even better. Brownies can be sticky and hard to cut if they are not cooled properly, and they may stick to the cutter.

Since these brownies use applesauce instead of oil, they are also lower in fat than a typical brownie recipe. To simplify the activity, purchase a pan of prepared brownies (unfrosted) at a local grocer or bakery.

The bouquet can be used for many different holidays and/or events, including Valentine's Day, Mother's Day, Administrative Professional's Day, 4th of July, birthdays, St. Patrick's Day, Easter, and so on. Any time you want to give a holiday-oriented gift that's not too expensive but shows you care, this is a great choice. They can be made to look masculine or feminine, so it need not be just a girly gift. Just imagine what a fun surprise this would be for a Sunday school class to do together to present to their moms (or dads) for Mother's Day or Father's Day!

You can give them as a gift in a flower vase, present them individually, or put them in a nice box and treat them as a special bouquet. Any way you give them, they are always well received.

Brownie Bouquet

1. Cut Brownies Using Cookie Cutter

Looking at the baking pan, estimate the number of flowers you'll want to get out of a single pan of brownies. With some cookie cutter shapes, it's best to alternate directions with each cut, allowing less "wasted" brownie trimmings.

Using a deep cookie cutter, cut brownies into shapes. Transfer cut shapes onto plastic wrap using a flat spatula to prevent cracking or breaking. Place the brownie so the plastic wrap will wrap evenly around the shape.

2. Make Stem

Take the floral stem wire, and fold it in half. Allow the wire to overlap at the top so it forms an X shape. Push the floral stem wire ends into the middle of the bottom of the brownie so that each overlapped end is in opposite sides of the brownie, 1 to 2 inches apart; this allows for more stability.

3. Wrap and Tie

Fold the top of the plastic wrap over the front of the flower, and roll the edges in, allowing the plastic wrap to seal at the edges. Using your precut ribbon, tie bows around the bottom edges of the plastic wrap, causing it to gather and seal tightly.

Your Brownie Bouquets are now ready to present in the fashion you've chosen. And you get to enjoy the leftover brownie trimmings!

Permission to photocopy this page from *Crafts Galore!* granted for local church use. Copyright © Group Publishing, Inc., P.O. Box 481, Loveland, CO 80539. www.group.com

Tuxedo Appearal

- $$
- Takes about one hour per pair of pears
- A creative bridal shower or anniversary gift

Supplies per pair of pears:

- 2 crispy pears with stems
- 12-ounce bag individually wrapped caramels
- ½ cup semi-sweet chocolate chips
- ⅔ cup white chocolate chips
- 2 tablespoons water

Supplies per table:

- small white round sprinkles
- toothpicks (pointy)
- parchment paper
- baking sheet
- microwave-safe bowls
- spoons
- silicone pastry brush
- plastic bags for piping
- scissors
- fondue pot (if doing as a group)

Food Crafts

Tuxedo Appearals are sweet treats for wedding showers, brides-to-be, and anniversaries. They can be served at the wedding shower or used as a decoration or centerpiece and then shared with the groom-to-be after the shower. They're also a great way to tell someone you're thinking of him or her on a special anniversary.

If these are being made as a group, you'll want to use fondue pots to keep the caramel in "dippable" form. Plan to microwave the chocolate chips in single-pair batches, or use the chocolate melting methods described on page 81. Also, make sure to keep the dipped pears separated until they're completely set; if they touch, you will have semi-sweet chocolate on the bride's white gown.

A fun addition to the pears is to glue or tape cut-out head shots of the bride and groom to the stems. These can be added just before presenting, so the photos don't have to be kept in the refrigerator with the pears.

Prior to your event, get in a little practice, and make a pair of pears to show. When setting up your room, place all supplies women will need at their tables. Thoroughly wash and dry pears. Allow them to come to room temperature if they've been refrigerated.

Place caramels and water in a microwave-safe bowl. Place in the microwave and heat on full power for 1½ to 2 minutes or until melted and smooth. Stir every minute during melting (if doing as a group, melt them in the microwave and transfer to a fondue pot to keep the caramels melted).

Tuxedo Appearal

1. Dip Pears

Dip both pears in caramel to the base of their "neck," spooning caramel over pears to coat. For smooth coating, make sure caramels are completely melted. Allow excess caramel to drip off, then scrape the bottom if needed. Place the dipped pears on a baking sheet covered with parchment paper. Allow the dipped pears to cool for about 15 minutes, or until caramel is set. While caramel is setting, melt both kinds of chocolate.

2. The White Chocolate

Dip one pear (the bride pear) completely in white chocolate, covering all but the last ¼ inch of the caramel. Use a spoon or silicone pastry brush to help keep chocolate smooth and completely cover the pear. Scrape excess off bottom if needed. Place this dipped pear on the baking sheet covered with parchment paper. Put baking sheet in refrigerator to cool for approximately five minutes.

Using a spoon or silicone pastry brush, coat the front of the second pear (the groom pear) with melted white chocolate to cover the area that will serve as the shirt front. Place this coated pear also in the refrigerator and allow to cool for about five minutes.

3. Decorate the Dress

Place 2 tablespoons of melted white chocolate in sealable plastic bag (this bag may need to be reheated to pipe the chocolate once dipped pear is cooled).

Once the bride pear is cooled, cut off a small corner of the bag, and pipe thin stripes of the white chocolate diagonally from top right to bottom left of the "front" of the pear, then from top left to bottom right, making a crisscross pattern along the front of the pear, implying it's a dress.

Using a toothpick, dip the point in the melted white chocolate, then use that to pick up a single white sprinkle. Using a clean toothpick, scrape the dipped white sprinkle onto the top edge of the white dress, creating the bride's pearl necklace.

4. Dressing the Groom

Place 1 tablespoon of melted semi-sweet chocolate in plastic bag for piping, and set aside.

Dip the groom pear in the melted semi-sweet chocolate chips in three steps. First dip one side diagonally

Permission to photocopy this page from *Crafts Galore!* granted for local church use. Copyright © Group Publishing, Inc., P.O. Box 481, Loveland, CO 80539. www.group.com

Tuxedo Appearal page 2

so that the white "shirt" forms a downward-pointing triangle (much like the front of a tuxedo would look when buttoned). Then dip the second side diagonally in the same fashion. You should now have a white triangle-shaped "shirt" in the front. Next dip the back side of the pear so that it's covered up to ¼ inch of the caramel edge. Use the silicone pastry brush to help cover and smooth the chocolate over the pear.

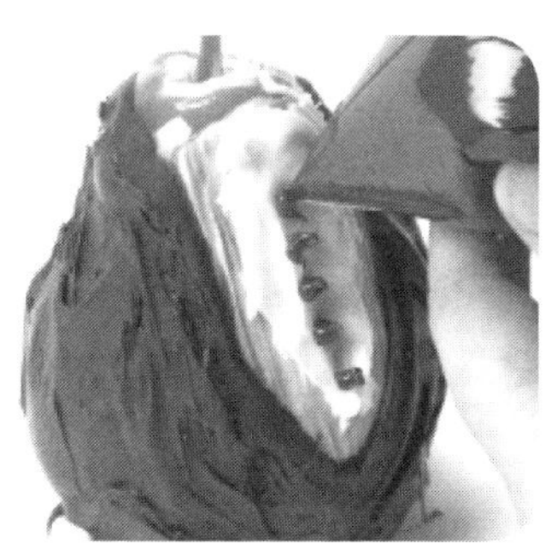

Using the point of a toothpick, or using the piping bag, make small buttons of dark chocolate up the front of the shirt.

Cut a small hole in the piping bag, and make a wide X-shape, closing both ends, which will serve as the bow tie for the groom. Fill in the X-shape to complete the tie.

5. Refrigerate

Place both pears in the refrigerator for 5 to 10 minutes for chocolate to set. If they are not going to be given away immediately, refrigerate until being presented.

Final presentation of the pears can be on a platter lined with parchment paper, which is being presented to the happy couple; in a nice gift box lined with parchment paper; or on pretty saucers you can give them to keep. They can also be enjoyed as a decoration and then given to the bride and groom to enjoy later.

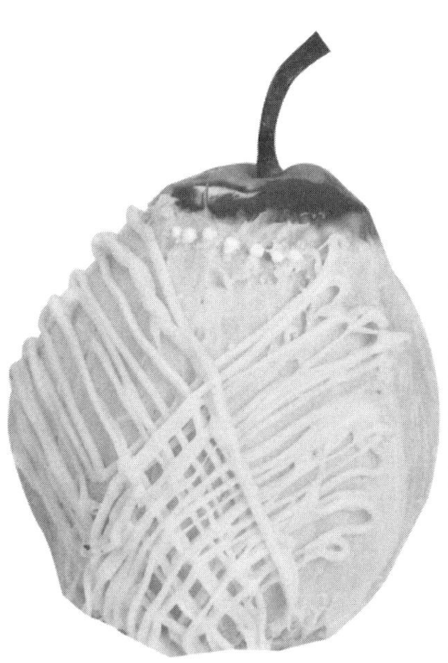

Permission to photocopy this page from *Crafts Galore!* granted for local church use. Copyright © Group Publishing, Inc., P.O. Box 481, Loveland, CO 80539. www.group.com

Tea (towel) and Scones

- $$$
- Takes about 30 minutes
- Tasty gift or fundraiser idea

Supplies per woman:

- 2 resealable plastic bags (sandwich size)
- 2½ cups all-purpose flour
- 1 tablespoon baking powder
- ½ teaspoon salt
- 2 tablespoons sugar
- ¼ cup dried cherries
- bowl
- 1 tea towel
- cloth ribbon
- scone/biscuit cutter
- thread to match tea towel
- printed recipe card or photocopy of recipe

Supplies per table:

- cutting boards and knives
- measuring cups and measuring spoons
- sewing machine
- scissors
- clear tape
- hole punch

Food Crafts

Tip

While the tea towel makes a pretty bag, this is really three gifts in one...scone mix, scone cutter, and pretty tea towel.

This craft is quick to make and really easy to do as an assembly line with a small group of women. You can make photocopies of the recipe card to include with the gift, or for an added personal touch, write the recipes on a card.

This tasty gift can be used for a holiday (or anytime you want to give a gift), and it is also great as a fundraiser. If using for a holiday, use a holiday tea towel and coordinated cloth ribbon. A great thing about this craft is that it can be made ahead of time and kept in the freezer for six to eight weeks, thus making the busy holiday season not quite so hectic.

Prior to your event, create one of these Tea (towel) and Scones sets for women to see as an example. When setting up your room, place the tea towels, thread, and scissors near the sewing machines, and place the supplies needed for the scones in another area. Invite some women to make bags from the tea towels, and ask others to make the scone mix.

Tea (towel) and Scones

1. Make Bag

Lay the tea towel out vertically on a clean, flat surface, wrong side up. Fold the sides of the towel into the middle. Flip the towel over, so the folded edges are tucked under. Fold the towel in half, bringing the bottom up to the top (the folded edges will now be on the outside). Line up top edges.

Using a thread that coordinates with the tea towel, sew both sides closed using the sewing machine's basting stitch. If the top edges already have thick seams, begin stitching just below that stitching.

When both side seams are sewn, trim threads and turn towel inside out so the colorful side of the towel is now showing. This is the bag for the scone mix.

2. Make the Scone Mix

To create scone mix, coarsely chop dried cherries, and place in one of the resealable plastic bags. Carefully push out extra air and seal tightly.

Measure flour, baking powder, salt, and sugar in a bowl; stir together. Using a measuring cup or large spoon, carefully spoon the flour mixture into the second resealable plastic bag. Carefully push extra air out of the bag and seal tightly.

Place bag with flour mixture into the bottom of the tea towel bag, and then place bag with chopped dried cherries into the bag.

3. Closing the Bag

Gather the top of the tea towel bag just above the cherries, and tie it closed with the cloth ribbon.

Wrap a 1-inch piece of clear tape around the corner of the recipe card. Using a hole punch, create a hole in the corner of the card, so the tape reinforces the hole. Pull the ribbon through the hole in the card, sliding the card up close to the bag, then slide the scone/biscuit cutter onto the ribbon and finish tying into a pretty bow.

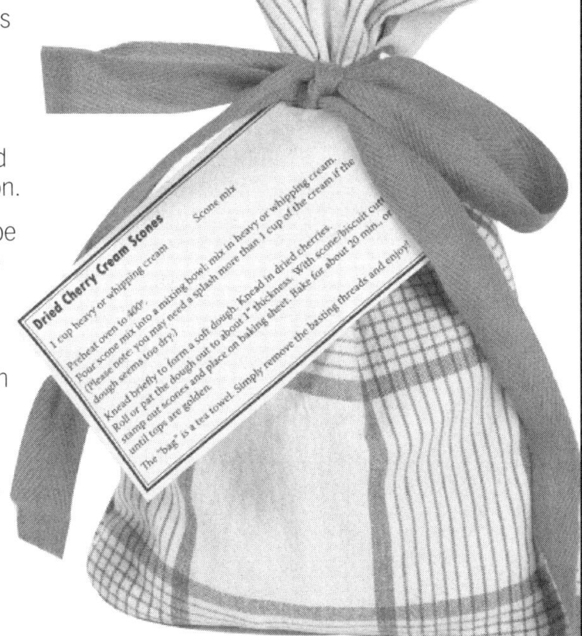

Permission to photocopy this page from *Crafts Galore!* granted for local church use. Copyright © Group Publishing, Inc., P.O. Box 481, Loveland, CO 80539. www.group.com

Dried Cherry Cream Scones

Dried Cherry Cream Scones

1 cup heavy or whipping cream

Scone mix

Preheat oven to 400 degrees.

Pour scone mix into a mixing bowl; mix in heavy or whipping cream. (Note: You may need a splash more than 1 cup of the cream if the dough seems too dry.)

Knead briefly to form a soft dough. Knead in dried cherries.

Roll or pat the dough out to about 1-inch thickness. With scone/biscuit cutter, stamp out scones and place on baking sheet. Bake for about 20 minutes or until tops are golden.

The "bag" is a tea towel. Simply remove the basting threads and enjoy!

Dried Cherry Cream Scones

1 cup heavy or whipping cream

Scone mix

Preheat oven to 400 degrees.

Pour scone mix into a mixing bowl; mix in heavy or whipping cream. (Note: You may need a splash more than 1 cup of the cream if the dough seems too dry.)

Knead briefly to form a soft dough. Knead in dried cherries.

Roll or pat the dough out to about 1-inch thickness. With scone/biscuit cutter, stamp out scones and place on baking sheet. Bake for about 20 minutes or until tops are golden.

The "bag" is a tea towel. Simply remove the basting threads and enjoy!

Permission to photocopy this page from *Crafts Galore!* granted for local church use. Copyright © Group Publishing, Inc., P.O. Box 481, Loveland, CO 80539. www.group.com

Joy in a Jar

- $$
- Takes about 30 minutes
- A sweet treat that's also a holiday gift

Supplies per jar:

- 1 quart-size wide-mouth canning jar with lid and rim
- ¼ cup granulated sugar
- ½ cup firmly packed brown sugar
- ¾ cup all-purpose flour
- ½ teaspoon baking soda
- ¼ teaspoon cinnamon
- ⅛ teaspoon salt
- 1½ cups uncooked oats
- ½ cup sweetened, dried cranberries
- ½ cup chopped walnuts
- photocopy of recipe card
- 8-inch square of holiday-print or pretty fabric
- 12 inches of ½-inch rickrack or ribbon

Supplies per table:

- hot-glue gun
- measuring cups and spoons
- bowl for mixing dry ingredients
- clear tape
- waxed paper
- pinking shears
- scissors
- mixing spoon
- hole punch

This is a great gift to give for the holidays, especially to teachers, neighbors, coworkers, small group members, and so on. Many people get lots of precooked treats over the holidays, and this one is a gift they can save until January or later, when they want a sweet homemade treat. It's not only pretty, but it is a much-welcomed and enjoyed gift. Plus, these are perfect to have on hand for those guests you weren't prepared for. They stay usable for several months if kept sealed tightly and stored in a cabinet or cupboard.

Joy in a Jar also makes a fun welcome-to-the-neighborhood gift, especially when a new cookie sheet is included…just in case they can't find theirs among the boxes.

Prior to your event, make Joy in a Jar for women to see as a sample. This is a good project to complete in an assembly line, so when setting up, be sure to put supplies out in the order they will be used.

Joy in a Jar

1. Prepare the Jar

Wash and thoroughly dry the wide-mouth quart jar, rim, and lid.

Using pinking shears, cut out an 8-inch square of fabric. Trim the rickrack or ribbon into a 12-inch length.

Using the hot-glue gun, attach the 12-inch strip of rickrack (or ribbon) to the edge of the metal rim, making sure ends meet to create a finished look. Set both fabric and decorated metal rim aside.

2. Mix and Layer

In mixing bowl, mix together flour, baking soda, cinnamon, and salt; stir well. Set aside.

The remaining ingredients will be layered in the following order (firmly packing each layer before adding the next): granulated sugar; firmly packed brown sugar; flour mixture; oats; sweetened, dried cranberries; chopped walnuts.

If there is room remaining in the jar, crumple waxed paper and place at the top so there's no room for jostling of the ingredients. To maintain the layers, the jar must be filled.

3. Cover

Place the lid on the jar, then the fabric square. Center the fabric square over the lid. Place the metal rim on the jar, making sure the fabric square is still centered over the lid. Tighten down rim.

Cut out the recipe for the remaining ingredients and baking instructions. Wrap a 1-inch piece of clear tape around the corner of the recipe card before punching a hole in it, and attach with ribbon.

Permission to photocopy this page from *Crafts Galore!* granted for local church use. Copyright © Group Publishing, Inc., P.O. Box 481, Loveland, CO 80539. www.group.com

Joy in a Jar

Joy in a Jar

½ cup (1 stick) margarine or butter, softened ½ teaspoon vanilla

1 egg

Heat oven to 350 degrees.

Stir together margarine, egg, and vanilla; beat well.

Using layered jar ingredients, remove top layers into separate bowl, leaving only brown sugar and granulated sugar in jar.

Add sugars to margarine, egg, and vanilla mixture; beat together until creamy. Add the rest of the layers from the separate bowl and mix well.

Drop by rounded tablespoonfuls onto ungreased cookie sheets. Bake 10 to 12 minutes or until golden brown. Cool 1 minute on cookie sheet; remove to wire rack. Makes about 4 dozen cookies.

Joy in a Jar

½ cup (1 stick) margarine or butter, softened ½ teaspoon vanilla

1 egg

Heat oven to 350 degrees.

Stir together margarine, egg, and vanilla; beat well.

Using layered jar ingredients, remove top layers into separate bowl, leaving only brown sugar and granulated sugar in jar.

Add sugars to margarine, egg, and vanilla mixture; beat together until creamy. Add the rest of the layers from the separate bowl and mix well.

Drop by rounded tablespoonfuls onto ungreased cookie sheets. Bake 10 to 12 minutes or until golden brown. Cool 1 minute on cookie sheet; remove to wire rack. Makes about 4 dozen cookies.

Permission to photocopy this page from *Crafts Galore!* granted for local church use. Copyright © Group Publishing, Inc., P.O. Box 481, Loveland, CO 80539. www.group.com

Bath Cookies

- **$$**
- Takes about 30 minutes
- A craft that actually gives you a mini manicure while you make it!

Supplies per woman:

- resealable plastic bag
- cellophane bag
- notecard

Supplies for 24 bath cookies:

- 2 cups of sea salt
- ½ cup baking soda
- ½ cup cornstarch
- 3 tablespoons light sesame oil (found in most grocery stores)
- 2 eggs

Supplies per table:

- a variety of fragrance oils (found at most craft and hobby stores, near soap-making supplies)
- food coloring (optional)
- 1-cup measuring cups
- hole punch
- curling ribbon
- markers
- cookie sheets
- nonstick aluminum foil
- access to an oven

Women will love making these clever gifts as much as the recipients will love using them! Make up several batches of the "dough," then allow women to add scent and color in resealable plastic bags. For more elaborate bath cookies, visit the soap-making aisle of your local craft store to find colorful soap chips women can mix into the dough.

Do note that while these Bath Cookies use edible ingredients, and they will look like edible cookies when they're done, these are not *for eating. These are used for adding to the bath to soften skin.*

Prior to your event, make up a batch of Bath Cookies to show as a sample. Premix bowls of the dough and place these on the tables. Provide supplies at each table for each woman to make about four or five bath cookies, as well as a notecard. While women wait for the cookies to bake, they can create colorful cards to accompany their craft.

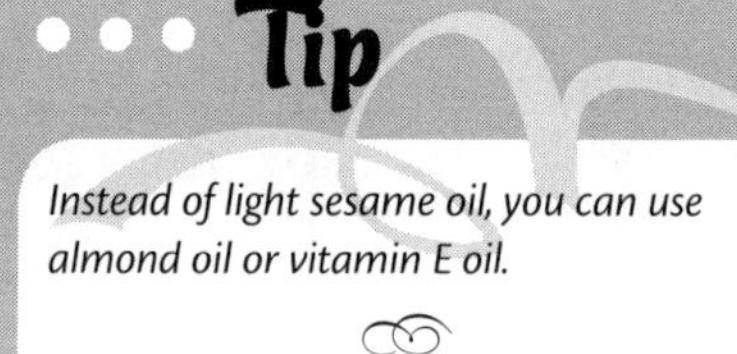

Tip

Instead of light sesame oil, you can use almond oil or vitamin E oil.

Bath Cookies

1. Fill Your Bag
Scoop 1 cup of "cookie dough" into a resealable plastic bag.

2. Customize Your Dough
Add about five drops of fragrance oil to the dough. Seal the bag and squish the dough to completely mix in the oil. You may want to add a drop or two of food coloring.

3. Roll the Cookies
Open the bag and take a small handful of dough (about 1/4 cup). Squeeze and press the dough into a ball. The dough is somewhat crumbly, so you need to press it together to form a ball-shaped cookie. Set cookies on a foil-lined cookie sheet.

4. Bake the Cookies
Bake the cookies for 12 minutes at 350 degrees.

5. Decorate Your Card
While the cookies bake, decorate a note-card. Include the instructions: "Crumble one cookie under running water into your bath." Punch a hole in the corner of the card. When cookies have cooled, place them into a cellophane bag. Tie the bag closed with curling ribbon and attach your card.

Permission to photocopy this page from *Crafts Galore!* granted for local church use. Copyright © Group Publishing, Inc., P.O. Box 481, Loveland, CO 80539. www.group.com

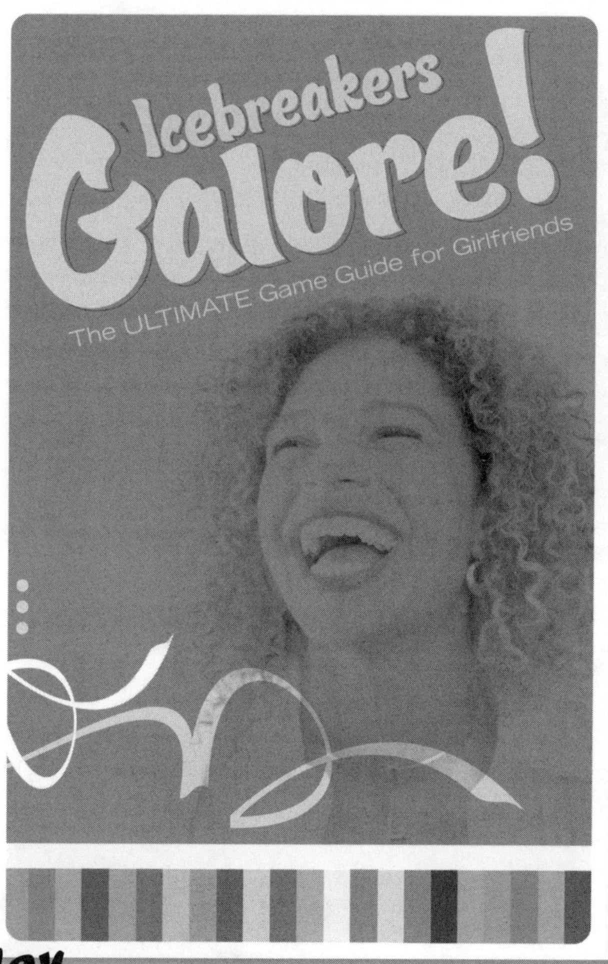

Discover ICEBREAKERS GALORE:

The ULTIMATE Game Guide for Girlfriends!

Help women feel connected, comfortable, and ready to have a fantastic time at your next event, small- or large-group gathering, party, or weekend retreat. Set the stage for fun and laughter with this game-filled resource. Great for Bible studies, road trips, slumber parties, and baby/bridal showers!

ISBN 978-0-7644-3625-3